DOUBLE EXPOSURES

Double Exposures

REPETITION AND REALISM
IN NINETEENTH-CENTURY
GERMAN FICTION

Eric Downing

STANFORD UNIVERSITY PRESS
STANFORD, CALIFORNIA 2000

Stanford University Press
Stanford, California
©2000 by the Board of Trustees of the
Leland Stanford Junior University
Printed in the United States of America

Library of Congress Cataloging-in-Publication Data

Downing, Eric
  Double exposures : repetition and realism in nineteenth-century German fiction / Eric Downing.
    p. cm.
  Includes bibliographical references.
  ISBN 0-8047-3678 2 (alk. paper)
  1. German fiction—19th century—History and criticism. 2. Realism in literature. 3. Repetition in literature. I. Title.
PT763.D69   2000
833'.709—dc21   00-029139

This book is printed on acid-free, archival-quality paper.

Original printing 2000

Last figure below indicates year of this printing:
09 08 07 06 05 04 03 02 01 00

Designed and typeset in 10/14.5 Minion by John Feneron

For Nancy

ACKNOWLEDGMENTS

The original idea for this study came to me one afternoon in the library reading room in Frankfurt am Main, where I was spending the summer preparing two courses for the following fall semester, one on nineteenth-century German literature and the other on contemporary literary theory. The evening before, I had seen Alfred Hitchcock's *Vertigo* with a friend; afterward we had discussed in detail and with great delight the film's exemplary representation of certain key concerns of psychoanalysis, gender theory, and aesthetics. That next afternoon I found myself reading Theodor Storm's *Viola tricolor*, and partway through I began to feel that power of attraction Nietzsche describes as belonging to everything contrary, everything antipodal: for "without ill-humor or impatience," Storm's novella seemed to pose a No, proposition by proposition and conclusion by conclusion, to Hitchcock's film. I put down the book to follow the thought through both my tracks of reading, and by the time I left the library several hours later I felt I had discovered, as Nietzsche says, my secret garden, the soil I could work as the ground of this study.

Since that afternoon much time has passed, and I have incurred many debts in bringing this book to its present form. I would like to thank Margret Guillemin, the first and always most gentle reader of my manuscript; and Dorrit Cohn and Robert Holub, the implied (as well as actual) readers toward whom this work was written. I need especially to acknowledge the help of Jim Porter, Catriona MacLeod, Eva Geulen, Judith Ryan, Thomas Pfau, and Ken Weisinger, all of whom read almost every chapter in its first draft and gave me detailed, invaluable comments and encouragement. Their conversation has made this not only a better book but also a far more enjoyable one to write. Two other readers and interlocutors, Richard Brinkmann and Christian Thomas, deserve special mention: each read several chapters in earlier versions and offered their critique and advice.

I thank my many former colleagues at Harvard University, including Elisabeth Bronfen, Gail Finney, Shlomith Rimmon-Kenan, and Maria Tatar, and my present colleagues at the University of North Carolina, Chapel Hill, in particular Alice Kuzniar, Lilian Furst, and Clayton Koelb. Each contributed in countless ways, both great and small, to the shape this book has taken. I would also like to express my gratitude to the graduate students at Harvard who first listened to my ideas about poetic realism, and whose own ideas about and inspired commitment to its study convinced me of the importance of this enterprise. I thank, too, the audiences at the University of Michigan, Ann Arbor; Stanford University; the University of California, Santa Cruz; Boston University; the Center for European Studies at Harvard; Duke University; and the MLA Annual Convention. Each heard some part of this study, and all gave useful criticism.

Finally, I need to thank my daughter, Jessica, and Nancy, whose love and support are the firmament spanning the ground of my work—and play. Thanks, too, to both Bo Rily and Emma. And to my father, who retrieved this book when my computer had lost it.

Some portions of this book have already appeared in print in somewhat different form. A version of chapter 2 appeared in *Colloquia Germanica* 28, no. 1 (1995): 35–53; part of chapter 3 appears in *History and Literature: Essays in Honor of Karl S. Guthke* (Tübingen: Stauffenburg Verlag, 2000); part of chapter 4 in *The Germanic Review* 73, no. 3 (1998): 221–38. Versions of chapters 5 and 6 appeared in the *Deutsche Vierteljahrsschrift* 65, no. 2 (1991): 265–303, and 68, no. 4 (1994): 506–48, respectively. I gratefully acknowledge these journals and their editors for their permission to include the essays in revised form in the current volume. I would also like to express my gratitude to the Institute for the Arts and Humanities at the University of North Carolina, Chapel Hill, where a Blackwell Fellowship during the 1998–99 academic year provided me the time and resources to bring this project to completion. And of course, special thanks to Helen Tatar at Stanford University Press for believing in this study and making it a book.

I should add that all citations from the German, except where noted, are my own. Since many of the German texts I discuss are not readily available in any standard English edition, my references are solely to page numbers in the standard German sources. However, I have consulted those English translations that are available, although I have often had to modify their renditions for reasons of both style and accuracy. Credit is given to the English translations in the appropriate footnotes. I refer to the texts themselves by their translated titles, but the first reference always gives the original German. All parenthetical dates refer to the first German edition of the works under discussion.

CONTENTS

1. Theoretical Introduction: Repetition and Realism in Narratology, Critical Theory, and Psychoanalysis — 1

2. Real and Recurrent Problems: Stifter's Preface to *Many-colored Stones* (*Bunte Steine*) — 24

3. Double Visions: Chiastic Mimesis and the Politics of Realism in Stifter's *The Mountain Forest* (*Der Hochwald*) — 41

4. Double Takes: Genre and Gender in Keller's Twice-Told Tales, the *Seven Legends* (*Sieben Legenden*) — 91

5. Second Wives, Second Lives: The "Ligeia Impulse" in Theodor Storm's *Viola tricolor* — 129

6. Double-Dealings: Trading Places in Meyer's *The Marriage of the Monk* (*Die Hochzeit des Mönchs*) — 170

7. Secondhand News: Boredom and a Motive for Murder in Wilhelm Raabe's *Fatso* (*Stopfkuchen*) — 216

8. (In) Conclusion: Second Thoughts — 260

Notes — 267
Works Cited — 321
Index — 331

DOUBLE EXPOSURES

1
THEORETICAL INTRODUCTION
Repetition and Realism in Narratology, Critical Theory, and Psychoanalysis

It has become a critical commonplace in almost every discussion of literary realism that it is nearly impossible to define the term itself, and that is particularly the case when the subject is German realism or, as it is also called, poetic realism. Already in the 1940s Rene Wellek had lamented, "In Germany everybody is on his own and looks for realism wherever he wants to find it."[1] And contemporary scholarship has done little to improve the situation: in one of the most recent surveys of the field, Lilian Furst is moved to recall the image of "that mythological beast, the hydra, which grew two heads for every one that was cut off."[2] The present study, which focuses on the problem of realism in several nineteenth-century German authors—Stifter, Keller, Storm, Meyer, and Raabe—does nothing to change this general state. It makes no claim to a notion of realism that will hold true for the entire range of writings commonly understood to comprise "realism," and limits itself instead to delineating a few narrow strains or properties within the general domain—a few of the monster's many heads, as it were.[3] Even so, the approach here taken will no doubt generate as many questions as it does answers about realism, in a truly Hydralike fashion. Nonetheless, this approach, and the property of realism described, do have the inestimable advantage of allowing us to confront self-consciously the critical commonplace of undefinability as itself characteristic, indeed symptomatic, of realism: both in its constant appeal to realism as exceeding any proffered, conventional definition, and in the eventual definitional status of that very commonplace.

This study begins with a simple but consequential pairing: repetition and realism. Repetition is a central concern of all three of the theoretical perspectives I engage in my analyses, namely those of narratology, psychoanalysis, and Critical Theory. Indeed, it proves a key point of juncture between these various discourses. And while there are many ways that repetition functions within these theoretical perspectives, and more important, within the texts on which this work is based, I have chosen to concentrate on those most acutely relevant to an understanding of the realism, or rather, the poetic realism at stake in these texts. Repetition is, after all, also a central, almost obsessional concern of many of the major thinkers of the mid to late nineteenth century period most associated with realism, thinkers such as Kierkegaard, Darwin, Nietzsche, Freud, and Marx. Equally important, it is also a dominant feature of most contemporary critical descriptions of realism itself. By bringing to the fore this single element of these various theoretical approaches, nineteenth-century cultural schemes, and contemporary critical descriptions, I believe we can discover not only a surprising consensus regarding the operation of repetition in realist discourse but also an equally surprising array of more or less self-conscious literary representations of this operation, and its problems, within realist texts themselves.

I

The basic analytical model of repetition and realism proposed by this study can perhaps most cleanly be introduced by considering the related formalist models for realism developed by Roland Barthes and Roman Jakobson. Once having established their structure, I can then go on to explore their affinities with and nuanced development in my other engaged discourses, those of Critical Theory and psychoanalysis.

Let me begin with Barthes and his seminal essay on "The Reality Effect," in which he argues for a twofold nature, or procedure, for the realist text.[4] First, Barthes shows how realist texts are heavily dependent on a certain redundancy, or repetition, that ensures their readability and marks their product as "realism." According to Barthes, the realist text displays a foreseeable predilection for the reproduction of the ritualized activities of everyday life, or more generally: it reproduces as its own that widely disseminated iconography of daily life, those established systems of rendering experience intelligible and recognizable operant in so-called real life as its own—indeed, the text reproduces them as the securities for its own reality.[5] To this extent, realist poetics are deeply invested in a principle of repetition, a representation of the world "the way it is," in all its own characteristic redundancies.

Second, Barthes describes how the realist text is also often characterized by a superfluity of detail, a notable excess of descriptive *realia;* but whereas the effect of this excess is frequently similar to that of the text's redundancy, its aesthetic intent is not—at least not initially. Rather, the realist's hypertrophic evocation of discrete details is intent on challenging, on *resisting,* meaning: on opposing functional assimilation to the established systems of intelligibility, whether these be conceived as primarily literary or as more broadly sociocultural. This realist practice also deploys redundancy of reference to extratextual reality, but actually aimed *against* readability, against the *vraisemblable*: and as Barthes notes, it is more this alleged resistance to or frustration of conventional structures of the sensible than its alleged extratextual referentiality that achieves the realist effect aimed at by this procedure. Of course, and as Barthes also notes, this interruption of readable structures by extraneous and excessive detail eventually evinces its own structure of intelligibility, its own conventionality. But more on that in a moment.

What we see, then, is that Barthes describes a necessarily double and conflictual structure to the reality effect, defined largely in terms of its relation to the principle of repetition. On the one hand, in its dependence on redundancy of the quotidian world "as it is," realism is firmly grounded in repetition, indeed in the repetition of repetition. On the other hand, in its resistance to the established conventions of making sense, realism is seen as opposing repetition, as its resistance, as difference.[6] Finally, Barthes hints at an inherent instability to the proposed structure, as the latter resistance to meaning threatens always to become in turn the former system of meaning itself.

Clearly, Barthes's model can be recognized as a specific formulation or realization of Roman Jakobson's equally famous but more general account of realism. And as with all such mixed structural and period-particular descriptions,

Barthes's raises certain well-known problems regarding the historical specificity to the concept of realism, problems that are perhaps inseparable from the concept itself. Jakobson's account is more circumspect in this regard: in his 1921 essay "On Realism in Art," he intentionally forgoes any attempt to delimit historically the idea of realism.[7] Rather, he chooses to stress both its extreme relativity and the need to situate it within the evolutionary context of literary history. For Jakobson, the problem of realism is played out in the ever dynamic process of the conventionalization and deformation of literary perceptions. Certain practices or codes of verisimilar representation become standardized and canonized within the literary tradition: new movements then arise that disrupt, disorder, and deform those codes, purportedly allowing for a closer approximation to reality or, perhaps better, for the articulation of a new truth. Within this process, there exist two competing claims to realism and verisimilitude: that which conceives of the adherence to and reproduction of the traditional codes as a faithfulness to reality; and that which conceives of the deformation or deautomatization of these same literary codes as an approximation to reality. That is, this description too proposes a double, conflictual nature for realism, and relates it to a principle of repetition: realism as grounded in repetition, in a commitment to repeating established convention—and as grounded in opposing repetition, in establishing difference. Moreover, Jakobson points out that these two possibilities are themselves doubled, both being possible perspectives for both the author and the reader, with the latter often situated at a later, and so different, moment in the literary historical process.

Jakobson does also address the more specific problem of poetic realism, or more generally, late-nineteenth-century realism. He identifies certain formal features that he, like Barthes, considers characteristic of the historical school that dominated the period from the 1840s through the 1890s, features such as contiguity, superfluity, specificity of detail, and consistent motivation. But for the most part, poetic realism is conceived as a specific instance of the general model, with both claims to realism operant. On the one hand, realism becomes defined by its effort to overcome or at least violate the literary codes of its traditional predecessor, here by and large identifiable with Romanticism—with all the misprision and simplification that effort requires. On the other hand, realism's own norms, devices, codes, and practices eventually become canonized in turn, and thereafter function as the model or set of conventions to whose faithful adherence later readers attribute, or deny, verisimilitude.

It will be noted that, unlike Barthes's, both aspects of Jakobson's paradigm are defined in purely literary terms: no correspondence to an extraliterary reality comes into consideration. Barthes's suggestive recognition of the textuality of the extraliterary realm, of the widely disseminated iconography of our daily social lives, provides the obvious and needed bridge for extending Jakobson's model, for spanning the two realms insistently linked by the concept of realism and so, too, for getting us beyond the limits imposed by a merely formalist analysis. However, as Jakobson's angelic trepidation should perhaps warn us, the bridge between the literary and extraliterary is to be trodden cautiously, and moreover to be traversed back and forth repeatedly. While the affinity and overlap between literary and social conventions and realism's stake in each remains an essential one, so does their difference and incommensurability. Similarly, while the recent critical propensity has been to emphasize how realism is where literary conventions prove themselves most social, most extraliterary in both their origin and aim, we need to emphasize the opposite as well—that realistic fiction is where social conventions become literary, that is, most identifiably fictional. For whereas social iconography in literature can be seen to lend the represented fictional world its sense of reality, literature can also impart to the socially constructed world its essence as fiction. In any case, and as I said, this remains a bridge to be trodden cautiously, and repeatedly in *both* directions.[8]

More important for our immediate purposes, however, is not how Barthes allows us to extend and refine Jakobson, but how Jakobson allows us to extend and refine Barthes. Whereas both theorists situate realism in its paradoxical relation to repetition—as simultaneously and contradictorily grounded in repetition and in opposing it—Jakobson stresses how this paradoxical structure will be itself, or is itself *repeatedly* repeated to achieve the same realist effect. That is, by stressing (as does Barthes) how realism's own norms and devices inevitably become conventionalized and automatized, and so subject to the realist operation of disruption and deformation, Jakobson opens up (as Barthes does not) an understanding of the operation not only as realism but also potentially within realism, and perhaps inevitably to realism itself, to its own demise.

Although advancing from a rather different direction, the most recent deconstructionist treatment of my topic—J. Hillis Miller, in *Fiction and Repetition* (1982)—also arrives at fairly similar conclusions regarding the definitional role of repetition in realism.[9] Admittedly, Miller claims not to be concerned with problems of realism per se. Nonetheless, he discusses the workings of repetition in exclusively nineteenth-century realist texts, in which he distinguishes two competing models of repetition, which following Deleuze he calls Platonic and Nietzschean.[10] Both are concerned with the issue of mimesis, a central tenet of any realist poetics. The Platonic model corresponds to the traditional view of mimesis as involving an original anterior reality and a faithfully re-presented literary copy. Of course, both Barthes's and Jakobson's models would force a slight sophistication on this description, involving the relinquishing of an anterior, original reality as the first term to this "Platonic" mode and introducing instead a set or chain of previous representations, whose status as representations has been forgotten or anaesthetically effaced. Otherwise, the match between this and the first part of each of their models for realism seems fairly precise.

As opposed to his Platonic model, Miller's Nietzschean model assumes no original paradigm or reality of which other things can be copies, but only intrinsically different things. It posits a world in which the tendency or desire to see identities between things—to say that Y repeats X—is ultimately mistaken and distorting. From this perspective, "realism" entails a recognition of the inherent loss of reality in the act of repetition (of tracing likes in unlikes), and the corresponding struggle to thwart the desire for such repetition. Miller at times implies the ascendancy of the Nietzschean over the Platonic during the course of the nineteenth century, and the Nietzschean model certainly proves of primary importance for his own textual analyses. But Miller also perceives that the two models imply and depend on each other, and that the nineteenth-century realist mimetic project rested upon two competing attitudes toward the relation of the real and repetition.[11]

II

Of course, the model of realism that informs most recent American-Germanist scholarship derives not so much from the formalist tradition as from that of the Frankfurt School: both Robert Holub's influential *Reflections of Realism* (1991) and Russell Berman's *Rise of the Modern German Novel* (1986) are notably representative of this approach.[12] Unlike the formalists, these critics tend to describe realism not as a discrete, discursive realm but as part of a broader social or ideological matrix, and in doing so they implicitly draw on the cultural analyses of bourgeois enlightenment elaborated by Horkheimer's and Adorno's seminal study *Dialectic of Enlightenment*.[13] Despite the rather different points of departure and emphasis, however, many of the major features of their analytical model still compare and contrast quite interestingly with those of the formalists.

Let me introduce this model by concentrating on "The Concept of Enlightenment," the first essay in Horkheimer's and Adorno's work, in which they develop their analysis of enlightenment in terms of two competing forces, myth and enlightenment proper. Although basically defined ahistorically, as an ever-repeating or progressing process from at least the time of the Greeks to the present, enlightenment is also identified by them with the specific historical period of the rising hegemony of bourgeois ideology and culture, roughly situated between the late eighteenth and early twentieth centuries—roughly the same period identified with the rise and rule of realism, which is often similarly associated with a specifically bourgeois culture. Most Frankfurt School critics of realism, including both Holub and Berman, tend to foreground and deploy only the more historically restricted model, narrowing and nuancing it to match more closely the particulars of the period; but we should note that the hesitation between the broadly structural and specifically historical that characterizes Horkheimer's and Adorno's definitions of "enlightenment" is the same as that which seems to haunt almost every definition of realism, from Auerbach to Jakobson. It is, I think, a hesitancy intrinsic to all models embedded in conflictual, antinomic terms with dialectical, temporally extended relations—or in other words, to all synchronic models with diachronic operators. For again, in the paired forces of myth and enlightenment driving Horkheimer's and Adorno's concept of enlightenment, just such a model is being mobilized.[14]

More important for our purposes, Horkheimer and Adorno also place the issue of repetition at the very center of the relation between myth and enlightenment; indeed, they see repetition as playing the "most decisive" part in their analysis of the enlightenment as a whole.[15] And as we will see, their understanding of repetition in enlightenment tends to reproduce that of repetition in realism from our formalist critics, but also to complicate and, at the same time, to flatten it.

Horkheimer and Adorno approach myth as the first term in their equation, and they define it as grounded in repetition: "[L]ike magical rites, myths signify self-repetitive nature . . . a state of being or a process that is presented as eternal, because it incessantly becomes actual once more by being realized in symbolic form" (19). Such a self-sustaining and stabilizing procedure or state, which perpetuates itself through the faithful reproduction of its symbols, or conventions—that is, through the mythical repetition of events, characters, and the world itself—has obvious affinities with the first half of the formalists' model. And as Horkheimer's and Adorno's use of the word "actual" makes clear, the mythical still functions as a form of reality; its mythical quality no more counts against it here than its conventional quality counts against its counterpart for Jakobson and Barthes.

Horkheimer's and Adorno's model also, however, differs at this point from the formalists'. As for Jakobson and Barthes, the half of the equation that is grounded in repetition clearly represents for Horkheimer and Adorno a conservative principle in world-formation. But the mythical also represents for them an acknowledgment of otherness, difference, or alterity, insofar as "power"—by which they mean the governance of events, significance, reality—is always conceived in myth as a property of the outside, nonhuman, natural world (15). In keeping with this, the distinctly human practice of mimesis is understood as an attempt, through its own repetition, to participate in and so to acquire some of that power (12), while still acknowledging the repeated reality's fundamental and fascinating otherness.

Over and against the mythical, Horkheimer and Adorno posit the procedure of enlightenment, which is first and foremost understood in Weberian terms as a demythologization, or *disenchantment* of the world. Enlightenment aims to expose the symbols or conventions of the world as just that, symbols and conventions, without intrinsicality or immanence in reality. Instead, they are seen as mere, and largely inadequate and distorting, systems of intelligibility, as constructed fictions with no real place in the outside world. Mythical mimesis is understood by enlightenment as the reverse of the procedure described within the mythical itself: it is not that men transform themselves or their artifacts into imitations or repetitions of some alien natural powers, but that those powers are themselves repetitions of distinctly human transformative procedures. The otherness of the world is eliminated along with its reality.

In its disenchanting or deautomatizing impulse and its frustration of traditional codes, what Horkheimer and Adorno call enlightenment can be seen to coincide with what Jakobson describes as the second claim to realism: both derive their "realist" nature primarily through a negative gesture of disabusement and a mortal resistance to the repetition of the inherited symbols or conventions. But again, Horkheimer and Adorno add a dialectical turn to the common model. While enlightenment thus represents an opposition to (mythical) repetition and a disruptive (reality) principle, its peculiar mode of disenchantment—namely, rationalization—also introduces its own principle of repetition and, rather than introducing difference (specifically, the difference between representation and reality), it eliminates it, imposing uniformity and similitude instead. In the paradoxical formulation so often favored by Critical Theory, we are told that while disenchantment turns myth into enlightenment by exposing it as a rational explanatory system, it also turns enlightenment into myth, by reinvesting it in a structure of repetition and equivalence that would fatefully determine the world "as it is."

As Horkheimer and Adorno explain it, rationalization—by which they frequently mean simply conceptualization—makes the dissimilar comparable by reducing it to abstract quantities. By conceptualizing the diverse, real phenomena of the world in terms of their conformation to uniform laws and principles, it works to reduce, eliminate, or repress the unique facticity of events, characters, and nature, in such a way as once again, as in myth, to make everything in nature repeatable (13), or exchangeable. "What was different is equalized," and equivalence becomes the perceptual rule: whatever obscures the transparent condition of likeness is written off as illusion or, as they also put it, as literature. As part of this, the mythical procedure of identificatory magical mimesis is replaced with a more objective one of detached scientific representation, in which the mythical linking of the unlike and the like "is exchanged for the fungible—universal interchangeability." At a single stroke, the alterity of the represented world and the subjectivity of the representing human are both eliminated, and power—the governance of events, significance, reality—becomes a (disguised) property of, and for, the equalizing procedure alone: a new immanence, which is external without being alien, and authoritative without being other.

Finally (and as the parenthetical question of disguise already suggests), Horkheimer and Adorno insist that a certain blindness or bad faith necessarily adheres to enlightenment, which at any given moment in its unfolding course cannot self-reflect on the contradictions of its own reality-breaking and -making apparatus, cannot conceive its own mode of conceptualization as a mythologizing construct, without ceasing to be itself and becoming instead its opposite, namely myth. Or perhaps better: it cannot do so without simultaneously initiating yet another moment in its ongoing relay of symbolic divestment, without becoming the latest victim of its own Saturnian appetite.

What we see, then, is this. On the one hand, Horkheimer's and Adorno's dual, conflictual model for enlightenment corresponds fairly closely with our formalists' model for realism. Myth represents a conservative claim to reality, is based on a faithful adherence to traditional codes, and is grounded in a principle of repetition and redundancy. Enlightenment represents a claim to a new reality, or truth, is based on the disruption or disenchantment of traditional codes, and so resists their repetition, their redundant equivalence with the world. On the other hand, however, Horkheimer's and Adorno's model also reverses the defining qualities of the formalists' model.[16] Difference and an acknowledgment of otherness, of the unlike, become characteristic of myth; uniformity and a new, more insidious principle of repetition and mimetic equivalence become characteristic of enlightenment. Mythical mimesis is seen as at least in part a flirting fascination with foreign, "natural" forces, a practice that remains largely self-conscious of its own magic and of the (almost) overwhelming alterity of existence; disenchanted representation is seen as a violent repression of uniqueness and otherness in both men and nature, a practice that remains largely insensitive to its own myth and to its own (almost) overwhelming leveling of existence.[17]

Admittedly, Horkheimer and Adorno also hold out an exception to this model, yet another dialectical turn that brings them back closer to the position of Jakobson and other formalists, and they do so by turning to art. In the midst of enlightenment uniformation, the authentic work of art "still has something in common with enchantment": it posits its own self-enclosed area and obeys its own unique laws of composition; closed off from actuality, it restores a "mythical" self-consciousness both of its own mimetic magic and of the engaging, and engaged, alterity of extraliterary existence (19). As such, what Horkheimer and Adorno call the great or true work of art always necessarily introduces in *its* moment of repetition not only self-reflection and an acknowledgment of otherness but also an awareness of its failure to achieve an identity between its representation and (outside) reality, and thus in a sense an insight into its achieved self-negation (131). This is, of course, a crucial qualification to their model, and one that becomes of even greater importance in the work of Walter Benjamin; it is also, however, a qualification that is almost entirely overlooked in most Critical Theoretical discussions of realism.[18]

Given the basic agreement among the more or less formalist theorists regarding the double, conflictual nature of the reality effect in literature, and given also the concurring sense in Horkheimer and Adorno that this double, conflictual nature is sustained by true literature even in enlightened culture, it is more than just somewhat surprising to have only half that nature ascribed to realism by both Holub and Berman. This basic disagreement, as well as the indisputable sophistication and reigning influence of each of their analyses, will encourage us both to challenge their readings by restoring the more paradoxical, double, and conflictual models of the formalists and Horkheimer and Adorno; *and* to confront the challenge they pose to those models—that is, to see how the double, conflictual model might turn out to be, or to become, one and the same thing.

For all their significant differences, Holub and Berman both enunciate the same fundamental, and insidious, structure for realism: both can be seen to transpose Horkheimer's and Adorno's general model for enlightenment into similar specific literary terms. Each sees realism in terms of ideology, specifically of bourgeois ideology: each sees it as a heavily normed discourse, or style, that purports to universal, transparent, natural, and ahistorical status, and that simultaneously and necessarily excludes or represses both self-consciousness and otherness. We are told that realist texts exclude self-consciousness because their bad faith is the "fiction that they are not fiction at all," that their conventions and representations passively mirror or reproduce homologously nonfictional "reality"; consequently, the self-conscious reflection on their own fictionality, on their own status as literary discourse, would subvert realism's structure or program. Similarly, we are told that realist texts exclude otherness because their bad faith claim to transparent universality and equivalence with the world is only maintained by repressing, or suppressing, all possible difference, all resistance to their own conventional norms. Berman describes this in terms of a purported "transparency, uniform perspective, and unified narration of the realist text that supplants the complicated variegations of earlier modes of writing," apparently an unconscious, reflective response to the Bismarckian politics of national unification.[19] Holub describes the norms of realism as "defined by a series of exclusions," most notably among them of the inconsistencies of its own theory; of the otherness of primeval desire;[20] and of the otherness of racial difference, whether outside Germany/Europe or within it.[21]

Both writers, of course, and especially Holub, discover evidence in the texts themselves for ruptures in the reputedly transparent, uniform normed discourse. Holub in fact foregrounds just those moments where realist texts "inadvertently" confront their own fictionality and conventionality, and he argues for the subsequent faltering of realism's "own shaky foundations, revealing its aesthetic as well as its political and social biases."[22] I very much agree with Holub's basic observations: but I also think we need to see that these moments of supposedly unwitting—or in Berman's phrase, marginalized—faltering, of exposed conventionality, are actually conscious, inherent aspects of poetic realism itself; that the reality, and fiction, that both these critics see exposed behind and within the text by their own extrinsic analyses are instead part of the texts' own intrinsic strategies, of their own double, conflictual nature. After all, the model of realism they impose upon their texts amounts to only half of the formalist model described above, and leaves out of account the authentically *literary* function suggested by Horkheimer and Adorno: it sees realism and verisimilitude only in terms of the adherence to and faithful reproduction of traditional, established literary and social codes, only in terms of uniformation.

They completely ignore, or rather, they appropriate only for their own critical perspective the other half of realism, the deformation and discrediting of literary and social codes as an approximation to a "truer" reality (which need only be that of a realized falsifying fiction).[23]

It is, then, to no small extent the attempt to restore an awareness of the dual nature of poetic realism that motivates this study: to see realism not only as grounded in a repetition or redundancy of the dominant discourse, but also in its resistance; to recall the self-conscious, somewhat self-deconstructive dimension that is intrinsic to realism, and almost inseparable from what we value as *literary* realism; and to explore the self-representations or -understandings of their realist dimensions that these texts yield, once we have redefined our own critical perspectives.[24]

Such an intent to restore an awareness of the dual, conflictual, and even self-deconstructive nature of realism motivates the necessity for what Adorno would call immanent critique: for the nonreductive, often exhaustive analyses of our chosen literary examples. This approach is called for, because my aim is to show how these texts actively resist a systematic (or in Adorno's terms, transcendent) account of their realist "program" or conventions, and also because it is frequently only by such careful attention to textual details and strategies that realism's own peculiar and often overlooked modes of self-reflection—and self-negation—can be adequately demonstrated.[25]

Let me also add that the same intent motivates my decision to focus on novellas rather than novels, and especially on novellas that are usually considered central to the canon of poetic realist works but are rarely considered central to the theory of poetic realism. I choose such works for at least two reasons. First, because novellas are, perhaps generically and certainly historically, more obviously given to the interruption of their own invoked interpretive strategies and deployed social iconographies. Indeed, Martin Swales persuasively argues for this simultaneous invocation and interruption of established "structures of intelligibility" as the hallmark of the novella.[26] What he (and he is not alone) evokes as generic features of the form I want also to consider as intrinsic features of the movement most associated with it, namely realism: after all, both the novella and realism find their florescence similarly situated between the Romantic fairy tale and modern short story, and it is not insignificant that almost all of Swales's own examples of his thesis are drawn from the corpus of identifiably realist works.

Second, I choose novellas (and in two cases not even really novellas, but rather anomalous short forms) that are both canonical and yet seemingly eccentric to the critical discussion of realism precisely because, unlike in France and England, German realism did tend to privilege the novella over the novel, did make this literary form its dominant mode of expression; and because many of the novellas produced by the German realists, and so that remain a part of what we call realism, *were* notably eccentric (even as novellas) and removed from any uniform, normed discourse easily identifiable as realism, and moreover *were* notably given to exploring more or less self-consciously the aesthetic and social problematics of their realist enterprise. To ignore *their* otherness, to marginalize their exoticism and their self-consciousness as somehow extrinsic to the definition of what realism is, and instead to privilege such more or less two-dimensional and programmatic works as Freytag's *Soll und Haben* (*Debit and Credit*, 1855) as decisive for "what realism is"—this is critically to perform the very operation of leveling, exclusion, and repression of which realism itself then stands accused. To restore an awareness of realism's full and fully self-contradictory nature, we must first restore its full, and fully eccentric, canon of texts.[27]

I say all this, and I mean all this in attacking what I take to be the reductively monological model of realism deployed by these representatives of the Frankfurt School of Critical Theory. But I also take quite seriously their challenge (and that includes their reading of Horkheimer and Adorno), and this study is no less motivated by the attempt to discover how, and to what effect, this dual, conflictual, and to some extent self-subversive nature of realism might nonetheless turn out to be in the service of sustaining a single, uniform, normed aesthetic discourse identifiable as "realism." But more on that in a moment.

III

Before proceeding to question how these models of repetition and realism might eventually self-destruct (might, that is, become unexpectedly monotonal or singular), I need first to outline how this same basic structure of repetition and realism manifests itself in my third critical discourse, namely psychoanalysis: that is, how repetition and realism function in terms of the discourse of desire. In engaging this third discourse, however, I need to make clear two fundamental points. First, that despite my employment of the names and systems of Freud and Lacan, I grant no more of an original, ontologically prior status of empirical, determinative (much less natural) reality to psychology or "primeval" desire than I do to (other) extraliterary social conditions. Rather, for me desire remains every bit as much a matter of conventions and structural effects as literary realism or social "reality": indeed, it is the very conventionality and constructed nature of desire that forms the basis for the interplay between desire, literature, and bourgeois ideology that this study undertakes in part to elaborate. The same, or at least homologous conditions are assumed to obtain for each discursive realm.

Second, despite the homology—or, if you will, the repetition and redundancy, the uniform conditions shared by all three—my assumption is that psychology (or perhaps better, desire) remains a discrete, largely irreducible discursive realm, as impossible to reduce to either literary or extraliterary/social terms as they are to each other. I assume that, for all the observable overlap, the discourse of desire also functions as a nodal point for maintaining a certain difference from and resistance to those of literature and ideology also governing the text; and that, for all the shared structure, the play of repetition and realism here might at times run counter to that found elsewhere in the same text. As with the bridge spanning the distance between literary and social conventions, the passages between these different realms must all be negotiated with caution and with frequent reversals: and in all cases, we need to recognize and respect both the structural repetitions and the discursive differences between them, and see both contributing to our common concern of realism.

Repetition functions to produce meaning in many different ways in psychoanalytic theory, and while many of these different ways figure prominently in this study, here in the introduction I want to concentrate on those modes specifically linked with the question of realism, or rather, with the play of the poetic and the real, and to articulate the common ground shared by those modes with the dual-natured, conflictual structure for realism already described.[28]

Let me begin with Freud, in whose thinking the relevant modes of repetition and realism are basically three in number, in compact relation to each other. The first mode is that of repression, the one implicitly assumed by such Frankfurt School theorists as Holub to be of almost definitional importance to realism. Freud's theory of repression imagines a given forbidding "reality," a censoring reality principle as it were, that prohibits the direct expression of another competing reality, the reality of desire, which it seeks to exclude or deny in order to maintain a suitably stable and controlled existence for the individual subject. The (almost) sovereign authority or force of this given repressive "reality" or reality principle is of course no more fundamentally real than, say, either the purported reality of inherited literary codes or of contemporary bourgeois ideology, and can in fact often be functionally equivalent to them—in any case, a fiction acting as a reality, a poetically real endowed with power and authority on the basis of its accepted working conventions.

According to Freud, however, another and different poetically real also emerges out of the same model. The given repressive fictional reality never truly succeeds in excluding or denying the competing reality of desire. Rather, in a reflex known as the return of the repressed, it merely succeeds in *moving it along*, in necessitating its displacement within the representational field (of reality, i.e., the text), its entrance into an ongoing chain of fictional, indirect substitutive manifestations—into a chain of repeating representations. And as a product of the combined pressures of the (repressive) reality principle and the (irrepressible) reality of desire, this chain or process of substitutive representations has its own claims on reality, a once again necessarily (but differently) poetic reality. As we will see, coming to terms with this ongoing, in some sense unmasterable and disruptive reality can constitute its own "realism" in the text. In fact, recognizing its ever-returning and repeating presence, its nonexcludability from the representational field, its "otherness" as intrinsic, constitutes a large part of the psychological realism and subjectivity often identified as new to the late nineteenth century.[29]

Freud's theory of repression, then, actually suggests a dual, complex, conflictual structure for (poetic) realism, a structure that is more than just roughly analogous to that already encountered in our discussion of Barthes and Jakobson: "reality" as the mobilization of certain (fictional and powerful) strategies for the maintenance of a stable, nondisruptive psychological relation to the world, and as the mobilization of certain (equally fictional and just as powerful) strategies aimed at disrupting and deforming that relation and expressing instead a different, denied reality. The major difference from, even reversal within, the earlier articulated models would seem to come in respect to the role of repetition. Whereas for our formalist theorists repetition seemed aligned only with the conservative fiction or strategy of realism, here it is also or instead the disruptive fictional strategy that is caught up in a process of representational repetition.[30] This was also, of course, the case in Horkheimer and Adorno. But whereas they saw repetition as part of the disruptive practice of rational consciousness, Freud sees it as part of the disruptive—and differently disruptive—practice of the irrational unconscious, which constantly accompanies and subverts the "enlightened" effort after controlled and complete representation, and reintroduces the excluded sense of otherness in a truly "uncanny" manner.

The second relevant Freudian mode is that associated with his famous notion of a *Wiederholungszwang,* or repetition compulsion; while it describes the same basic drama as above, it does so from a different perspective or end-point. Freud's explanation of the repetition compulsion begins with the act of repression, with the fact of a repressed anterior memory—and it is worth stressing that, from Freud's point of view, it makes no difference whether the memory repressed is real or fictive, and it is even more likely to be the latter. The compulsion then obligates the patient "to *repeat* the repressed material as a present experience instead of, as the physician would prefer to see, *remembering* it as a piece of the past."[31] Again, if the original memory is a fiction, the compulsion paradoxically becomes to repeat in the present something that never actually happened in the past, that exists only, as it were, in its fictional dimensions.[32] As one can see, the patient's compulsive, pathological construction of a stable, uniform, and faithfully self-reproducing "apparent reality" clearly corresponds to the first half of Jakobson's and Barthes's models for realism (and Miller's for the Platonic mode, and Horkheimer's and Adorno's for the mythical mode), wherein difference is eliminated in favor of an original anterior reality and its endlessly and unfailingly represented mimetic copies. And this might suggest how, from a larger socio- and literary-historical perspective that would combine Freud and the Frankfurt School, realism itself could seem a pathological construction, subject to and sustained by its own repetition compulsion, its own ever-repeating imposition of a single, sustained, and repressive fiction designed to conceal a feared, ever-changing reality.

This is, however, still only half of Freud's own model for the repetition compulsion. The second half begins with the therapist, whose task becomes to get the patient to where "he recognizes that the apparent reality is in fact always and again only a reflection of a forgotten past."[33] In other words, the therapist's (or patient's) distinctly realist task becomes to thwart the vision that sees persons and things as repetitions ("the apparent reality") and to instill a recognition of the unique difference (i.e., reality) of the present. The process shares notable features with Freud's related notion of *Trauerarbeit,* the work of mourning: realism becomes a process of divesting the present of the projected psychic investments of the past. It also has something in common with Weber's notion of disenchantment, but still differs—fundamentally differs—in not equating disenchantment with rationalization and its leveling. Instead, and as one can see, this process corresponds to the latter half of our dual-natured model, the half that Miller called Nietzschean—where Y cannot repeat X—and that insists on the recognition of difference rather than the imposition of similitude. Notably, however, within Freud's own model both moments or movements to this compulsion arise out of the same sustained chain and process of repetition. Under the therapist's care, the patient's *Wiederholungszwang* becomes a fictional reality perpetually launched toward the recognition of its real fictionality, even as, from another perspective, it still remains a fiction forever aimed at repressing reality and repeating itself.[34]

A third Freudian mode of repetition explored in this study is that associated with what Freud calls the death drive. In his eyes, the death drive is related to the repetition compulsion. It is however differently evaluated, and while perhaps of dubious value for psychoanalysis itself, it has proved, especially in the hands of critics such as Peter Brooks—working almost exclusively with realist texts—to be extremely useful for literary analysis.[35] In this model, the desire for repetition, the desire to maintain a same-state, sustained identity, is associated with a death instinct, and is contrasted with a desire for difference, which Freud identifies with the life instinct.[36] Again, as in the case of the repetition compulsion, I would say that the emphasis on difference as central to a life impulse aligns this description with the realist impulse associated only with the second half of our proposed model. But the characterization of the desire for repetition as in the service not of the production and maintenance of a fiction—as is the case for the repetition compulsion already discussed, for the other, conservative half of realism described by Barthes and Jakobson, and for the mythical enlightenment model proposed by Horkheimer and Adorno—but rather in that of ending, of annihilating its own existence, achieving its own death, is somewhat of a different and unexpected turn of events.[37] In any case, it once again suggests that repetition and redundancy function not only as part of the construction of realism but also of its deconstruction, its self-pursued demise—quite apart from, or even including, its ongoing, repeated need for difference.

Lacan is evoked in this study mostly for the nuances he brings to our engaged Freudian models. Still, there are two aspects of his thought that are of independent importance to our model for reading realism. The first of these concerns his ideas about identity-formation. As Lacan and others argue, the concept of the self is to a large extent a specific, historically limited construct that, like realism and enlightenment, is tied up with the rise of bourgeois culture, in particular with the rise of the nuclear family—although it is also, and again like realism and enlightenment, a concept that proves unusually resistant to historical delimitation and that reappears across time with the same recurrent regularity as the other two. In any case, as Richard Brinkmann argues, subjectivity, or rather the subject pole of the subject-object relation, is absolutely central to the project of poetic realism; and as Leo Bersani argues, the "myth" of a significant, coherently structured self is central to realistic fiction, and both contributes to and draws support from realism's literary and social orders of coherence, significance, or intelligibility.[38] Lacan provides us with a way to conceive subjectivity itself in terms of the subject-object relation, and as part of that in terms of the play between the poetic and the real; moreover, he offers an especially suggestive model for self-structuring that both establishes the coherence demanded by Bersani and displays its intrinsic flaws.

Lacan's model consists of two basic parts, which are often presented as if they were diachronically related in a progressive movement from one to the other, but that actually—much like Miller's model of the Platonic and

Nietzschean, or Jakobson's of the established convention and its deformation—always remain mutually dependent and always function without logical or genetic priority.[39] The first part is associated with the mirror-stage, or what Lacan also identifies as the Imaginary. It consists of the attempt by the child (or simply, the self) to compose or forge a unified, singular, and encompassing identity through a complex specular process of equating models and copies. In Lacan's own figure, the hapless, fragmented child identifies itself with its own happy and whole re-flected image in the mirror. It then (mis-)takes this representation as its own reality, thus effecting a critical reversal: the mirror's representation/copy/image becomes the real/model/self, and the child becomes a representation of its own representation, its sense of its own reality based on its detour through its unreal representation.[40] As one can see, the process is ruthlessly engaged in repetition, and endlessly played out in the exchanges between the fictional and the real. Moreover, as Samuel Weber stresses, while it is not aimed at the "real," it is aimed at a reality, which would be its self-contained and autonomous legitimation.[41]

The second part of Lacan's model involves the move into what he calls the Symbolic: a move out of the "illusion" of wholeness, stability, and coherence vouchsafed in the Imaginary and into a new reality—again, not "real," but still a reality—in which the subject becomes defined not specularly but instead by being taken up into a system of difference: where the self is defined *as* difference, the subject by what it is not (and in some sense by what it is not *allowed* to be—that is, by frustration). Rather than a structure of endless repetitions and seemingly transparent exchanges, the Symbolic introduces one of thwarted repetitions and seemingly opaque, discrete positions that the subject is no longer able to hold—that's reality.

Given Lacan's own indebtedness to Jakobsonian models, it is not surprising that his descriptions of identity-formation seem to match Jakobson's for reality-formation.[42] This is true of the model we have been discussing, where Lacan's dual-natured, conflictual model for the self corresponds fairly exactly to Jakobson's for realism—where the Imaginary, with its easy verisimilitude and exchange between reality and representation and its dependence on repetition to maintain its stable and unified world can be associated with the first half; and the Symbolic, with its disruption of the established identity (now especially declared a fiction), its tactic of frustration (of the fiction-maintaining repetition), its movement away toward a supposedly more "realist" but no less conventionally constituted state, is associated with the second half. But it is no less true of Jakobson's other literary-historical model for realism, which we have so far ignored but that is more overtly relevant to Lacan and that can also be shown to be based on repetition. In his famous essay "On Two Aspects of Language," Jakobson associates metaphor, with its desire for a kind of repetition (substitutability, identity, and so on), with Romanticism (which, as we mentioned before, as realism's literary predecessor also functions at least at one stage as realism's own first term); and he associates metonymy, with its avoidance of metaphor and insistence on deferral (on meaning as further along), with realism.[43] Similarly, Lacan associates the metaphorical and the metonymic with the Imaginary and the Symbolic, respectively, making the latter, or the transition to the latter, representative of a kind of realism. That is also of course roughly analogous to Miller's description of the move from Platonic to Nietzschean, where learning not to see things as metaphors, not to see likes in unlikes, is equated with a realist impulse. But again, the two tropes, the two tendencies, remain indissoluably linked, as ultimately inseparable and mutually dependent as the Imaginary and Symbolic or, in Miller, the Platonic and the Nietzschean.

The second aspect of Lacan's thought relevant to my discussion of realism makes clear this continued inseparability: this is his notion of the lure, which comes up in his own discussion of aesthetic representation, and which has the added virtue of articulating with unusual clarity Lacan's understanding of the structure of desire.[44] The drama of the lure, and of desire, apparently takes place completely within the Symbolic realm, but it nonetheless continually (re)produces the Imaginary and, with it, the play between reality and representation according to the following basic script.

With the absenting of the original, "real" object of desire found in the Imaginary (the Mother or, more generally, the narcissistic self-reflection, lost under the forbidding law of the Father or the Symbolic), desire—the drive to recover this lost reality—begins its endless relay along an ongoing repeated chain of signifiers or representations. Each representation is approached by the subject *as* a representation, as an embodied repetition of the original real, which will stop the chain, secure identity—both between the representation and real, and between that real and the desiring self—and so stabilize both the subject and the (lost) object of desire. This is the lure, the promise of the restored Imaginary, with all its wholeness and stability: its reality.

However, there immediately follows, or perhaps better, there immediately accompanies another moment, the moment not of promise but of disappointment. The subject recognizes that the representation does not adequately embody, or repeat, the (lost) real (object of desire), and this recognition is loaded with two realizations, or if you will, with two realisms. First, the subject is forced to recognize the re-presentation in its difference, in its non-re-presentative reality or quality: arriving at this recognition is, I think, much like the Freudian realist task of mourning mentioned above.[45] Second, and intimately related: he or she is forced to recognize the "real" as lost, as not there, as essentially unattainable. And in both of these realizations, we find realism once again defined as the acknowledgment of the failure of its project of "realist" representation—that is, of the imaginary drive motivating desire to (re-)discover a self-contained and sustaining reality.

And yet: and yet. As Lacan stresses, despite any and all awareness of its faulty logic of representation, the reality of desire is still powerful enough to sustain the chain, the hopeful search for the lost real that imagines that the real is always just further along, and so moves desire along and in this way perpetuates the endless, contradictory interplay between the imagined mimetic utopia of matching model and copy, signified and signifier, reality and representation, of the faithful repetition or reproduction of the prior illusion in and as the present; *and* the realization of its impossibility, of its failure, occasioned by the loss of the one, and the inevitable difference of the other—by the recognition that Y never repeats X. What we see, then, is that whereas at one moment (the second moment) Lacan's model seems, like the mourning part of Freud's therapeutic cure of repetition, to associate realism only with the process of disillusion (or disenchantment), in the end, like Jakobson's, his model restores the more dynamic, conflictual structure that endlessly repeats itself, driven by its own inherently flawed logic of representing the real. As both Lacan and Jakobson seem to insist, the internal contradictions to realism's structure not only continually undo it: they also sustain it.

Theoretical Introduction

Such, then, are some of the most basic points of congruence and difference about the role of repetition in realism evident in the three theoretical discourses most engaged in this study, namely narratology, Critical Theory, and psychoanalysis. Each can be seen to evoke and elaborate a dual, conflictual model for realism that turns on issues of repetition, or rather, on repetition and the failure of repetition. But each also articulates differently, and often even contradictorily, the precise workings of repetition within that conflictual model, and so too different consequences for the realism at stake in its operation or failure. There is, that is, a high degree of redundancy between the models of repetition and realism elaborated by these various discourses, but there is an equally high degree of difference, not least in the role assigned to repetition and difference in realist discourse. All of the various overlaps and undercuttings here identified will reappear in my analyses of specific texts and problems in the following chapters; indeed, they will multiply as I also engage other aspects of repetition and realism in each of these discourses not yet discussed. Nor for that matter will I be exclusively concerned with only these three theoretical approaches; subsequent chapters will also draw on work inspired by feminists and by Foucault, in order both to further extend my dual conflictual model for repetition and realism, and to engage the challenge posed by Holub and Berman, and that is to challenge the viability of this dual conflictual model altogether. But I suspect that by this point our Hydra has sprouted enough heads from this particular limb of our monster. It seems time to cut and move on to another.

2 REAL AND RECURRENT PROBLEMS

Stifter's Preface to 'Many-colored Stones'
('Bunte Steine')

> What is evident is violent, even if this evidence is gently, liberally, democratically represented; what is paradoxical, what does not follow of itself, is less so, even if it is imposed arbitrarily.[1]
> —Roland Barthes

Much like the conversation about art—the so-called *Kunstgespräch*—in Büchner's novella *Lenz* (1839), the preface to Adalbert Stifter's *Many-colored Stones* (*Bunte Steine*, 1853) is often considered an early expression of poetic realism's aesthetic, a prophetic formulation of many of the principles, and problems, of the literary movement that would dominate German letters for the next forty years.[2] It certainly shares some central features with Büchner's *Kunstgespräch*: the unstated polemical stance against other, earlier aesthetic programs; the central issue of God, including the crucial paradox of both his importance to and threatened irrelevance for the proposed realist endeavor; and more positively, the common call for careful attention to small details and for the inclusion of previously excluded classes in the represented world.

Nonetheless, despite this commonality, Stifter's preface is clearly very different from the *Kunstgespräch*, and not least insofar as it also represents a quite different, and in some sense more explicit, political program. Written in 1852, and by Stifter's own account formulated in response to "the experiences of the past few years" (16)—namely, the failed revolutions of 1848, it plainly registers Stifter's political conservatism in the wake of these violent upheavals. In this respect its unstated polemical stance seems diametrically opposed to that implicit to Büchner's text. In fact, Stifter's polemic is directed not only against the common foe of Romanticism, but also and perhaps even more against Büchner's own school of radical Young Germany (*Junges Deutschland*) aesthetics.³ As an early document of poetic realism, then, the preface suggests a fundamentally different orientation from that foreseen by Büchner's work, or rather, the former joins the latter to yield a more complex, paradoxical inheritance for the realist tradition to come: a dual desire both to maintain the world the way it is and to dislocate it in the name of some new "reality."

The conservative political character of the preface and its significance for poetic realism are by now critical commonplaces. My interest is slightly different. What I find most significant, characteristic, and consequential about the political program of the preface is *how* it is presented, namely as nonpolitical. As Walter Benjamin notes, historical reality and ideology are almost always presented in Stifter as simple descriptions of the laws of Nature and of human nature.⁴ That this is not simply the case, that Stifter is not merely describing the objective, real workings of Nature and humanity but is instead inscribing a specific set of subjective and ideological values onto the site of these phenomena and then presenting them as immanent natural laws—this is signaled by Stifter himself, both at the end of the preface, where he explicitly links "my just explicated views" concerning natural law with "the experiences of the past few years," and at its opening, where he writes, "If there is something noble and good in me, then it will repose of itself in my writings; but if that something is not in my disposition, then I will strive in vain to represent elevated and beautiful things" (9).⁵ Stifter openly announces here the origin of the moral and aesthetic principles animating his texts not as immanent or proper to the world of these texts, but as projected by the individual author. It is, paradoxically, within the framework of this self-conscious procedure that Stifter proceeds to disguise his aesthetic discourse as "Nature" and as "reality," committing the defining realist act of denying the fictionality of his constructed world—wherein he needn't preach "virtue and morality" because these will be effected in his works simply through "what they are" (9)⁶—even as he first calls attention to the process of disguise. Similarly, it is within this framework that Stifter engages to present his political program as a way of *not* presenting politics or history, as a way of suppressing history and of defining the real in nonpolitical, nonhistorical terms, even as he calls attention to the suppression.[7]

This mode of not presenting real history or historical reality as part of the real, but nonetheless still *as* a mode for expressing the historical and ideological at the site of their supposed absence, will have significant consequences for the subsequent tradition of poetic realism.[8] Indeed, the "nonpolitical" strategy of realist aesthetics, where politics proper is circumscribed and placed off-stage—made discrete, discreetly—and then replaced by other, nonpolitical discourses that carry on the political function by other smaller, pettier, less overtly identifiable means—this same strategy is also already evident in Stifter's own literary works from the period before 1848, namely in the *Studies*, and perhaps most clearly so in *The Mountain Forest* (*Der Hochwald,* 1841).[9] But for both these reasons—because of both the peculiar, intrinsically nonpolitical nature of his realist mode and its active presence in the pre–1848 *Studies*—I also hesitate to characterize it as "political" in any simple or direct sense. After all, the nonpolitical nature of Stifter's program asserts itself not only in negative terms, in the discursive practices it avoids, but also in positive ones, in those it elaborates instead. And as I expect my reading here and throughout this study will confirm, the staging of a political, ideological program elsewhere, in supposedly nonpolitical discursive fields, is always a dangerous, highly ambivalent affair, as potentially threatening to the authority that inscribes it as it is supportive, and never as simply redundant as it might initially appear.[10]

What I would like most to work out in the following brief analysis of the preface, then, is the *kind* of realist program here presented, namely that of "the gentle law" (*das sanfte Gesetz,* 12). In particular I want to show the consequences of such a program for a reading of Stifter's works and in general to show the repercussions of considering realism as grounded in the politics or, rather, in the nonpolitics of this gentle law. This will, I believe, allow me to raise many of the thematic issues that prove central not only to the discussion of *The Mountain Forest* in the next chapter but also to that in most all of the subsequent ones as well.

Real and Recurrent Problems 27

I

The most notable aspect of the program described in the preface is that it is first articulated in the realm of Nature, or what Stifter calls "external nature [*die äussere Natur*]," and only subsequently in that of the "inner nature" of humankind (12). That Stifter supposedly privileges the world of Nature over that of man is irrelevant here, even misleading. For once we acknowledge that, in depicting the world of Nature, Stifter is not describing its real objective workings but rather a set of inscribed social (and psychological) values, the actual priority of the world of men and society becomes clear and the question of the rhetorical or strategic priority of the natural more focused. This rhetorical strategy is a specific form of repetition, namely that of a reflective chiasmus, a tactical reversal of terms in the interests of a somewhat deceptive, mirroring confirmation by an objectified authority. Nature will serve as a legitimizing power, as a "reality" that, once established, will establish the reality of Stifter's vision of human nature.[11] Such a projective strategy of reflective repetition is central to Stifter's supposed valorization of the nonhuman natural world and to its deployment vis-à-vis his human social one. It is also central to his realism, both in its external projection of an immanent authority, or reality, and in its subsequent shaping reflection back upon the human reality from which it nonetheless originates.[12]

The first characteristic, then, of Stifter's realist program is its rhetorical tactics of chiastic mimetic equivalence. Its second is the dual-natured, conflictual world that strategy projects. This characteristic emerges in Stifter's discussion of how his vision of the great and small differs from that of his nameless detractors. In the most famous and oft-quoted sentence from the preface, Stifter draws the distinction between "the flowing of air, the trickling of water, the growing of grain," and so forth, all of which he considers grand, and "the magnificently approaching storm, the lightning that splits houses, the tempest that drives the surf," and so on, all of which he considers small (10). Besides the distinction between the general and the individual, the true issue seems plainly to be between a certain static or hypostasized peacefulness and an agitated violence (each of the particular effects Stifter lists is patently disruptive). Implicit to the distinction are, of course, two competing visions of what counts as significant reality, the quarry of realism; and as my preceding chapter has shown, Stifter is quite traditional not only in proposing such a conflictual model but also in portraying one part of it as more realistic than the other.[13] Those who concentrate only on such natural upheavals are characterized as the "uninformed and inattentive," that is, as those who neither know nor perceive nature for what it really is. On the other hand, those who concentrate on the whole and the general (*das Ganze und Allgemeine*) are the true realists, able to recognize and embrace the order that maintains the world "as it is." Here especially, I think, we sense the inscription of Stifter's political program, his association of violence with the "uninformed" (= Young Germany) and of peacefulness with his own realist aims; here especially we see the embeddedness of his program in the conservative principle of realism posited by Jakobson and others, and his rejection of the claims of that other, competing principle of intentional disruption.

However, as Stifter elaborates his notion of the "higher laws" of the whole and the general (10), the simple terms of his distinction begin to break down. Stifter introduces the example of a man who daily measures the minute vicissitudes of a magnetic compass's needle. Although apparently insignificant, when joined with similar measurements taken from all over the world, the results reveal "that a magnetic storm goes over the whole earth, that the whole surface of the earth, as it were, feels a magnetic shudder at the same time" (11). The point is crucial: the general, world-maintaining forces turn out to be as violent as the individual ones; it is simply violence on another, more monstrous (*ungeheuer*) scale and on a less visible plane. The repetition is almost involuntarily registered in Stifter's language. His first example of violent individual upheaval, the magnificently approaching storm (*Gewitter*), is now countered by a magnetic storm (*Gewitter*) that goes over the whole earth.

There are at least two different ways that we can read this repetition, and while they overlap, they also suggest different things about the realism at stake in Stifter's description of the natural world. On the one hand, the reemergence of this storm and its epexegetical shudder can be seen to reveal that the higher law or force (*Kraft*) is itself a form of violence, indeed a greater, more organized, if less tangible or visible form—which is to say that perhaps Stifter's realism is based on a more hidden, but pervasive, even systematic violence of its own.[14]

And as part of this, the repetition of the word "storm" here can also be understood as what Freud would call a return of the repressed—which is to say both that there is some repression at issue in the hidden whole of the world-maintaining forces and that there is some violent, disruptive reality that persists and returns to the site of representation, despite its alleged effacement. But on the other hand, the appearance of the "storm" on both the individual and general level suggests that perhaps Stifter instead considers the specific disruptive violence to be a consequence of the general sustaining law, to be a "natural," systemic effect, and not in the sense of an accidental, unwanted by-product, but more or less the opposite: its logical, even immanent manifestation. This is certainly the relation implied by Stifter's accompanying example of the electrical force that produces the lightning; and this in turn implies a fundamentally different relation to the several violences in Stifter's program—one that avoids all issues of repression and sees instead a certain inclusive continuity between the principles of world maintenance and disruption. (The relevance of this, and its critical difference from the preceding model, will emerge as we proceed.)[15]

Besides its rhetorical strategy of chiastic repetition and its intended effacement of disruptive violence in favor of a stable world of law—which however quickly yields its own chiastic repetition—there is another way that Stifter's description of nature can be construed as peculiarly realist: in his depiction of the artist recording this description as a *Forscher,* or investigator. A similar designation can be found throughout realism, including many of Stifter's own works and works by both Storm and Raabe discussed in this study. It has two especially important aspects here in the preface: the relation to God and the relation to vision.

The realist conception of the artist as mere investigator might seem, or be, in tension with the image of the poet, or *Dichter,* that prefaces Stifter's account of the natural world and especially in tension with his notion of the quasi-religious status of poetry, or *Dichtung,* proper. Stifter writes, "Art is for me . . . the highest thing on earth after religion; . . . There are very few poets in the world, they are the high priests"; for which reason "I have never held my writings to be poetic works" (9). Although the distinction seems primarily based on grounds of modesty and to apply only to Stifter's own small, insignificant artworks, the conflict between art conceived religiously and realistically is in fact to a great extent intrinsic and general. For example, we see the same conflict in Büchner's *Kunstgespräch,* indeed in the whole novella, where (as here) an aesthetic procedure that purports simply to record objective, empirical observations runs counter to one that is more or less divinely creative or productive; and where a realist orientation that appeals to a world of natural law and forces seems to call into question certain notions of transcendence, particularly Christian ones.[16] However as Holub has shown, none of this prevents a religious dimension from haunting the image of the realist artist in Büchner's novella; and the same turns out to be the case in Stifter, although for revealingly different reasons.

For Stifter, the problem of the realist artist as investigator might be formulated something like this. The object of his pursuits is the whole and the general. However, due both to his restriction to the observable, phenomenal world and, further, his particular restricted place within that world, the investigator and his brother artist can only ever observe and record the potentially endless individual details of that world. This is implicit in Stifter's example of the magnetic readings, where the individual's minute recordings need to be complemented by a more or less impossibly omniscient appeal to "observations being made simultaneously all over the world" before the general "reality" can be perceived or realized: the realist alone cannot compose the text, or table, recording reality. And it is explicit in one of the more syntactically and logically twisted sentences in the preface. Stifter writes:

But because science only obtains grain after grain, only makes observation after observation, only compiles the whole out of particulars, and because finally the number of phenomena and the field of the given are infinitely large, so that God has made the joy and happiness of investigation inexhaustible, we, too, in our workshops can only ever represent the particular, never the general, for that would be Creation. (11)

What this amounts to is the observation that "the whole and the general" is empirically not there, is absent, that as both scientist and realist artist the investigator sees only discrete, unconnected pieces and fragments without immanent, intrinsic meaning or connection. In fact, he is limited to the perception of the same mere particulars and phenomena (or appearances, *Erscheinungen*) as those "uninformed," those nonrealists whom he would oppose. From within the realist's empirical sphere itself, there is no general law-giving or meaning-giving reality.

This is precisely the state of affairs that is described in the famous opening pages of *Abdias*, that Swales sees again in the opening chapter of the *Studies'* version of *The Album of My Greatgrandfather* (*Die Mappe meines Urgrossvaters*), and Berman behind all the pedantic descriptions of *Indian Summer* (*Der Nachsommer*): not that meaning, significance, or "law" are immanent in Stifter's world, whether natural or human, but that they quite possibly are not, that reality is itself insignificant or incoherent, or perhaps better, that coherence, significance, or law must be derived from somewhere else.[17] This is one of the key, inherent moments of self-consciousness in Stifter's realism; it is also a moment at which, in this instance, the appeal to Christian religion becomes both unavoidable and highly embarrassing for his program. God supplies the general reality that realism itself cannot, but still needs: God supplies the missing unity, or rather Stifter supplies God to supply the missing unity and law—the law of unity—that guarantee that the pieces and fragments function *as* pieces and fragments, as signifiers of a common, but empirically absent, reality. It is, finally, faith in or obedience to this unseen order and general law that alone distinguishes the realist's particulars from those of his nonrealist counterpart. Realism becomes a matter not of scientifically recording what is there but of religiously believing in what is not.[18]

To be quite clear on this point, for it is an important and often misunderstood one: it is not, or not simply, this appeal to a uniform signifying reality behind the "infinitely large field of the given" that characterizes the realism of Stifter's program and the privileged objectivity of his artist qua investigator. Rather, it is the perceived fragility and even fictionality of that appeal, the awareness of the empirically resistant, frustrating "reality" that also keeps the appeal notably belated and forced, even doomed—and so far removed from the Christian or even from the classical Goethean world it might otherwise wish to recall.[19] And while it is certain that if the discrete heterogeneous pieces of the realist's natural world do not yield "the whole and the general," then their forging together into a uniform order becomes something in itself violent and repressive and anything but gentle or natural; it is still equally certain that this potential failure, this fiction and the simultaneous violence and fragility of the fiction themselves remain part of Stifter's realist vision—and not only Stifter's, as we shall see.[20]

The second aspect of the artist as investigator that is of importance to Stifter's realism, indeed to poetic realism itself, is the privileging of *vision*, and especially of "the eye of science." It is common at this point to mention Stifter's own training in painting, a training shared by several other realists, particularly Keller; to explain Stifter's famous nature descriptions as the extension into literature of a visual, pictorial impulse, thus upsetting the distinctions inherited from Lessing and the eighteenth century and heralding a new nineteenth-century poetic that aims more at spatial stasis than temporal or narrative movement; to argue that the realist program of mimetic reproduction almost inevitably appeals to the visual arts, where the ideal of faithful imitative representation seems more credible and avoids the obvious objections of arbitrariness and conventionality inseparable from signification in the literary linguistic realm; and also to cite Benjamin's observation on Stifter's style that he can represent only the visual and that his realism thus shuts out or excludes the more central truth or reality, the revelation of language itself.[21]

There is of course considerable truth to all these points, and no discussion of poetic realism can risk ignoring them, perhaps especially any discussion of Stifter's realism. But their truths tend to obscure another, equally important one, which is particularly conspicuous in the preface, namely that the emphasis on vision persists even after the visible is no longer the object of realist attention. In fact, as in Büchner's *Kunstgespräch*, the preface presents an apparent tension between those who stay on the surface, who are restricted to the empirical, natural details that "the bodily eye" reveals, and those who penetrate beneath these appearances to "the whole and the general," who are in this case focused on the connection that "the spiritual eye of science" (11) alone perceives. That is, the Stifterian realist vision is not about the visual at all, or only in the second place. It too is about the imposition of law, order, and meaning behind or within the visual; it is about the unseen. In Lacanian terms, we would say that it is more about the gaze and desire than the look; in Foucauldian terms, that it is more about supervision and power than objective scientific truth. In our terms, we should note that the investigator's "eye" is both the source and effect of God in the constitution of hidden reality. His vision first posits the order of God so that it may then in turn become its reflective repetition, and it is in the chiastic coordination between the questioning investigator and the answering deity that this posited order behind the natural world is confirmed, and closed.

One last point about Stifter's description of Nature—a sort of coda in response to his own coda. Although the preface follows the *Kunstgespräch* in positing this distinction between those whose vision stays on the surface and those whose eye penetrates to the reality beneath, it goes further in casting this distinction in terms of an *historical* development, an historical unveiling of sight toward the real, a sustained retreat from the distorting representations of the past. Implicit in this is a rejection of Romanticism and Young Germany as earlier, more naive stages of vision, where the focus on "what was near at hand and striking" betrayed "humans in their childhood" and blinded them to the reality of the natural world. But note how, by designating the process of seeing as part of history, Stifter manages to depict a natural world that seems itself to exclude history—by which I mean not any concrete history, but the very idea of history, of temporal unfolding, development, embeddedness, or maturation. For all the acknowledgment of its own ongoing development, the ideal of Stifter's realist vision still rests upon a model of a static, spatial, unchanging reality, as does the exchange between God and investigator in piecing together "the edifice of the eternal." As a result, Nature itself in Stifter has no development; it seems instead to have only a childhood, or else a fully realized form.[22] History becomes a quality intrinsic only to representation, not reality, and which in fact disappears even from representation as it comes adequately to approach reality. History becomes precisely what realism would somehow leave out of the natural world.[23]

The exclusion of temporality, of history in this sense, from natural reality causes nearly insoluble problems for Stifter's realist program, and, as Benjamin notes, the problem becomes particularly acute in his representation of women, who cannot grow up without violating his concept of Nature or natural law, as Nature becomes a repressive standard that actually excludes nature, a reality that denies reality.[24] Given the patriarchal order of Stifter's natural world—confirmed in the male gender of both his Christian God and his scientific investigator and secured in the chiastic coordination between them—this role of women should come as no surprise. We will see it graphically in the case of both Johanna and Clarissa in *The Mountain Forest*, but it is no less evident in that of Ditha in *Abdias*, of both Anna and Chelion in *The Castle of Fools* (*Die Narren-*

burg), or of Margarita in *The Album of my Greatgrandfather*. However, the problem is also not peculiar to Stifter. In fact, even in the *Kunstgespräch* the ideal of realist vision is represented by the famous image of the Medusa's head, which is figuratively aimed at two young girls going down a hillside, freezing or petrifying them into static dead representations in the very course of aesthetically ordering their living reality.[25] Something similar can also be seen in Keller's *Green Henry* (*Der Grüne Heinrich*), where the protagonist's painterly attempts to capture natural reality in a realist fashion are strangely but significantly coordinated with the denied sexual maturation and subsequent early death of Anna, the privileged subject of most of Heinrich's paintings. Many of these same problems arise in many of the works addressed in this study as well; for as we will see, the paradoxes of stasis and temporality and even of life and death are intrinsic to almost any program of realist representation, not only Stifter's. But as we will also see, the arrest of poetic realism on issues of female sexuality seems also to reveal something intrinsic to the realist program—and again, not only Stifter's.[26]

I I

From his discussion of the natural world, Stifter proceeds to one of the human, social world. He insists from the outset that the relation between the two is one of equivalence, or repetition: "As it is in external nature, so is it also in the internal, in the nature of humankind" (12). And he rhetorically structures his representation of the human world to repeat that of the natural, describing the same explicit contrast between peaceful normality and violent upheaval, with the same implicit historical and political resonances: the same rejection of movement and of desire and history as primary, even related forms of movement, and the same embrace and elaboration of a supposedly quite different gentle law (12). But while his account of the natural world prepares us for the essential paradox that this gentle law proves violent in the human sphere, it does not fully prepare us for *how* it proves violent and how it relates to the more open violence it both opposes and repeats.

Let me attempt to explain this and its consequences for a realist aesthetic more clearly. The distinction between the peaceful and violent life is again presented in terms of the general law versus the individual. However, in this case, the distinction is also between radically different forces, or *Kräfte,* the one individual and the other social, with only the latter qualified as law, a law that explicitly and exclusively manifests itself through the repression of the individual and his or her appetites: "There are forces that aim to sustain the individual. . . . [But] therefore there are forces that work to sustain mankind as a whole that may not be restricted by the individual forces, that, on the contrary, act restrictively on the individual forces themselves" (12). Critics regularly point out how different this model is from that of Goethean classicism. My point is a slightly different one, and that is how different this model of the "gentle law" and its relation to the individual is from that of Stifter's own description of Nature. For all the covert play of repression and difference, the individual instances of disruptive violence in Stifter's external nature are still primarily conceived as consequences of the general sustaining law, as natural systemic effects. This is perhaps most apparent in Stifter's example of the relation between the lightning and the omnipresent electrical force, where the perceived disruption is seen to be an expression of law, in fact of the same law (or reality) governing the magnetic storm. However in his human world, we see no such continuity. Instead, Stifter expressly presents two different, opposed forces, one violently individual, the other repressively (and only repressively) social: the idea of the individual force, in all its disruptive violence, as nonetheless a consequence, an effect, or simply a part of the social, general law (of reality) is, apparently, excluded.

And yet despite this crucial distinction, Stifter still rhetorically presents his social world as a repetition of his natural one, even as he has first presented that natural world as a reflection of his social and aesthetic program. He still intends to make the functioning of law seem identical in both spheres, and for the one to regulate the other in a moment of chiastic equivalence. This contradiction raises the real issue for Stifter, to some extent for realism in general, and to a very great extent for *The Mountain Forest* in particular: whether "the forces that aim to sustain the individual"—and so too the eruptive assertion of difference—are part of the "law" of realism or not, whether realism seeks to exclude or to include them to define itself, and so whether their eventually emergent reality is to be read as a return of the repressed or as an immanent effect.[27] Paradoxically, Stifter seems here to want to have it both ways at once. But I would suggest that this paradox is inherent to much of realism and finally characterizes it far more accurately than either alternative taken alone.[28]

Besides its inherently flawed chiastic structure and its hesitancy between an inclusive and exclusive self-definition, there are two further aspects to Stifter's description of his "gentle law" that can be construed as fundamental to an emergent realist aesthetic: the privileged attention paid to quotidian social reality and the description of the realist artist as an investigator of human beings (*Menschenforscher*).

Like Büchner's Lenz in the *Kunstgespräch,* Stifter also advocates a reorientation of aesthetic focus onto the lower classes and their daily activities, "the ordinary, everyday, countlessly recurring acts of human beings" (14). However, Stifter's rationale for the focus is quite different from Büchner's, though no less consequential for realism in general. Whereas for Büchner the justification for including the mundane human world is that "the vein of feeling is the same in nearly all human beings," but that it is somehow more palpable, less obscured in the common people, for Stifter the justification is that "the law reposes wherever people live beside people" (13), but that it is particularly evident in common everyday activities, "in which this law lies most securely as a center of gravity" (14).[29] Stifter's realist quarry is not life but instilled convention. Reality for him is not something ontologically given, but culturally and historically installed.

There are two aspects of the identification here of the gentle law with the functioning of everyday society, or reality, that are of particular importance for Stifter's (and not only Stifter's) realism. First, much as Stifter supplies God to enforce the unity and law that guarantee that the empirically discrete particulars (*Einzelheiten*) function as signifiers of a common, empirically absent natural reality, so does he supply the community to enforce the law that guarantees that discrete individuals function as representatives of a single human reality. Reality itself becomes defined as an order of similitude, of ever-repeating, normed identities that eliminate individual differences, and it is only insofar as they display proper faith in or obedience to the conventions of this order that individuals partake of reality.[30]

Second, as Stifter makes clear, perhaps the most important site for the enforcement of these conventions and their concomitant repression of the individual is the family, which is privileged as the truest locus of commonality (:of reality) because it is the most forceful sphere of regulation. More precisely, within the family, the gentle law and its norm-inducing conventions achieve their first and finest expression, and they do so in the form of love (*Liebe*): "This law reposes everywhere . . . it reposes in the love of spouses for one another, in the love of parents for their children, of children for their parents, in the love of siblings, of friends for one another, in the sweet inclination of both sexes," and so forth (13). The point is crucial: "love" is the purest manifestation of law, of conventionality itself; it is the very embodiment of the "political" agenda inscribed and promoted by Stifter's realism; it is the unseen significance and order that realism makes its end and means. Much as in Nature the investigator's vision functions to establish the otherwise absent unifying divine reality, so here does love establish the required social reality. In both cases, the policing, order-imposing function remains the same.

Of course, it is not quite so simple. As the rhetorical embedding of "the sweet inclination of both sexes" in the exact middle of this long list (truncated in my quotation) suggests, the realist's love-as-law also stands in a complex relation to a potentially different reality, that of desire, which threatens subversion of the intended, orderly reality.[31] According to Stifter, it is desire that interrupts and opposes the common ground that upholds the world "the way it is." It is the privileging and emergence of pleasure (*Genuss*) and the sensual (*das Sinnliche*), the sensuous (*das Sinnenreizende*) and, finally, desire (*Lust*) that are to be guarded against and resisted at all times. We should, of course, note the paradox of a realist program that appeals directly to the sensible world and yet fears the sensual one, the paradox of a program that would ground itself precisely on that which it would also deny. But we should also note that this paradox is only the particular symptom of a more general problem. Stifter seems himself to formulate the more fundamental question when he describes the *Lust* that destroys the social fabric as an effect "of its inner disarray or that of an external, more savage but more powerful enemy" (16), a distinction that expresses quite well the essential ambivalence adhering to "the sweet inclination" in the list of loves quoted above. For on the one hand, *Liebe* and *Lust,* love and desire, seem radically different forces, or realities, and love seems (much like Nature vis-à-vis female sexuality) to function primarily as a repressive, gently violent force, as a reality that excludes or denies another reality.³² From this perspective, the rhetorical embedding of "sweet" sexual desire in the quoted sentence seems a gesture of containment and repression, a would-be exclusion through a strategy of neutralizing enclosure or assimilation.³³ Similarly, its disruptive reemergence at moments of the collapse of conventionally maintained reality appears as "that of an external enemy," as a decisively other, but more powerful reality that persists and returns to the site of its supposed elimination. But on the other hand, desire also seems very much a product of *Liebe,* and not accidentally or unwantedly, but logically and immanently so. It emerges as a systemic effect of the constructs of familial love, as part of the self-sustaining force of the gentle law itself. From this perspective, its disruptive reality seems a result of love's own "inner disarray," as the expression not of some other extrinsic and repressed reality but of the same intrinsic and encouraged reality. We need not (and perhaps cannot) decide between these possibilities, nor for the moment need we decide on the precise nature of the latter's inner disarray, or *Zerwirrung*.³⁴ For now, we need only observe this structure of love and desire and its prominent place in Stifter's program: as *the* privileged site of realist concern, as reality (even, we might say, as politics)—in its stabilizing, maintaining, norm- and identity-inducing role, and in its disruptive, resistant one.

The second, related aspect of Stifter's description of the gentle law in human society that is of importance for his realism comes in his account of the artist as an investigator of human beings (*Menschenforscher*). Repeating his earlier history of the unfolding stages of vision vis-à-vis Nature, Stifter now provides a history of views vis-à-vis social, human reality, wherein an initial aesthetic focus on and valorization of overt physical violence, including political action, warfare, and powerful "sensations and passions," eventually yield "a survey [*ein Überblick*] of something greater: . . . the suppression of sensations and passions came to be considered grand and great" (15). There is not, that is, so much a lessened concern with violence by the present-day realist artist as there is a shift to its more systematic and effective, but less visible expression. The overt, external violence against others is turned inward against itself, is chiastically reversed and repeated in a more covert, internal sphere.³⁵ The realist's privileging of a restricted, quietly prosaic subject matter is in fact based on a conviction that this is where the "victorious and great" regime of the gentle law is most forcibly present. The representational mode that keeps itself similarly small, restricted, and nonremonstrative is privileged precisely for its capacity to describe and inscribe this more general violence (this law, this love) behind and into human events.

This gently violent suppression of sensations and passions is not only the condition of realism in relation to the artist's chosen subject matter, but also in relation to himself: he too experiences the same suppression. And if we connect this back with Stifter's earlier history of human views regarding Nature, we can see how its elimination of the marvelous in Nature is a result of the elimination of marvel, of imagination, and its corresponding passion in the observer. The structure, and perhaps too the flaw, of Stifter's chiastic, reflective strategy is particularly conspicuous here. The posited natural world seems not so much the noninscription of a subjectivity as the very definite inscription of a would-be nonsubjectivity, which is then reflected back, as reality, to deny the nature of the subject from which it nevertheless originates. The very reality the realist artist envisions seems both predicated on and aimed at his own annihilation, his own self-effacement, his own self-denial. Its law, its violence claims him as its foremost victim.

The consequences of this gently violent elimination of subjectivity, desire, and imagination in the realist artist himself are somewhat complicated, certainly more so than most critics allow. On the one hand, we might simply speak of the repression of the subject's imagination and desire, indeed of the poetic itself, as the condition and project of poetic realism. In support of this we might look to Stifter's own sense of diminished powers (*Kräfte*) in the two closing paragraphs of the preface, his characterization of the proto-realist narratives in the *Many-colored Stones* as "the products of modest powers," and his mistrusting his own power (*Kraft*) to produce anything more poetically ambitious (16). Such a sense of severely lessened imaginative powers accords well, and only apparently paradoxically, with the frequent outbursts of almost uncontrolled, even pathological emotion, violence, and fantasy that so familiarly characterize those same modest tales. Both are the expected outcome of the same model of realism as repression, as the necessarily impossible exclusion of a reality that inevitably returns.

On the other hand, using a slightly different though not unrelated model, we might confirm how, in the very gesture of their elimination, both imagination and desire assert themselves in Stifter's realism. The suppression of imagination is an inherently imaginative effort, that of desire a fervently desired outcome. The difference may seem small, but it matters greatly. Desire and imagination do not simply inhabit realism as unwanted by-products, as realities that won't stay away, but as intrinsic forces in its own project: realism as based not on the repression of desire but on the deployment of a new, different desire—based not in the elimination of imagination but in its displaced, more dispersed, less conspicuous but no less powerful exercise.[36] This is, I would say, the necessary corollary to our recognition of the inherent if hidden violence to Stifter's program, a violence critics might more readily admit; but where we find the one, we find the others, too.

Let me briefly sum up in more general terms what the preface reveals to us about a realist aesthetic, before proceeding to my particular concern with *The Mountain Forest*. The preface has shown some of the ways that realism can be described as a fiction aiming at a stable, law-governed uniformity and based on exclusion and repression: of singularity, difference, and nonconformity, of violence, desire, and imagination. And where there is repression, there is also of course a return of the repressed: the preface seems constantly to betray a certain built-in fragility to realism, which is endlessly threatened by its own repressed reality. But the preface has also shown us another possible basis for realism that skirts issues of exclusion and repression and rests instead on inclusion and expression: of violence, imagination, even difference, and even desire. Repetition works slightly differently here, both within the work and over the projected course of realism itself: realism as the ever-ongoing possibility of more imagination, more desire, more reality—and more violence. Both models conflict and collaborate, conceal and reveal each other. If I hesitate to choose between them, it is because, I think, the hesitation is realism's own.

3

DOUBLE VISIONS

Chiastic Mimesis and the Politics of Realism in Stifter's 'The Mountain Forest' ('Der Hochwald')

> Every breath you take,
> Every move you make,
> I'll be watching you.
> —The Police, "You Belong To Me"

Although one of his most popular, *The Mountain Forest* (*Der Hochwald*, 1841) is hardly one of Stifter's best stories, nor one of his most successfully realist ones. Even in the *Studies*, several texts evince their superior quality, most notably *Brigitta*, *Abdias*, and *A Walk in the Wood* (*Der Waldsteig*); and many of the novellas collected in *Many-colored Stones*, especially the first three, more obviously achieve a consistent realist effect. In comparison with these, *The Mountain Forest* is a very uneven work, fundamentally flawed in design and uneasily combining elements of the Romantic fairy tale and the incipient realist novella. However, it is also one of the very few tragedies, or unremitted tragedies, in Stifter's oeuvre, one of the very few complete ruptures in the serene façade most often associated with his realist world: and as I hope to show, this tragic outcome is deeply, intrinsically related to the story's aesthetic flaws, which similarly rupture the usual, well-regulated fiction. Moreover, these same flaws expose many of the essential features and problems of Stifter's realist enterprise far more tellingly than his supposedly seamless tales: in fact, I will argue that both the flaws and the story's tragedy are related symptoms of Stifter's self-conscious exploration into his project of poetic realism.

Besides this self-exposing dimension to the story's realism and its tragedy, there is another feature to *The Mountain Forest* that makes it peculiarly well suited to function as a focal point for our own exploration into Stifter's—and not only Stifter's—poetic realism. The story concerns the attempt by the Knight of Wittinghausen to sequester his two daughters, Johanna and Clarissa, away in the woods during the Thirty Years War. But Clarissa's lover finds his way to her, and both father and lover are subsequently killed during a siege of the father's castle by Swedish troops.[1] In some indirect but still central manner to be worked out in our analysis, the tragedy in the narrative follows from a certain fatal conjunction of female desire and history, from their joint intrusion into the constructed realist world. As I said earlier, the perceived threat and consequent suppression of both these elements—but also their irrepressible (re)emergence—are characteristic not only of many of Stifter's own, other texts but also of much of poetic realism in general: *The Mountain Forest* will allow us to articulate more distinctly some of the chief relations between realism, history, and female desire.

I

The Mountain Forest is a frame story, and, like the preface to *Many-colored Stones*, it begins with Nature. Unlike in the preface, however, it is initially almost impossible to get a satisfying sense of the opening description of Nature, which even on a first reading proves extremely confusing and disorienting. This confusion is unquestionably an early symptom of the story's flawed design. But it is also intrinsic to the intended realism, and so worth considering in some detail.[2]

Certainly amid the confusion of the opening description of the frame we can discern several basic patterns and themes that will have significance for the novella as a whole. Most of these structures or patterns initially assert themselves in terms of *directions*, for, interestingly enough, the dominant sense of disorientation results largely from the narrator's opening excess of directional orientation. So, for instance, we note that the narrator begins with Nature for much the same reason as Stifter does in the preface to *Many-colored Stones*: he is setting up a rhetorical structure that moves first from the natural world to the human, historical one within the frame, that is, from the "high woods" to the Wittinghausen ruins outside of Friedburg, and then from this Nature-dominated frame on to the human, historical world of his primary narrative, that of the Wittinghausen family during the Swedish War, some two hundred years earlier. In this way, the narrator contrives to double the tactical function of Nature we already encountered in the preface to *Many-colored Stones* with that often associated with the frame in realist texts, wherein the frame-world acts as the "real," as the setting into and against which the story proper is introduced and tested.[3]

Second, we note that the narrator not only follows the same movement from the prioritized natural world to the subsequent human one as in the preface to *Many-colored Stones*. He also traces the same implicit, back-and-forth mirroring movement between them. We see this broadly in the two points (*zwei Punkte*) of his description, namely of the woods and their lake, which represent the natural, and of the town and its castle ruins, which represent the human locus of his tale.[4] But we see it more specifically in the moving track of his narration, as he travels—and narrates as he travels—first from the town westward, along the Moldau, up to the lake and woods, and then re-turns eastward, again along the Moldau, back toward the castle and town. Admittedly, the reflective symmetry here seems not quite to work, to be somewhat frustrated by the recalcitrant "facts" of his description, since the point at which he begins (Krumau) and to which he returns (Friedburg) prove not to be the same; but the intended recursive relation between the human and natural spheres still seems recognizably the same as that more cleanly established in the preface to *Many-colored Stones*.[5]

In part, then, the confusion to the opening description of the frame follows from the more forced unfolding of a familiar pattern or directionality between the two established spheres. But it also arises from the presence of other non-reflective directionalities and relations, and the sense of a unified whole that the narrator so apparently desires his opening description of Nature to represent is further strained by these other competing patterns. These patterns or directions are two in number, the one linear and the other circular, and in the first paragraph, even before his introduction of the pattern of mirroring repetitions, the narrator suggests both through the movements of his description itself. First, he seems notably intent on tracing a linear, descending movement from some natural origin down into human history. This is reflected in two apparently separate instances. He initially depicts the forest "beginning at the sources [*Quellen*] of the river Thaia, and stretching forth to that juncture of borders where the Bohemian land joins with Austria and Bavaria" (211), a crucial point in the Thirty Years War that provides the novella's historical setting. Then, in a sudden and unsignaled shift in perspective, the juncture of borders (*Grenzknoten*) becomes a massif (*Gebirgsstock*) that itself sends down streams to the three countries, now located both away and below. The effect of the shift in descriptive location is undeniably disorienting, and seems to thwart the narrator's overt intent of our spatial orientation. But he makes it in order that the basic movement of his description remain the same: irrevocably downward and away.

Second, the narrator's entire opening paragraph seems to follow an almost classical ring structure of composition. It begins *An der Mitternachtsseite,* that is, on the north side of the country, and ends with the mountains and woods going "many a day's journey further northwards [*mitternachtswärts*]"—in a seemingly different, back-turned (*abgebeugt*) direction from that followed by the descending waters: while the streams go down into a human, historical world, the woods go back into themselves. As with the first movement—as in fact also with the back-and-forth symmetry setting movement of his subsequent scouting mission—the circular one is carried more by the rhetoric than by the facts of his description. In all three cases, the narrator can be seen to impose a structure not quite empirically there. As we will see, he will continue to trace these two uneasily contradictory movements—one circular, turned back, stable, and closed, the other linear, descending, labile, and open-ended—throughout the narrative; both together represent a major, even insuperable complication to his subsequent, in some sense belated effort to inscribe a pattern of reflective repetition onto the same two spheres.[6]

The reason for all these confusing, apparently contradictory directionalities, even the logic of their common relation, can be found in one of the two simple themes to the frame, indeed to the whole story, namely: the originality of the woods, or rather, their virginity (*Jungfräulichkeit*). While the motif might seem a literary commonplace, and has often invited comparison with the works of James Fenimore Cooper, it is in fact almost uniquely here in Stifter's own works, where it serves a highly specific function in the novella quite foreign to anything in Cooper. "The virginity of the woods" (241) becomes in *The Mountain Forest* the narrator's functional equivalent of the gentle law in Stifter's preface to *Many-colored Stones*, the natural law and hidden, ordering reality that not only organizes and motivates the individual details of his natural world but also determines the relations between the natural and human worlds, or more specifically, between the forest and the female protagonists, Johanna and Clarissa.

The semanticization of the woods as virginal is almost insidiously obvious: it is predicated on two conditions, that of a self-sustaining origin and that of its precipitate, disruptive loss, which correspond fairly precisely to the two movements defined in the opening paragraph and to the relation they establish between the spheres of nature and men. But the very obviousness of the inscription tends to conceal both its covert design and its inherent aporia. We see the first condition when the narrator sums up his opening description of the woods with the line "No trace of human hand, virginal silence" (213): all the minute, specific details of his preceding account are calculated to yield this general conclusion. For the narrator, the purest, truest, most real state of Nature (and Nature is here the purest, truest reality) is that untouched, unviolated by the "hands" of man, which in fact knows nothing of the human: reality is, as it were, innocent of human reality. The paradox here is not, as some critics suggest, that the narrator violates that virginity by his own human presence, or that his own tracing hand and speaking voice undo the very reality they represent.[7] Rather, it is that this virginity is itself the perceptible trace or mark of his hand, its silence the echo of his projecting voice: for in the ideal of a natural virginity, the narrator constructs a recognizably human fiction as reality, but which nonetheless excludes human reality. And whereas such a construct or fiction might seem worlds away from other examples of realism, we should note that it also perfectly embodies two of the defining, bad-faith fictions of all realism: that its proffered world is uniform, stable, and unchanging; and that it is untouched by human agency, is immanent, pure reality (and not just reality as pure).

The second basic condition of the woods' virginity is that of its inevitable and irretrievable loss as one enters the world of the human and of history. This is conveyed by, and linked with, the same descending movement of water from its origin depicted in the opening paragraph. As the narrator first enters the woods, he re-encounters the waters of the Moldau he left below, "except here they are even more youthful and nearer their origin" (212)—that is, before their descent into human society. In the story proper, but with a momentary retreat to the narrative perspective of the frame, his language becomes more explicit: "At that time there was neither village nor path, but only the valley and stream, and these were even more beautiful, more fresh, more virginal (*noch jungfräulicher*) than now" (233)—that is, before the descent into human history.[8] Human reality, and perhaps especially historical reality, is conceived as a perpetual falling away from an original, stable reality: its meaning is the perpetual loss of meaning.

Again, the representation of virginity vis-à-vis the human world seems commonplace to the point of inconspicuousness. But the problem arises when, similar to the rhetorical gambit in the preface to *Many-colored Stones*, this virgin law of Nature—supposedly untouched by and actually excluding human reality—is then extended to include, even to police the human, which is nonetheless defined by its inevitable falling away from that law: when the stable and closed order is asked to repeat itself in the open, labile one via the third—that is, the mirroring order of repeating realities. In the gentle law of virginity, the narrator sets up an inherently dual-natured, conflictual reality, and as a result all his subsequent belated efforts after coherence and uniformity between the two spheres can seem only contradictory and doomed to frustration from the start. This is, we might say, one of the most flagrant "flaws" to the story's aesthetic: but as we will see, the story's realism lies not in the realization of its aesthetic but rather in that of its flaw, of the necessary failure of its attempt to construct a simple, identical, uniform, and pure reality.

Exactly how this last movement to the theme of virginity comes about, wherein its natural law or reality is made to repeat in the quite different reality of men or women—this is mediated through the agency of the second simple theme of the frame and story, namely glances, and especially reciprocal glances. The theme picks up on the same central role of vision and the gaze in realism already elaborated in my analysis of the preface to *Many-colored Stones*, and combines two aspects previously discussed separately: supervision and communication.

Within the narrative proper, this theme will be carried by the telescopes connecting the story's two points (*zwei Punkte*), and for various reasons I will want to return to them later. Within the frame, the narrator lays out the thematics of vision in the following way. His incursion into the woods is perhaps best seen as a sort of advance scouting expedition, as a scopic reconnaissance setting the groundwork or sightlines for his upcoming tale. And as a crucial part of this preparation, his description of the virgin woods comes to concentrate on the central point (*der eigentliche Punkt*, 212) of the forest lake, which he then subjects to one further act of imaginative projection: "One and the same thought often occurred to me as I sat on its shore:—as if it were an uncanny eye of Nature [*ein unheimlich Naturauge*] that regarded me here—deep black— overarched by the forehead and brow of rocks, edged by the lashes of dark pine—the water within motionless, like a petrified tear" (214). In the preceding paragraph, the narrator fancied that the lake's fixedness (*Unbeweglichkeit*) made it seem a monstrous black mirror-glass (213); here, its motionlessness turns it into an uncanny eye. This almost deathlike stillness or petrifaction is one of the chief and highly ambivalent features of the virginity that he would inscribe into the entire woods: its concentrated incorporation in the lake serves to figure the lake as the *unheimlich* embodiment of that virgin law, which the narrator then imagines reflectively to look out of Nature, and back at him.

Once he has established the forest lake, "the *one* of the two previously mentioned points" (Stifter's emphasis, 214), the narrator proceeds to the other, the castle ruins. This too he describes as an eye, although again the symmetry is a strained one, somewhat violently imposed on the facts of his description: it is not the castle itself but "a bright valley that is opened like a delicate eye" (214)— whereas the castle seemingly functions as this second eye seen from afar (i.e., from the woods), it is actually the point from which it is perceived (215). In any case, having set up this second eye, the narrator can inaugurate between the two sites that proliferated exchange of glances by which he most seeks to fix the mirroring, reciprocal relations between the wooded lake and Wittinghaus castle ruins.

Within the thus mobilized circulation of gazes, there is also a curious, somewhat unexpected asymmetry to the exchange. This is most conspicuous when the narrator describes the view from on top of the ruins:

For whoever climbs to the top there is a view that, although in complete opposition to the monuments of grief all around, still immediately lets it be felt that this is what marks the completion of his rising sensation; for over the top of all the dark pines, an immeasurable view flows toward you from every direction, streaming into your eyes and almost crushing them with brightness. (216)

It is not so much that one sees the view of surrounding nature as that the view, in all its dazzling oppression, sees—*you*. The reversal of perspective seems both confusing and contrived: nonetheless, it is also insistent and maintained throughout the novella. It is the belated motivation for the figuring of the lake as an uncanny eye of Nature, a conceit maintained in "the black startled little eyes of a nesting robin" (216) and the many "dark-eyed flowers" that oversee and witness (and even accomplish) Nature's invasive, gently aggressive destruction of the castle ruins; and again, in the story, in such circumscribed instances as Johanna and Clarissa in their morning chamber, "watched by the peaceful festival of Nature outside" (230; cf. 247, 241) or in such extended instances as the narrator's rather daring description of the Wittinghaus family's trek through the woods from the perspective of the forest itself, which ends "Our dear little patch of woods had seen its first human beings" (235; cf. 259).

What we have here, of course, is the same chiastic structure I delineated in the preface to *Many-colored Stones*, the same projective strategy of reflective reversal that proved so central to Stifter's realist program, both in its external projection of what then becomes an immanent reality of Nature, and then in its subsequent reflection back upon the human social reality from which it nonetheless originates. And again as in the preface to *Many-colored Stones*, we note how vision is not really about the visual at all, or only in the second place: rather, it is about the imposition of law, order, or meaning behind or within the visual. As the semanticization of the woods in general and the lake in particular makes clear, the law and order here is virginity, and by incorporating the vision thematic into his overarching chiastic strategy, the narrator contrives to have that law or reality look out from Nature, and then enter into and govern the repetitions implicit in all the subsequent exchange of glances.[9]

What we see, then, is that vision serves two related functions in the novella, one covert and the other overt. First, vision reflects a covert intent of supervision, as through its gaze Nature seeks to have its law repeated, corroborated, or imposed on the human realm, or rather: as through Nature the narrator seeks to have *his* gaze and *his* law chiastically reflected and then repeated in the human sphere, by first supervising the disposition of the natural world, and then (and thereby) that of the human as well. Second, the constant exchange of glances—not only between the two specific points of lake and castle or the two general spheres of nature and men, but also within the latter sphere, between all the various characters themselves—reflects the overt intent of communication, of a shared reality between everyone and everything. It is however a shared reality that is first predicated on a shared purity or virginity, between both nature and man, and man and man (or better, woman)—or in other words, a visual communication based on an internalization of the broader, more insidious and one-sided project of surveillance. Any transgression of the law of virginity and the structure of repetition and similitude in both communication and supervision is bound to collapse: reality depends on repetition, and repetition on maintaining the law.

Such is the apparent "realist" structure for the ensuing tale announced in the frame, the structure that governs and maintains its narrative world. But there are two other elements to this structure that also need to be recognized. First, for all the chiastic investment of an external, immanent authority or reality in Nature and its virginity, there is also the signaled acknowledgment of its fiction, of its origin in the imagination, desire, and power interests of the narrator and his human world. We see this in how none of the various patterns or directionalities of his description quite fit the given facts, but rather always seem conspicuously, even tortuously imposed. We see it in how his description of the lake as an uncanny eye of Nature is explicitly presented as his poetic fantasy, so that how it looks at him is clearly the effect of how he looks at it. Moreover, his fantasy is itself presented as caught up in "that double dream, the dream of youth and of first love" (211), so that not only is Nature's supervising "reality" recognized as his enchanting fantasy (*Zauberfantasie,* 212), but its perceived virginity is, however paradoxically, an acknowledged reflection of his desire. And we see it most clearly, in the story, at such moments as this, when the narrator again foregrounds his own presence and intelligence: "There is a seemliness, I would say an expression of virtue in Nature's aspect when still untouched by human hands, before which the soul must bend low, as before something chaste and godly—and yet again it is finally the soul alone that transposes all its inner greatness into the likeness [*das Gleichnis*] of Nature" (241). "And yet again it is finally": the reality is the fiction, and the narrator seems both to realize and to work to represent this truth.

Second, as implicit both in the image here (in the just quoted passage) of the soul contorted before itself in its own, reflective fiction, and in that of one of the two "points" to the structure (the castle) already in ruins, in fact apparently ruined by the other (the incursive surveillant woods)—as implicit in both, there is an acknowledgment of the disaster, the failure, the flaw to this supposedly sustaining structure of mirroring repetitions. If in the first case we are given to realize the fiction of the reality, in the second we are made to suspect the nonetheless real effects of the fiction. And it seems to me to be this double reality that Stifter works self-consciously to expose in the realism of his novella: the "flaws" to his realism that, in however disruptive and difficult a fashion, are still a part of that realism.

II

The whole semanticization of the woods as virginal, the establishment of the mirroring repetitions between the two nonetheless competing conflictual realities, even the implicit self-conscious effort to include the disruptive subverting reality as part of the overarching project—all this is done in preparation for the introduction in the primary narrative of the two women, Clarissa and Johanna, or rather, of the two women and their father. In many ways, the story, and the story of its realism, come down to the relations between these three characters. Let's look at them closely.

The daughters are introduced and described first, and their description also introduces the first problem into the story itself. At the outset of the tale, the narrator regularly describes Johanna and Clarissa in two competing, apparently contradictory ways: as interchangeable doubles, or repetitions of each other, and as embodiments of two quite different, even conflictual realities.[10] The narrator's paradoxical procedure can clearly be seen to repeat and extend the practice that he already followed in the frame, where he imposed the structure of a dual-natured reality onto the spheres of Nature and man, and then obstinately sought after a uniform coherence between them: this same structure and search seem now transposed onto the characters of and the relations between the two female protagonists, or more precisely, onto the constellation of themes associated with each of their characters and the possible, or impossible, common ground between them.

Johanna is described first, and although everything thus far in Stifter has taught us to suspect the priority of the first term, I will nonetheless begin with her as well. Johanna is identified with the visual arts, and through them with both the figure of the father and the realm of Nature: she sits at the window embroidering a picture of a rose, knowing that "her father takes pleasure in beautiful flowers" (221). This initial emphasis and its double association are then repeated in the description of her clothes. Although it is still early morning, Johanna is completely dressed "in that particularly picturesque manner that we still occasionally see in paintings from the time of the Thirty Years War" (217); her head "peers almost blissfully young out of the old-fatherly cloud of clothing" (*der altväterischen Kleider*wolke, my emphases). The painterly quality of her appearance and especially of her clothing produces a decisive pleasure in both the narrator ("Everything is nice") and Johanna, and is itself further expressive of a certain ideal immobility and purity: Sleeves and bodice are neatly buttoned (*schliessen reinlich*), every fold and lace sits perfectly in place, while her eyes are set pure (*rein*) and round in their frames (*Rahmen*), untouched by pain and passion (218).

Given the foregrounded focus on its painterly quality and on Johanna's highly conventionalized purity, this hardly seems a "realistic" description, an impression further strengthened by the narrator's accompanying efforts to figure Johanna as a house, complete with gable and windows (217f.). However, while not a realistic description, it is still very much a description of a realist program found throughout Stifter's work. The privileged prominence of the visual arts and their positive evaluation; the association of the visual arts with the father, or more generally with a patriarchal male and his pleasure (an association furthered here by the imagery of the house, which in this novella always evokes the father's presence and will); and especially the deployment of the visual arts to try to achieve a certain static repression of the female body and so to inscribe a requisite purity, or *Reinheit,* as female reality—this constellation is at the center of Stifter's work, where painters are almost exclusively male, and the intended objects of their artistic gaze female.[11] Moreover, the parallel between the representation here of Johanna and that in the frame of Nature, which also serves as a site for the visually projected, immobilizing ideal of purity by a decidedly male gaze—this parallel is patent, and helps determine the conjunction of visual representation, Nature, and the feminine that Johanna can already be seen to embody.[12]

Whereas Johanna is closely associated with the pictorial arts, with architecture, and with Nature, her sister Clarissa is descriptively linked with writing, with music, and with history. That is, as with Johanna—as in fact with all the major characters in *The Mountain Forest*—what we have in Clarissa is not so much a realistic figure as a figure for certain key elements in Stifter's realist program. These elements are far more ambivalently conceived than those configured about Johanna, beginning with the papers and scrolls of parchment that somewhat mysteriously surround Clarissa as she lies, still undressed, in bed.

Exactly what these particular papers are we do not know: what we do know is that, while visual media are almost uniformly valorized in Stifter's world, narrative media, including writing, are for the most part dangerous, or rather double-edged therein.[13] We see this already in the first scene, where, along with its connection with Clarissa, writing is most prominently linked with the various correspondences concerning the approaching war that the father so assiduously solicits and studies. On the one hand, such written reports clearly complement the visual project of stabilizing mastery of the world that we see in the representation of Johanna (and, in the frame, of the woods), and this is underscored by the faith the father places in their narratives in his efforts to maintain a predictive hold over the unfolding historical events. On the other hand, writing thus also becomes associated with just those historical forces whose uncontrollable forward course threatens the stability of the narrative world, and this is underscored by the vehemence with which the father tries to keep not only this history but also these narratives away from his daughters, fearful that not only history (*die Geschichte*) but also the story of history (*die Geschichte der Geschichte*) will upset their secure, unchanging world.[14]

Clarissa is also associated with music, which represents something equally threatening.[15] This is partly because music is identified with what is abstractly the most threatening predicate of writing (or of language, *Sprache,* in general) and also most removed from the visual: a temporality that marks music as the most historical art form.[16] But its danger more obviously arises because music is identified with desire, a good part of whose own danger is its identification with temporality: with movement. We see the first point in music's identification with Clarissa's erotic preoccupations; the isolated notes of a submerged melody that Clarissa strums on her harp here are, we learn, signifiers of her hidden desire for Ronald (219). And we see the second point, the association of desire with movement, in the lability associated with the body of the "still undressed" Clarissa. Her hair, we're told, "is loosed and cuts a wide downfalling stream across the ruffled snow of her nightgown" (218), and the image clearly recalls the descending stream introduced in the frame, and so too its association with movement, with a falling away from some ideal of original purity—and hardly incidentally, its association with history as well.

Music and desire, then, like writing and history, clearly pose a threat. This threat touches Clarissa herself, as graphically conveyed by the image of her trapped behind the barlike strings of her harp; but the real threat of both music and desire, indeed their death-threat, is to her father. We see this in the words of the song Clarissa sings, "There lay white bones/beside the golden crown," which prompt Johanna to say, "You know of course that Father doesn't like to hear you sing that song" (219)—in stark opposition to his pleasure in her embroidery.[17] In any case, the contrasting prominence of the nonvisual, temporal arts of writing and music and their primarily negative evaluation; their association with history, desire, and the unclothed female body; and especially their potential threat to the father, and his would-be repression of their presence—all this finds itself, in the figure of Clarissa, at the center of Stifter's text.

Given the extremely different constellation of thematic elements clustered about each daughter, we can understand more fully the problems and stakes at issue in defining that common ground or equivalence that allows the narrator also to describe them as identical, even interchangeable images or representations. Both are perhaps best illustrated in the sisters' own exchange on nature imagery, as they work together on a flowered embroidery for their father. As we have seen, Nature is the privileged site for the codification of the reality that will then chiastically determine their own human reality, and we see both Johanna and Clarissa themselves projectively encoding Nature through their discourse, but in radically different ways. Johanna describes a world "good from the very beginning . . . just like today, without a cloud as far as you can see, clear blue and unsullied blue, the purest and friendliest blue" (219f.). In contrast to this world of repetitive and virginal sameness, Clarissa proposes and defends as nature precisely what Johanna's Nature would exclude, a world that includes clouds and fog ("men wrongly call them passion [*Leiden-schaft*]," 220), which obscure and frustrate the pure and uniform visual field advocated by Johanna, and significantly enough also introduce a certain historical narrative into Nature's course, as in Clarissa's account the story of desire moves from rising vapors through lightning and rain, and so forth.

The key question woven into this exchange—and their common artifact of nature imagery, the embroidery—is very much like that we discovered in the preface to *Many-colored Stones* and the novella's own frame: whether the Nature or reality that can encompass both women will be such as Johanna's, an inviolable, stable, and childlike purity that excludes the labile forces of passion and maturing (female) nature, or such as Clarissa's, a more inclusive field that not only admits the reality of desire but also its defining movement, its history and narrative.

Certainly our first (and perhaps also our final) answer to this question has to be the former, that Johanna represents the inscribed realism or Nature governing the tale, to which Clarissa must conform if reality itself is to be maintained—and this despite Reddick's incontestable point, that the narrative's real, principal concern is with Clarissa, which it merely hides behind the foregrounded façade of Johanna (e.g., by describing Johanna first, or having her lead the way into the woods). But to a great extent, its "real" concern with Clarissa *is* with her hiding, with assimilating her to the protective, replicative cover of Johanna. We see this in how it is only once Clarissa leaves her music and manuscripts and joins Johanna working on her embroidery that they become mirroring repetitions of one another; or in how it is only when, as they embroider together, language can be reduced to the purity of the visual that it can support the requisite similitude for reciprocal exchange ("when now we look at their two beautiful countenances, hear their words, each one a transpar-

Double Visions 55

ent diamond set in the silver clarity of their glances, then this simple room seems to us consecrated and pure, like a church" [224]).[18] But we see it most clearly in how the narrator, when describing the two daughters as one, seems to repeat Johanna's position, albeit with a revealing complication:

> So immeasurably precious is the pure work of the Creator, the human soul, that so long as it is still unsullied and unsuspecting of the wickedness that hovers about it, it is unspeakably more holy to us than any rectification [*Besserung*] obtained with tremendous force; for nevermore can such a man extinguish from his face our pain over the earlier disruption [*Zerstörung*]—and the force he exerts to overcome his evil appears almost threatening to us, however gladly he performs it. (223f.)

The echo of Johanna's just preceding description of Nature would seem decisive for establishing the governing principles regulating the story's "reality," but so too would its newly added dimension. While sharing with Johanna the valorization of the "still unsullied" as the best and truest, most natural reality, and inscribing it here as the basis for the common representation of the sisters, the narrator also indicates both its violence and its fiction as soon as it would also include what exceeds it, what escapes its originary stasis with the disruptive movement of both desire and history (cf. "earlier"). Far from the gentle reality in which Johanna would keep Clarissa whole and untouched, the narrator recognizes its violent, futilely repressive fiction, its merely but furiously poetic reality—even as he perpetuates it. The fiction, violence, and futility of the program of similitude and virginity were already, of course, implicitly marked in the frame, in the prescribed resemblances between the spheres of nature and man. They become explicitly so here, in the enforced mimetic equivalence between the two sisters.[19]

III

Although first introduced in the figurative descriptions and gnomic generalizations of the narrator, this contradictory, violent, and ultimately futile poetic realism is most emphatically associated in the story proper with the figure of the father, in whom it is also translated out of the narrator's mostly poetic, allegorical, and even religious terms and into more recognizably realist ones. As already suggested in the description of the daughters, the father is the moving force in the story behind the visual project and its related changeless, timeless ideal, the supervisory gaze enforcing and maintaining the shared reality and communication between them;[20] he is also the one most threatened by the moving forces that seem to exceed or oppose it, and the one most desperately engaged in their belated repression through a necessarily violent fiction of maintained reality or similitude. But a close look at the father not only exposes the violence, fiction, and perhaps final futility to this ideal of a pure, immutable reality;[21] it also exposes the forces that arise in opposition to it to be intrinsic and systemic to the ideal itself. We see this in respect to both of the realities he determines for his daughters: that of the family and its love, and that of the forest and its virginity.

As already indicated by both Johanna's and Clarissa's concern for his pleasure or displeasure, the father is very much the source for the circulating love, or *Liebe,* that binds this family in the stable community that, for Stifter, is always the privileged site for social reality: for the proliferation and enforcement of those shared conventions or laws that protectively join the separate individuals in a single, uniform identity.[22] Moreover, as was implicitly the case with the painterly conventions modulating the representation of Johanna, the conventions, or better, the law of this love that governs both daughters is explicitly linked with his vision, and even especially with his unseen supervision. So for example we are told, "Both children fasten on his eyes. He tells them to continue embroidering—and as they do, his gaze, unseen, lingers on them with earnestness and love." (225).[23] It is precisely because gazes are an expression of his love that they function as the vehicle for establishing the common and stable familial field: love itself is the expression of his law, and insofar as the various glances express this love—not only those between the father and daughters, but also between the sisters themselves—they convert his supervision into the common ground of their own communication and similitude.

However, as our analysis of the preface to *Many-colored Stones* has already alerted us, there is something inherently precarious in the attempt to ground the sustaining, shared reality of the family on the principle or law of *Liebe,* and this precarious something is particularly conspicuous in the Wittinghaus family. We see the problem right away in the father's far from simple relation to his daughters. He is first introduced as "the girls' father, who entered their morning chamber so discreetly and reverently, *like a stranger* [wie ein Fremder]" (224); a bit later we are told, "Along with a father's care for his daughters, he also displayed almost a bashfulness toward them, *like a beloved* [wie ein Geliebter]" (226, my emphases). The very love he awakens to keep them safely familiar also becomes something "strange" and potentially threatening—becomes, that is, the erotic passion that in Clarissa seems already to court paternal displeasure, already to disrupt the pristine and well-regulated domestic sphere, and already to threaten the ideal of sustained similitude between the sisters—but that, as we see here, nonetheless has its origin in that familial sphere, in just that paternally determined ideal that would exclude it.[24]

As a result, without at all forfeiting its original innocent nature—after all, this alone begets the subsequently threatening eroticism—the father-centered familial love also eventually becomes something of a repressive force, repressive of its own issue. The unfamiliar, unlawful desire—which is of course both familiar and lawful—must either be contained within the original paternal structure, or destroy that structure. And we see the somewhat contradictory and literally perverse consequences of this project of containment in the manifestly erotic relations not only between the daughters and the father but also (and even more so) between the sisters themselves.[25] In any case, the incestuous "inner disarray" of this family is hardly incidental to the father's express desire to maintain its stable common ground. Rather, it is a direct expression of both the original bid at protectively joining the sisters in a single, shared reality through love and the subsequent attempt to maintain it once it has been threatened by itself. Or to put it in the narrator's terms I evoked before: the creation of the valorized pure and common ground itself engenders both the desire that exceeds and disrupts it, and the subsequent violence that would reclaim it.

The same simultaneous, albeit inadvertent creation of the desired reality and its potential subversion evident in the love the father awakens in his daughters is also apparent in the security, or rather, the virginity he arranges for them in the woods. Although proleptically echoed by the narrator, the father is still very much the original source for determining the law and reality of the woods' virginity, which is now to protect his daughters from all the ravaging forces that threaten his own, no longer secure world at home.[26]

As with love, the inviolable virginity of the woods is also linked with the father's vision, or unseen supervision, although in this case in a manner even more obviously translated into realist terms. The father constructs a vast surveillance network, supported by both advance scouts and written reports, and extended into both the threatening war zones and the woods; his purpose is to ascertain the absolutely objective separation of the two spheres and the absolutely real, intact inviolability of the latter. The empirical manifestations of his supervisory precautions—his provision (*Voraussicht,* 228), foresight (*Vorsicht,* 229), outlook (*Absicht,* 230), etc.—extend to great lengths: he makes certain that those who help construct the refuge in the woods are "three-times bound" to preserving their silence and its seclusion; he seals off the way that originally led in and out of the spot, leaving it physically unapproachable save over the water in a bullet-proof raft; he even takes care to determine that no threatening wild animals inhabit the woods, and nonetheless installs protective fences about the house and an armed guard at its gate. By all of these means, the father transforms the abstract, slightly idyllic inviolability of the woods into a concrete, objective, rationally determined reality.

For all its rationally calculated, empirical determination, however, the father's realist version of the woods' security very much remains a fiction, indeed a notably fantastic fiction. The basis for the fiction is this: while the motivation for establishing the inviolability of the woods is overtly to thwart the external danger posed by the historical war, it is also covertly but still undeniably to thwart the internal danger posed by *Liebe*—hence the continued identification of its promised safety with virginity. The father seeks to determine, in fact to govern and control the reality of the woods, to transform them by means of his objectively projected gaze into an inscribed repetition of his love and law; but only so that the woods will then in turn fantastically inscribe or repeat this law or desire—this determined reality—in his daughters. Theirs is the "historical" force he fears, theirs the virginity he wishes to determine—but indirectly, through the detour of an external projection and recursive reflection. He does not, that is, seek to determine the woods as a reality, but as a repetition, a representation—of him, and for them.

We see this in any number of ways. We see it for instance in the "almost frightening" (249) identicalness of the rooms he has constructed for his daughters in the woods with those in his original house: the repetition is intended to maintain the conditions of his authority, law, or reality, to forge a mimetic equivalence between the two spheres so as to extend the common ground encompassing, including, and keeping his daughters, and thus to maintain *their* selfsame, unchanging identity via the second repetition, the shaping, recursive coercion enforced by the rooms themselves. This latter effect is particularly conspicuous in the father's outfitting of the rooms: "Everything was arranged in the most careful way, not the slightest little thing was missing, and every day they discovered that their father had often *foreseen* [*vorgesehen*] what until then they themselves had still not thought of" (255f., my emphasis; cf. 225f.). The loving attention to the smallest details, so typical of the realist orientation, becomes a means for inscribing a desired order into the surrounding world and so back upon his daughters, whose subjective reality—and not the things' objective one—always remains the primary focus of his scopic concern. And we see the same thing on a far larger scale in the natural objects outside the rooms that the father provides for his daughters' safekeeping, and that convey even more forcefully the fantastic nature of his designs.

The father's strategy for their protection is especially invested in two features of his chosen site, namely the towering rock wall that secures the house on one side, and the lake that seals it off from another. But I would argue that it is invested not so much in the physically real properties of these objects as in their fantastically representative ones: the towering erection of the rock repeats and incorporates his patriarchal authority every bit as much as the mirroring house, and more important, its reflection "like a fantastic picture" (*wie ein Fantasiebild,* 248) is mirrored in the deathlike, virgin stillness of the lake, which then and in turn reflects back to the daughters an image of themselves shaped in the image of that same virgin stillness (and of course, behind it, that same towering erection). The forest lake's virgin mirror is very much *his* uncanny eye of Nature, his *unheimlich Naturauge,* expressing his supervisory gaze, power, and desire in its fantasy of mirroring virginity: this is the true intent of his realist calculations, of all his foresightful surveillance. His realism is, that is, an inherently poetic realism, which invests itself in the external, real world only for the sake of its representative effect. Its real effect is always elsewhere, even as its intended mimesis is always elsewhere, namely in the similitude established in the moment of chiastic return.

However, as with love, the father's fantasy of a secure, stable reality based on virginity immediately produces the threatening reality it would exclude. This is primarily because that imagined virginity depends on the very forces it would deny, chief among them fantasy itself: for while the father's designs are clearly based in his own imaginative projection into the woods, they must also erase all traces of this in order to function as the objective order he intends his daughters to reflect, *and* in order that his daughters do not themselves reflect or repeat this moment of subjective, imaginative extension—this part of the project is not to be repeated, is in fact what the project is particularly working to prevent. We see this in how the very written reports and surveillant scouts through which the father seeks "realistically" to determine the inviolability of the woods and to prevent the intrusion of any ravaging human-historical forces, he also tries to keep from his daughters, to secure their inviolability and prevent any intrusive ravaging imaginings on their part. And his fears prove well founded; when the reports nonetheless do reach his daughters and his spies are espied, the very media for the father's controlling realism—for his fantasy—become the source for their decidedly uncontrolled fantasy. This is particularly so in the case of Johanna, herself the human embodiment of the father's inscripted ideal: word of his reports and scouts in the woods immediately arouse in her "fantasies of robbers and enchantment" (223), romances of ravishment, magic, and danger generated by the same phantasmatic mechanisms as for his romance of innocence, reason, and safety.

We see the same thing more concretely and centrally in the figure of the poacher, or *Wildschütze* (literally, "shooter of wild game"), who is rumored to inhabit the woods and who forms the particular object of Johanna's erotically tinged fantasies. The poacher—in its first publication the novella was entitled *The Poacher* [*Der Wildschütze*]—brings out the other dominant paradox to the father's realist designs: while they are obviously an expression of his desire, they are also intended to prevent desire in the daughters. As with the role played by his fantasy, this part of his project is not to be repeated, but rather deleted as part of the realist equation.[27]

The father's plans for his daughters' security are most especially invested in the protection offered by his friend Gregor, who will watch over Johanna and Clarissa in the woods while the father returns home to his castle. Gregor is thus in many ways the most forceful expression of the father's empirical realist strategy for their safekeeping. But he is also the most concentrated manifestation of the father's more poetic strategy of repetition: that is, Gregor offers protection not or not only for any objective reasons, such as his concrete knowledge of the woods (244) or his rifle (252), but also and even especially for projected reasons, insofar as he is a double for the father, who will reproduce the original conditions of the father's own love and law. As the father tells Johanna, "If there is a *Wildschütze* out there, then it's a handsome old man who will be at your service and whom you will soon love as your own father" (230).

But again, the strategy can be seen to occasion the very crisis it was meant to prevent. For even as there is an inherent ambiguity to the original love-of-the-father, so necessarily too to the subsequent figure of the *Wildschütze,* which reproduces that original ambiguity by evoking at once the character of Gregor and that of Ronald—both the protecting father *and* the threatening stranger or beloved (*der Fremde, der Geliebte*: for the father as both, see above). The father's displacing of the secure realm to the woods has eliminated none of the inherent dangers encountered closer to home: projecting his desire into the external world has not effaced any of its troublesome features but has merely reproduced and repeated them in that external world. Concealing the fact that desire lies at the center of his vision has only made the desire still lurking at the center more concealed, but no less there in either his daughters or the woods; indeed, its concealment seems actually to contribute to and augment the play of desire. And once again I should emphasize how it is Johanna, the human representation of the father's contradictory desire to stop desire, who produces the erotic fantasy of the violating *Wildschütze* behind the protecting one in the woods: the one produces the other with the same infallible fatality that adheres to the magic bullets of this ambivalent, uncanny figure.

IV

Thus, while the father's enterprise is a recognizably realist one, it is also a recognizably flawed one. His attempts to determine a common, undisturbed ground for his daughters and to keep them in it—first through the familial love of his house, and then through the natural virginity of the woods—seem doomed from the outset, and for at least two related reasons. First, because his efforts at creating stability immediately create, indeed are based on the very labile disruptive forces they would exclude, whether that be the shared familial reality that produces erotic desire, or the reassuring, reality-determining writing and surveillance that produce threatening, uncontrolled fantasy. Second, the father's enterprise seems doomed because it always seems already too late, an attempt to restore through a tactic of similitude and repetition what has already been irrevocably lost: whether that be the familial love that returns (supposedly as the same thing) to repress the erotic desire it has itself already set loose; or the natural virginity that is to repeat and extend the stable, secure reality of the father's house—of his love and law—but only once, and only because, that reality has itself already proved neither stable nor secure.

Recognizing both the repetition and the inherent failure at the heart of the father's exclusionary, repressive realism helps us better understand the dual function of Gregor as well as the need for Gregor, who represents both a repetition of the father and a new, quite different attempt at defining his and the novella's realist aims, that is, at determining its governing laws, and so salvaging or maintaining its stable realm and its program of mimetic equivalence (or communication). The narrator describes the father and Gregor as "so radically different and yet so alike" (238), and this paradox has significant consequences for the issues at stake in the novella's realism.

The similarity, or repetition, between the father and Gregor is most easily seen: it lies in Gregor's role as patriarchal representative, as supervisor and so protector of the two sisters; and it lies more specifically in the means by which he attempts his protecting supervision. Like the father, Gregor is very much the purveyor of the forest, the interpreter of its meaning, and so the governor of its reality: and in his case, too, the projective inscription of the forest is intended to be reflectively repeated in the women—all hopes for their safekeeping are invested in this deposited "reality" of the woods and its recursive effect (cf. 259).[28] In keeping with this, when the daughters enter the mountain forest proper and are entrusted to Gregor, they are also entrusted to his gaze, as the source both of their new community and of the forest's nature (238f.). He repeats, assumes, and sustains the authority and governance of the father, and the desired protective reality of the woods is the result of that sustaining repetition.

Double Visions 63

The difference lies in Gregor's new gambit in his attempt at control, that is, in his new and different interpretation of the nature of the woods, as the first step in the continued project of keeping Johanna and Clarissa within the imposed "reality." As with the father's and narrator's, Gregor's Nature is still that of the pure and unsullied, and its patriarchal character is still evident in the repeated evocation of "God" as its ultimate transcendental guarantor. But whereas for the father the forest's virginity and its promise of safekeeping lie in its exclusionary nature, for Gregor they lie instead in its all-inclusive nature, a Nature that would encompass all those forces—and chief among them fantasy, narrative, movement, and desire—which the father's Nature sought simply and unsuccessfully to repress. As Gregor says, in Nature "there is no weed [*Unkraut*], because the Lord loves and treasures every little plant [*Kräutlein*]" (242), in marked contrast to the father's earlier command, "Throw the weed out of your hearts" (230). Similarly, Gregor maintains, "[T]here is no defiance or depravity in the [animals and] plants of the earth . . . rather they simply follow the laws of the Master [*den Gesetzen des Herrn*], and in accord with them progress to flower and fruition—therefore they are all loved by him" (246); and again, "Everything speaks, everything narrates, and people will see that in fact there are only pure, good, and loving words" (243). That the motivation of containment is still behind this inscription is emphasized—"In everything here there is sense and feeling; even the stone lays itself about its sister-stone and holds it fast" (243)—but so too is its difference. In fact, it is the same difference already broached by Johanna and Clarissa: that between a conception of the shared reality that can encompass both sisters as repressively exclusive—the conception associated with Johanna and the father—and one based on a more encompassing vision, that not only admits the would-be excluded forces but even admits their formative role in constituting that vision, that reality—the conception associated with Gregor and Clarissa.[29]

In terms of its redetermination of the common ground and reality represented by the woods and for the daughters, the most important examples of Gregor's inclusive mode of poetic realism come in two of his own narratives, that of the aspen tree and that of the forest lake itself. The first is overtly presented as an example of Gregor's authoritative, informed reading of "the signs and the language of the woods" (245): it not only focuses on the decisively realist orientation of Gregor's vision, and on the apparently paradoxical inclusion of language in his fictional world;[30] it also focuses on the general question of the inclusion of movement, and the specific one of the inclusion of desire in that world. Significantly enough, the story also represents a shift in focus from Johanna to Clarissa as the admitted object of the recursively directed realist discourse: Clarissa initially solicits the story, and Gregor closes it by handing her one of the aspen leaves he has just finished describing, or rather, inscribing.

Clarissa asks Gregor to account for "the eternal unrest" (245) of the aspen tree, and he offers two apparently opposed interpretations, one traditional and from his grandmother, the other recent and from his own empirical observations. The grandmother's tale is one of sin and punishment, and for all its religious and fairly-tale elements, it still seems governed by the same exclusionary principles championed by the apparently more rational and enlightened father. According to the grandmother's account, because the aspen tree refused to display proper obedience to the Lord and Master on earth (*der Herr auf Erden*, 245), it or rather she was punished with ceaseless uncontrolled movement of her leaves, and so banished from the common, law-bound realm, "the remaining calm and solitude of the woods." Her lability bespeaks both her original crime and her punishment. Gregor, however, in his more mature and intimate knowledge of the woods, insists instead that in its trembling, or *Zittern*, the aspen is actually displaying her proper obedience to patriarchal law ("her leaves simply follow the laws of the Master," 246); that there is a natural order behind and so explanation for its movement ("the trembling is no doubt only a consequence of the leaves' rather long thin stems," 246); and that therefore its movement is pleasing to and included in the Master's love (*die Liebe des Herrn*) and any account of punishment and exclusion is out of place. Moreover, the "human" parallels are emphasized throughout, highlighting the necessarily allegorical dimension to Gregor's realist account, whose real effect is only achieved elsewhere—that is, insofar as it points back to Clarissa: the tree is gendered female, its leaves are described as "like hearts," and the word "trembling" (*Zittern*) is specifically linked throughout the novella with Clarissa's own displays of desire.

It is crucial for the subsequent unfolding of the entire narrative that Gregor is presented here as both the demystifying realist and the defender of an inclusive realm: that he describes as natural, systemic effects what previously, in the system of both the grandmother and father, appeared only as transgressive violations. To some extent, the issue posed by his twofold tale seems very similar to that in Johanna's and Clarissa's first exchange about nature imagery: that is, the question of which version of the aspen tree will turn out to be authoritative or real in the story, which inscription of the woods will most succeed, and so which discursive system will reflexively govern the unfolding course of events and desire. But we also note how the narrator's evaluative perspective has shifted since that first exchange: the realist hope now seems firmly tied to the inclusive interpretation, and the exclusive reading—including its notion of an original purity and then subsequent disruption—now appears not only as a fiction but also as the threatening, destructive force itself, as a fiction nonetheless capable of inflicting real and harmful effects on men's perceptions of the real world, both outside and inside themselves.

To some extent this is the issue posed, the danger identified, and the new realist allegiance declared in the competing tales of the aspen tree. But to some other extent, more intrinsic issues seem posed, more inherent dangers identified *within* Gregor's own tale, and so the realist allegiance left far more ambivalent. We see for instance the internal opposition, or contradiction, to Gregor's account in how he is first motivated to include the labile aspen within the law-abiding common sphere only insofar as she too proves capable of radical stasis and silence, her leaves "so horribly immobile . . . and she herself frozen into solid glass" (246)—that is, only insofar as her movement and "speech" can be controlled and reduced to the same deathlike, virgin stillness implicitly represented by the first tale, and explicitly by both the father and narrator before. And we see even more clearly the contradictions to Gregor's vision, and their consequences both for this story and for realism itself, in the closely parallel tale of the forest lake—which, in its role as "the uncanny eye of Nature," remains the privileged site for the projected, reflexively protective reality of the woods. Much therefore is at stake in Gregor's account of its nature.

As with the story of the aspen tree, Gregor's account of the forest lake is actually two accounts: one fantastic and associated with the grandmother, which conceives of the lake as bewitched (*ein Zauberwasser*), its blackness the mark of God's rejection; the other realist and grounded in Gregor's own observations, which dispels the inherited fantasy, substitutes natural law and explanation ("as for its black color, that probably is only caused by its reflection of the dark pines and mountain peaks"), and installs a benign, embracing Lord, or *Herr,* where the traditional tale had only an excluding, punishing one. That Gregor's new realist vision is also again meant to be inclusive is conveyed not directly in his defense of the lake, but indirectly in the juxtaposed defense of the hawk that circles the lake throughout Gregor's account, casting its reflection on the waters' mirror. Gregor describes the hawk's rapacity not as a transgressive violation but as simply part of the innocent natural order: "It clearly must be so ordained on earth that one thing lives through the other" (264). The parallel with the earlier example, as well as the parallel aim, is further secured when Gregor offers Clarissa one of the hawk's tail-feathers, as before he offered her a fluttering, heartlike aspen leaf. Clarissa remains the intended object of Gregor's recursive discourse.

For all the parallel, there is also a noticeable redistribution of emphasis in the tale of the lake: far more weight is placed upon the tales of the grandmother. Gregor actually recounts at length three such tales, in all of which history and fairy tales freely interplay against the common backdrop of Nature and its supporting Christian order. We are told of kings from Saxony, Bohemia, Bavaria, and Austria who make their ways into the woods, and impress their presence in the formation of the very rocks, most especially in the rock wall of the Blockenstein overlooking the lake and woods. We are told of how the first of these kings, fleeing out of Saxony before the advancing forces of the Kaiser, brought with him gold and silver, precious tableware and red carbuncles (265), and magically concealed them in the rocks; of how these hidden treasures inspired the greed, imagination, and desires of men who came after, some of whom were magically imprisoned inside the rock wall and the rest of whom were magically frightened away, by both the spirits of those imprisoned and the curses of those departed. Afterward, we are told, these fantastic stories themselves function as guards (*Wächter*), keeping men away from the cursed forest (267).

Gregor elaborates these three tales as a prelude to his own, comparatively brief account of how he eventually came to discount them and to venture exploratively into the forbidden realm: "[F]or I gradually came to know the woods and recognized how wonderful they are, without any need of people first weaving into them their stories . . . and so I climbed up here and found this beautiful, lovely lake" (267). As in the case of the aspen tree, his rejection of the obscuring myths and introduction of exclusively natural explanations leads to the reacceptance of the previously rejected objects within the law-abiding common ground: "By that time I already knew full well that the forest did not produce outrageous or transgressive wonders but rather purely calm and unpretentious, but therefore far huger and more monstrous ones than human beings comprehend, who for that reason poetize into the woods their own coarse tales. But the forest produces its wonders with a little water and earth and with air and sunshine. Other than that there is nothing there, nor has there ever been, take my word for it" (268).

For all the apparent simplicity and clarity to Gregor's new "ecological" realism, it is still, of course, hopelessly complex and confused, in irresolvable tension with its own intentions and ultimately subject to the same fatal flaw already exposed in the father's realism. The major problems to Gregor's position can, I think, best be approached indirectly, by first noting how, with one crucial exception, the grandmother's fantastic representation of the woods and lake once again repeat the father's supposedly more realist one. As in the grandmother's account, the father's "story" is very much about a man who hides his treasured possessions in the woods and then fantastically installs himself in the towering rock wall to watch over them, projectively inscribing the woods with his express and sovereign wish that men stay away—so that when Clarissa suddenly looks at the stone and woods as watchmen (*Wächter,* 266), she is responding as much to the present reality dictated by her father as to the remote fairy tale conveyed by Gregor. In both cases, the project remains the same, to keep intact the human valuables sequestered in the forest, and the procedure remains the same, to inscribe the woods themselves with a meaning, a reality, that will function immanently to secure that inviolability.

What alone distinguishes the grandmother's account from the father's is of course the free circulation of history, fantasy, and desire throughout her representation of the woods: throughout the meaning or reality she poetically attributes to the forest, and that the forest then immanently reflects back to her human auditors. These are, we know, the very forces that the father's supposedly more realist representation of the woods so self-defeatingly and unrealistically tries to exclude from itself; and with the critical exception of history, these are also the very forces that Gregor seeks to include in his arguably more realist and less immediately self-defeating poetic world. For like the grandmother (but unlike the father), Gregor would include the marvelous and wonderful as part of the reality of his woods; and as the earlier example of the aspen tree and the present juxtaposed one of the hawk make clear, he would also include some form of desire ("trembling," "unrest") and even of rapacity in his woods. Indeed, the distinguishing feature of his gambit at keeping Johanna and Clarissa safe within the woods derives from the inclusion of just these elements.

Despite this similarity with the grandmother, Gregor is however forced to reject her world, and all the inscribed history, fantasy, and desire that go along with it.[31] And I would argue that the contradiction comes as a necessary consequence of Gregor's realist strategy, from within the construction of his natural order. For in order to represent desire and wonder as part of the natural order, Gregor must present them as just that: as natural, as immanent and pure, and so too as not of human origin or agency, as not merely "poetized in" (*angedichtet*)—for only so do they acquire the necessary authority to shape and assimilate the human world of Clarissa and Johanna to their own representative reality. The motive for discovering or inscribing these forces is firmly located in the human world, but this must be just as firmly concealed or effaced in order to achieve its desired recursive end in that same human world. However, the "flaw" is that the resultant representation of Nature ends up having to exclude exactly what it was designed to include, and thus, in the moment of its chiastic return, to deny in the human realm what it also denies in itself, namely the distinctly human forces of desire and imagination—whether manifested in the "poetic" world of fantasy or in the "real" world of history.[32] In a curious but characteristic way, Gregor's poetic realism ends up excluding both the poetic and the real: if the father's ended up having to include what it would exclude, Gregor's ends up having to exclude what it would also include.

Recognizing the inescapability of the paradox does not, however, lessen the problem or its effects: Gregor's all-embracing and benign realism proves as exclusive and repressive as the father's, and just as fatally flawed. His world, too, has to suppress the human—fantasy, desire, and history—in order to realize its uniform, law-governed order—*its* fantasy, its desire—that is protectively to secure the human. And it too seems inevitably to produce the very danger it would eliminate, because it too depends on the very forces it would undo: even as before Ronald appeared in the very figure of the *Wildschütze* by which the father would eliminate him, so now does he covertly appear alongside the very narrative that would deny him ("Other than that there is nothing there, take my word for it").

V

As with all the other major characters, Ronald is not so much a realistic figure as he is a figure of key elements in the novella's realist program. He represents everything that the father's construct first of familial love and then of the virgin inviolable woods would exclude; that Gregor's construct of the woods would both include and exclude; and that seemingly everyone's construct of Clarissa would exclude to maintain her mimetic equivalence with both Johanna and the woods and which, when admitted, destroys both mirroring repetitions and so too the common ground of the story's increasingly fragile reality. In Freudian terms, we would say that Ronald represents the return of the repressed—as he himself says, "it is *not* overcome" (286)—the Other or stranger (*der Fremde*): the reality that the various fictions of the woods and of the women would deny, and produce in the very process of its exclusion. In our own terms, he seems the undeniable and now emergent flaw in the several realist designs of the father, Gregor, and the narrator; he seems inextricably present in every fantasy of the reality of the forest, and yet remains what no version seems capable of admitting or containing.

We see this paradoxical inside/outside, a part of/apart from, quality in every major aspect of Ronald's character, indeed of the whole scene on the forest meadow in which he appears. Ronald primarily represents the crucial and now repeated combination of poetry, desire, and history. His identification with poetry, and especially fantastic poetry, is perhaps most overt: Gregor first describes him by saying, "He does only things that are without goal or purpose, and strives after the unattainable. He's often wanted to pin the sunshine to his hat, to embrace the sunset" (271f.); the adjectives he recurrently attracts are "poetic," "rapturous," "fabulous," and "magical." And his association with desire, or rather of poetry and desire, is no less obvious: his scene on the forest meadow is after all, and in however abstract a fashion, a love scene, and the threatening, magical power he wields clearly combines the two forces of the erotic and fantastic. This combination and this aspect of his figure are of course highly conventional, even romantic, and the narrator evidently stylizes the scene in such a way as to emphasize rather than downplay its romantic conventionality; and this forces the question of belonging, of what Ronald and this scene are doing here in the middle of Gregor's—and the father's, and the narrator's—woods, or more generally, in the middle of a supposedly realist work, where they can only appear as out of place, as a jarring fault in the text's design. But the jarring is intentional, the seeming fault itself at issue: for it is just this question that Clarissa herself asks ("Why are you here?" 283), that Ronald repeats and makes his own ("*Why am I come??*" 284), and that Stifter makes key to the entire scene.

The scene itself gives us two quite different ways of answering the question of why Ronald is here. On the one hand, as lover and poet, he seems to emerge out of some prior, or at least remotely situated sphere that the novella's woods and realism wish to overcome and keep in abeyance. This impression is supported by the "romantic" nature of both Ronald's desire and his imagination, which associates him with the same pre-realist world already introduced (and banished) with the grandmother; by the situating of the origin of his love for Clarissa in some much earlier, less mature moment of her life, a moment thought long past and overcome; and by his arrival from the remote, foreign world of "the new country on the other side of the great glistening sea" (282)— or alternatively, from the alien, other land of the invading Swedish army. As such, in both his patently unreal, fairytale-like poetry and his wild, unruly passion, Ronald seems to represent something fundamentally foreign to the novella's realism, something in fact that acquires its reality, power, and presence in the text only insofar as it has proved irrepressible by the various realist constructions that would oppose him. From this perspective, his appearance in the woods seems very much a return of the repressed, the interrupting and unwanted disorder that suddenly appears from elsewhere to undo the stable governance of the realists' world.

On the other hand, however, and as we have seen, love and fantasy are not only what the novella's woods and realism would repress, they are also that which would repress, that which in fact is most nurtured. The father himself mobilizes his own highly conventionalized love to determine Clarissa's domestic reality, and so it makes sense that Ronald's love is depicted as originating in his, the father's, house (cf. the father as himself "the stranger," "the beloved"). And Gregor mobilizes his own, equally conventionalized fantasy to determine her natural reality, and so it also makes sense that Ronald—*der Wildschütze*—is depicted as uniquely at home in these, Gregor's (also *der Wildschütze*), woods— or alternatively, that Ronald argues that "there is no difference between Swedish and German" (291). Here of course, in Ronald's appearance in this family and woods, these same two forces or realities return to undo those constructs. But in so doing, Ronald represents not (only) some prior reality, extrinsic and repressed by the father and Gregor, but (also) some present reality, intrinsic and employed by them. His unreality is realism's own, his desire that of realism itself.

Ronald's association with history, which is equally insistent and if anything even more threatening to the various fictions of reality forged by the father, Gregor, and the narrator, partakes of the same ambivalent, inside/outside, a part of/apart from, status. Concretely, he arrives in the woods as a representative of the Thirty Years War: as the scion of Gustav Adolf, king of Sweden; and as a would-be warrior, yearning for action (285), thirsting after human blood, eager for adventure and danger (303), etc. As such, he very much belongs to that empirical human realm that both the father and Gregor—and the narrator— would read out of the empirical natural realm, whose nature is in fact designed to exclude just that other reality. In this respect, Ronald as history seems again a threat, and reality, arising from outside the world of the woods.

However, Ronald also represents history in a more abstract sense, as movement, and especially movement in its temporal manifestation, as transience (*Vergänglichkeit*); and in this, both the threat and the reality he embodies seem again to arise as much from within as from without. We see the menacing transitoriness his figure evokes in Clarissa's repeated complaint, "*Then you departed [Da ginget Ihr fort]*" (286); we see its compelling reality in Ronald's reply, "Yes, I departed, because it was *ordered* by one who was more powerful than you and I, and than your father and king" (287).[33] The intrinsicality of this more powerful compulsion or law is perhaps especially evident in the primary force that constantly endangers the intended mimetic equivalence between Johanna and Clarissa, namely that of time itself, of their age difference and Clarissa's emergent maturation, which all by itself is taking her away from her younger sister and self. But it is no less evident in the historical, necessarily temporal dimension to the (narrative) poetry and desire variously deployed by the narrator, father, and Gregor, an intrinsic aspect to both narrative and desire first suggested in the opening description of Clarissa and now reasserted in the figure of Ronald and his onrushing speech and equally precipitate desire—the inherent reality of temporality, or *Geschichtlichkeit,* and so uncontrol that confronts all efforts to achieve a stable, uniform, unchanging world through language or love.[34] *Fortgehen,* movement, proves itself an intrinsic, irrefutable law of all nature, all narrative, and all desire, and this spells disaster for all those who would use them to establish a different law, one devoted to stability and stasis—but again, it is a disaster that arises from within, a reality that is its own.[35]

VI

The counterpart to the question of what forces or danger Ronald represents is, of course, what crime or sin Clarissa commits in accepting him. And as with the case of Ronald, the answer is in some sense fairly clear and straightforward. By yielding to her desire for Ronald, Clarissa immediately disrupts the system of mimetic equivalence on which the common ground of reality to the novella depends. She explains how, when she first met Ronald, "in the madness of bliss I clung to you, sinfully forgetting my father, my mother, my God" (286). Similarly now, as she submits again to the "superior power of emotion [*Übermacht des Gefühls*]": "The entire forest, the eavesdropping maples, the shining rock wall, even Johanna and Gregor dissolved about Clarissa like insubstantial simulacra, nothing was in the world except two pounding hearts—forgetting everything she bent ever more toward him her face, shining with love, and her dark streaming eyes (289)." By heeding her desire, Clarissa takes herself out of the system of love, language, and glances that maintained her commonality with both the woods and Johanna, these two complementary representatives of mirroring, protecting virginity; she falls deaf to the inscribed, surveillance law of the forest, and she asserts her difference from her sister.

The crime of Clarissa's yielding extends not only to her destruction of the virgin serenity of the woods but also to her destruction of the father's house. In fact, the system governing the reality of the novella reveals itself most surely in the necessary relation between these two events. As soon as Clarissa yields to desire and asserts her changed self, she initiates an ongoing relay of broken equivalences repeated back along the entire chain of reflecting mirrors that ultimately rebounds upon their origin in the father, and thereby destroys at once both him and his constructed world. Admitted desire destroys Clarissa's virginity, or rather the father's proscribed law of virginity; this in turn destroys her mirroring identity with Johanna; this in turn destroys both of their identities with the woods, or rather with the reflected fantasy of the woods inscribed by both Gregor and, before him, the father; and this in turn destroys the woods' identity with the father's house; and this in turn destroys him. In a very direct sense, Clarissa is being completely realistic when she says, "I was the one, I killed father and brother" (315), although in an indirect sense, it would be even better to say that, through its structure of repetition and recursion, the father's house destroys itself—through the woods, and through its defensive construct of virginity.[36]

The basic nature of Clarissa's dual-sited transgression is, then, fairly straightforward, as clear in its way as the identification of Ronald's threat with the transgressive elements of poetry, desire, and history. However, even as with Ronald's threat the truly interesting question was whence it came (from inside or outside the poetically real realm), so with Clarissa's crime the truly consequential issue is what becomes of it. That is, after the abrupt emergence both of Clarissa's self and desire and of history and the war, and so too after the failure of the constructed "natural" world either to contain them or keep them out, there is a renewed, concerted effort to renegotiate the relation between these variously ravaging human forces and the poetically real natural sphere in order to include the disruptive elements—concretely of desire and history, but more abstractly of temporality, transitoriness, and destruction, even death—within the definition of the virgin order of the woods.

To some extent, this effort is first initiated or necessitated by Ronald when he insists that he is by blood not other but a part of this (German) people and land; when he begins imaginatively to inscribe himself within the present community ("It seems to me as if there were no 'out there,' no human beings except those here, who love each other and learn innocence from the innocence of the woods," 292); and especially when he begins metaphorically to refigure the woods as a reflective repetition or representation of the forces he himself embodies ("for man is ephemeral [*vergänglich*], like the leaf of a tree," etc. [292]). However, it is primarily carried out by Gregor, who particularly works to inscribe both Clarissa's emergent self and desire and the destruction of the father's castle as natural, law-governed events, and so to maintain the stability and uniformity of the represented world. And as part of that, we're told, "He poetized and narrated . . . and transported himself in fantasies and feelings into the wilderness [*die Einöde*]" (302), in order to project into the woods the newly required laws and order that will maintain the desired common ground and mimetic equivalence between them and the newly transpired events. In this, he has obvious (and needed) support from the narrator: for immediately after Ronald's sudden appearance and disappearance from the forest meadow, there follows an extended description of the woods that presents them almost exclusively in terms of seasonal change, as poised between a moment of late summer and the onset of early winter.

The shift is quite startling—even the narrator exclaims, "How changed was the forest!" (303)—but it allows Gregor to read the woods as embodying just those forces now loose in the novella; for from this point in the story on the natural world becomes conceived as inherently temporal, as movement and transitoriness par excellence; as an unfolding course or narrative that includes as natural realities both the processes of maturation and fruition and those of destruction and death. And given the system of reflective repetition underlying the novella, this new representation allows Gregor simply to point out "the frost's devastation" (305) in order to establish the law also governing the destruction of the father's castle; "the protruding [plant]shafts hanging down, so to speak, desiccated and limp" (305), in order to suggest the naturalness of the father's loss of power; and especially, together with "the falling of the last raspberries and the shriveling of those not yet mature . . . already on the branches the preliminary forms of the coming blossoms of Spring" (301), in order to ensure that the death of the old and the emergence of the new are all part of Nature's sustaining sexual narrative—intrinsically sexual, and necessarily a narrative—and do not violate but rather help maintain the world "as it is."

Despite this admittedly belated, somewhat forced, and even artificial attempt by Gregor and the narrator to maintain the common ground between the natural and human realms, the desired reconciliation is nonetheless left unrealized.[37] We see this in the novella's final chapter, which even in its title, "Forest Ruins," establishes the two contradictory patterns for the natural and human worlds we discovered already in the novella's first paragraph, and which now fall out of the system of mirroring similitude in its next to last: the one movement circular, turned back, stable, and self-sustaining, the other linear, descending, labile, and irretrievable. The shared order of virgin nature is lost forever: Gregor destroys all signs of the human intrusion into the woods, namely the forest house that so perfectly mirrored the father's original house; he plants new woods, and "they had numerous descendants and overgrew the whole place, so that once again the deep virgin wilderness [*die tiefe jungfräuliche Wildnis*] arose as it was before, and as it still is" (318). Meanwhile, the sisters leave the woods, return to the father's burnt-out castle, which we are told is never restored; the war goes on long beyond the winter season, "the sisters continued to live on there, both unmarried," and so without renewing, self-sustaining progeny; and with time, all traces of their existence disappear from the narrative world—"no human being knew [the whereabouts] of their grave" (318).

I said at the outset that these two uneasily contradictory movements represent an almost insuperable complication to the effort to maintain a pattern of reflective repetition between the two spheres, and we have just seen how their reassertion here signals the abandonment of that effort. But what we can now also see is that the pattern of mirroring repetitions has nonetheless *produced* each of these conflictual realities, the impossibility of their reconciliation, even the tragic issue of the latter, human reality. The point is most evident in respect to the representation of the natural realm, which clearly reflects the problem or paradox of the human one: the father's fantasy of a static, in some sense timeless and law-bound virginity is represented and inscribed there, joined with the emergent and apparently contradictory reality of sexuality, temporality, and wildness, also inscribed. The paradox is resolved, of course, the uniform but dual-natured reality established, by eliminating the human component altogether and introducing instead a certain recursive circularity into the representation of Nature itself, a kind of self-contained and self-reflecting system of repetition that can both include and exclude time and movement, change and death, and so too can retain both sexual maturation and purity.

The easily perceptible point, however, is that the very conditions of this natural reality, both its paradox and its needful reconciliation, have all their origin in the human sphere, which produces the other through its own projection, even as it eliminates all traces of itself, of its participant role, from that projection: the replicative forest house is completely effaced, the sisters forced out of the woods, all traces of them, even of their death, deleted from the represented real world. For once again, the novella seems to have fallen victim to its own realist designs. What makes the natural world might well be the human projection, but what makes it "real" is the effacement of that human dimension. And for that very reason it cannot be real for the men or women for whom it was nonetheless intended, that is, in whom the real effect was desired in the moment of the second reflective representation or repetition. The one reality destroys the other, from which it nonetheless originates—even as, already in the opening frame, the woods were undoing the human dwelling of the father, in whom the fantasy of their nonhuman nature began. The very narrative designed to integrate the sisters into everything sweet and sustaining, everything divine and natural, instead ruthlessly destroys and denies them, leaving Johanna, Clarissa, and the father all dead, all absent, all effaced from the surviving "reality."

This, then, is the one reality that the novella leaves us with, that of the disaster, the flaw to its realist structure, the undeniably real effects of its self-denying fiction. But it also goes one step further, fully exposing the consequences of its own realist logic. The novella leaves us, that is, not only with the absent corpses of Johanna, Clarissa, and the father, but also, in its final sentence, with a most present ghost: "One still often saw an old man like a phantom [*wie einen Schemen*] walking through the woods, but no one could tell of a time when he still walked, nor of one when he walked no longer" (318), a line that significantly echoes the temporal cadence in the description of the forest "as it was before, and as it still is." The natural reality of the woods has failed to eliminate the human phantasm at their center: the fantastic remains a reality, because the reality remains fantastic. These two realities, then—the fiction of the reality, or conversely the reality of the fiction, and the nonetheless real effects of a fiction that would become real at the expense of itself—these are the realities that Stifter works self-consciously to expose in the realism of his novella, the flaws to his realism that he still makes a part of his realism. The pure, innocent, and self-sustaining woods are not the only reality he leaves us with: their hidden corpses and haunting phantom are part of his realist legacy as well.

VII

I said at the outset that I would return to one of the central motifs of the novella, namely telescopes, and I would like to do so now. For telescopes incorporate many of the most critical issues to Stifter's realism, both in *The Mountain Forest* and in his work as a whole; and while we have encountered some of these in other contexts and constellations, most obviously vision, patriarchy, and chiasmus, others have forced themselves upon us only here at the end. Chief among them is the issue of death, which we need now finally to confront, and so too to acknowledge its place in the program of this novella in particular and of realism in general.

But let me begin with vision, and let me expand the scope of my own vision in this last part of the discussion to include a wider range of Stifter's texts, while still retaining my particular focus on *The Mountain Forest*. We see both the import and importance of telescopic vision throughout Stifter's work, starting with his first published story, *The Condor*, which opens with the protagonist gazing through his *Objektiv* at a hot-air balloon hovering at dawn on the eastern horizon. Again in the *Studies*, in *A Walk in the Woods* (*Der Waldsteig*), we find the protagonist gazing through his telescope (*Fernrohr*) as he forges his way into the woods, in his first—and then continued—step toward recognizing, mastering, and embracing his natural surroundings; in this, his practice adumbrates that, in *Many-colored Stones*, of the protagonist in *Limestone*, who similarly surveys his initially unfamiliar and forbidding environment through his scope, and so comes to perceive, appropriate, and appreciate it.

Moreover, all three of these protagonists share in the close association of telescopes and pictorial representation that we see once more in the late novella, *Descendants* (*Nachkommenschaften*), where the painter-protagonist carefully and repeatedly observes the landscape setting through his *Fernrohr* in preparation for its definitive "realist" reproduction; for in each of these earlier tales, the protagonist is also engaged in transforming his telescopic vision into either a painting or sketch. As we'll see, telescopes also appear in many other of Stifter's works, but nowhere so constantly as in *The Mountain Forest*, which is, significantly, set in the time of their first invention and deployment. The Wittinghaus family first looks out and discovers their intended retreat with a telescope from their castle, and then Gregor and the daughters regularly look back with another telescope from that retreat to discover the same castle, marveling, especially at the outset, about the novel modes of vision opened up by their new device.

How are we to read this broadly thematized mediation of vision, and what does it tell us about Stifter's realism? As the so-called *Objektiv* from *The Condor* might suggest, the realist telescope seems to function differently from its romantic counterpart, for instance the *Perspektiv* through which E. T. A. Hoffmann's Nathanael views the lifeless puppet Olimpia and imagines her to be real. Such an awareness of the psychological perspectivism of all vision is of course—and despite the frequent critical denial of this—not unknown to Stifter and other realists, nor its challenge to, and so needed place in, a realist program. Indeed, Stifter's own decided preference for first-person, even if nameless narrators such as in *The Mountain Forest*, directly incorporates such a perspectivism into his fictional world.[38]

Nonetheless, this does not seem the primary focus of Stifter's telescopes, although it remains a closely related one. Rather, as the examples above confirm, telescopes seem to convey the same specific import of realist vision we discovered in the preface to *Many-colored Stones*, namely vision as not about the simple objective recording of an empirical reality but instead about the complex—and not *only* psychological—imposition of a meaning, law, and order behind that reality. For all Stifter's protagonists, telescopes become their means for mastering the world, for establishing that initially unperceived, and so also in a sense absent, order that transforms the view into something real for them. Significantly, in their character as both artificial, mechanized eyes and as supposedly neutral scientific instruments, these telescopes render ambivalent whether the law and order they assist in determining is a quality of the perceiver or the scene. But as we have already seen, and will again, such an ambivalence is actually characteristic of poetic realism, both in its overt, if partial, display of its mechanisms of artifice and imposition, and in its covert, if also partial effacement of those same mechanisms, and the concomitant ascription of an objective immanence to its law and order.[39]

Telescopes not only concretize and self-consciously thematize the "objectifying" mediation of Stifter's realist vision, the mechanical and external nature of his "spiritual eye" (*geistige Auge*). They also, in a slightly different sense, instrumentalize and aim that vision. To explain what I mean by this we should note that telescopes can, of course, always be pointed in one of two directions. They can be directed either horizontally outward to survey the immediate or distant terrestrial surroundings and activity, or vertically upward, to survey the distant celestial world and movement. Both directions and their somewhat different employments have been part of the history of the telescope from the beginning—Galileo, for instance, immediately proclaimed their usefulness for military surveillance as well as astronomy[40]—and, more important, both appear in Stifter's work. Besides the outward, earthbound examples already mentioned, there is the example of Prokopus in *The Castle of Fools* (*Die Narrenburg*), who builds a tower to aim his telescopes at the sky. There is the scientific expedition in *The Condor*, which rides its balloon into the upper atmosphere to aim its instruments at the stars. And there is also Stifter's own report on *The Solar Eclipse of July 8, 1842*, in which he climbs up on his Viennese rooftop to observe the astronomical event through his celestial telescope (*Sternenrohr*). Aimed in either direction, telescopes reveal "reality," reveal that is a certain otherwise unperceived law and order to the external world. Indeed, based on the evidence of history, namely of the Baroque science that is contemporary with the world of *The Mountain Forest*, when telescopes first opened up the heavens to rational scientific investigation and so dispelled centuries of established illusions in a newly enlightened, more realist age—based on this, one might argue that telescopes aimed skyward would more fully corroborate and affirm Stifter's realist ideal of a revealed meaning, order, and law to the world.

And the example of *The Solar Eclipse of July 8, 1842*, which is contemporary with the publication of *The Mountain Forest*, might initially seem to confirm this expectation.

However, despite these two possible directions, and despite the arguable superiority of the skyward one for the establishment of an immanent external order, the vast majority of Stifter's telescopes are aimed earthward, and there is even an implicit reproof against those who would look upward instead. We see this in the fateful figure of Prokopus in *The Castle of Fools* and the tragic events that later unfold in his tower. We see it too in the aborted balloon expedition in *The Condor* and the circumstances surrounding its failure. But we see it most clearly in Stifter's comments in a letter on Johannes Kepler, about whom he secretly hoped to write a book.[41] Kepler belonged to the same Baroque world as the protagonists of *The Mountain Forest*, and he was a (if not the) major figure in its scientific revelation of the rational order and law of the celestial spheres. But this is not what mattered most to Stifter. Rather, Stifter emphasizes that, at the time of his most important telescopic discoveries, Kepler was employed in Linz as a land surveyor (*Landvermesser*), but like his later Kafkean counterpart, he spent all his time surveying the upper realms and none of it surveying the more earthly ones—much to the righteous anger of the people of Linz and, apparently, of Stifter himself.

As we gather from the land-surveying in *Limestone*, this neglected but also preferred surveillance was conceived by Stifter as equally a matter of telescopic vision, equally a matter of discovering and establishing order and law by means of this device. So we need, I think, to ask what in particular distinguishes the lawfulness, or *Gesetzlichkeit,* made available through the earthbound telescope from that obtained through the starbound one, and more especially, what increases its usefulness for Stifter's realist program. And I should stress again the specific relevance of this issue and question for *The Mountain Forest*, where, after an initial brief period of focal adjustment, the telescope is always directed earthward and never skyward—an omission made all the more conspicuous by the novella's Baroque setting (as well as by the nearly simultaneous appearance of Stifter's *The Solar Eclipse of July 8, 1842*).[42]

To answer this question we need first to ask another, namely what else, besides the world of (merely) natural phenomena, Stifter's earthbound telescopes capture in their scopic field. And the answer is, perhaps predictably, women. This is again most conspicuous in Stifter's late novella, *Descendants*, where the telescope that is first aimed at mastering the landscape for the projected realist painting soon becomes simultaneously focused on mastering the woman for what becomes the projected, and realized, marriage. But we see the same basic constellation in many other, earlier works as well. In *A Walk in the Woods*, the protagonist also coordinates his telescopic surveillance of the natural landscape with his growing visual cognizance of his female companion and his steadily improving sketches. In *Two Sisters*, the protagonist, another sketch-artist, climbs a hill to look back through his telescope at the estate where the recalcitrant object of his affection, Maria, awaits; and in *Indian Summer* (*Der Nachsommer*), Heinrich does much the same thing when he climbs into the hills to look back at Sternenhof and so fix Natalie's place with his telescopic gaze.

More pointedly, in *The Condor* we witness the same constellation in its failure. The painter-protagonist seeks to fix his beloved but rebellious Kornelia in his telescopic sights, and in so doing to achieve a number of different but interlinked ends: to impose on her both his personal desire and the established social constraints for female behavior; to reassert the standard contours, dimensions, or order of the "normal" natural world; and to complete the realist painting that sits framed on the easel before him. But Kornelia is not to be seen or fixed through the scope: by joining the skybound expedition she has (fatefully) exceeded the boundaries of both her womanly role and the natural world, and as a result the protagonist's desire goes unanswered and his "realist" painting must be abandoned.

What we see, then, is that Stifter's earthbound telescopes generally embody a fairly familiar but still decisive cluster of themes: a male gaze, its association with visual artistic representation, and the association of both with the project of establishing a certain identifiably "realist" mastery over the natural world and the female body and soul. As such, these telescopes all embody and express a peculiarly patriarchal, or at least male program of lawful order, or *Gesetzlichkeit:* they serve simultaneously to concentrate male imagination and desire into a properly focused vision (or representation), and to bind nature and female nature to the law and order of that vision.

The telescopes in *The Mountain Forest* also clearly associate themselves with the male order, in particular that of the father. For instance, the first telescope in the story belongs to the father and is set up in his castle to determine the location of Clarissa's and Johanna's future home in the forest—but only once they have dressed themselves to his full visual satisfaction ("Look, how beautiful—now we will set up the scope and look through it," 232). The second telescope, which is brought into the woods with Clarissa and Johanna, does not belong to the father but rather to the mysterious knight, Bruno. It is, however, introduced as the last item in the father's litany of his foresightful precautions for his daughters' security, and as such firmly linked to his law and love. Moreover, the shift in possession of the telescope from the father to Bruno and then Gregor—who immediately takes charge of it in the woods—largely parallels the movement of succession we see elsewhere for the keeping of Clarissa from the father to Gregor and then, wishfully, to Bruno: Stifter uses the same device again in *Two Sisters*, where the shifting possession of a telescope from Franz through the father to the narrator-protagonist signals the intended shift of Maria along this same chain of possession. Finally, we can note that in *The Mountain Forest*, the telescope is always and only taken out and extended from atop the towering erection of the otherwise patriarchally semanticized, protecting, and law-imposing Blockenstein, and is also, with one exception, always and only aimed and deployed in the direction of the father's house.

What is of course exceptional about *The Mountain Forest* is that the women in the tale are not the objects of this patriarchal telescopic vision. Instead, they are the subjects, the viewers themselves. But as the fact that the focus of their scopic project is almost exclusively the father's house, from which the first telescope—his telescope—was aimed out at their present location makes clear, far from negating the standard identification of Stifter's telescopic vision with the male gaze and its realist project, the example of *The Mountain Forest* confirms and furthers it by incorporating into it another characteristic tactic of his realism, namely that of chiastic projection and reversal. By constantly fixing their gaze back on the father's house, Johanna and Clarissa ensure that they themselves will constantly remain fixed by its gaze; while seeming the free and controlling subjects of telescopic vision, immanently desirous of sustaining communication, they nonetheless remain the determined, controlled objects of their father's surveillance, precisely through their sustained desire and linked vision.[43]

This is basically the same chiastic arrangement—and arrangement by chiasmus—that Stifter describes so explicitly in *The Solar Eclipse of July 8, 1842*, which represents another seeming exception to his standard pattern. In his account of the eclipse, Stifter focuses not so much on the divine law deciphered in the heavens by the telescopic viewers as on the *same*, reciprocal law solicited in the human viewers by the heavenly sight (which too, of course, proves specifically patriarchal—that is, Christian). And it is also basically the same arrangement that Stifter evokes in *The Mountain Forest* for nontelescopic, "natural" vision, through the parallel motif of the forest lake as an eye of Nature, which looks back at the castle, or alternatively at the women, and in so doing projects and enforces its "natural" law on its object—but only once, and only because it has already been transformed by the father's super-vision into an embodiment of his surveillant law. (One might interpret the need to trek up into the mountains in order to look back at the house in both *Two Sisters* and *Indian Summer* as motivated by the same chiastic tactic, the same desire to associate the lawful order of the telescope with that of Nature, the two reciprocating fields enclosing and defining female identity.)

The parallel is actually thematized in *The Mountain Forest*, and so too the desired naturalization aimed at by putting the telescope in the women's own hands. Johanna, the more successfully "naturalized" sister, regularly spots and establishes the link with the father's house by means of her "natural" vision, while Clarissa, in whom the desired "nature" remains more overtly strained and *un*natural, manipulates the artificially supplemented one—thus bringing out even more the artifice and strategy of self-policing attached to the telescope's use.[44] And the same arrangement is also maintained in the only apparent exception to their usual practice, the only time the sisters really look at anything besides their father's house, namely when they once look back through the "wrong" end of the telescope at their own house, an exact duplicate of their father's, so that it appears as distant as his. This performs the same chiastic function of reversal, repetition, and equivalence that the telescope "rightly" achieves by keeping the father's house so near.

Telescopes, then, thematize several motifs that we have discovered elsewhere to be of primary significance for realism: vision, and vision as a matter of law and order; patriarchy, and its supervisory, surveillant determination of female nature and Nature together; and chiasmus, that is, the (chiastic) projection and displacement of vision, law, and patriarchal desire into the subjects of scopic concern, namely Nature and women themselves. This last facet of Stifter's realism is somewhat uniquely incorporated into the telescopes of *The Mountain Forest*, which also more or less uniquely thematize several other motifs of central importance for realism, namely those of stasis, exclusion, history, and death.

The association of telescopes with stasis, and stasis with realism, is particularly insistent in *The Mountain Forest*. It is also particularly problematic. The first time the sisters set up the telescope and aim it at their father's house, we are told, "They couldn't sate themselves of always looking at one and the same thing" (*Sie könnten sich nicht ersättigen, immer das eine und das eine anzusehen*, 256). Thereafter, "whenever they looked through the scope, there always appeared in it the same beautiful, pure, intact image of their father's house" (*immer dasselbe schöne, reine, unverletzte Bild des väterlichen Hauses*, 258). "In the same beauty, as often as they sought it out, their father's house appeared in the glass lens of their telescope" (261); or again, "the scope was set up, and pure and clear as always the diminutive copy [*Nachbild*] of their father's house appeared in it" (276). The reproduction of the same representation, and the repeated reproduction of the same representation throughout the narrative, even in the language used: all this serves to negate a sense of narrative progress or change, to insist on the represented reality as still, and its still-ness and reproducibility as the guarantors of its reality.

It is worth stressing, however, that this clarity, purity, and ordered uniformity of vision, which provides an image and intelligence at once both accurate and aesthetically pleasing, is not an immediate effect or accomplishment. Rather, as the narrator remarks, the sisters' telescopic vision is initially fantastic (*abenteurlich*) and dreamlike (*träumerisch*), everything seen appears utterly strange (*wildfremd*) and enchanted (*gezaubert*), the telescope itself bewitching and inexplicable, and the father's house first appears "trembling in the orb of the wonderful glass" (*zitternd im Runde des wunderbaren Glases*, 256f.). The eventual clarity, familiarity, and repeated regularity of its vision (that is, once the sisters become properly adept at its manipulation) can, of course, be understood simply as the subsequent elimination of these inchoate labile elements of fantasy and desire (*zitternd*). But it can also, and equally appropriately, be understood as their obtained concentration or focalization. After all, we are told, "[T]hey couldn't *sate* themselves of always looking at one and the same thing," and then again later on, "It was as if they couldn't pull themselves away from [the scope and its always pure and clear image of the father's house], and as if they *must* be able to see their beloved, beautiful father" (276). Especially this last example illuminates how the sustained stasis and repetitiveness of the sisters' telescopic vision remains a function of their (increasingly desperate) desire and imaginations.

While the emphatic clarity and reliability of this ever-repeating vision underscore the link between its achieved stasis and realism, the equally emphatic focus on the father's house and the combined beauty (*Schönheit*) and purity (*Reinheit*) of the vision underscore the link to its other, or rather its real focus, namely the female viewers themselves, and especially Clarissa, who regularly takes charge of the telescope and who just as regularly remains the intended object of the tele-scopic desire for and fantasy of an untouched ever-sameness, a *Reinheit* that is a *Schönheit*, a stasis that (desperately) wants to be real. As we've seen, this fantasy and desire originate with the father and his gaze or regard. But it is represented here in its chiastic realization, in the fantasy and desire reflected in the daughters, their consistently reproduced vision, and their "glass"—which is, appropriately enough, at once a looking device, a mirroring device, and a peculiarly frozen medium of enclosing transparency.

The complex associations between clarity, purity, and uniform order that are achieved through telescopic vision are not, however, the sole extent of the telescopes' relations to realism in the novella. For in a manner that is, I believe, unique to *The Mountain Forest*, realism is associated here not only with what the telescopes capture in their field but also with what they fail to capture, what in fact they actively exclude from their scopic concern. This is emphasized from the outset, and from the outset the excluded reality is history. When the father first reveals the spot in the woods they will see through his telescope, and from which they will subsequently see him through theirs, he describes it as so ever-silent, untouched, and unchanging that "it takes real effort for one to believe that for many years now the din of war and destruction has raged in the world of men" (227). The static and silent natural realm that is to secure the daughters and ground the future visual exchanges is defined by the temporal and noisy historical realm it keeps at bay. When Johanna and Clarissa arrive in the woods and, as instructed, look back, then "in the same beauty, as often as they sought it out, their father's house appeared in the glass lens of their telescope . . . even though they knew full well that out there, where their gaze no longer reached, lay the smoky haze of war that at any moment could appear in their field of vision" (*der jeden Augenblick an ihrem Gesichtskreise sichtbar werden könne*, 261). The beauty and uniformity of their arranged natural setting reproduces itself in their equally arranged telescopic vision or report, but again the reality it so clearly represents is rendered eerily incomplete by the smoky, unclear reality that hovers just out of sight. Finally, when the sisters look back again for the last time and espy only "an altogether faint layer of blue haze over the ruins" of their father's house, we're told, "It was an uncanny thought that, at this very moment, the violent tumult of war could be raging there, and deeds be occurring that could tear apart a human heart; but one perceived absolutely nothing of the tumult of war" (306). For all the clarity and purity of their vision, telescopes finally fail to render reality at all, insofar as reality proves to be precisely what Stifter's realism has worked from afar to eliminate from their scopic field. Reality becomes what his telescopes do not, cannot represent, and yet what nonetheless emerges to destroy and inhabit their static representation; the off-scene, the unseen. And as a result, for his female protagonists, "realism" becomes a seeing what they cannot see, a realizing of the failure of their telescopes to either capture or exclude the reality on which they sought to fix its sights.

The historical reality that thus both escapes and ultimately destroys the project of telescopic vision is not, we should note, defined only in terms of gross political movements, such as the passing Swedish troops that destroy the father's house. It is also defined in more minor, intrinsic terms. Most obviously, perhaps, there is *Geschichte* as *Geschichte*, the noisy narrative of "what else has happened [*was noch geschehen ist*] that [they] cannot see with the telescope" (306): the attempt to assimilate the narrative world to visual practices falls apart once the real proves temporal and eventful—at which point the narrative not only fails to coincide with visual representation, but actually works to negate its founding equation of stasis and realism.

Equally important, however, and more centrally related to the chiastic focus of this telescopic realism, there is the *Geschichte* of maturing female sexuality, that historical reality which the father's tele-scopic fantasy of a pure stasis so desperately tries chiastically to control. Stifter suggests this dimension to the history threatening the telescopes' visual representation early on through the leitmotif of trembling (*zitternd*), which is consistently applied to Clarissa's desirous nature and which, through her hands, rocks the telescopic view of her father's house in the beginning as surely as the hands and weapons of the Swedish troops do at the end. But he thematizes it more fully later on as well, through the motif of the clouds and smoky haze that obscure the visual field once the destructive forces reach the father's house and prevent the telescope from rendering a clear account of what has happened (*was geschehen ist*). As we remember, clouds were metaphorically linked early on by Clarissa with emerging sexual desires, joining together changes in Nature and female nature in ways that potentially challenged the elsewise enforced visual ideal of an unchanging, translucent stasis for both. Here near the end, once Clarissa has revealed her desires for her beloved Ronald, the fogs of early autumn conspire with the pluming smoke of warfare to frustrate the visual connections that up to this point had sustained and determined the common unchanging reality of the women, the woods, and the telescopic report. For once she admits her awakening desires into the woods and her heart, Clarissa breaks her father's surveillant, policing hold over those woods and herself, shatters the uniform identity between the woods, herself, and his scopically imposed, realist wish for virgin sameness, and so too virtually requires the destruction of his house, the recursive blanking of his controlling vision. History—as politics, narrative, and female sexuality—emerges as the common reality excluded from, interfering with, and finally even invading the established field of Stifter's telescopic realism.

This history, then, that the telescopes seek to exclude, fail to capture, and that nonetheless comes eventually to dominate their visual field—this history reveals a complex logic of desire at the heart of telescopic vision. On the one hand, in the form of both the political rapacity of the passing army and the female sexuality of the maturing Clarissa, desire emerges as a labile, uncontrolled, and destructive force that telescopes seek to exclude from or negate within their represented realm. On the other, in the form of the surveillant, policing fantasy of the father's gaze and its reflective reproduction in the daughters', desire emerges as the operant condition for the controlling construction of the static field of the telescopes themselves. As we've seen, the contradictions occasioned by finding desire on both sides of the realist equation are many, and become increasingly conspicuous as the story progresses. But more immediately pressing for us now: the contradictions and identities that emerge between the two competing realities of Stifter's realism appear again when history is conceived in terms not of desire but of death—or rather, in terms of both death and desire, for our novella insists upon this linkage, this identity as well.

That the external, political reality that the telescopes seek both to distance and to determine is to be associated with death is patent; history is war. That the internal, sexual reality that the telescopes seek chiastically to keep away and fixed is also to be linked with death might seem less immediately obvious, but it is just as insistently maintained. The natural maturation of Clarissa is forcefully joined with the theme of transience, or *Vergänglichkeit,* as is the object of her desires, Ronald; moreover, the moment of their meeting and of her emergent sexuality is closely paired with the imminent decline of autumn, whose own death-dealing *Reif* (that is, hoarfrost, but the word inevitably recalls Clarissa's own *Reife,* her maturing) is itself paired with the similarly death-dealing passage, or *Übergang,* of the Swedish troops. On both sides of the telescope, the excluded reality is that of death. But the included field of telescopic vision, the very project of telescopic stasis, is no less clearly and insistently linked with death. Like the motionless silence of the woods' virginity, or the petrified stillness of the lake's reflecting eye of Nature, the ever-repeating clarity, fixity, and uniformity of telescopic vision—including its chiastically inscribed purity and virginity for the female telescopic viewers—represents a consistently thematized stiffness (*Starrheit*) that itself proves deathlike precisely through its elimination of movement and difference and its insistence instead on stasis and sameness. So for example, even before the arrival of the Swedish troops, the "always the same beautiful, pure, intact image of their father's house" becomes described as the "always the same, long familiar and lifeless [*unbelebt*] image in the glass lens [*im Glase*]" (276). Death haunts Stifter's telescopic vision not only as that which it will not or cannot see, but also as its seeing itself; as the reality it desires to deny, and as the very form of its desiring.

This central conjunction of death and desire on both sides of the realist equation that we see expressed in the (already and then again) "lifeless image" of the father's house we see expressed again in more allegorical terms for the figure of the telescopic viewer herself, Clarissa, shortly after the sudden appearance and disappearance of Ronald. On a walk through the woods, Johanna, Clarissa, and Gregor chance upon a group of butterflies called "mourning-cloaks" (*Trauermanteln*, 299) playing in the late autumn sun. Johanna laments that they have prematurely emerged from their childhood (*Kinderstube*) and cocoon (*Puppenschlaf*) only to freeze to death in the coming winter. But Gregor rejects this scenario and describes instead two alternative accounts of their fate, which he claims depends solely on whether or not they marry (*sich vermählen*, 300). According to Gregor, these creatures die soon after their wedding; the realization of their sexual nature is almost immediately followed by their death; both are expressions of the same troublesome transitoriness of all life, all history, and all narrative. On the other hand, "If instead they do not marry, then they become stiff and still [*so erstarren sie*], and look! . . . often frozen in ice and snow, these fragile beings survive the harsh winter." The alternative, then, should these creatures avoid their sexual course and its death, is itself a kind of death, even a double death: committed to a sterile, nonprogressive virginity, they are petrified into a frozen, eerily lifeless *Starrheit*, and in this double death they seek their life. The allegory here specifically applies to the figure of Clarissa, and the medium for its privileged stasis is ice; but it applies equally well to the model of realism found throughout the novella and its privileged medium of glass. Stifter's telescopic realism, on both sides of its apparatus, pits one form of death and desire against another.

In *The Mountain Forest*, the outcome of this struggle yields yet another crucial combination of death and realism, which is again thematized by the work's telescopes, and with which I would like to close this chapter. Once Clarissa's maturing sexuality has broken the father's surveillant, arresting hold over her, has broken the uniform identity between herself, the woods, and his scopically inscribed realist wish for virgin ever-sameness, and so has also more or less broken the edifice and structure of his controlling power; that is, once her death-promising desire destroys his, a slightly different, if still the same, stasis and reality comes to dominate the telescopic field.[45] The uniformity and ever-repeating sameness of the view of the castle before, enforced as the chiastic realization of the father's tele-scopic law and order, is succeeded by more uniformity and sameness once that order has been toppled, the law violated, and his castle destroyed. "Clarissa threw herself once more in front of the telescope's lens and looked into it for a long time—but the same report was always there, doubly alarming because of its same mute uniformity and clarity" (307). That is, the failure of the father's telescopic project does not, strangely enough, yield a negation of its ideal but rather its repetition; the desire for stasis, uniformity, clarity, and a constant, unchanging reality is defeated not so much in its frustration as in its fulfillment. And the same of course is true in the end of the daughters, who pass from their deathlike virginity to their deathlike, unmarried old age almost without transition.

We are left, I think, with two different ways of describing what we finally glimpse through Stifter's telescopes, two different versions of the "realism" they make us see in this moment of repetition. On the one hand, we are left seeing the necessary sameness of these two represented states of ordered uniformity, the inherent if self-negating identity between the realist wish for a pure, regulated, identical world and a wish for death, indeed for the death of the very reality it wishes to keep alive. On the other, we are left knowing the undeniable difference between these two states, realizing the death-dealing difference that makes all the difference in the world between the one and the next, same "mute uniformity and clarity"; the realized difference that is itself, however brief the moment of its appearance, the lasting trace of the real in Stifter's world. But it is to be hoped that, as we gaze through Stifter's scope, in however contradictory and unclear a fashion, we see both.

4 DOUBLE TAKES

Genre and Gender in Keller's Twice-Told Tales, the 'Seven Legends' ('Sieben Legenden')

The world of Keller's writings is a mirror-world, and that includes the sense in which something is fundamentally inverted, even perverted in it, with what is right and left transposed. While what is important and active preserves its order apparently intact, the masculine imperceptibly changes into the feminine, and the feminine into the masculine.
—Walter Benjamin[1]

I know very well what you're up to! You think you can make a fool of me and keep putting me off, so that I let you run around forever in this in-between condition? Well, it won't work!
—Mirror, the Cat

Stifter's *The Mountain Forest* has often been recognized as a retelling of an earlier narrative, namely of Goethe's *Novella*. Nor is it unusual in this regard. In *Many-colored Stones,* for instance, the second story, *Limestone,* is sometimes seen as a retelling of Grillparzer's *The Poor Musician* (*Der arme Spielmann*), the last story, *Mountain Quartz* (*Bergmilch*), as a retelling of Kleist's *The Marquise of O—*. And Stifter is not at all alone among the poetic realists in his practice of basing his fictions on earlier fictions. In fact, two more of the novellas discussed at length in this book are re-presentations, or repetitions, of other literary works: Storm's *Viola tricolor* repeats the tale already told in Auerbach's *The Stepmother,* and Meyer's *The Marriage of the Monk* (*Die Hochzeit des*

Mönchs) repeats a tale told in Boccaccio's *Decameron*. The list could, of course, be easily and almost endlessly extended.

The circumstance that so many realist stories are twice-told tales is not in itself surprising. What is surprising is the quite obvious challenge this circumstance poses to any traditional, programmatic realist aesthetic, and the equally obvious lack of response to the challenge by most contemporary critics of realism. For most traditional accounts, realism derives its quality as "realist" by virtue of its faithful mimetic reproduction of an original, anterior, extraliterary world. However, when a narrative overtly undertakes to reproduce not an extraliterary original but a literary fiction—and so at best becomes a representation of a representation—and yet still lays claim to a realist intent, then we must look elsewhere and otherwise to account for that claim. We must, that is, look for its realism not in the original but in the representation, the repeated fiction itself.

I

Of all the poetic realists, Gottfried Keller offers not only some of the most interesting examples of twice-told tales, but also some of the most interesting self-reflection on his practice. There is, for instance, the case of the two different versions of his famous novel *Green Henry* (*Der Grüne Heinrich*, 1854/55; 1879/80), which offers irreconcilably different representations of supposedly the same, real events, and so introduces the possibility of radically revising the represented world through its retelling. Even more famously—and more germanely for our concerns—there is Keller's retelling of Shakespeare in *A Village Romeo and Juliet* (*Romeo und Julia auf dem Dorfe*, 1856), whose opening paragraph explicitly ruminates on the problem of retelling for a realist poetics.[2] Keller describes his novella as an imitation, or repetition, not so much of Shakespeare's tale as of a certain primeval fable, an *Urfabel*, that both Shakespeare's work and his own repeat, and that not unincidentally is also constantly repeated in real life. In fact, Keller presents his tale as simultaneously a repetition of Shakespeare's earlier drama and of a contemporary actual occurrence (*wirklicher Vorfall*), each of which is in turn conceived as itself a repetition of an original *Fabel*. As Keller says, "There are a limited number of such fables, but they are constantly reappearing in new clothes and, when they do, they force the [writer's] hand to hold them fast." Thus, his tale derives its realist quality from its retelling both of the "actual event" and of the reality that constantly reveals itself as a repetition of an *Urfabel.* Or to employ Keller's own terms, we might say that he bases the realism of his retelling both on its contemporary or "new" clothing and on its strangely elusive original body—elusive, because even as an original it seems only to manifest itself in its re-presentation, in its appearance, in its ever-changing costume.

Because Keller's *A Village Romeo and Juliet* grounds its realism at least in part on some extraliterary actual event, even if it does conceive of that actual event as itself a manifestation of some underlying and possibly more real "fable," this novella does not present as fit an example of our topic as we might like. One could still argue for realism as the faithful mimetic reproduction of an original extraliterary world rather than as a particular mode of repeating fiction. Far more suitable for our purposes are Keller's perhaps lesser known realist retellings of Christian fables in his *Seven Legends* (*Sieben Legenden*, 1857/58; 1871). Keller bases his retellings of these legends—which consist of three medieval tales of the Virgin Mary and four conversion stories set in the late Roman Empire—exclusively on their prior retellings by the romantic poet, Ludwig Kosegarten (1804). No attempt is made to ground the tales in any actual extraliterary occurrences; nor, strictly speaking, in any "original" version of the legends. Still less does Keller attempt to ground them in any contemporary setting. In fact, Keller claims to select his material in deliberate protest against "the terrorism of the *externally* contemporary" (*dem Terrorismus des* äusserlichen *Zeitgemässen;* Keller's emphasis).[3]

The challenge that these retold tales pose to a traditional understanding of the realist enterprise was registered almost immediately in the critical response that followed upon their publication. Almost all the critics, both those who liked and those who disliked the retellings, seemed united in regarding them as motivated by a realist impulse. And almost all, in the absence of any direct relevance to actual contemporary events, ascribed their realism to one or the other of two related, but also different, operations. On the one hand, the retelling of these religious legends was imagined to be inspired by a more or less Feuerbachian interest in secularizing the Christian tradition, in preserving but transforming the inherited fictions by reinterpreting and refunctioning their original transcendental orientation back into the concerns of the present, real world. So, for instance, one disapproving critic describes how Keller "transforms the ascetic features of the holy into a mask, behind which hides a worldly face"; another who praises the work, Emil Kuh, describes basically the same procedure but for "worldly" substitutes the concepts of the "real" and "natural."[4] On the other hand, Keller's retellings were felt to aim not so much at preserving the inherited conventions by binding them to the new and "real" as at evacuating or discarding them by detaching them from the real—where the narrative repetition is more exclusively in the service of parody, and the intended realist effect more narrowly in the nature of disenchantment. So the Viennese author Ferdinand Kürnberger lauds Keller: "Without moving even a hair's breadth away from the basis of belief in these legends, he carries this belief almost to the point of absurdity by pretending to be naïve. . . . He has only to present himself as credulous in order to confound all credibility. He lets belief be condemned by its own account."[5] Theodor Fontane, who attacks the retellings, does so on much the same grounds. He claims that Keller's more or less parodic style renders the legends "antilegends," so that the re-takes represent not so much a "turn of the inherited figures in another direction" as a "wringing of their necks, as if they were pigeons."[6] The two operations are not, of course, necessarily mutually exclusive, and one could certainly see that the automatization of the inherited Christian conventions is an integral moment in their transformation to accommodate the newly invested "reality." Nonetheless, they also indicate quite different functions for the repetition at issue in Keller's realist enterprise, posing Kuh's sense of reanimation against Fontane's of death. But more on that later.

Both of these operations and their service in the contemporary *Kulturkampf* regarding Christian conventions, ideals, and authority are undeniably central to any discussion of the realist impulse behind Keller's retellings.[7] However, Keller himself, in the foreword to *Seven Legends,* identifies a slightly different motivation for his realist impulse, a more focused and circumscribed field for its exercise, and a more layered model for its project of re-production. Keller reports how, in reading the legends, it seemed "as if in the handed-down mass of tales it was not only the churchly art of fabulation which asserted itself, but that, if one looked attentively, the traces of an earlier, more profane story-pleasure or 'novellistic' was to be noticed as well." These traces in turn are said to arouse "the desire to reproduce the handed down figure[s]," albeit with a "turn" in a different direction. That is, beneath or behind the Christian fables there is felt to lurk another earlier, and in some sense opposite, genre of tales, which also somehow simultaneously represents an earlier, in some sense more original "story-pleasure," or *Erzählungslust* (expression of desire, or desire of expression). The possibility of stripping away the concealing Christian trappings from the handed-down figure (*die überkommene Gestalt*) and so exposing this other genre and releasing the hidden *Erzählungslust* arouses, as he says, Keller's own desire for a reproduction (*Lust zu einer Reproduktion*).

It is, I think, well worth drawing out with even greater clarity the specific claims for realism made in the foreword, and the specific way in which repetition functions to achieve that realism. First of all, like Stifter in his preface to *Many-colored Stones*, Keller seems here to designate erotic desire as *the* privileged site of realist concern; it is, as it were, the *internally* contemporary with which the tales are fully concerned.[8] However, unlike Stifter, Keller does not identify the realist program with the stabilizing, maintaining, and norm-inducing role of the erotic, but rather with its disruptive, liberating one. The role of normative and largely antierotic conventions is here placed upon the churchly art of fabulation (*die kirchliche Fabulierkunst*), whose representations are felt to conceal or even exclude (albeit unsuccessfully) the underlying reality of desire, which Keller's retellings aim to restore through his promised deformation, distortion, or dislocation of the inherited material. Hence, realism is identified with desire, and the operation by which desire can be re-presented is identified with the liberating introduction of difference into the representation.

Second, the desire that is identified by Keller with realism—both that which the prior Christian representations conceal or distort and that which his representation will release—manifests itself not in or as any particular subject matter, not as any "thing" to which his or earlier narratives might refer and thereby acquire (or forfeit) their quantity of reality, but rather in or as the narrative form itself, as an *Erzählungslust* and *die Lust zu einer Reproduktion*. One consequence of this is that the desire here associated with realism remains closely linked with the issue of the genre-shift from *Fabulierkunst* to *Novellistik*. In Keller's program, desire and genre are inseparable.⁹

Finally, the realism at issue in Keller's *Reproduktion* is not only dependent on the newly released desire that accompanies the genre-shift (itself conceived as more realistic), but also on its coincidence with an earlier version of both this desire and this genre. In fact, in the absence of any reference to some "actual occurrence," the coincidence of his representation with this earlier, anterior basis behind the Kosegarten representation—that is, the repetition by his reproduction of that representation—becomes the primary ground for its realism. But at the same time that this coincidence in repetition is made the primary support for the work's realism, its own main prop seems to be taken away. There is, conspicuously, no *Urfabel* to which the new narrative can refer, no original "body" to the legends, but only different prior representations. Indeed, given Keller's sole dependence on the "churchly" retellings—and more specifically, on Kosegarten's—even the prior "more profane" versions are nothing but a projective reproduction out of their later (Christian) reproductions. In other words, the supposedly more original, essential version is recognized as a fiction projected onto the site of an absence—an irony underscored by Keller's image here of the painter who completes a landscape picture not according to any original reality but out of "a small engraving of some forgotten master" alone. A further unexpected consequence of this that we might note is that the Christian or Kosegarten retellings, far from presenting distorting or different versions of the legends, must in fact coincide with or re-present the other (opposite, original) version, such that the one can be read into and out of the other.¹⁰

This is, then, the troublesome, self-contradictory way that repetition functions here in the realist project. On the one hand, Keller's realism depends upon the generic trappings of his representation corresponding with some "original" of the legends, and certainly far more fittingly than their previous, in some sense opposite generic trappings, which need to be shed for the disguised reality or truth to be exposed. The realism requires the repetition that mimetically equates the new representation with the earlier "reality." On the other hand, this original reality is understood to be not "really" there, to be instead itself a fiction reproduced out of a fiction and reproduced as a fiction. In this case, the repetition seems not so much to essentialize the new representation, to endow it with reality, as it does to draw the whole question of such a privileged ground into view.

II

Such are some of the problems, and the terms of the problems, identified by Keller in his foreword for the realist impulse operant in his project of twice-told tales. It is crucial that we recognize the self-conscious reflection on his realist practice, and so reconfirm the ever-present, foregrounded awareness by the realist author of the inherent paradoxes and problems of his enterprise. But it is equally crucial that we recognize that the self-conscious reflection on his project does not end with the foreword. Rather, the retold tales themselves are so structured and contrived as to repeat, or represent, in their subject matter the very terms, conditions, and problems of their narration, or more precisely, of their renarration. For whereas from one perspective the seven legends that Keller retells can hardly be considered realistic tales in their plots and characters, they can still from another quite clearly be seen as tales of realism, almost as allegories of realism, that translate the terms and operations of their "realist" representation into those of their characters and plots. So, for example, all but one of the tales present as a major theme or event the reclothing or even refiguring of the protagonist (or of the Virgin Mary), and so incorporate into themselves the issues of changing trappings and even bodies raised explicitly by Keller at the beginning of *A Village Romeo and Juliet* and implicitly here. In three of these tales, the change of clothes is accompanied by a shift out of the "churchly" sphere into a "more profane" one; and in each case the shift into what we might call the "real" world is accompanied by the release of the protagonist into the realm of erotic desire. Moreover, and perhaps most significantly, explicitly in two of the legends and implicitly in the third, the shift in clothing and cultural spheres is also accompanied by a shift in gender, which neatly translates the shifts of genre thematized in the foreword. Finally, in all of the first five legends, the very process I am here describing, namely the translation of the figures of its artful dimension into the living, "real" sphere of the story, is also self-consciously represented in the form of statues that in various ways can be seen to come to life in the tales—and in so doing to thematize the issue of the representation versus the real/original that is also so central to Keller's musings in the foreword.[11] All of these features—new clothes and new figures, shifting spheres and the play of desire, shifting genders and the play of art and reality—all are prominent, even determinative aspects of the *Seven Legends*, and most notably so in the first story, "Eugenia," which opens with the biblical injunction, "A woman shall not wear that which pertaineth unto a man, nor shall a man put on a woman's garment," and forcefully brings the focus to bear on issues of cross-dressing and -gendering and their implications for a realist aesthetic.

Keller's concern with transvestism and its gender play is not of course limited to *Seven Legends*. It also shows up in several tales inculcated into *Green Henry* as well as in a novella inculcated into *The Epigram* (*Das Sinngedicht*, 1881), "Regine." And he is far from alone among nineteenth-century authors in his interest in the practice; even among the other poetic realists, we have the examples of Meyer's *Gustav Adolf's Page* and Stifter's *Brigitta*. But in *Seven Legends*, because Keller somewhat uniquely translates the terms, conditions, and problems of his "realistic" retelling into the issues of cross-dressing, gender-play, and so on, we can in our turn mobilize these same terms in order to explore Keller's understanding of his project of poetic realism. In doing this, we can avail ourselves of some of the tremendous amount of theoretical work devoted in recent years to the issues of gender-play and transvestism, in particular that of Judith Butler, whose interests in these topics have led her to explore several questions that also prove central to our concerns: the question of the representation versus the reality, or if you will, the clothing versus the body; the question of how the re-presentation—"drag"—can shift or displace the inherited discourse and reality; and the most vexed question of the role of repetition in both the establishment of "reality" and its displacement or subversion. Considering briefly her representation of each of these questions will, I hope, allow us to suggest not only the role that gender and cross-dressing might play in any realist program but also more specifically the way Keller might be playing out his realist program—and even more specifically, his retelling realist program—in the role he has gender and transvestism play in these tales, and especially in "Eugenia."

Butler represents gender as a sedimented, disparate congeries of actions, gestures, postures, and desires that produce the effect of an internal core or substance "through the play of signifying absences that suggest, but never reveal, the organizing principle of identity as a cause."[12] These bodily representations or significations, she argues, are "performative" in the sense that "the essence or identity that they otherwise purport to express are *fabrications* manufactured and sustained through corporeal signs and other discursive means."[13] This suggests that the gendered body has no ontological status apart from the various representations that constitute its reality and that, if this reality is fabricated as an interior essence, then its interiority is an effect and not a cause of its bodily representations—its gestures, postures, desires, and so on.

Butler is clear about the interests she sees being served by this engendered illusion of an interior determinative core, and they are those of cultural and ideological regulation. As she puts it:

If the "cause" of desire, gesture, and act can be localized within the "self" of the actor, then the political regulations and disciplinary practices which produce that ostensibly coherent gender are effectively displaced from view. The displacement of a political and discursive origin of gender onto a psychological "core" precludes an analysis of the political constitution of the gendered subject and its fabricated notions about the ineffable interiority of its sex or of its true identity.[14]

The basic relevance, even homology, of this model with our general model of poetic realism is, I believe, quite evident. As we've seen, realism can also be described as a set of culturally established conventions that produce the effect of an anterior, original "reality," a disparate collection of signifying practices that fabricate the world of which they are fictively the copy or expression. As with gender, the interests served by this feinting maneuver can be understood as those of ideological regulation: by maintaining the fiction that it is not *just* a fiction, but instead a faithful representation of some originating reality, realism effectively disguises and removes from view its own normative practices, presenting as real and natural what is in fact conventional and cultural.

The basic relevance of Butler's model to that specifically invoked by Keller for *Seven Legends* is also evident, albeit with a significant complication. Here too we confront a practice that produces its anterior reality out of the representation that supposedly only reproduces it—although, because it does so self-consciously, we confront both the assertion of this preceding essence and a display of the allegedly self-disguising mechanism for manufacturing it. This is a minor complication; the more significant one is that, as mentioned, Keller associates not his realist but Kosegarten's "churchly" representation as the site for the set of conventions engaged in promulgating through its fictions ideological norms and disciplinary practices. Keller's representation is, quite to the contrary, intended to displace and interrupt the established conventions and regulations, precisely by divesting them of their claim to reality, by prying their representation apart from "reality." This is a problem to which we will have to return.

We can, however, already address one part of it by turning to Butler's discussion of the role of cross-dressing or "drag" in the politics of gender. For like Keller's understanding of his re-presentation as in the service of a dislocation of "reality" and its sedimented conventions and norms, Butler depicts the practice of transvestism as engaged in exposing "one of the key fabricating mechanisms through which the social construction of gender takes place."[15] Drag does this through its subversive complication of the relations between imitation and original; in place of the law of coherence or equivalence between "natural" internal core (i.e., sex) and gestural representation (gender), we see these two "denaturalized by means of a performance which avows their distinctness and dramatizes the cultural mechanism of their fabricated unity."[16] As a result, the gender parody that cross-dressing performs aims to reveal itself as an imitation without an origin, or more precisely, it aims to reveal the original "natural" identity after which gender fashions itself as itself an imitation without an origin, an effected representation without (being) a causal reality. It works to denaturalize or derealize the normative ideals and practices of gender, to drive a wedge between the "phantasmatic" and the real, even as it also works to open up those same conventions to resignification and recontextualization, to expressing or performing a different reality, or more cautiously, a different ideology from that of the previously dominant culture.

Again, I believe the correspondences between the intended function of transvestism and that of realist "defamiliarization" described by Jakobson are clear. For Jakobson, this other modality of realism seeks to automatize the inherited literary conventions and so disrupt the established identity between them and reality, in order to redeploy them in allegedly more authentic ways;

the claim to realism rests both on the exposure of the inessentiality of the previously naturalized conventions and on the redirection of the inherited material toward a different, more authentic ideal. And again, the specific appropriateness of this model to Keller's realist practice in *Seven Legends* seems clear—but again, with a complication. Like that of Butler's transvestite, the purpose of his reproduction of the inherited (Christian) cultural material is subversively to displace it by detaching its representation from reality, that is, by problematizing the identity of its representation with an original reality, while simultaneously opening it up to recontextualization. But the complication arises when, looking at the legends themselves, we recognize how transvestism is depicted just as often as a displacement of identity *into* the allegedly normative and regulative (Christian) culture as it is a displacement out of it. That is, transvestism itself—and with it, of course, the project of retelling—does not seem to be a guaranteed marker of realist subversion in Keller's work, and can be equally indexical of further ideological, normative regulation.[17]

There are, I think, at least two factors to Butler's account of natural, normative gender and parodic, disruptive transvestism that help to explain this ambiguity, and that simultaneously reveal a central homologous problem for realist fiction, especially realist retellings. The first and most important of these concerns the role of repetition. According to Butler, the performance that constitutes gender is necessarily a repeated performance: "[T]his repetition is at once a re-enactment and re-experiencing of a set of meanings already socially established; and it is the mundane and ritualized form of their legitimation."[18] It is precisely through a "*stylized repetition of acts*" (Butler's emphasis) that the illusion of gender—and with it, the illusion of the identity between gender acts and reality—as an abiding, natural ground is produced. In other words, representation, through repetition, is the very form of cultural regulation.

This repetition compulsion is, for Butler, not only the basis for the legitimating performance of gender. It is also the basis for its disruption. As she says, it is only *within* the practices of repetitive signifying that a subversion of identity or reality becomes possible: "[T]he task is not whether to repeat, but how to repeat or, indeed, to repeat and . . . to *displace* the very gender norms that enable the repetition itself." Butler's argument is that practices of parody, including those of transvestism, "can serve to re-engage and reconsolidate the very distinction between a privileged and naturalized gender configuration and one that appears as derived, phantasmatic, and mimetic—a failed copy, as it were."[19] This is an important point, and the emphasis on the realization of the failure of the representation to reproduce the real accords well with our own understanding of realism as at least in part based on recognizing or realizing the failure of its mimetic program. But the fact that the same logic of repetition of the same set of "stylized acts" underlies both the legitimating and the subverting practices and performances of gender seems also to indicate the possible impossibility of successfully distinguishing the two, or rather, the necessary hesitancy of any representation between the reinforcement of and resistance to the normative reality it engages.[20]

The second complicating factor to Butler's account of natural, normative gender and parodic, disruptive transvestism that accounts for their unexpected similarity is the role of what we might call, for lack of a better word, ideology.[21] As Butler describes cross-dressing—and as many describe realist disenchantment or defamiliarization—it functions to denaturalize and/or displace normative conventions and ideological codes: as such, it derives its own quantity of reality both from its subversive exposure of ideological fictional constructs and from its own alleged freedom from ideological constraints or programs. But while the former claim might hold, Jakobson and Barthes have alerted us that the latter certainly will not. Rather, the practice of disruption represents its own set of normative gestures in the interests of its own mimetic program. Indeed, to paraphrase Butler, we can say that the subversive repetition represents its own regulated process that both conceals itself and reinforces its rules precisely through the production of *liberating* effects. Gender parody and/or realist disenchantment, by maintaining the fiction that they are *not* representative of some ideology, effectively disguise and remove from view their own normative practices, and in this they are structurally identical with (and repetitive of) the inherited cultural reality they would discard. Moreover, since the basis for the subversion remains the same as that for legitimating inscription—namely, repetition of the same stylized conventions—the question arises as to the actual difference between the two ideological positions: whether they do not necessarily remain as consonant as they are dissonant—indeed maintain consonance through the illusion of dissonance.

III

These preliminary considerations provide us with a specific set of questions with which to approach our analysis of the first and most programmatic of the *Seven Legends*, "Eugenia." Most generally, we will want to ask: what can Keller's representation of gender-identity, cross-dressing, the play of desire, and the play of art and reality reveal to us about his realist program of retelling literary tales? Again, what enables this question is not only the role these terms and relations might play in any realist program but also the way Keller specifically transposes the terms and conditions of his narrative enterprise into these terms in his tales. Second and more particularly: what can Keller's exploration of these concerns reveal to us about the problem of a realist representation without an original, or, more precisely, about the problem of a representation that both produces an anterior original out of itself where "in fact" none exists *and* calls attention to the phantasmatic or fictional quality of this ground even as it produces it? Finally, we will also want to ask: what can Keller's tale tell us about the relation between the competing claims to realism, as normative and as subversive, as stabilizing and as disruptive, as a repetition that reinforces the same and as one that enables difference?

The opening paragraphs of the story explicitly present the tale of the cross-dressing Eugenia as representative of a certain timeless, or rather, constantly repeated reality or truth. Its biblical motto is followed by a declaration in the gnomic (or iterative) present: "When women renounce the ambition of beauty, charm, and femininity . . . the matter often ends with their putting on men's clothing." This is followed in turn by a more specific, but still general point, that "more than one female saint in the pious legend-world of early Christianity was driven by the desire to play the man." And the tale of Eugenia herself is said to exemplify not only this (doubly) common desire but also "the not uncommon consequence" of an ensuing embarrassment and subsequent, salvaging reliance on "the resources of her natural sex" (12). Clearly Keller—or more cautiously, his narrator[22]—repeatedly and almost excessively insists upon the iterative nature of his narrative material; and he clearly does so because the exemplary and realistic status of his tale rests upon its redundant nature. As with the very project of retelling tales, repetition seems the mark or symptom for the reality or truth of the story he represents.[23]

For all the insistence on the repetitive nature of Eugenia's story, however, and for all the underlying reality acquired by her story because of its redundancy, it still remains fundamentally unclear what reality it is that the tale allegedly repeats and exemplifies. As might be expected, the indeterminacy asserts itself most forcefully in respect to the central matter of the story, the status of feminine gender and its sartorial transgression. On the one hand, the narrator describes women who wrongfully neglect their proper femininity, or *Weiblichkeit,* before falling back, almost by necessity, on their natural sex (*ihr natürliches Geschlecht*). On the other hand, he sees women who work only, and actively, to free themselves "from the inherited custom [*Herkommen*] of home and society." This basic hesitation about whether gender is natural or conventional, "real" or constructed, and hence whether its semiotic subversion is perverse and doomed to failure or somehow authenticating and impossible to repress—this hesitation is evident in, even irremoveable from, numerous other details of the introductory paragraphs as well.

Still, for all the ambivalence and its ineliminability, the decisive impulse here seems to be toward the former position, the assertion of the "reality" of gender and hence, too, toward the dominance of a normative realist program rather than a disruptive one. This is most patent in the sense of a false or premature conclusion built into the story's introduction. We are first told that when women neglect their femininity, the matter often "ends" in their taking on male clothing. But then Eugenia is presented as an example of the not uncommon "end-result" (*Endresultat*) of a recursion to the succors of her natural sex. It is, that is, not the repeated challenge of transvestism but rather its repeated and only apparently exceptional failure that Eugenia's story is said to illustrate or represent. Its repetition is in the service of reinforcing as "real" the regulatory norms and conventions of gender, not in that of disrupting them; indeed, one can even see how the initial illusion of disruption partially conceals, and so abets, the reality of final regulation, precisely through its (double) gesture of liberation.

The apparent dominance of a normative poetics of gender, and of the repetition employed in its service, should not of course surprise us. After all, Keller criticism rarely tires at underscoring the author's culpably conservative attitude toward women, and many of the studies in this book can be taken to confirm the essential threat posed by women to almost every poetic realist program, not only Keller's. But what should surprise us is the contradiction with the supposedly more subversive impulse informing the foreword, which presents its program in much these same terms and even, as I said, intends to transpose it into these terms in the story proper. There, Keller's repetition was purported to release desire and identity from the ideological and generic trappings that had excluded or repressed them. Here the repetition seems poised to reinforce just such repressive trappings.

In retrospect—that is, from the perspective of the introduction, not the foreword—we can no doubt bring the two programs more closely into agreement by recognizing how Keller's structural arrangement of an original or earlier genre and desire, a following distorting outfitting in different, Christian trappings, and his own restorative reproduction of that more original genre and desire corresponds with the arrangement here of an original femininity, its sartorial Christian travesty, and a concluding return to the "natural sex"; so that Keller's apparently dislocating repetition was also (always) in the service of reasserting a proper genre and gender identity for "Eugenia." But in either case—whether we perceive the two programs as unexpectedly dissonant or consonant in their repetition and realism—the indeterminacy of the roles of normative reinforcement and subversive displacement again comes to the fore. And this in turn prepares a more critical issue, the issue of whether the story itself can be said to fit or perform either of the programs it is asked to repeat and uphold; that is, whether Keller's realism can possibly maintain itself as a program or poetics of either regulation or subversion, indeed of any uniform or singular program at all.

Let me attempt to stage my discussion of the story proper in terms of the triadic arrangement just mentioned: the depiction of the early profane Eugenia, followed by her displacement into the cross-dressed Christian Eugenius, and concluding with the return of Eugenia to both the profane world and her proper or "real" feminine identity. Since it is in the simple frame of this common plot, with its highly signaled moments of displacement and its final recursive moment of mimetic equivalence, that the twinned programs of the tale and its telling most evidently converge, it is also here that we can most clearly follow the normative or subversive intents to the story's play of desire, gender, reality, and representation.

There are two points to stress about the Eugenia we encounter at the very outset of the tale, both fairly obvious but decisive for the subsequent story. First, despite the association made by Keller in the foreword of the earlier profane world with the real or true—with the unperverted in respect to genre and *Lust*—and despite the strictly coordinated association made by the narrator of an original femininity with the real or natural in respect to gender (and, implicitly, desire), the profane Eugenia at the beginning of the tale neither conforms to the expected conventions of gender nor displays any real erotic desire. Instead of cultivating the virtues of beauty, charm, and femininity, she devotes herself to the pursuits of knowledge "like a [male] student" (*wie ein Student,* 12) and "as a man of learning" (*als ein Gelehrter,* 15). And as a consequence of this, Eugenia abstains from those practices that should evince a governing, natural femininity and erotic desire, both of which would properly draw and bind her to her male suitor, Aquilinus. Rather, when Aquilinus first declares himself and his love to her, Eugenia simply doesn't signify: "Eugenia smiled imperceptibly and never even blushed, so thoroughly had her learning and spiritual development [*Geistesbildung*] bound all the finer impulses of ordinary life in her" (14).

In the original profane stage, then, the anticipated or posited "real" and natural, in terms of both gender and desire, are quite simply not there, are absent; or more cautiously put, they are represented as already subverted, repressed, or excluded. That is, the narrator does indicate that behind the already abstracted Eugenia there lurks a "real" woman, whose femininity inevitably betrays itself in her desires (e.g., "But Eugenia too had secretly cast her eye upon him," 13). These desires are, as it were, the mark of the real, and not least insofar as, by directing her toward a man, they signal her own denied identity as "in fact" a woman. Moreover, and perhaps contradictorily, the narrator also indicates that Eugenia is unable to keep desire from informing her more spiritual, immaterial pursuits (e.g., "[S]he had already begun to stroll pleasurably [*lustwandeln*] in the mysterious labyrinths of neoplatonic doctrines," (13); like the hot and fervent prayers of the "naughty-holy" Vitalis at the bedside of prostitutes, the supposedly absent or repressed eroticism presents itself in the very discourse of its repression.[24] But in any case, the point remains: the original or early profane Eugenia is decidedly not the gender norm, and is instead already the supposedly subsequent subversion. The origin is displaced from itself, and the real deferred.

Second, we need to note not only that the original or early profane Eugenia does not conform to gender norms, but also how this comes about; or, more precisely, we need to note the structural arrangement or mechanism by which her original, supposedly unnatural gender identity is constituted. Eugenia is constantly accompanied throughout her studies by a bodyguard—or literally, a body-watch (*Leibwache*)—of two lovely young boys her own age, both of whom curiously have the same name, Hyazinth.[25] The two are never distinguished from one another, and remain throughout mimetic equivalents, or repetitions, of each other; and it is in the chiastic reflection of these two ever-accompanying mirror images that Eugenia's identity is narcissistically or imaginarily formed. The dependence of her identity on their mirroring representation is underscored not only by the inseparability, nor only by the exactly identical opinions and activities of all three figures. It is also underscored by the somewhat peculiar feature that the two Hyazinths always carry about with them inscribed copies of all the poetry by the bookworms of Alexandria devoted to and depicting Eugenia's muselike appearance (*musenhafte Erscheinung*, 13). Even as she constitutes her self through an identification of her reality with these fictional representations, wherein the usual relation between model and copy, reality and representation, becomes somewhat reversed or even annihilated (in Butler's terms, she becomes the effect, the poems the cause)—so too does she constitute herself through an identification of her person with those of her mirroring body-watch. And the result of this imaginary constitution of the self through the reflection of the other is an abrogation of the difference that normally marks gender: the common ground between them is such that "a stranger would have been unsure whether he saw three beautiful tender boys or three fresh blooming girls before him" (13f.). This gender indeterminacy is, moreover, sartorially reinforced through the basically unisex outfit of all three.

If the identity manufactured for Eugenia through this mirroring arrangement resulted only in gender neutrality or indeterminacy, the disavowal of her femininity might seem stark enough. But it results in more than just neutrality. The mirroring relation established between Eugenia and the two Hyazinths maintains not only equivalence but an equally evident difference; and with this difference comes power, and with power gender reenters the equation. We are told that the two Hyazinths always go "on her left side and her right . . . or gracefully along behind her, while their mistress, walking backwards, disputed with them"; similarly, "they were never of a different opinion from Eugenia, and they always remained a little behind her in their learning" (13). The slight dislocation in the mirroring arrangement signaled here conveys the power relations that inform the apparent equivalents; and it is this difference, this power that allows the relation both to secure a "masculine" identity for Eugenia and to render the two Hyazinths not only gender neutral, but more plainly emasculated, with her masculinity, or in other words, her power and superiority, necessarily coming at their expense.[26] And it is for this reason that Aquilinus perceives a threat to the presence of the two Hyazinths and also refuses Eugenia's request that he participate in her intellectual or spiritual life (*Geistesleben*). He sees Eugenia's reflective existence with these mirroring males to be the source of her power, and he quite rightly recognizes the gender and power reversals to which he would immediately become subject were he to assume the proffered position.[27]

This structural mirroring arrangement that mimetically and phantasmatically and chiastically manufactures Eugenia's identity is, then, important to us for two reasons. First, because it seemingly opposes the model of gender as natural (*natürliches Geschlecht*) that is broached in the opening paragraphs. Instead, it presents a model of gender—and with gender, identity, and with identity, reality—as not biological but positional, that is, as structurally determined or imposed: as a matter not of nature but of imaginary power and authority. Second, and more unexpectedly, because it so obviously agrees with, even reproduces, the model of narration as repetition broached by Keller for his own tale, his own "Eugenia." That is, Keller's narrative retelling can be seen to position itself in an identical relation to its slightly anterior, Kosegarten model as Eugenia does to her cozy, garden-flower companions, with the same self-constitution through mimetic reflection and the same superiority (in knowledge, power, and reality) based fragilely on identity and difference. The parallel can perhaps be even more highlighted by recalling the already established equivalence between the Hyazinths and literary texts in the mimetic fabrication of Eugenia's identity.

Admittedly, this unexpected repetition might appear as an instance of so-called false friends, of a structural sameness that belies a substantive difference. After all, the arrangement in the story has resulted in an aporia, in a seeming perversion of gender identity and exclusion or suppression of desire, and not, as proposed in the foreword for the telling, in a solution, a setting aright of genre identity and release of desire. Nonetheless, we need to note both the procedural similarity and the intentional difference, and to include both in the early crisis or embarrassment (*Stein des Anstosses,* 15) effected by this identity-, gender-, and reality-producing mimetic structure.

IV

It is the aporia arrived at in the early profane stage that motivates the event of the following Christian stage, as Eugenia abandons her unhappy standoff with Aquilinus and, with the two Hyazinths in tow, converts to Christianity by joining a monastery, having first adopted male dress and the name Eugenius in order to effect the transformation. This is of course the story's self-declared complication. But given the unforeseen complications entailed by the first stage, we should not be too surprised to find that this middle, transvestite stage also produces some undeclared complications, not the least of which is the apparent absence of complication. That is, Eugenia's Christian transvestism seems to represent both what Marjorie Garber would call a "category crisis" and just as much a noncrisis—and this represents a crisis all its own.[28]

The noncrisis to Eugenia's transvestism arises for a very simple reason: it merely repeats, or represents, Eugenia's earlier profane reality. As a monk, Eugenia is able to maintain both the (ambiguously) male identity she has constructed for herself and the neutral or repressed relation to erotic desire she has already adopted; and so the difference between her original heathen existence and her converted Christian one proves no difference at all. The continuity is further underscored by the ease with which Eugenia's previous training in profane studies is transferred to the new cultural sphere, actually securing for her

her new identity: when the monastery's abbot quizzes the three new recruits, "because she was well instructed, Eugenia knew how to answer his probing questions so suitably that he . . . permitted all three to assume the monastic habit" (17). The much anticipated crisis between the spheres or realities fails to materialize, and the expected moment of normative displacement fails to come about—in large part because the moment of normative enforcement was never realized in the first place. What we find instead is a sense of the governing equivalence between the signifying practices—the genres, so to speak—of the profane and Christian cultures, a ruling repetition between the "original" Eugenia and the redressed Eugenius. And as I suggested, this seeming noncrisis represents a very real crisis, both for the model of transvestism described by Butler and for the model of realism proposed by Keller. Both insist on the shift signaled by the change in gender-habit as producing a real difference, the former in the disruptive release from cultural conventions, the latter in a repression by such imposed conventions. But both would seem equally disappointed by the dominating sense of sameness.

The crisis-causing disappointment to Eugenia's cross-dressed Christianity is, I believe, even more extensive than this. Not only does it not seem a subversive displacement from pre-established gender norms, nor a shift into a cultural or ideological repression of erotic desire. Rather, it actually appears to function as a move toward reinforcing "proper" gender identity and desire. That the shift here is *toward* femininity and its prescribed, "real" erotic inclination is clearly indicated in the words of the psalm that initially inspires Eugenia's conversion: "As a doe yearns for the water's spring, so my soul yearns for you, O God! My soul thirsts for the living God!" (16). This is, as it were, a call for Eugenia to heed the reality of desire, the thirst and yearning of her real inner self; that is, to (re-)turn to some (mythical poetic) origin, to acknowledge and adopt a feminine role ("like a doe"), and so too implicitly to submit to male authority. The irony is exquisite, the paradox decisive: for Eugenia to adopt the ascetic Christian faith is for her to begin to acknowledge the "more profane" erotic desire previously repressed; to adopt male clothing is for her to begin to acknowledge a "real" femininity she had earlier denied.[29] As with Eugenia's pleasurable stroll (*lustwandeln*) in the gardens of neoplatonic philosophy, the erotic presents itself precisely in the supposed mechanism of its repression, in this case the Christian religion, or more accurately, the churchly art of fabulation.

At the same time, the supposed mechanism for phantasmatic liberation from gender conventions, namely transvestism, instead presents itself as an instrument for their reinforcement. Exactly how this occurs can be explained in terms of its relation of repetition, of mimetic representation or equivalence with the earlier stage just described. For by donning masculine clothing, Eugenia enters into a new relation to her masculine inclinations (*männliche Liebhabereien*), a more clearly representative or performative relation. And in this new relation, Eugenia's new outfit does not so much allow her to express some supposedly masculine part as essential to her identity as it allows her to represent or perform that part as inessential, as assumed, or better, as "put on," and so too capable of being "taken off." The point is perhaps best illustrated in terms of Eugenia's learning, that noted mastery of her culture's discursive practices that has proven the source of both her opposing power and her "masculinity." As I said, this easily transferred knowledge-power is crucial to maintaining the continuity or repetition between the two (generically opposed) cultural spheres and the two (genderly opposed) Eugenias; it allows Eugenia to answer all the interrogating abbot's questions, pass his identity or reality test, and so secure the right both to enter the monastery and to assume male clothing. At the same time, however, in their repetition, Eugenia's discursive powers also here become fundamentally false, performed, unreal; and this in turn occasions a new relation between these powers and Eugenia, one that emphasizes the split or incongruence between the represented and the real. This is, as it were, part of the logic to the seeming coincidence that the male clothing Eugenia here assumes is simultaneously described as a monastic or "spiritual" habit (*der geistliche Habit*). The association not only confirms the already implicit identity in the story of spirituality (*Geistlichkeit*) and masculinity. It also deconfirms the essential relation of both with the "real" Eugenia. For once *Geist*, like masculinity, becomes a mere matter of external trappings, it ceases to represent an inner reality; and this neatly prepares for the possibility of its being subsequently discarded.

Far from acting as the expected perversion away from the supposed reality of gender conventions, then, Eugenia's transvestism seems to be an operation for facilitating their eventual (re-)inforcement, for an admittedly still deferred turn toward the admittedly still not governing conventions of femininity, through a rendering unreal or phantasmatic of all her "male" identity—even as her Christianity seems not the anticipated ideological repression but rather a promised release of profane, "real" desire, which itself seems more and more the decisive apparatus for ideological repression and control. And again, both points are crucial not only to our appreciation of Eugenia's narrative but also to that of Keller's narration, insofar as his generically cross-dressed "Eugenia" is perhaps also operating not to subvert the governing conventions but to reinforce them, his desire for a re-production (*Lust der Reproduktion*) working not to dislodge some sedimented, repressive norms but to install them.

Still, for all its perceptible contribution to her normative regulation, Eugenia's transvestism does not cease to be perverse, socially disruptive, and ideologically subversive; by the same token, the self-identity and desire it produces do not cease to threaten the established conventions or discourses defining "reality," even if they also repeat and secure them. The same event, the same act of representation—and again, whether we refer to Eugenia or "Eugenia"—presents itself with an almost alarming indifference in terms of both regulation and resistance, of both the competing claims of realist poetics.

V

The middle, mediating phase between the early and late profane Eugenia is actually bifurcated into two parallel and simultaneous events, each of equal and related importance for negotiating Eugenia's intended transition toward a more normative gender identity and desire. For while the real Eugenia disappears into the Christian sphere and becomes transformed into the cross-dressed monk Eugenius, heathen priests persuade her father that she has been abstracted into the heavens and transformed into a celestial goddess; he in turn persuades Aquilinus to have her represented in a statue and installed in the forecourt of Minerva's temple. The power play between the two spheres for the significance or "telling" of Eugenia is firmly in force here; but perhaps more important than the differences between their competing versions of Eugenia are their similarities. That is, there is a crucial functional equivalence between the transvestite monk arranged by Eugenia herself and the profane marble statue arranged by her father and Aquilinus, an equivalence not least secured by their similar transposition of Eugenia's earlier real identity into the realm of representation—which is to say, by their similar logic of repetition. Even as the early heathen Eugenia becomes repeated in her sartorial artifice among the Christians, so too in her marmoreal artifice among the profane.

Along with the functional identity between Eugenia's transvestite and Aquilinus' statue comes another of equal consequence: that between the aesthetic program behind Aquilinus' statue and the one behind Keller's own narrative. In his authoritative and overtly political supervision of the statue's fabulation, Aquilinus is explicitly presented as motivated by a realist impulse. Unlike the father, he is wary of the abstracted, etherealized version of Eugenia proposed by the priests; and unlike many other Alexandrine youths, he is not able or willing to fall in love with their representation of Eugenia as a heavenly body. This refusal to participate in the power structures that maintain Eugenia's spiritual life (*Geistesleben*) and his insistence on desiring only what he calls "a woman of flesh and blood"—that is, a "real woman"—are, we know, characteristic of Aquilinus, characteristic in fact of his allegiance to an identifiably normative program for gender and desire. Here, that allegiance expresses itself in Aquilinus' asserted condition that the commissioned statue be made to resemble the departed Eugenia (*der Entrückten ähnlich gemacht würde*). That is, the statue is to embody a realist program: it becomes perhaps the clearest instance of Keller's translation of the terms and conditions of his narration into the subject matter of his tale.

Given the central representative importance of the statue for the realist program at stake in the novella, we need to look closely at the structural arrangements and signifying practices that it embodies, that is, at the mechanisms and procedures through which it asserts its realism. Most pressingly, we need to see how, although both Aquilinus and the narrator insist upon the "speaking resemblance" to Eugenia, the statue still remains a resemblance without an original. It is fashioned in the absence of the real Eugenia—whose absence is in fact the prerequisite for its construction—and is based instead on "a whole collection of busts and portraits of her"; it is a re-presentation of other, earlier representations. This is, we know, the same operating condition underlying Keller's own realist project of representation here. But we also know it to be the same structural arrangement underlying the earlier construction of Eugenia's identity through the two Hyazinths, or rather, through the copied lyrics devoted to Eugenia they constantly carried about with them. Even as Eugenia manufactured her self-identity through an identification of her reality with those poetic representations, so too does Aquilinus manufacture his statue through an identification of its reality with these visual representations.

In the earlier instance, this mimetic arrangement resulted in the aporia of an unnatural, artificial existence (*künstliches Wesen*) that thwarted the desired expression of those gender and erotic norms associated with Eugenia's real self. Here however, when the same mechanism is mobilized in the service of a realist program, it is also clearly put in the service of regulating and imposing those same gender (and erotic) ideals. That the mimetic realist program embodied in the statue represents an ideology is not really at issue: the narrator explicitly relates, "In spite of its speaking resemblance, it was an ideal work [*ein Idealwerk*] in features, deportment, and clothing." What is at issue is how the same mirroring strategy first employed to subvert the ideal can now be redeployed to enforce it; in other words, how what seemed to yield a repression of reality can now seem to secure it.

Two different factors contribute to the shift in the signifying effects of the same mimetic procedure. First and most perceptibly, the two male Hyazinths, whose mirroring presence abrogated Eugenia's distinctive femininity, have been unobtrusively removed from the equation. The statue Eugenia is thus more cleanly constructed in the chiastic reflection of images of Eugenia alone, yielding or reinforcing a more acceptable female identity by subjecting the statue to the usual consequences of a woman identified with the fictional images of a male imagination. Second, Eugenia herself has been replaced by Aquilinus as the controlling authority over the phantasmatic mechanism forming her—that is, the statue's—identity. In a somewhat paradoxical manner, the mimetic arrangement has produced something both more female and real precisely because it has become at once more male—in terms of both the model images and their deployment—and more fictional. Hence the irony that, as with Eugenia's own gambit of taking on male clothes, the move into artificial representation facilitates the loosening of her previous "artificial existence." In any case, what makes the statue "real"—far more so than Eugenia—seems to be just this perceived shift in the mimetic power arrangements that reestablishes male control.[30]

The statue, then, is presented as a fiction based on other, earlier fictions; as an embodied ideology; and as part of that, as an instrument of patriarchal powers. All three of these points are important for our understanding of its role in representing Aquilinus'—and by extension Keller's own—realist program. But even more important is our recognition of the real object of the statue's chiastic mimesis, namely Eugenia herself, *and* the tactic deployed for realizing this design, namely the production of an anterior, earlier reality or gender identity where in fact none ever existed. That the (realist) mimesis should be achieved at the site of Eugenia plainly involves a reversal of the more traditional understanding of the relation between model and copy in the realist aesthetic. But in this case (and not only in this case), the traditional understanding merely serves to conceal the actual realist operation; clearly, it is far less important that the statue be "like" Eugenia than that she be "like" it. She is to be a representation of its original; in Butler's terms, she is to be the statue's effect, not its cause. The implicit relation of chiastic mimetic equivalence is, I might add, quite similar to that described in the last chapter for the relation in *The Mountain Forest* between Nature and the two women: here, significantly enough, it is not so much the "natural" features of the statue as it is the deportment (*Haltung*) and clothing (*Gewänder*) that embody the ideal and the law of femininity that Eugenia must assume in order to herself become real, that is, to become the embodiment of the "speaking resemblance." The nearer parallel, with Keller's own project of realistic redress, can also be noted: it is of course the (new) generic trappings of his artwork that are similarly to restore the realism to the original narrative of "Eugenia."

The second point is equally important. As mentioned, the "ideal work" and "speaking likeness" of the statue that Eugenia is herself to resemble is based on a collection of other, earlier artifacts, that is, on a supposedly earlier Eugenia, one familiar from before she disappears into the monastery and her transvestite Christian costume—or alternatively, into the heavens and her divine celestial body. In a decisive association, in coming to be like her statue Eugenia is also to become "like" her earlier self. Here too the parallel with Keller's own program for retelling the legend can be noted; his realistic rendition of "Eugenia" is also intended to revive its former, more profane identity. But in the case of Eugenia herself, this earlier self clearly never existed, in particular this earlier ideal of womanhood. Rather, the distance between Eugenia's earlier self and the statue is enormous, even unbridgeable; and, as soon becomes evident, the statue is meant to dislodge Eugenia as much from her earlier philosophical self as from her present Christian and/or divine self. As with Keller's own realist program, the identification of the statue's rendition of Eugenia with some earlier, more original version is nonetheless absolutely essential to the self-legitimating claim that the dislodgement it encourages is into something more natural, real, and liberated—while in fact it remains something manifestly ideological, constructed, and restrictive.[31]

V I

That Aquilinus' statue (and by extension, his realist program) *is* aimed at Eugenia, and as such represents an annihilatory threat to her reality—this is vehemently borne out in the novella's central scene, the encounter between Eugenia qua Eugenius and the statue qua Eugenia. Eugenia seems instinctively to realize the threat posed for her by the statue, much as Aquilinus seemed instinctively aware of that posed for him by Eugenia's *Geistesleben*. Soon after learning of its existence, she takes a strong and thick (*stark*) hammer and leaves the monastery to smash the image (18 f.) And her fears prove justified, for in the encounter the statue strips Eugenia of all the power implied in that thick hammer and her male Christian dress, and even more important, it robs her of her sense of self as well. The details are worth quoting:

Eugenia saw her image, white as new-fallen snow, standing there in wonderful charm and beauty, the delicately folded garments drawn virtuously about the shoulders, and looking straight forward with an inspired gaze and gently smiling mouth.

Full of curiosity the Christian walked towards it, the raised hammer in her hand; but a sweet shudder passed through her heart when she saw the image in all its distinctness; the hammer sank down and she soundlessly feasted her eyes on the vision of her own former existence. A bitter sadness enveloped her, a feeling as if . . . she was now an unhappy shadow wandering through a wasteland; for while the image had been elevated to an ideal, for that very reason it represented Eugenia's original inner being, which had only been veiled by her pedantry. (19)

The moment's bitter and even violent power struggles are played out not so much behind as through its sweetness, delight, and feeling: the (feminized) emotion to the scene is very much part of the desired effect of the program and chiastic mimetic procedure being brought to bear. Eugenia's phallic hammer droops and falls, and the morally clothed and constrained feminine ideal takes over the cross-dressed monk; Eugenia herself becomes the shadow, the mere image, the unreal, and the statue becomes the real, Eugenia's "original being" (*das ursprüngliche Wesen Eugenias*), which in a most insidious way evacuates and then replaces her, as she becomes the copy that repeats, or fails to repeat, its "original" ideal. Significantly enough, it is Eugenia's pedantry (*Schulfuchserei*) that is said to have disguised the original inner being or, as it is also called, the earlier being represented by the statue. This pedantry was itself of course a quality of the earlier Eugenia: the mimetic realist ploy here not only replaces the real present Eugenia (reduced to a mere shadow) with the present ideal of the statue, it also replaces the actual earlier Eugenia (reduced to a mere covering) with a new anterior reality. Indeed, it largely accomplishes the former through the detour of the latter.[32] Again, the parallel between Aquilinus' realist statue and Keller's realist narrative vis-à-vis both the Christian *and* the earlier manifestations of "Eugenia" is apparent, and intrinsic.

Three points in particular need to be further stressed about this encounter. First, we need to note how the two different representational ploys of the middle phase—the supposedly subversive transvestism of Eugenia and the norm-reinforcing statue of Aquilinus—actually converge here to accomplish the desired displacement and anticipated restoration. As mentioned, it is Eugenia's cross-dressed Christian existence that transforms her pedantic and masculine *Geistesleben* into something put on, false, and unreal, that derealizes the essential identity between Eugenia and her earlier subversive self and so prepares the disjuncture (*Zwiespalt*) between the real and represented Eugenia that the statue now—with its morally upright, or *sittig,* vestments—takes advantage of by posing as that essential original identity and relegating Eugenia in her pedantry and unfeminine guise to the status of "shadow" and disguise. The mechanisms of the supposed subversion and the opposed ideal collude to achieve the desired realist effect; in fact, the moment of successful regulation or conventionalization depends upon the prior moment of supposedly transgressive disruption.[33]

Second, we need to note how the political regulation and disciplinary practice enacted in this scene—and again the explicitly political character of the statue and of Aquilinus' role in its production should be emphasized—pose as something of a psychological process and encounter, that is, as a narcissistic moment of self-confrontation. Indeed, this is the characterization of the scene, and especially of the kiss Eugenia subsequently plants on the statue's lips, most often embraced by critics, even feminist ones.[34] This is, however, and as even the narrator is forced to admit, precisely what the encounter is not.[35] Rather, as Judith Butler would insist, the *appearance* of a narcissistic moment of self-encounter becomes the very manner by which the ideological program of the statue—Eugenia's better self (*ihr besseres Selbst*)—conceals and legitimates its regulative procedure. By displacing the political origin of its gender ideal onto some interior psychological (and so ostensibly nonpolitical) core of Eugenia through the fiction of a mimetic self-confrontation, the scene overtly enacts the maneuver realism is usually assumed to keep hidden in order to achieve its intended effect, namely the ploy of disguising and removing from critical view its normative practices, of presenting as natural and inherent what is instead artificial and externally invested.

This is not to say that narcissism plays no role in the scene; but what narcissism there is belongs to Aquilinus, who soon approaches with "quick, manly tread" while Eugenia "involuntarily hid herself in the shadow of a column [*im Schatten einer Säule*]," (19). Even before Eugenia does so, Aquilinus places a kiss on the statue's lips; and when he does so, Aquilinus is clearly kissing not Eugenia, but *his* own ideal, *his* own image. The statue answers to his desire because, in its refiguration of gender and power roles, it not only imposes Eugenia's identity as a woman, it also reinforces Aquilinus' own as a man ("manly tread") and dominant force (a "tall figure [*hohe Gestalt*]," 19). That the statue that chiastically reflects Aquilinus' male identity should be female is not so paradoxical as it might first appear: in fact, it corresponds quite neatly to the way that gender differentiation and heterosexual desire in the story seem always to bespeak a one-sided patriarchal ideal, which it would impose on others in order to secure its own valorized sense of reality and self-identity.[36] In any case, when Eugenia then kisses the statue after Aquilinus' departure, she is not so much kissing "herself" as she is *his* image, or what amounts to the same thing, *his* lips and implanted kiss, a point nicely made in the possessive: "breaking out in tears, she too impressed a kiss upon its/ his lips [*seine Lippen*]" (20). In either case, she is quite right to burst into tears: both signal the same submission to his ideal of gender and desire, the same surrender of her real self to his realist image.[37] Far from being a narcissistic moment of Eugenia's self-absorption, the kiss proves to be her absorption into Aquilinus' self-reflecting project, which establishes his identity (his gender reality) by repressing and replacing hers.

Finally, for all the undeniable, active repression and exclusion of the real—of Eugenia's deviant desire and gender identity, of her flesh and blood and otherness, and so on—and hence all the confirmation of Holub's reading of realism as a repressive, coercive program of normative regulation and exclusion, the scene still remains equally undeniably saturated with erotic desire—expressed, *not* repressed—and an erotic desire of the most "unnatural," deviant, and disruptive kind. The perversion is evident in respect to both Eugenia and Aquilinus, each of whom sensually embraces an object that is, after all, a statue and moreover whose (grammatical) gender identity remains provocatively unstable throughout the encounter.[38] The statue certainly solicits a desire in Aquilinus in a way that the flesh and blood Eugenia never does; and the statue—which again and always must be read as realism—arouses a desire in Eugenia equally deviant, for not only does she too erotically embrace a piece of chiseled marble, but she also clasps—along with the statue as "herself" and as Aquilinus—the statue as an (other) woman, and she does so with her own gender identity always still ambiguously double. The corrective intent inherent in the embrace of the statue's normative ideal entails its own intrinsic per-version, its own unexpected but unavoidable "turn" in a different direction. The situation is actually very similar to that described in *The Mountain Forest* for the father's familial love and its self-defeating project of erotic and female containment. For far from (only) repressively constraining and policing desire and gender, Aquilinus' statue and its mimetic realist program thoroughly and necessarily release and lose control of them—and this occurs not so much through a return of the repressed as through and as the controlling mimetic program itself.

VII

The tactical availability of the same event or discursive material to competing (re)tellings, readings, and programs that we see in the encounter between Eugenia and the statue we see again in the "wild" seduction scene between Eugenia and the widow and, more forcefully, in the final decisive encounter between Eugenia and Aquilinus, the encounter that most explicitly manages the transition of Eugenia "back" to the profane sphere and her feminine identity. Significantly enough, the whole latter scene is emphatically placed under the sign of repetition, or rather retelling. Shortly after her nighttime tryst with the statue, Eugenia had visited a young heathen widow who, imagining Eugenia to be Eugenius, had lured the beautiful young monk into her bedroom and then into her wild, passionate embraces. When Eugenia finally resisted her advances and the widow realized the failure of her seduction, we're told that "all at once she transformed herself and took the way out that once was taken by Potiphar's wife and has been taken a hundred and a thousand times since" (21). The repeatedly deployed expedient she selects, of course, is her retelling of the event, with all its concomitant reassignment of the reality and truth of what happened. She claims the monk seduced her, and reinforces her version of the event through her quickly summoned household, who read into the available signs her representation and, in the immediately following scene, second it before the judging authority of Aquilinus. Her renarrational strategy ironically but still significantly recalls Keller's own project, his own retelling of the event: both are made possible by the same discursive shiftiness to the "stylized repeated gestures" we see in the scene itself, and which appears yet again in Aquilinus' own strategic retelling of the encounter near the end.

The representation, and in particular the widow's representation, of the seduction scene is not, however, the primary repetition at issue in the encounter between the officially presiding Aquilinus and the accused Eugenia, even as the transgression the widow identifies is only of secondary importance to the "reality" Aquilinus is called upon to determine and redress.[39] The real repetition here is of the statue scene, albeit translated into terms at once more fleshly and more narrative (and so too more "proper" to poetic realism); the real crime is still Eugenia's transvestism, the real reality her disavowed femininity.[40] The fact that the statue scene is *repeated* here in this, the decisive meeting between Aquilinus and Eugenia, is itself decisive in two different, and perhaps incompatible ways. On the one hand, the repetition—and I should add that the encounter between the widow and Eugenia can also be read as a repetition of the statue scene—underscores the specific gross manner in the tale through which power is exercised and reality secured; not only through the repeated manifestation of the same structural ploys but also through their apparently dispersed, unrelated manifestations.[41] On the other hand, however, the repetition also perhaps underscores the opposite point, namely the continued manner in which power *fails* to be successfully exercised through this procedure, and so reality fails to be secured—that is, the way the same structural operations *need* to be repeatedly deployed, precisely because the reality they would enforce never really succeeds.

Before deciding which of these explanations seems the more relevant, let me first describe the encounter itself: its repetition of the statue scene, its structure, and the role played by gender and desire in determining its outcome (i.e., in arriving at the determined truth and reality of Eugenia's identity). Aquilinus and Eugenia leave the public, overtly political arena of the trial and enter into the supposedly more private space of Aquilinus' room, where Eugenia immediately declares, "I am Eugenia, whom you once desired for your wife [*die du einst als Frau begehrt hast*]!" (23). Aquilinus recognizes her at once and is persuaded "that it was she," thus rendering (almost) moot the question of the truth to the widow's tale. This does not, however, put an end to the scene: rather, "he determined to carry through to the end and to ascertain whether, in regard to proper discipline [*Zucht*] and pure manners [*reine Sitte*], he had the old Eugenia before him" (24). That is, the reality test now becomes not whether he has Eugenia, but the earlier Eugenia before him: only if an equivalence can be established between the pre-Christian Eugenia and the present one can the latter claim to be real. In order to pass the test, however, Eugenia must show herself not to be the actual earlier Eugenia, but instead the properly disciplined (*Zucht*) and conventionally regulated (*reiner Sitte*) new one—although the trick remains, for Aquilinus' as for Keller's own enterprise, to present this new version as the earlier version, since it is only through this fiction that the new can stake its claim to being real or true. To be the true Eugenia (*die wahre Eugenia*), she must prove herself to be the woman she never was. And to be real, she must show herself a fiction, indeed the same fiction and the same intended substitution as that promulgated in the statue scene.

It is not just that in this encounter Aquilinus proposes the same fiction and intends the same substitution as in the statue scene. The same chiastic, ostensibly narcissistic procedure is also evoked. Aquilinus himself assumes the role of the statue. He confronts Eugenia "with apparent cold-bloodedness"; for as men so often do in Keller's fiction, Aquilinus puts on the appearance of coldness, turns himself into an artifact of marblelike coldness, in order to control and discipline not only his own desire but ultimately also the object of that desire, Eugenia.[42] And in his cold fiction Aquilinus has exactly the same desired effect on Eugenia as does the statue.[43] He "feminizes" her by weakening her, and brings her "back" to herself by initiating a moment of reflection that ostensibly allows her to assume a more natural self, while actually imposing on her his image and his regulating fiction:

At these [apparently cold-blooded] words, Eugenia blushed and looked at the ground in embarrassment; still, it seemed to her not so unpleasant to be here and finally once again . . . to speak of herself and her life; she didn't hesitate, she reported in natural words [*mit natürlichen Worten*] everything that had happened to her since her disappearance, except that, strangely enough, she didn't say a word about the two Hyazinths. (24)

The narrative that Eugenia produces, or better, the self that Eugenia produces as narrative is explicitly marked as "natural" in style, and it is the style of her tale—*die ganze Art der Erzählung*—that renders it persuasive and so real for Aquilinus—as Butler might say, its realism is a matter of performance rather than content or subject matter, or as Keller's foreword would have it, a matter of Eugenia's story displaying the proper genre-trappings. But while presented as "natural," Eugenia's narrative is also explicitly presented as not wholly true, but rather exclusive, in fact exclusive of precisely what was most objectionable about her earlier self, namely the two Hyazinths and their implicit complicity in Eugenia's unnatural identity. Her "natural" narrative does not reproduce or repeat the real Eugenia, but only pretends to; instead, it replaces the real with the more conventional ideal in reflexive response to the cold Aquilinus—such that the realistic genre comes actively to *produce* Eugenia's supposedly real gender:

genre becomes gender. Moreover, as the foreword suggests, a crucial part of the supposed realism to Eugenia's story lies in the pleasure, the *Erzählungslust* aroused by the performative *Reproduktion*; but insofar as the decisive pleasure in the tale seems clearly to be Aquilinus' (e.g., "the story pleased him right well"), and Eugenia's only insofar as it reproduces his, we would have to say that even as the realistic genre inserts itself as Eugenia's real gender, so too does Aquilinus' pleasure insert itself as Eugenia's real, released desire.

The potentially fatal threat to Eugenia implicit in this replacement of her real self with the narrative's realistic self, all done in the name of her liberation from the distorting disguise of her cross-dressed Christian identity, is more or less realized in the climactic moment to the scene, when Eugenia seems finally to submit to Aquilinus' demand that she show herself to be indeed his Eugenia, that is, a woman: "[S]he ripped her monk's robe in two, pale as a white rose and collapsing in shame and despair" (25). As might be expected, the basic ambiguities regarding both desire and gender that have dominated the tale and its telling from the outset are firmly in force here as well. On the one hand, Eugenia's gesture seems highly eroticized as it reveals the feminine body and physical sensuality that lie cloaked beneath the repressive Christian garb, or, from a slightly different perspective, behind the Christian legend. In the terms proposed in the foreword, the original profane *Lust-* arousing reality hidden behind the constraining trappings of its Christian *Gestalt* (and genre), has been released and revealed; the provocative, liberated disruption implicit in the torn vestments and displayed body is itself the sign of the real. On the other hand, her gesture seems anything but liberating or subversively disturbing. Instead, it seems simply to reinforce the conservative norm: in response to Aquilinus' repressive demands, Eugenia accepts the desired identity of herself as a woman, and discards the transvestism that had kept her identity truly disturbing, because unfixed and uncontrollably eroticized.[44] If in the first case Eugenia's body appears as the repository of the disruptive erotic and the real, and her clothing as the rejected repressive norm, in the second the clothing seems the site of the disturbing erotic and her "body" the regulatory principle par excellence. The resultant dual and contradictory status of her body is beautifully captured in the simile, "pale as a white rose," which evokes at once a warm, emerging sensuality and the cold, devivified marble of the statue—as if beneath the covering artifice of her clothing might come but another artifact and not the real.[45]

Both readings of Eugenia's revealing gesture can and perhaps should be simultaneously maintained; nonetheless the latter, of the moment as one of normative reinforcement, does receive added emphasis. Insofar as the body beneath Eugenia's clothing is gendered female and so in a sense becomes the statue, the disturbingly ambiguous Eugenia is annihilated; and reflecting this, Eugenia herself seems metaphorically to perish at this moment, losing consciousness and passing out as she and her clothing are replaced by (Aquilinus') regulatory femininity.[46] Moreover, as soon as Eugenia collapses in her deathlike faint, Aquilinus "pressed her to his heart and covered her with his cloak; for he well saw that she was an honorable woman" (25). He then lays her out on a bed, wrapping her "to the chin" in purple covers, and quickly (but also covertly) has brought in all the clothing "that at that time an elegant woman required to array herself from head to foot" (26). It is not the naked Eugenia who is presented here as a woman and who inspires Aquilinus' desire and approval, that is, his acceptance of her as real. Rather, what makes Eugenia "a woman" is that she has now assumed the proper clothes, which in the first place are, explicitly, *his* clothes. What is embraced is not Eugenia but the properly and completely conventionalized representation, which, as with both her statue and self-narrative, is always somehow more him than her, more fiction than fact, and more phantasm than flesh.

And yet: and yet. For all the emphatic embeddedness of this decisive moment in a normative program of repressive convention, and especially for all the obvious denial of the physical, living, and naked Eugenia that accompanies Aquilinus' enshrouding of her body with his cloak and his imposed conventional covering, it is still and again a moment, just like the statue scene, almost uncannily alive with a sense of perversion, and especially of perverse eroticism, and we would be misrepresenting the scene (and the model of realism at stake in the scene) if we failed to mark this. It is not just that Aquilinus' desire persists, if not as love for Eugenia then as love for himself, as we see him embrace his clothes here much as he did his statue in the earlier scene. Nor is it just that clothing continues to be the instigator of erotic desire, that Aquilinus has not succeeded in (nor did he ever intend) eliminating the perverse eroticism aroused by Eugenia's clothes: rather, he has just changed the clothes that continue to solicit, and not repress, desire. Quite beyond his desire for himself and for clothing, Aquilinus reveals a quite definite desire for the (almost) dead here, one that manifests certain tendencies that were already, perhaps, latent in his earlier embrace of the lifeless statue. As we already saw in Stifter and will see again in both Storm and Meyer, there is a profoundly suggestive necrophiliac impulse to much of poetic realism, especially conspicuous in the representation of women and often, as here, coupled with the themes of self-reflecting male desire and the (would-be) controlling superimposition on women of established governing conventions. Precisely why such a love of the dead should prove so inseparable from poetic realism is an issue to be addressed elsewhere.[47] Here we need only to stress how, far from somehow eliminating all troublesome erotic desire and aberrant behavior through the suppression of both Eugenia's naked body and her transvestite garb, Aquilinus' normative realist efforts have necessarily given rise to their own continued eroticism and perversion. Desire is shifted, but it does not disappear from the realist equation; and although the originally anticipated subversion of conventional norms might fail to materialize and prove instead a reinforcement of the same, nothing can keep this reinforcement from emerging as its own transgressive, subversive force.

VIII

If we were to end here, with the image of Aquilinus' unnatural enjoyment of his corpselike and statuelike wife, we might well have managed to call into question the achieved normality and erotic repression of Eugenia's recovered identity, but we would have done little to question the balance of discursive or phantasmatic power that itself represents the decisive authority over the real in this tale. Aquilinus with his programmatic (albeit also perverse) desire and his knowing determination of Eugenia's "true" identity would still be in complete control, and Eugenia thoroughly silenced and all but eliminated; the tripartite program announced in the opening paragraphs for the re-production of Eugenia's true and exemplary character would be, for all its revealed violence and artifice, realized, and a stable, "happy" end to its realist allegory reached.

But even as these opening paragraphs included a false, premature conclusion, before shifting the force of the narration's repetition away from disrupting the norms of gender and toward reinforcing them, so too does the moment of Eugenia's recovery and revealed "true" feminine self prove a false and premature ending to the tale. There follows a coda that once again redirects the force of the work's repetition, and further undermines the tale's ability to maintain or represent any singular uniform realist program at all.

The undermining of the achieved realist ideal embodied by Eugenia at the end is already suggested in the supposedly conclusive moment of this falsely concluding scene, and it is done by Eugenia herself through the very silence and covers that were finally to fix her. Aquilinus asks with the utmost self-assurance, "'Will you now, finally, be my woman?' . . . to which she said neither yes nor no, but certainly shuddered faintly beneath the purple covers in which she lay wrapped" (26). The silence that seemed to signal the exclusion of Eugenia from the reigning discursive field, and so too the uncontested dominance of that field's version—which is to say of Aquilinus' realist version—of her essential identity, becomes instead a signifying practice of its own, and a radically disturbing one at that, one that drives its own wedge between the imposed phantasmatic identity and the "essential" self.[48] Indeed, her nonsignifying "neither yes nor no" proves as subversive of Aquilinus' authority and desired ideal for Eugenia as did her refusal to display the expected signs of femininity and desire at the outset. In the same way, we see that Eugenia does not simply disappear behind her enshrouding, defining cover. Rather, the very covers that are to keep her under wraps do keep her under wraps, covered, concealed, unknown—and unfixed, an always possibly failed equivalent with her bodily presentation.[49]

It is not, however, only through covered silence and its suggested nonsubmission that Eugenia retains her sense of self-identity and (in)determination. She also does so in more outspoken and assertive ways, through her active participation in the normative conventions made available to her. In particular, Eugenia never really seems to relinquish power, authority, or self-identity in her role as either "woman" or "corpse," the twin positions to which Aquilinus' realist designs have apparently reduced her. Rather, Eugenia dis-poses both through their very assumption, and redetermines (or retells) her own fate in so doing.

So, for instance, having ostensibly submitted to becoming Aquilinus' woman, "without making many words about it, Eugenia gave herself over to the study of marital love and fidelity, with the same fundamental perseverance that she had previously devoted to philosophy and Christian asceticism" (27). Much like the conversion of Vitalis from wayward martyr to upstanding husband, the ease with which Eugenia shifts her behavior from one cultural field and set of practices to another betrays their similarity far more than their difference. Here as there, the shift is made possible not because of the unreality of the one identity and the more "natural" correspondence with an essential interior core of the other, but because of the superficial imitativeness of both, their common existence as stylized, repeatable, representable gestures—indeed even as more or less the same repeatable gestures.[50] "Marital love and fidelity" prove just as much a matter of assumable spiritual, or *geistlich*, habits as the discarded trappings of Christianity (and neoplatonic philosophy), and Eugenia adopts the same essentially inessential, performative relation to her new role or identity as to her disposed one(s). For this reason, her study (*Studium*) proves just as subversive of the essence of marriage (*das Wesen der Ehe*) as it does submissive; indeed, it proves subversive by being submissive, because it discounts that essence's essence, the difference that would mark it as real, in the very possibility of its assumption. Or to put it more cautiously: Eugenia's *Studium* reveals how the very procedure deployed for the normative regulation of her identity depends on the same logic of repetition and representation that also occasions the subversive derealization of that identity. Thus, not only does her assumed representation as woman and wife fail to control, confine, or define Eugenia; it seems to also invest her with a certain "knowledge-power" over the easy exchangeability of the supposedly opposing cultural conventions that enables her, as woman and wife, subsequently to shift not only herself but Aquilinus back into the Christian sphere.[51]

Eugenia's reinscription of herself as corpse is in some ways more interesting and even more decisive for our understanding of the repetition and realism at stake in the novella. After having become Aquilinus' wife and then converting him to Christianity, Eugenia, together with the reclaimed Hyazinths, deliberately seeks out a martyr's death in Rome. Once dead, we're told, "[*Ihre*] intercession is supposed to be especially useful for indolent schoolgirls who are backwards in their studies." There is a crucial ambiguity to that initial *Ihre*, which, as both a singular and plural third-person possessive, can be taken to refer to Eugenia, the Hyazinths, or all three together, so that in death, a certain gender indeterminacy once again adheres to Eugenia's figure; again, Eugenia seems impossible to fix in a stable uniform identity, impossible even to identify as a singular unified entity. This gender ambiguity, however, is only a secondary effect of Eugenia's more conscious project. In seeking out her martyr's death, Eugenia works at, and succeeds at, inscribing her corpse with her meaning, her identity—even if you will, with her allegory. She is, so to speak, a corpse twice told in this tale, first under the representative control of Aquilinus and then again and "at last" under her own authority. She retells her dead body, struggling with the powers that be to determine the reality it signifies. Indeed, in a manner that applies equally to the tale and its telling, the story of "Eugenia" comes down to a struggle not over erotic bodies or even gendered ones but over corpses. Such corpses, however, refuse to stay dead, refuse to relinquish their power of arousal, whether over dull schoolgirls or clever tellers of tales. Their continued reality is secured, no doubt, by their power to compel their own repetition—even if their repetition forever fails to compel or secure their reality.

5

SECOND WIVES, SECOND LIVES

The "Ligeia Impulse" in Theodor Storm's 'Viola tricolor'

"The likeness! o, the likeness!"
—*In the Neighbor's House to the Left*

Theodor Fontane, perhaps the most sensitive critic among the German realist writers, referred to Theodor Storm's *Viola tricolor* (1874) as "a model-piece [*ein Musterstück*], perhaps his finest novella."[1] The high estimate of the work was a common one among Storm's contemporaries, but Fontane's evaluation does not simply direct our attention to its quality: "model-piece" means something both more than and different from "masterpiece [*Meisterstück*]."[2] Fontane does not specify exactly what he considers the tale to be a perfect example or model of; to some extent, we assume, of the novella form itself, but no doubt also of the poetic realism of which Storm, and Fontane, were major representatives.[3]

To approach *Viola tricolor* as a model of poetic realism is in some respects merely to obscure rather than clarify our focus. The difficulties inherent to the problem of defining poetic realism are by this point almost axiomatic, and few of these can be expected to be resolved in Storm's novella or in the various critical theories that seek to identify its peculiar, exemplary claim to realism. Still, confronting some of the variety of approaches to the realism in the novella seems a promising way to approach the work itself; and as Fontane suggests, our understanding of the realism in the novella should have consequences for our understanding of poetic realism per se.

I

One approach to the realism in Storm's novella is to see it as a peculiar, private variant of the "social realism" characteristic of Storm's non-German, European contemporaries. This is more or less the approach adopted by Tschorn.[4] Concentrating on the depiction of the patriarchal nuclear family and its reflective relation to the broader social reality, he explores the typical division of labor that perpetuates the authority of the man and the economic dependence of the woman. He notes the social need for a woman in Rudolf's household after the death of his first wife: to raise the child, to manage the servants and housework, and to fulfill a certain *Repräsentationsfunktion*. He emphasizes the generic titles to the characters—the husband (*Herr*), wife (*Frau*), master and mistress (*Herrschaft*), and so on—the attention paid to the servants, and Rudolf's formal handing over of the house to Ines. He quotes the line, "The servants readily submitted themselves . . . and anyone who came in from outside felt that once again a woman well matched with the master reigned inside" (278).[5] He recognizes the special difficulties encountered by Ines as the second wife, whose social conditions are even more impersonally structured and restrictive than usual, insofar as she must manage as a re-presentative (*Stellvertreterin*) in a role already scripted by the first wife. Nonetheless, Tschorn seems to imply that this merely accentuates the general fate of woman in the patriarchally structured nuclear family. The woman is assigned to a role prescribed by the economic requirements of the household; her difficult and, although unacknowledged, tragic task is to internalize the authority of capitalistic production and so restabilize the familial order, which is the foundational realm of bourgeois society.

Such an approach does much to situate Ines's dilemma within the broader social context, and the focus on the familial order as the primary enforcer of bourgeois norms accords well with what we have seen already in Stifter. Still, the perspective as here presented seems very much to belong to "one who comes in from outside"; that is, it recognizes a reality as central to the story that the characters themselves only recognize peripherally, and even as by and large extraneous to the reality with which they privately struggle. Certainly Ines's position as representative, or *Stellvertreterin*, is decisive for our and her understanding of her situation, as is the crucial issue of possession. But to define these economically is unnecessarily reductive. One ends up identifying only a very marginal part of the narrative as constituting its realism, and nothing that would particularly recommend it as a "model-piece."[6]

Another common approach to the novella's realism is basically biographical; to see it as a peculiar, private variant of historical realism (which will more directly be my concern with C. F. Meyer in chapter six). While more commonsensical and less abstract, it shares with the sociological approach the characteristic referential appeal to a nonliterary, extratextual realm as the touchstone for the story's realism and authenticity.[7] Storm's first wife, Constanze, died in May of 1865; in June of the following year Storm married the friend of his youth, Dorothea Jensen. Dorothea had difficulties adjusting to her new responsibilities in managing the household and raising Storm's many children; these difficulties were compounded by Storm's unwillingness to allow the children to address her as "Mother." The tensions began to resolve two years later, after Dorothea gave birth to a daughter; she wished to name the child Constanze, but Storm vetoed this, too. Some five years later, Storm composed *Viola tricolor*.

Despite the degree of general, and at times detailed, correspondence, there are problems with assuming the realism in the work to be biographical realism. Most important, this approach forces us to ignore both changes to the biographical details (e.g., the "colors" of the respective wives, or the number of children) and the inclusion of invented material; to treat a very partial version of the text as a whole, and to regard the literalizing process itself as inessential to the story's realism. On a more particular basis, the biographical approach encourages us to identify Rudolf with the author, and by extension to endow him with a similar degree of insight and authority. And yet as I hope to show, this would lead us to ignore one of the central dramas in the novella. Clearly, we do not wish to deny the importance of the author; but clearly we do not wish to deny the importance of his text, either.

A more promising approach to the poetic realism at stake in Storm's novella would seem to come from a more formalist perspective, and particularly from that of Roman Jakobson, which I have introduced in chapter one. It will be remembered that Jakobson offers two accounts of poetic realism, one more general and situated within the broadest possible context of literary history, and the other more specific to the peculiar instance of mid- to late-nineteenth-century fiction. In the more general discussion, Jakobson defines the problem of realism as played out within an ever ongoing process of the conventionalization and deautomatization of literary codes and perceptions, and as continually giving rise to two competing claims to realism and verisimilitude: that which conceives of the deformation and disruption of literary conventions as an approximation to reality; and that which conceives of the adherence to and reproduction of the traditional codes as a faithfulness to reality.[8] For the more specific case of the nineteenth century, Jakobson describes both these claims to realism as again operant. On the one hand, realism becomes defined by its effort to overcome or violate the literary codes and conventions of its traditional predecessor, in this case by and large identifiable as Romanticism—with all the misprision and simplification of Romanticism that this effort requires.[9] On the other hand, realism's own norms, devices, and codes eventually become canonized, and function in turn as the model to whose faithful adherence later readers attribute, or deny, verisimilitude. We should note that, as opposed to the models of social or historical realism discussed above, both aspects of Jakobson's paradigm for poetic realism are defined in purely literary terms; by the disruption of one paradigm and by the introduction of another, no less literary one. Correspondence to an extratextual reality, whether social, biographical, or whatever, need never come into consideration.

Although Jakobson's model intends to identify only formal features, in fact it also accounts for many of the central thematic concerns of *Viola tricolor*. Indeed, the novella comes closer to being a "perfect example," or *Musterstück,* of this realism than of either of those others so far considered. Romantic motifs dominate the narrative. Overlooking for the moment the fairy-tale topos of the stepmother, the most prominent and important of these motifs is that of the second wife, which provides the basic framework for other romantic topoi, such as the cult of the dead woman; the dead woman as picture; the dead woman as Muse; the haunted garden, the fantasizing male protagonist, and other assorted residues of a supernatural fairy-tale world, all significantly located in the past. But more decisive than the dominance of these motifs is the sustained, and perhaps only partially successful, effort to overcome that dominance; to make room for a new reality and present through the deformation of these traditional conventions. As we will see, this effort is especially conspicuous in the case of the topos of the second wife. Not only do we see Storm invoke and yet impede the conventional, romantic enactment of this motif. Within the motif itself, we also witness the effort of the second wife, Ines, to free herself from the canonized codes of the romanticized first wife, Marie, an effort that parallels the author's literary realist project and thematically incorporates Jakobson's model into the story itself.

Interestingly enough, Jakobson's literary historical model can also be applied more particularly to the case of Storm's own writing. As Hildegard Lorenz argues in *Varianz und Invarianz*,[10] Storm's prose works can be analyzed in terms of a set of repeatedly engaged motifs or elements. Many of those elements recur in *Viola tricolor*, such as that of the picture coming true, or alive; the threat of death by water; the haunted garden; the brown-haired girl with the red object; and so on. And yet as a comparison with his other works reveals, the decisive factor is not the presence or dominance of this personal stock of literary topoi but rather again the sustained effort to deconventionalize their application, to restructure their functions. That is, we can see Storm, as author, striving to overcome his own literary, romantic conventions, his own fairy-tale, or *Märchenwelt*, and fictional norms.[11] From both perspectives—that of the broader, literary historical tradition and that of the personal, literary authorial one—Jakobson's model suggests a way of looking at the realism in *Viola tricolor* that both speaks to central concerns of the novella in particular and accounts for the difficulties of definition to realism in general. It suggests that realism is not something given but rather something that only gradually emerges, or strives to emerge, in the struggle against the given; something that does not, and cannot, exist at the beginning of the narrative, and that might, even must, exist at the end as only another literary, conventional world. But that might not be the point; the effort is, the desire to realize and release difference.

Mention of Storm's personal literary tradition indicates one way by which Jakobson's model might lead us back to something resembling biographical realism—that is, to a perception of the novella as evidence of a personal crisis or turning point for the author. But I would like to suggest that the model can also take us much further in the direction of reclaiming an extraliterary dimension to the realism at stake in Storm's work, namely, a psychological realism and, finally, a kind of social realism as well. This becomes clear when we emphasize the conservative principle in Jakobson's model, which conceives of the faithful adherence to the traditional literary codes as constitutive of reality; and when we recall Jakobson's insistence on the inevitable conventionality of all, and not just literary, perceptions. What this helps explain is the determinative role that romantic conventions have for individual psychology, that is, the literary determinants to supposedly nonliterary reality. Both Holub and Martini note Storm's realist tendency to associate the romantic and supernatural dimension with the psychological.[12] The association not only grounds the fantastic conventions in the realistic context of an individual's psyche; it also reveals the grounding of individuals' psyches in fantastic conventions. That is, Storm's literary realism can be shown to have a strong realistic basis not so much because reality permeates the literary, but rather precisely because the literary permeates reality. As we will see, one of the most critical struggles both Rudolf and Ines engage in is that against their own romantic psychology and the way it shapes their respective fears, imaginations, and desires.[13] Again, we can argue that the psychological struggle to overcome this romantic psychology, to deconventionalize it, represents the competing and emerging realist psychology active in the tale. Moreover, the romanticization of the individual psyche that we encounter in *Viola tricolor* can be shown to have an essential sociohistorical dimension. In fact, the social dimension to romantic psychology is perhaps nowhere more consequently explored than in our critic Fontane's own *Effi Briest*. From the opening pages of that novel, we witness a protagonist whose imagination, especially erotic imagination, is constituted by the romantic conventions and expectations presented to her by society; whose romantic psychology is the most prominent mark of her membership in that society; and whose ironic tragedy is that it is precisely her romanticism that seduces, betrays, and expels her from that society. Insofar as Storm, too, is exploring the texture of an embedded romantic imagination in his characters in *Viola tricolor*, he too exposes a fundamental social reality behind the supposedly personal and private crises of his protagonists.[14] We might even say that his figures are far more obviously caught up in this authoritarian economy and system of possession than in the labor and material ones assumed by critics such as Tschorn.

I I

While these preliminary considerations manage to recuperate an approach to realism that can facilitate a reading of *Viola tricolor*, they do so without as yet confronting the central and in some ways insuperable paradox to all literary realism. That is the problem of representation itself, a problem that almost inevitably leads us back to our other major concern, the problem of repetition. For in this respect, too, realism is often considered to depend on a poetics of repetition: it re-presents an original reality anterior to it. And yet in the very act of repetition and representation, the realist enterprise thus comes to defeat itself, because it fails to recognize the essential difference between its two spheres. As Jakobson noted, and countless critics since have insisted, "[V]erisimilitude in a verbal expression or in a literary description obviously makes no sense whatever."[15] Whereas painting can pretend to an objective and mimetic relationship between signifier and signified, the arbitrary character of the linguistic sign excludes any such claim. To enter into literary representation is essentially to leave the realm of "reality" altogether. For this reason, and as we have already noted in regard to Stifter, many of the realist writers themselves chose to explore their claims to realism through looking at painting rather than writing; and yet even in this case they almost unwittingly come up against the same paradox. If the repetition is to represent "life," it must cease to be itself; and yet when life becomes representation, it must cease to be itself.

There is no way out of the paradox; and yet perhaps realism does not so much depend on finding a way out as it does on the angle from which the problem is approached. Again, Jakobson's model suggests a way to reconceive the issue; and again, Storm's novella can be seen to incorporate the problem thematically into the story itself. The act of representation, or repetition, is what subverts, and ultimately deconstructs, realism. And yet as Jakobson's model and our own earlier discussions would suggest, perhaps realism should not be identified with a poetics of repetition, but rather with the exact opposite: with a desire to frustrate, avoid, and disrupt repetition, to thwart the life-annihilating act of re-presentation.[16] This involves relinquishing the notion of an original, anterior reality as the first term in the realist's project, and introducing instead a chain of previous representations, whose status as representations has perhaps been forgotten; but this is the move that Jakobson's model has already had us take in respect to the conventionality of perception per se.[17] As we will see, *Viola tricolor* thematizes the problem of representation and repetition in a number of ways, but chiefly in two, which are closely interrelated. First, the painting of the first wife, Marie, which dominates the novella from the very beginning, problematizes the issue of representation directly; it has the added function of presenting the anterior, "original" reality as a representation. Second, the stubborn desire for Ines, the second wife, somehow to become the first wife—and so in some way also to become the painting—problematizes the issue of representation and repetition more indirectly, but also more tellingly. The desire for (and fear of) repetition belongs very much at the center of the romantic psychology that governs both Rudolf and Ines; the effort to avoid or frustrate repetition and realize difference is almost definitional for the competing, emerging "realist" psychology.[18] As we will see, this struggle loosely corresponds to the Jakobson-derived, Lacanian model for the transition from the (metaphorical) Imaginary to the (metonymical) Symbolic that I described in chapter one, which seconds my operating assumptions here: the association of the literary and psychological, and the movement of both away from a metaphorical, imaginational state toward a more "realist," but no less conventionally constituted one, with the emphasis in all cases on the movement, the struggle and transition itself. But rather than continuing in these theoretical considerations, let me turn to an analysis of the work itself, beginning with a look at Storm's use of Romantic topoi.

III

For comparative purposes, let us first consider what I take to be the conventional "romantic" treatment of the topos of the second wife, with the emphasis on its supernatural, fantastic, and uncanny enactment. Doing so will allow us better to understand both the constant pulls behind Storm's novella, and the significance to its breaks with convention. We can take Bronfen's analysis of Edgar's Allen Poe's *Ligeia* as establishing the paradigm for the motif's romantic realization, at the head of a tradition that she shows to include in our time Alfred Hitchcock's *Vertigo* and, I would add, Vladimir Nabokov's *Lolita* as well.[19] At the other end of the spectrum, on the far side of realism's struggle with the romantic tradition, would be, for example, Hauptmann's *Flagman Thiel* (*Bahnwärter Thiel*, 1888), where the excessively flesh and blood second wife so dominates the scene that she threatens to expunge all traces of the ghostly, spiritualized, and worshiped dead first wife.[20] But in Poe's *Ligeia*, the opposite threat dominates. The beloved and spiritually endowed first wife, Ligeia, grows ill and dies, but continues to exert, even to strengthen, her presence through both the idealizing adulation of her husband and the oft-repeated, fantastic promise that somehow she shall escape death. The mourning male protagonist takes as her successor the fair-haired and blue-eyed Lady Rowena, who dreads his obsessiveness and shuns him, while he in turn loathes her and thinks only of Ligeia. Largely from the pressures of her husband's desires, Rowena too grows ill and dies. Then, at the site of her corpse and under the influence of grief and opium, the husband witnesses a "hideous drama of revivification," in which the corpse comes back to life, however not as Rowena, but rather as Ligeia, as much to his delight as horror. Although not as fantastic as *Ligeia*, both *Vertigo* and *Lolita* can be seen to repeat the same pattern. In each case, the second and somehow common woman is transformed into a representation, or repetition, of the first woman, at the price of her own reality and, frequently, of her life as well—because ironically, part of the repetition is always of death.

A number of Storm's own fairy tales (*Märchen*) and novellas play with a similar pattern of repetition, wherein the first figure/beloved is repeated in a second figure, at which point the story usually ends. *The Mirror of Cyprianus* (*Der Spiegel des Cyprianus*), *In the Castle* (*Im Schloss*), *A Corner of the Forest* (*Waldwinkel*), and *Eekenhof* all enact different variations on this motif; however, in each case the repetition in some way crosses generational bounds, for which reason I will postpone their discussion. For now, I'd like to concentrate on how the "Ligeia impulse" permeates *Viola tricolor*, that is, the desire on the part of the various characters for Ines to repeat the first wife, Marie, and so, too, to repeat the romantic convention; and on the various modes of impediment to that desire that make this tale so different.

Of course, to some extent the story does not admit to this (forbidden) desire, and so we detect it first through its denial and frustration. Interestingly enough, it is the child, Nesi, who initially and most insistently resists the impulse toward repetition and substitution. When Ines first addresses Nesi and asks, "You do know that now I am your mother?" Nesi glances to the side and offers to call Ines "Mama; but not Mother." To Ines's reply that "Mama and Mother are of course the same" (276), Nesi says nothing, but nonetheless manages both to identify the illicit, unspoken desire for repetition and substitution driving the exchange, and to institute the opposing drive to realize difference.

The husband, Rudolf, seems to support Nesi's shifty solution, or *Ausweg*, and a similar poetics of difference. However, his own investment in maintaining the distinction between "Mother" and "Mama" seems somewhat suspect; not so much meant to guarantee Ines's individuality, her uniqueness and authenticity, but rather to keep Marie intact and untouched—as if Marie should somehow take over Ines, and not Ines Marie. For despite his pretenses, and perhaps even despite himself, the "Ligeia impulse" silently dominates Rudolf's desires and psyche from the beginning, and he only slowly arrives at the position the child seems to attain almost immediately. For instance, when Rudolf and Ines first enter the house, he leads her quickly into the ground-floor, twilit room: "'Here we will live together,' he said, as he pressed her down into a soft armchair. 'Do not leave this room without having found your first rest [*erste Ruhe*] here in your new home!'" (275). As we soon find out, this is the room where Marie's corpse was laid out, where Marie went to her "last rest." The ambivalent and slightly alarming oppression to Rudolf's gesture ("pressing down"; "do not leave") betrays the moment's uncanny significance.[21] The second wife is being forcibly placed into the place of the dead first wife, that the "hideous drama of revivification" might be staged at the site of her body, with all the suggestions of Ines's own death that this drama entails.

This is perhaps the most subtle but disturbing example of Rudolf's desire for illicit repetition; there are others. When Rudolf first shows Ines the portrait of Marie, he says, "She was once my happiness; now it is to be you" (277). In that "it," Ines is essentially effaced and refigured as another Marie, a threat that Ines immediately recognizes and responds to. Rudolf's desire is made even more explicit a moment later when, looking at Ines, he thinks, "If it were only the Mother!" (278). Or again, after Rudolf puts Nesi to bed and promises, "'I will say good night to Mama for you.' . . . He meant to go down to his wife" (284); he goes instead to the portrait and exclaims, "Good night, Marie!" (286). Each of these cases confirms the dark desire behind his enlightened façade, the romantic fantasy behind his realist rationality. He claims Marie "was nowhere" (287), but the problem is that through his desires she is everywhere. He claims that Ines is to take possession from the dead woman "of all the rooms of this house" (276), but it seems clear that Ines is the one to be "possessed" by the dead woman who still possesses the house ("This dead woman still lived, and there was not room in one house for both of them!" 277). In this respect, Ines is completely justified in questioning her husband's pretensions to superior wisdom and saying, "I know better, Rudolf!" (288). Over and again, we see Rudolf anxious to perpetuate the canonized codes of his thoroughly romanticized first wife, and so, too, to perpetuate the romantic version of the topos of the second wife: to force Ines to repeat the given, and the present to represent the convention.

Even Rudolf's "baby solution," which is supposed to display his insight (*scharfer Blick*) and belief in the necessity of difference seems instead to betray his blindness and need for repetition. He maintains that only when Ines has her own child will she become "Mother" in her own right; but an additional implication is that only then will the desired parallel with and repetition of the first wife be complete. The narrator of course seems to identify with and so second Rudolf at this and similar moments. But we should note that, at least at the beginning, the narrator appears also to facilitate the threatened, or desired, effacement of Ines. We see this in the overall delay in providing proper names for the two women, which deprives them of individuality and invites appropriative conflation; we see this in the persistent and almost exclusive use of the same two adjectives—"beautiful" and "young"—to describe Ines that are consistently applied to Marie and her portrait; we see this in the repeated focus on Ines's "portrait" features, her face and head. That is, the narrator seems tempted discursively by the same "Ligeia" topos that seduces Rudolf psychologically.

Perhaps unexpectedly, the character who proves most susceptible to the desire for repetition and substitution is Ines herself. Our literary expectations would have this desire emanate exclusively from the male; our ideological expectations would have it be imposed from without on the unwilling female victim. But it is Storm's insight and innovation to describe the infiltration and penetration of this desire for virtual self-effacement into Ines's own psychology, so that in a sense she victimizes herself, from within.[22] Certainly this resituation of the determining desire to the second woman is far more the novella's distinguishing feature than the somewhat misleading claim that the story is told from her perspective.[23] For instance, it is Ines who first wishes to be called "Mother" and says, "Mother and Mama are of course the same." Later on, it is again Ines who insists on the appropriation of the role, crying, "But I am supposed to be her Mother!" (280). That the desire to be Nesi's "Mother" is intimately connected with the desire to be Rudolf's "wife" is apparent in her reply to his rejection of her first claim: "If you can say, She is not your child, why then don't you also say, You are not my wife!" (280). The logic here is not rational, but precisely for that reason it reveals the irrational, unconscious logic motivating Ines's desires. She feels that the only way for her truly to become Rudolf's wife is to become Marie. She understands herself in the position of *Stellvertreterin*, of representation, and desires to succeed in that representation, even at the price of self-annihilation. The "Ligeia impulse" becomes her own. Moreover, the same basic desire is still at work in Ines, even after her own crisis is past, when she suggests that the newborn baby become Marie—a "poetically fit" repetition that Storm exploits in the fairy tale *The Mirror of Cyprianus*, but significantly thwarts here.

IV

The woman toward whom these various desires are directed is, of course, not only present as a psychological presence but concretely as a portrait as well. The dead woman as portrait—or more generally, the beloved as artifact—is a romantic motif in its own right, for example in Poe's *The Oval Portrait*. It is also a persistent romantic motif in Storm's own oeuvre: most notably in *Eekenhof*, but variations on the beloved as portrait also occur in *In The Castle*, *In the Neighbor's House to the Left*, *Aquis submersus*, and, as statue, in *Psyche*. Especially in *Viola tricolor*, the identification of the dead woman with a portrait is hardly accidental. Rather, the problems and paradoxes associated with the dead woman are doubled in those surrounding the painting, or representation, itself.[24] The portrait is consistently described in terms that repeat those used to describe the dead woman. It is first described as "the life-size, half-length picture of a young woman" (273), and a bit later as "the sweet, life-full picture" (277); and yet as artifact, it is also described as essentially "lifeless" (273). The conflation of the woman and portrait in this paradox is further secured by a number of details. For example, even during her life, Marie was described by her friends with "'beauteous,' that antiquated word" (273), which in a sense already assimilates her to an ideal, literary-romantic, nonliving "other" world. The fact that the painter anticipates her death by including in the portrait "a slight trace of melancholy, which no one had seen on her in life" (272), has the same effect. It, too, informs us that Marie herself is only completed, or realized, in death and as a painting: only then does she truly become the woman represented. We should note that this amounts to something of a double death for Marie: even before her literal death, there is this appropriation of her person to the lifeless realm of representation. In fact, her literal death seems in some ways simply a metaphor for, or repetition of, this figured death.

More important, we should also note how the conditions pertaining to the portrait of the dead woman are also those that traditionally threaten to undo the realist enterprise. As Holub observes, "Capturing life in art unavoidably involves a removal of and from life, because the nature of aesthetic reproduction is representation in lifeless appearances."[25] That is, the very act of realist representation involves a problematic relation, a destabilized limen between life and death. In the aesthetic reproduction (or repetition), the reality represented is effaced and becomes lifeless; at the same time, however, the representation itself is effaced so that the thing represented appears immediately "alive." In a perverse way, every realist representation embodies the problem about Marie and her portrait, that the dead still live: the way in which the lifeless, represented Marie takes over the present site of her portrait, even as the representation/painting has already overtaken her, exposes the persistent threat to the present reality posed by representation, or repetition, itself. (The threat that the lifeless Marie might somehow also take over the present site of Ines merely continues the same chain of destructive representations, and this makes clear how the same problem, that of realism itself, is incorporated into both topoi, that of the living portrait and of the second wife.)

Of course to some extent, the portrait also exceeds its status as realistic representation, insofar as for Rudolf it functions as something of an icon, and for

Ines as a model. For Rudolf, the portrait is situated at the center of the "chapel" he constructs in his study, with the lamp, flower, and vase beneath, and the westward-facing window with the "shimmer of evening's gold" coming through to the side. For him, the representation primarily serves the purpose of recollection: the painting is ignored in its own presence and simply points beyond itself to the thing other than itself that it represents. This brings into play an allegorical dimension to the portrait, a dimension that Holub shows to be part of every realist reproduction.[26] But as the chapellike setting underscores, the allegorical function is not limited to pointing to the dead woman to be recalled; perhaps inevitably, she becomes an allegory for death per se. And insofar as both the painting and Marie are deprived of their own reality and function as allegories, the realistic dimension is overwhelmed and gives way to the decidedly romantic and fantastic.

For Ines, the portrait exceeds its realist status and undergoes a romanticization in a different way. For her, too, the painting becomes charged with allegorical significance: it not only points to Marie and to death; it also paradoxically points to her. It becomes an allegory for what she should become, a model of which her life should become a copy or representation. To use the image the novella itself exploits, the portrait becomes a mirror for Ines, but with the conventional relation of model/life and copy/representation chiastically reversed. And yet the model is still a decidedly unreal one: death and representation imbue the image of Marie with a "romantic" completeness and power essentially alien to real life.

In these two different ways—as icon and model—the painting thus exercises a control over the life and reality of the two major protagonists. To some extent, this can be read as the work's central romantic/realist crisis, where the representation threatens to overwhelm the narrative world, so that the present reality itself gets lost. This threat, which is closely related to the one posed by the father's vision of the woods for Clarissa in Stifter's *The Mountain Forest* and by Aquilinus' statue of Eugenia for Eugenia in Keller's *Seven Legends*, is very much present in *Viola tricolor*. Equally important, it is also present in quite a number of Storm's other novellas, and the similarities and differences in his handling of the motif in general and here reveal what is at stake in *Viola tricolor*, and how its use of the motif is "realistic."

I mentioned before that a number of Storm's own stories play with a narrative structure of repetition, wherein the first figure/beloved is repeated in a second figure. What I didn't mention is that this first figure is frequently a picture, so that the movement is simultaneously from the representation to reality, where the painting somehow takes over, or comes true, at the site of the second living figure. For example, in *In the Castle*, the female narrator recalls her fascination as a child with "the fantastical wonders of the fairy-tale world," chief among them the life-size portraits in the so-called knights' room. One of these portraits represents some of her own noble ancestors as children; another represents a twelve-year-old whipping-boy (*Prügeljunge*) from a lower class. Anna falls in love with the portrait, even kisses it on occasion; one day a young boy from a lower class arrives who resembles the painting. The boy, Arnold, turns out to be a descendant of the whipping-boy in the portrait; the subsequent romance between Anna and Arnold both fulfills the initial romance with the portrait and overcomes, or reverses, the original social slight among the respective ancestors. In two ways, then, the narrative is structured about the principles of representation and repetition. The characters in the original paintings are repeated in those living in the story; and Anna's desire for the original portrait is repeated in her desire for Arnold. In both cases, the representation takes over, or is repeated in, reality; in both cases, the coming true of the paintings creates a decidedly romantic, antirealist ending, much like that achieved through the repetition of names in the fairy tale *The Mirror of Cyprianus*.

The same basic movement from representation to reality constitutes the narrative structure to *A Corner of the Forest* (which Storm called a counter-piece to *Viola tricolor*, and Fontane a "model-piece" of how a realistic novella should *not* be written).[27] A painting hangs on the wall in the room of the male protagonist, Richard, depicting two young figures wandering through a landscape while an older man stares after them. At the end of the story, the painting comes real or true, when his lover, Franziska, leaves with another man and leaves Richard standing alone, thus repeating not only the picture but also, ironically, the scenario surrounding Richard's first wife, who also left him for another man. In this case, the repetition of both the painting and the first-wife scenario is not desired but rather feared. However, this merely emphasizes on the one hand the romantic sense of fate dominating the repetition, and on the other the functional identity of fear and desire in motivating it. The same basic structure is also evident in *Aquis submersus*, where the eyes and curse of the portraitured ancestress come true and repeat in the figure of the dead child at the end.[28] Again, the repetition is feared and "fatefully" determinative; and again, the repetition of the representation is the main source for the fantastic and supernatural in the tale.[29]

Although ultimately frustrated, the same narrative impulse is also at work in *Viola tricolor*, a "romantic" movement from representation to reality through a moment of repetition, in which the painting comes true and effectively takes over the present reality. The impulse manifests itself mostly through Ines, in the form of both desire and fear, and leads to a crucial compounding in the logic of her "Ligeia impulse." Ines's desire somehow to become Marie, to become Nesi's mother and Rudolf's wife, is simultaneously a desire to become a painting; that is, her desire to become a representation is also a desire to become a representation. Ironically and yet essentially, this also involves a compounded desire to die. First, in order to become the dead woman, Marie, Ines must effectively efface herself that the substitution or repetition might take place, that Marie might "possess" her. Second, in order to become Marie as painting, Ines must allow herself to be appropriated to the lifeless realm of representation. And in addition to these figural deaths, there is always the sense in which Ines must become actually dead in order to become Marie, whose very figure is inseparable from death, is, as I said, even an allegory for death.

Altogether, then, there are three interrelated impulses to Ines's romantic desire for repetition, her "Ligeia impulse" to become Rudolf's beloved, Marie: to become Mother, painting, and dead. It is a desire so strong that it nearly destroys Ines; and it is the struggle to impede and overcome this desire that constitutes the hard, slow road to realism and life in the novella.

We see this decisive constellation of impulses, and the attendant struggle to overcome them, in two of the psychologically most complex scenes in the novella: in the dream sequence, and in the childbed/deathbed scene. The dream sequence itself falls primarily into two parts: the actual, depicted dream, followed by Ines's account of a second dream she had as a child. Although the two dreams are seemingly very different in content, Ines claims that they are somehow the same dream: the only distinction between them is between her fear and her desire in dreaming them. To some extent, it is precisely the identity of fear and desire in both dreams that secures their similarity. But once seen as the "same" dream, each part can also be seen as motivated by the same fear and desire: to become Mother, dead, and painting—Marie.

We see the interplay of desire and fear in becoming mother and dead already in the introduction to the dream sequence, which begins, "A seed-corn had been laid in the ground, but the time of germination was still remote" (289). This is immediately juxtaposed with the announcement "that she too was to become Mother [*dass auch sie Mutter werden sollte*]." The anticipated moment of repetition ("she too") also has its dark side, however. The "seed-corn" of the first line, which seems to echo Ines's expecting, is also traced with an earlier line applied to Marie: "Death had secretly sown his seed" (286). Becoming "Mother" and dying are equated by the same imagery. It is this equation that seems to underlie the double, "uncanny" nature of Ines's "delight" ("to her delight [that she was to become Mother] there was soon allied a different one [*gesellte sich bald ein anderes*]," 289). Both "delights" go into the making of her dream, and both of course are tied up with becoming Marie.

The dream itself continues this complex mixture of fear and desire that attends her complex drive to become at once Mother and dead. For example, the description of Ines's physical appearance consistently stresses both its sensual and its deathlike character. The narrator focuses from the outset on her naked feet (290, 291); he describes how "the wind was playing with her light nightgown," but by the end he has her "almost undressed, her lovely hair moist with the night dew" (291). The image of the dew-dripping trees and the mythically resonant image of "a shower of yellow leaves" (291) falling on the "almost undressed" Ines combine with that of the large, pursuing dogs with "red tongues hanging out of their steaming jaws" (291), which eventually come to lick her naked feet, to secure the unmistakably sexual nature to her dream.[30]

At the same time, her deathlike appearance is also emphasized, as is the role of death in general. We are told that "her usually so elastic figure seemed as if sunken" (290); the approach of the fantastic dream-hound brings with it a fear of death (*Todesangst*); especially Rudolf's vision of the "dark water" clarifies that the direction of the dream is not only toward sexual fulfillment but also toward death. The two are not, however, opposites, but neither is their identity a simple one: it is not just that sexual desire veils itself as life threatening, nor that *Todesangst* exposes itself as erotic. Rather, as the initial description of Ines's "beautiful countenance fully lit by the moon's pale gleam" (290) suggests, the identity of the two depends on a third term. "Beautiful countenance" emphasizes the sensual, "pale gleam," the deathlike to her appearance, but both also point to Marie ("beautiful countenance," 273; "moon/ lit/ beautiful/ pale head" 285–87), and reveal the direction of the dream to be single: toward Marie and repetition.

The logic of the dream leads us to basically the same conclusion.[31] Ines wants to go "to her mother, never to return!" (290). In the dream, this involves the key and the gate into the open (*das Freie*); when she half-awakens inside the large garden, "one of her hands still held the latch of the grated iron door" (291). The surface sense suggests that Ines is fleeing from Marie, but the deeper logic of images suggests rather that she is running toward Marie. The image of the key and gateway come from the last part of the scene immediately preceding the dream sequence, where Rudolf offered Ines the key to the garden, or "grave," of Marie (288 f.). The image of her hand on the latch comes from an earlier scene in which Ines tried to enter the same garden (281). It is there, on the other side of that gate, that she can enter into the space of her desire for "Mother," "never to return," and "the open [*das Freie*]." It is there that she can enter into the space of Marie and death.

Rudolf's vision, or version, of the dream contributes other elements essential to its interpretation. As mentioned, his image of "dark water" juxtaposes death with Ines's notion of "Mother" as the goal of her quest. But significantly, the desire for death by water is here also described as a desire to pass through to the other side of the "black water-mirror [*Wasserspiegel*]" (292). The already established juncture of Mother and death as pointing to a desire to become Marie allows us to interpret this detail as generated by the same logic of desire, and as securing the necessary third term to its constellation. That is, it is the desire to enter into the lifeless, life-annihilating realm of the image, of representation; again, to enter into the space of Marie, whose image, as painting, functions as a mirror for Ines, for what she desires to become. And of course, the logic that links entering the realm of representation with death was already established in relation to Marie long before it is linked here in relation to Ines's desire to drown in the mirror.

If this seems a strong reading of the image of *Wasserspiegel,* the second, "nice" dream related by Ines—which she calls the same dream as the "terrifying" and "fearful" one just experienced—foregrounds even more indisputably Ines's desire to enter into the picture, and again features the crucial constellation of painting/mother/death, all pointing to the desire to become Marie. Ines recounts how, when she was thirteen, "my mother had given me a picture, a Madonna with Child; it hung in a pretty frame over my little work-table" (293). Besides the obvious, though unvoiced, link in the names of the painted figures (Madonna/Marie), several details underscore the parallel with the significant present: the identity of the figure as mother, the focus on the painting's pretty frame, and especially its placement over the work-table (*Arbeitstisch;* cf. 273). Ines further relates how she conceived a passion for the painting ("I felt just as if it were alive") and how she desired the "Christ-child," or more precisely, how she desired to become the Mother in the painting ("[If] I could only have taken the child in my arms like the mother in the picture!" 293). The desire culminates in the dream proper: the child Ines takes the painting into her bed, into her arms, and presses her head against its glass, exactly as if trying to enter into the picture itself. Again, the parallel with the present is obvious, and it is from the present that the dream draws its significance.

If the first part of the dream sequence foregrounds the elements of Mother and death and only hints at that of the painting at the end, the second part foregrounds the elements of Mother and painting but insists on that of death at its end. Immediately after Ines tells of her attempt to enter into the picture, we are told, "For a while it was dead quiet in the room" (*totenstill im Zimmer,* 294), a response that would seem incongruous, except for the meaning already attached to such an attempt. "With dawning awareness," Rudolf asks, "'And now?'" to which Ines, again otherwise incongruously, replies "—O Rudolf! Let me die; but don't reject our child!" (294). "But" functions here as much as a conjunctive as a disjunctive: the desire to die is the inextricable "third" in the desire to become the representation, and so the legitimate mother and wife. In these many interconnected ways, then, the dream, the realm of unchecked fantasy and desire, repeatedly exposes the (illicit) urge for representation and repetition that threatens to overwhelm Ines's waking reality.

An effort is made during the dream sequence itself to thwart this urge and disrupt its fantasy. Just before Ines recounts the second part of the dream, Rudolf goes to the window and pulls back the curtain, so that light pours into the room: "'I must see your face,' he said" (292). The need to see Ines, to keep her individuality and reality present as she narrates her dream-wish, reintroduces the competing, "realist" desire that would turn away from repetition and fantasy. Rudolf's resolve in the last sentence of the scene, "Now everything, everything must change [literally, "turn"]!" (294), draws on the same desire for deformation. But the effort made is not yet enough, the fantastic drive not so easily untracked; in the narrator's words, "The dark powers were not yet overcome" (294). For this reason, the same decisive set of impulses reappears in the childbed/deathbed scene; and it is only here, at the moment where the repetition, the "Ligeia impulse," comes closest to realization, that the struggle to overcome that desire and to realize difference finally manages to achieve some type of decisive dominance.

Again, the introduction to the scene displays the operant conditions and impulses. We are told, "Already the first storms of spring were raging about the house; the hour neared" (296). The resonances are ambivalently precise. "Spring" points on the one hand to the season of giving birth and becoming Mother, and on the other to the season of Marie's death: the hour threatens, or promises, Ines a moment of double repetition. The moment comes—"a second little daughter" is born, and "in the room the young Mother lay pale and disfigured" (296)—in both ways, both as Mother and as pale, Ines is closer than ever to becoming Marie. That her nearness to death is not accidental, but rather essential to her desires, is emphasized in the thought that precedes her condition: "If I don't survive . . . will he *then also* remember me? [*ob er* auch *meiner* dann *gedenken würde?*]" (296, my emphases). Death, or rather repeated death, is crucial to Ines's desire to become Rudolf's beloved.

It is, however, the third element to the constellation of desire that dominates the scene itself. Already Mother and anticipatingly dead, Ines has "one more request": that now a portrait be painted, or at least a photograph be taken, since the child "has to know how *the Mother* appeared [*wie* die Mutter *ausgesehen*]"

(296, my emphasis).³² When Rudolf attempts to defer her desire, Ines suddenly, and climactically, demands a mirror:

The sick woman seized it hastily; but as she looked into it, an intense terror painted itself [*malte sich*] in her features; she took a cloth and wiped at the glass; but it didn't change anything [*es wurde nicht anders*]; only ever stranger stared the sick, suffering countenance back at her. —"Who is that?" she suddenly cried. "That is not I!—O my God! No picture, no shadow for my child!" (297)

It seems clear that, when she looked into the mirror, Ines fantastically expected to see herself as Marie; so close was she to fulfilling all the conditions of her desire for repetition. But the representation fails; the real resists. The fact that she does not see Marie, but Ines, that she must acknowledge that she is not and cannot be Marie, but is and must be herself; that is the anagnorisis that shatters the "Ligeia impulse" in Ines, and the uncanny, fantastic, "romantic" drive to the story itself.

The anagnorisis is also, however, a peripeteia. That is, it is at this moment of impediment to the plot of repetition that the new, realist poetics of difference comes to dominate. As at the outset, Nesi is again the agent who instigates the counterplot. When she exclaims, "[My] dear, *sweet* Mama!" (297), Ines acquires—as "Mama" and *not* as "Mother"³³—the one adjective that had been exclusively reserved for Marie and her portrait, thus affirming, even desiring, Ines in her difference, not in her parallel. Similarly, Rudolf now comes to desire "a completely *new* pleasure" instead of a repetition of his past happiness ("now it is to be you"), and he finally says the "good night!" to Ines herself, thus affirming and desiring Ines, as Ines, as his true, or "real," beloved wife (cf. the reference here to their wedding day, 301). Most important, the frustration of the desire for repetition in Ines herself allows her to desire to live, and in living to disrupt the uncanny, romantic topos. In this respect, it is important to see that the desire for life is as overdetermined as was the opposing desire for death, and as decisive for the new realist direction as the death drive was for the romantic one. "Life" here bespeaks the thwarting of the desire for representation; the surviving of the desire for death; and the embracing—by all the characters, including Ines herself—of the living, present Ines in all her difference. As Rudolf says, "Ines too exists for me but once in the world and never again" (303). Each aspect of the "life" drive rejects repetition; each signifies the struggle that constitutes the work's realist impulse.

V

While the related topoi of the second wife and of the portrait constitute the two dominant romantic motifs that need to be disrupted, or deformed, in the story and by Ines for the new poetics to emerge, there is another pair that the story also takes on. These are the related topoi of the dead beloved as Muse and the haunted garden. Each constitutes a source for the romantic and fantastic in the tale; and as we will see, each points to a romantic/realist crisis connected to one of the other main characters besides Ines.

As the dead beloved, Marie appears not only in the role of artwork but also in a sense in that of the inspirer of artwork. In this latter function, she joins other, more famous figures such as Dante's Beatrice, Poe's Virginia, and Novalis's Sophie; that is, she functions as, and so repeats, a recognizably literary, and romantic, convention.[34] We see this motif associated with Marie from the very outset. Her portrait hangs in Rudolf's study (*Studierzimmer*), directly over his large writing-desk, covered as it is "with all the apparatus of a learned archaeologist; bronzes and terra cottas from Rome and Greece, small models of ancient temples and houses and other things risen up out of the debris of the past filled almost the entire top of it" (273). The collection of aesthetic artifacts from a distant past gives a crucial twist to the significance of Rudolf's "chapel" and cult: Marie is to inspire not only her artwork but also that of her beloved husband. And so it was from the beginning. Marie was first seen by Rudolf looking up from his books through the window of his study: she, too, was engaged with books and study, her schoolwork (285f.). His work becomes dependent on her inspiring presence, insofar as she first "takes away" his thoughts and then gives them back to him once she enters his house as wife. We are told, "Years of *happiness* and joyful *productiveness* had entered with her" (285, my emphases). Rudolf's creative productivity becomes inseparable from her and from the happiness he associates with her. The motif is pushed to almost grotesque proportions at the moment of Marie's death, when Marie's deathbed actually is moved to occupy the space of Rudolf's writing desk in his study—as if through the conflation of images we were to imagine Marie dying to sustain her husband's work, or conversely Rudolf writing on the space of his dying wife.

The depiction of Marie as Muse is significant not only insofar as it presents yet another romantic topos identified with her figure that the story's realistic impulse has to overcome. It is perhaps even more important insofar as it highlights the role of Rudolf's imagination in engendering the romantic, fantastic world in the story. To some extent, this is merely to reiterate something said before, namely that it is largely Rudolf's (unacknowledged) desires that keep Marie everywhere alive and present, and that even threaten Ines with murderous intent. But the designation of Rudolf as artist introduces an added dimension that links the issues surrounding his psychology with those surrounding art and literature per se.[35] This linkage is analogous to, in fact parallel with, Ines's linkage of the desire to become Marie and the desire to become a painting or representation: each associates the personal, psychological crisis of the protagonist with the general, literary crisis of the work, or realism, itself.

Let us begin by noting those instances of Rudolf's imagination actively intruding into the narrative. In each case, decidedly literary, fantastic tropes invade the story. The most conspicuous example comes when Rudolf retreats to his study at night and lights a small bronze lamp from Pompeii below the portrait (284f.). Dark clouds crowd out the moonlight, and suddenly, "out of the fantasy of the man who looked down into this solitude there walked a lovely figure who no longer belonged among the living" (285). Again, what is significant here is not only how Rudolf's imagination and desires are responsible for keeping Marie present but also how they are responsible for keeping the supernatural, romantic topoi present in the story. The aesthetic significance to the scene is evident in the decisively art-ful character of the altar, which in turn inspires Rudolf's "creative" fantasy. But as the cloudy, moonlit night and wandering ghost underscore, the inspired fantasy is emphatically conventional—and romantic. In this respect, it is important to note that while Rudolf's imagination is almost always connected with recollection and death, and so in this sense involves repetition and the supernatural, in his imaginative recollection death is almost always literalized and romanticized, and so in this other sense involves repetition (i.e., of "the supernatural") as well.

We see the same combination of fantasy, desire, death, and convention in Rudolf's contribution to the dream sequence. The passage has to be read as one of the pieces to the logic of the dream itself, but it also has to be read as one of the pieces to the logic of Rudolf's imagination. His vision of "a dark water" introduces into the narrative one of Storm's stock literary conventions: death by water.³⁶ Thus, the issue of death and repetition is also doubled here. On the one hand, Rudolf's fantasy exposes his (unacknowledged) desire for Ines's death. This is, of course, the flip side to his desire and imaginative effort to keep Marie alive: it is his desire to have Ines repeat Marie, which inevitably and necessarily involves her dying. On the other hand, his fantasy poses the threat to the given reality by literary convention; Rudolf cannot help but desire and imagine the tropological. That is, through Rudolf's imagination we again encounter the movement from representation (Storm's stock motif) to reality (the narrative world of *Viola tricolor*) through a moment of repetition (reusing the motif). We see Ines threatened by a different kind of death, a figural deprivation of her living individuality through an imaginative assimilation to the lifeless realm of representation; threatened, that is, by this form of representation and repetition as well.

The climactic instance of Rudolf's imagination invading and threatening to control the narrative comes during the childbed/deathbed scene, just after Ines has apparently overcome her repetition crisis and has fallen asleep. Rudolf's fantasizing at this point combines both of his desires—to make Marie present, and to see Ines dead—and so brings the story as close to the "Ligeia" plot as it comes:

Already long since [*Längst schon*] he sat again at the bed of his beloved wife, in brooding expectation; thoughts and images came and went; he didn't look at them, he let them come and go. Already once before it had been as it was now; an uncanny feeling came over him; he felt as if he were living a second time [*zum zweiten Mal*]. Again he saw the black tree of death rise up and cover his entire house with its dusky branches; ... in the blooming lilacs beneath the window a small bird sang incessantly; he didn't hear it; he was intent on driving away the deceptive hopes that wanted now to spin their web about him. (298)

The essential ambiguity to Rudolf's desires is evident throughout this passage. The ambiguity begins already with the phrase "Already long since he sat again at the bed of his beloved wife." We are momentarily left unsure whether we have not already entered the fantasy, whether "again" and "beloved" do not already signal Marie; and it is only once the fantasy and its repetition are formally announced with "Already once before" that we realize the subject was in-

Second Wives, Second Lives 153

deed Ines. Nonetheless, this opening gives the tone-setting ambivalence to Rudolf's "expectation" here. It is critically unclear whether he expects and desires Ines to live or die; whether, in true "Ligeia" logic, he desires Ines to die and so repeat Marie, and in repeating Marie, in reviving her death, fantastically to revive her and to bring her—Marie, and not Ines—back to life. The ambivalence is maintained all the way through to the last line, where it remains uncannily open as to what constitutes his deceitful hopes, what his efforts to thwart them.

An equally important aspect of this passage is the close connection between Rudolf's desire for repetition and his imagistic, metaphoric imagination. His brooding expectation (*dumpfe Erwartung*) is accompanied by an animated and yet impersonal circulation of thoughts and images (*Bilder*); his yielding to the one corresponds to his yielding to the other. His "uncanny feeling" of repetition, that he is back at Marie's bedside, is accompanied by the fantastic, unreal, metaphoric vision of the black tree of death; the one blinds him to the presence of Ines even as the other blinds him to the presence of the real, living tree outside the window. Both desire and imagination efface the "real": both threaten to overwhelm the narrative world with re-presentation.

As suggested by his role as artist, the issues surrounding the role of Rudolf's imagination are also those associated with one of the chief paradoxes of realism per se. This is the problem of the necessary intercession of human, aesthetic fantasy between the given reality and its "realistic" representation.[37] For example, in his discussion of the realist painter Johannes in *Aquis submersus*, Holub notes the ideal of the artist as a transparent medium, a mechanical mediator between object and representation, world and sign, whose own personality and wishes are totally effaced for the sake of the faithful, accurate reproduction. And yet as Holub also notes, the central examples of the infatuating painting (*sinnberückendes Bild*) of Katharina and the picture of Lazarus with Gerhardus's features both point to the necessary subversion of this ideal. In the latter case, the unconscious fantasy of Johannes unwittingly intercedes and informs, or deforms, the representation; in the former case it is his unconscious desire that invades and possesses the painting. Although Holub does not say so explicitly, his argument indicates the essential identity of imagination and desire as the disrupting factor that subverts the realist ideal, a conjunction that also appeared in our analysis of Stifter (which also foregrounded the specifically male identity of both the operant imagination and desire).[38] The same link is also evidently operant in the case of Rudolf; and yet his case also adds an element that both complicates the aporia and points a way to its resolution. Again, his imagination and desire essentially inform one another and disrupt his perception of the "neutral" reality. And yet here we note that his imagination, far from being something individual, indefinable, and freely creative, is instead something deindividualizing, defined, and profoundly conventional. It does not, that is, occasion the failure of the realist ideal because it fails to represent the world, but rather precisely because it does represent the world: it subverts the "real" precisely through a kind of mechanical re-presentation, through its deadly conventionalization—its romanticization. And the same can be said about his desire. Rudolf's desire does not distort or frustrate his perception of reality simply because it is there, but rather because it aims at re-presentation; because it is so fundamentally coded, so fully shaped and scripted by an established tropology.[39]

The introduction of the question of convention allows us, however, to reformulate the crisis facing realism in general and Rudolf in particular in a manner that allows for its at least partial resolution. The task is no longer to efface or eliminate fantasy and desire altogether, to reduce to nothing the interceding human agency. It is not their presence that thwarts the realistic representation; rather, it is their re-presentation that thwarts the present reality. The task, then, is to redirect imagination and desire, away from the established tropes and conventions and toward the new and unscripted; away from the desire for repetition and toward the desire for difference. It is this *movement* to desire and fantasy that becomes the definitional dilemma for realism, not their elimination.[40]

As Rudolf's case makes clear, the movement is not simple, but rather a struggle. Moreover, in some sense the struggle is never entirely successful; however, it need not be, since the realist impulse secures itself more in the ongoing struggle itself than in any teleological outcome. And the impulse, the struggle is certainly there for Rudolf. We might already detect it in his efforts to escape his enveloping deceptive hopes during his "Ligeia" fantasy. But the struggle comes to dominate only once it is clear that Ines will survive; it is the heavy burden (*schwere Last*) that Rudolf now bears as his happiness. As he sits by her bed, Rudolf calls his wife: "'Ines!' he whispered; 'Ines!' He couldn't desist from calling out her name." The desire for Ines expresses itself in what amounts to an imaginative invocation of the real; an invocation of her (and it) as the inspiring Muse for his desire and fantasy; an invocation for her to occupy the site of her body—at which point, significantly, Ines wakes up as if from death, "as if her soul had first to climb up to reach him out of the depths of sleep."

The same direction is also indicated in regard to Rudolf's vision. The realist impulse already present in his desire to "see" Ines during her narrative in the dream sequence also asserts itself at her bedside: "He looked at her and couldn't satiate himself with the sight of her." Again, desire is very much present in his vision, and not at all eliminated: but rather than expressing itself in a fantastic, metaphoric vision that replaces the real, his desire expresses itself in a vision that privileges the present, the "real." In keeping with this, the (unreal) branches of the envisioned death-tree now yield to a perception of the real tree present outside the window. And finally, Rudolf's new desire—"I want to watch you eat"—also indicates the new direction taken by both his desire and his vision, away from the romantic and toward the real, the natural, the everyday.[41]

In this respect, it is important to note that the new ideal of life (*Leben*) at the story's end has special significance for Rudolf as well, and that its recognition is as difficult and newly won for him as for Ines. When he rejects Ines's proposed repetition in naming—that is, the impulse to "paint over [*übermalen*]"—he is resisting his own previous imaginative tendencies as well; the declaration that "Ines too exists for me but once in the world and never again," signals the new orientation to his desires and imagination as well. More tellingly, when Ines expresses her fantastic, religious vision of their meeting Marie in the "other world" (of the living dead), Rudolf's response shows that the problem indirectly has as much to do with him as Ines: "He enclosed her firmly in his arms and said, 'Let us attend to what is close at hand [*das Nächste*]; that is the best thing a person can teach himself and others'" (303). Ines's fear, and her desire, are still directed at the unreal and the conventional, and it is precisely this tendency to allow the conventional and unreal to determine fantasy and desire that touches on Rudolf's case, too, and calls forth his need to teach himself. The new lesson is to desire *das Nächste*, with all its varied resonances: to desire the "next," the different, the state on the far side of the Ideal that was before; and to desire the "nearest," the most immediate, what is present and before one's eyes.

This is the double movement to Rudolf's desire caught in the double phrase "Life, Ines," where both "life" and "Ines" signal his new imaginative, realist impulse.

One final point on this. The same realist impulse we recognize in Rudolf at the end in his embrace of "Life, Ines" we recognize in the narrator at that point beyond the end, namely in his embrace of the story's title, "Viola tricolor." The designation of Rudolf as artist suggests something of a functional identity between him and the narrator; and as mentioned, early on the narrator seems tempted discursively by many of the same tropes that tempt Rudolf psychologically. In this regard, the *kind* of artist Rudolf represents is of crucial importance. As an archaeologist, or, more literally, an investigator of antiquity (*Altertumsforscher*), he straddles two worlds and two competing impulses. In the concern with antiquity (*Altertum*), we see the engagement with a past, dead world, a world of art, established conventions, and ideals. It is a world in every way removed from the everyday, the present, and the real, in every way a traditional poetic world (*Dichterwelt*), and so in this sense fully symptomatic of his imaginative fixation on death, convention, fantasy, and Marie. On the other hand, in the concern with research (*Forschung*), we see that scientific, realist way of looking at these same things that depoeticizes them, in a sense by making them fully "dead" by distinguishing the conventions they embody from those with which the present "artist" views them, with "sight" rather than fantasy characterizing the view.

It is this role as investigator, or *Forscher,* that Rudolf shares with so many of the protagonists in Stifter's works, including the narrator of the preface to *Many-colored Stones*; it is this same role that he shares with that archrealist in Storm's own works, the uncle in *In the Castle*; and it is, apparently, also this role that Rudolf shares with the narrator of *Viola tricolor* and that comes to dominate both of their imaginations at the end. Editors' notes tell us that "Viola tricolor" signifies the same (pansy) flower that the Germans call "little stepmother" (*Stiefmütterchen*); and yet of course there is a significant difference between the two that has Storm, or his narrator, purposely choose the one and reject the other. *Stiefmütterchen* is the common, conventional, we can even say fairy-tale designation for the flower:[42] to "name" the story with this name would be to overpaint it (*übermalen*) with established convention and romantic, fairy-tale codes; would be to assimilate the story to a realm of literary trope; would be to see it as a (romantic) repetition. "Viola tricolor" suggests the narrator's struggle with and break from literary convention, suggests, that is, his own realist impulse. A different and defamiliarizing way of seeing and naming the same thing, that directs us away from the literary and conventional and toward a new, deromanticized and "realist" way of seeing, of imagining life—that is how the botany behind the title expresses the "life" behind the story's newly won poetic realism.[43]

VI

The final romantic topos in the novella, that of the haunted garden, is in many ways the easiest to identify, and yet it introduces perhaps the most difficult problem for an understanding of the work's realist impulse. Many features indicate the garden's fantastic, romantic character. It is intimately connected with Rudolf's study and the "chapel" about the portrait. The window next to the writing-desk overlooking the garden faces west and lets in "the shimmer of evening's gold" that illuminates the portrait and contributes to its allegorical significance; looking out this window from his desk, Rudolf fantasizes the ghost of Marie walking the garden paths. This association of what Rudolf calls "the garden of the past" with both allegory and fantasy does much to impart its romantic character. It is further secured by certain features of its own. The garden is closed off by a high surrounding wall that separates it from the space of the everyday; it is also described as a "garden wilderness," which again signifies its extraordinary, uncontrolled, and fantastic character. Dominating the rank-growing shrubbery are the black, pyramid-shaped conifers, which ingeniously join the images of art and death that determine the work's romantic poetics; at one point we are told that "a great night-moth was just flying over them" (288). Altogether, then, the garden quite explicitly represents both the space of Marie and the space of the romantic. In many ways, it functions as an analogue to the portrait, transposed into three dimensions.

Deliberately juxtaposed with the fantastic, haunted garden is the large, open garden of the house. This other garden is visible through the other window in Rudolf's study; the contrast between the two windows and their respective gardens is emphasized twice at the outset, when Nesi and then Ines first enter the study. Each time, the significance of this other garden is indicated not only by its contrast with the haunted garden but also by its association with "the mighty baying of a dog" (272; cf. "the mighty voice of a dog," 277). The vibrant, virile register contributes to the semanticization of this open space with an opposing power: that of "life." The window of the room in which Ines gives birth also looks out over this garden.

The presence of these two oppositely semanticized spaces, however, presents us with a problem. The logic of the argument to both this analysis and the narrative proper would want the story to end up in the open, unromanticized garden, looking through the other window, as it were. But that is not what happens. Instead, the movement at the end is from the large garden back into the small one; the final scene and resolution are emphatically staged in the "garden of the past." This movement would seem to be against the direction of my reading; to be, at the end, a retreat to romanticism and repetition, and away from the story's own emerging realism.

There are certainly other indices that the movement toward realism is an illusory one, and that convention and repetition prove the dominant forces to the end. This is especially clear at those crucial moments of quotation in the novella. At the very end of the dream sequence, after Ines has revealed her desire to become the picture of Mother Mary (*das Marienbild*) and has exclaimed "Let me die!" Rudolf whispers, "Now everything, everything must change [or literally, "turn": *Nun muss sich alles, alles wenden*]!" (294). The line should function as evidence of the new realist impulse, the turning away from the illicit and fatal desire for repetition. But the line is not original: it is in fact a quotation from Uhland's "Spring Faith" (*Frühlingsglaube*). Both the act of citation and the source of the citation point against its realist reading. The act of citation shows Rudolf still assimilating all his experience to aesthetic models, to established, and romantic, conventions. He does not negate Ines's desire to become a representation; he repeats it. The source of the citation "Spring Faith," while apparently pointing to the hope for the new and for life, points instead to a desire for repetition and death, insofar as spring is also the season of Marie's death. In this respect, Rudolf does not negate Ines's desire to die, he repeats it, too. The "turn," then, turns out to be no turn at all: convention and repetition simply return in realist guise.

We see a similar subversion of the apparent realist impulse at the moment it is determined that Ines will live. The moment is meant to signify the successful struggle against fatal repetition and an escape from the established literary topos, but the word chosen to mark this moment—Saved! (*Gerettet!*)—simply assimilates Ines to a different topos.[44] And while this single word (*einziges Wort*) twice repeated might by itself escape notice, Rudolf's immediately following response is explicitly marked out as the "words of the poet": "Fortunately for her / It dragged her up" (*Es ward ihr zum Heil, / Es riss sie nach oben!* 299). Again, the act of citation shows that Rudolf's imagination will not allow us to escape from literary convention; and again, the source of the citation—Schiller's "The Diver" (*Der Taucher*)—points away from the apparent promise of life and toward a more disconcerting threat of repetition and death. Both examples are in a sense the functional equivalents of the narrator's "And it was again the time of roses" (301), one of Storm's stock literary motifs.[45] Rather than leading us out of the romantic, tropological, and repetitive, they seem to lead us right back into them—and so back, as it were, into the haunted garden.

Still, there seems to be sufficient evidence of a genuine realist impulse in the rest of the novella for the ending to pose a different kind of problem for us: namely, how can we read it as evidence for, and not against, "realism"? One way, of course, would be to say that in the end, romanticism proves itself to be a powerful, perhaps too powerful reality: that both psychology and literary discourse prove too deeply embedded in the romantic ever to be able successfully to escape its truths and its conventions; that in the end, the romantic proves itself the real. Another way would be to say that, even if the work's realist impulse should manage to escape romanticism, that does not mean that it could ever escape literary convention; that "reality" can never be reached, only another, "more authentic" stage of artificiality; that in the end, entrapment in the conventional proves itself the real. Each of these approaches has its validity and truth, and I hope to have respected these "realities" in my analysis. But the major thrust of the argument here requires us to take on the problem from a different direction, to seek "realism" from a different quarter; to ask, that is, how can we read the ending of the novella in the small garden as evidence for the overcoming of the illicit urge for repetition and re-presentation?

We find the beginnings of an answer to this question when we consider the other designation for the small garden operant in the story. Whereas Rudolf refers to the garden as Marie's grave (*Grab*), and in this sense as a garden of the past (*Garten der Vergangenheit*), Nesi consistently refers to it as "Grandmother's garden," and so in this other sense as a *Garten der Vergangenheit*.[46] In this respect, we should note that it is not only Ines who wants to enter the garden, but also, and in fact first, Nesi; it is also Nesi who first identifies for Ines the gate "to Grandmother's garden," and who when asked "And to whom, then, does the garden now belong?" replies "'To us!' . . . as if that were self-explanatory" (281). But nothing in the story is less self-explanatory than what is meant here by "us." For the designation "Grandmother's garden," by Nesi, reminds us that there are actually two competing notions of succession at work in the tale; and this in turn alerts us to the possibility of two competing structures of desire, repetition, and possession at work as well.[47]

Once our attention is turned toward Nesi, other details in the description of her character take on added significance. Nesi is the first major figure introduced, and Nesi is the first one to enter the "twilit room":

To one side, above the sofa, a Venetian mirror shone like silver on the dark-green velvet wall-hanging. In this solitude it seemed intended solely to reflect the image [*Bild*] of a fresh bouquet of roses that stood in a marble vase on the table by the sofa. But soon the small dark head of the child also appeared in its frame. (272)

In a narrative in which mirroring plays such a crucial role, it is quite telling that the first mirroring should be of Nesi. Moreover, the details of "image"/ "small child's head"/ "in its frame" depict the mirroring as in some ways similar to becoming a picture, especially a portrait; and of course, the first character we see try to climb into a, or rather the, portrait is again Nesi. Like the reference to "Grandmother's garden," these details foreground for us the way in which Nesi, and not just Ines, is cast into the role of successor, replacement, or substitute for Marie. And as the fact that the rose in the mirror-image is about to be stolen by Nesi suggests, the competition between these two patterns of repetition is not necessarily a simple or innocent one; and this in turn warns us that the rose motif throughout, and the "time of roses" at the end, might not prove so simple or innocent, either.

But first, we need to note that this mirroring relation vis-à-vis Marie is not the only mirroring relation in which Nesi is involved. At the very end of the story, Ines reveals to Rudolf that she has discovered something:

> "Just take the first letter of my name and put it at the end. Then what does it become?"
>
> "Nesi!" he said smiling. "What a wonderful coincidence." (302)

The transposition, or reversal, of the *i* neatly secures an identity, or rather mirror-identity, not only between Nesi and Marie but also between Nesi and Ines. Two points need to be stressed. First, Ines's "discovery" points to an extremely complex pattern of (illicit) mirrorings *across* generations that competes with that complex pattern of (illicit) mirrorings between the wives of the same generation. But second, the *non*discovery, the *non*recognition until the very end by the main characters of this quite obvious mirroring in the names points to an equally complex pattern of suppression in the story. We have similar indices of suppression and nondiscovery at the beginning as well. In the opening scene, Nesi barely manages to catch the drop of blood pricked from her arm by the stolen rose—"for it had almost fallen on the pattern [*Muster*] of the precious table-cover" (272). Moments later, she is again shown effacing the traces of her crime (or complicity) when, after putting the rose in the portrait over the desk, "she quickly climbed back down and, with her handkerchief, carefully wiped the traces of her feet from the desk-top" (273). This conspicuous effacement of Nesi's illicit involvement from the pattern (*Muster*) and writing surface is essential to an understanding of the story. For in a tale ostensibly and properly about doubles, there seems to be an almost compulsive evocation of triples: from the house clock that always strikes twice but is still crowned by three gilded knobs (271), to the title, which seemingly hides behind it the double theme, but actually hides in it the triple one. In a complex way, the story keeps revealing a pattern it wants to conceal, and telling a tale it does not want told.

The general outline of the tale, and the reasons for its repression, are not difficult to discover. When the pattern of substitution in which child replaces mother repeats features properly belonging to the pattern in which wife replaces wife, it becomes properly suspect. We have such an "improper" repetition in the first description of Ines and Nesi together: "Her hair and eyes were almost as dark as those of the child, whose stepmother she had become; indeed, at a fleeting glance one might have taken her for the actual mother, if she had not been too young for that" (275). The logic here is striking: what keeps the mother/daughter identity between Ines and Nesi from working is that they are actually *too* much alike, *too* identical in their attribute of youth. This alerts us to the somewhat disconcerting fact that Rudolf has married a woman who resembles, and so repeats, not so much his first wife as his child.[48]

Once we look closely, however, we see that Rudolf's desire has always tended toward children, and equally important, that these children have always been sexually charged.[49] For example, when Rudolf first sees Marie, she is "the barely fifteen year-old girl . . . and the *child* with the blond braids had carried off the thoughts of the serious *man*" (285, my emphases). Marie retains her childlikeness after she becomes wife to this "man": her blond braids "like a crown of youth" and her blue eyes-of-a-child (*Kinderaugen*) are the distinguishing features to her portrait (273). Similarly, Ines is only thirteen—just two years younger than Marie—when she has the *Marienbild* dream that reveals her sexual desire. And although Nesi is only eleven—just two years younger than the dreaming Ines—Lorenz has shown how the opening image of the pricked red blood and stolen rose mark her, too—even especially—as a sexually vital child.[50] The persistent tendency of Rudolf's desire to cross generational bounds; the complex (and often unrecognized, or repressed) pattern of mirrorings across generations that competes and colludes with the pattern of mirrorings between the wives; and finally, the recognition of the erotic nature of Nesi and the (again repressed, effaced) "crime" or robbery associated with her sexuality—altogether, these indices suggest that in an involved and indirect way, the tale not told, the repetition not revealed, partakes of the pattern of incest.[51]

Like most realist writers, and unlike the romantics, Storm rarely wrote about incest per se.[52] However, patterns of incest do appear in a number of his other novellas; when they do, they tend to be between fathers and daughters; to be indirect and deferred; and to occur in conjunction with several other patterns also operant in *Viola tricolor*. One example is *A Corner of the Forest*, the counterpiece to *Viola tricolor* in which the movement from representation to reality succeeds, as the painting is repeated in the concluding action. In a coda to the story, Kaspar-Ohm claims that Richard's lover, Franziska, "was his own blood," and outlines Richard's strategies for concealing this. Another character notes that the facts contradict the claim but still finds it "a powerful story"; and we are certainly required to consider why Storm would want to introduce the incest motif, especially since it has no factual basis in the story.

The novella in which incest plays the most explicit role is *Eekenhof*, one of Storm's most complex works and one that also plays with a constellation of motifs similar to that found in *A Corner of the Forest* and *Viola tricolor*. Like both, *Eekenhof* joins the themes of the "painting coming true" and the "first beloved repeated in the second." However, it complicates the association, and not least by splitting the function of the first beloved/wife between two women. The first, actual wife dies in childbirth but lives on in a portrait that haunts the house, as well as in a son who resembles her. The second woman, a mistress taken before the protagonist's, Hennike's, second marriage, also dies in childbirth, and leaves a girl-child in whose eyes her own eyes are repeated and live on (even as the eyes of the first wife are repeated and live on in the portrait). Hennike's relationship to his second wife and her children is completely loveless; all his desire is directed at this girl-child, in whom he loves her dead mother. His incestuous desire for repetition is ultimately frustrated, but only by another repetition that proves equally incestuous: under the aegis of the portrait, the two children of these two "first" women develop a relationship and flee together.

There are a number of ways to approach the function of incest, or the incest taboo, in Storm's writings, and perhaps in poetic realism in general. One would be to describe incest as an *Urfabel* that his realism attempts to free itself from and not repeat. In this approach, incest would function as a traditional (and perhaps even fairy-tale) plot that threatens to overtake and conventionalize the "reality" of the narrative world. The realist task would be to deform this plot and to realize a different story. Another way—the way I adopted in my analysis of Stifter's *The Mountain Forest*—would be to describe incest as a desire for sameness, where desire is directed at a mirror-image and fails to recognize the reality of the other. In this approach, the realist task would be to disrupt the mirroring pattern, to redirect desire away from the sameness of the imaginary and toward the difference—that is, the reality in difference, of an other.

Both the literary and the psychological are productive ways of describing the function of incest in Storm's works. Both conceive of incest as presenting the problem of repetition, and the overcoming of incest as the realization of difference; both together secure the association of (literary) convention and (psychological) desire we have pursued throughout; and both justify the association of the incest motif with those other motifs of repetition with which we find it here, namely the "picture coming true" and the "first beloved repeated in the second." However, the specific form of incest on which Storm tends to focus (father/daughter) reminds us that we also need to consider incest in the context of another of his repetition motifs, namely the repetition of and across generations within a family. This pattern of repetition has certain unique features that introduce different concerns, among them that of a future, and not just present, dimension.

As Holub points out, Storm seems to have had some rather set, semi-Darwinian ideas about heredity; Lorenz notes that certain constellations of figures (*Figurenkonstellationen*) tend to be repeated in his stories across generations.[53] Certainly Storm was very concerned with the problem of generations, and particularly the way in which natural succession could become unnatural repetition. The repetition across generations could be either positive or negative. For example, in both *The Mirror of Cyprianus* and *In the Castle*, the later generation repeats the pattern of an earlier generation, and in repeating it reverses an original wrong and so allows a "happy ending." In *Aquis submersus*, the story surrounding Katharina's ancestress is repeated in her own experience, even as the ancestress's eyes are repeated in those of the dead child.[54] The repetition in effect amounts to an evil curse, or fate, that dominates and determines the present (and future). (All three stories play with both pictures/mirrors and repeated names as well.) What is important to note is that in both cases, both the positive and the negative, the repetition propels the story out of the realistic and into the romantic, either in the form of a fairy-tale happy ending or of a supernatural, tragic fate. And in both cases, desire is decidedly not free, but rather condemned to desire the same, and so to repeat a primal, familial pattern.

In some ways, the incest impulse seems merely an intensified, compounded example of this "antireal" desire for one generation to repeat another: for natural succession, which should include difference (in both plot and desire) to become unnatural, romantic re-presentation.[55] Another example of this desire can be seen in *In the Neighbor's House to the Left*, where it occurs in conjunction with the same constellation of motifs found in these other works; but this time, significantly, the desire is explicitly thwarted. In the story, the grandfather of the narrator possesses a miniature copy of a portrait of his first beloved, which he keeps wrapped up in "a symbolic burial," and whose subject is presumed dead. Years later, the narrator finds both the original picture and the original, still living subject in the house next door. This neighbor is filled with a desire for repetition that expresses itself in the conflicting wish to make her heir either her niece, who resembles her, or the descendant of her first beloved, whose resemblance to the narrator first attracts her to him. The first option would allow for a repetition/fulfillment of her own, realized life-pattern, the second for a repetition/reversal of her own original wrong: both would inscribe on the succeeding generation a set plot and pattern of desire. While not actually or directly incestuous, the operant pattern and desire pose the same basic threat: the narrator feels himself to be somehow both her grandchild and the representative of her youthful love (*Jugendliebe*); and the motif of inheritance (*Erbe*) merely casts in economic terms what in, for example, *Eekenhof* is cast directly in biological and erotic terms.

In this case, however, the narrator frustrates the desire for repetition. He deceitfully denies his resemblance (and identity) with her youthful love, and so denies and escapes his neighbor's inheritance; and because the old woman dies soon after, before her will can be altered, the niece escapes her inheritance, too. She marries a man different from both her forebear's chosen husband and wronged *Jugendliebe*, moves away, and, apparently, lives happily. The happiness, however, is fundamentally distinct from the "happy ending" based on repetition/reversal seen in *The Mirror of Cyprianus* and *In the Castle*. Rather, this happy ending is based on difference, on thwarting the perverse mirroring of desire across generations, on freeing the future from the familial plots of the past.

All these considerations would be beside the point if we did not find evidence in *Viola tricolor* of similar incestuous desires for repetition that threaten to impose their plot-pattern across generations, and equally, evidence of similar realist efforts to thwart those patterns and desires. We do: but we need to note that this desire for repetition is not simply centered in Rudolf (as, for example, in the isolated elder figure of both *Eekenhof* and *In the Neighbor's House to the Left*). Instead, it is again essentially interpersonal; in fact, even as the "Ligeia impulse" proves strongest in Ines, so the incest impulse proves strongest in Nesi. And this introduces another way of reading Nesi's initial reluctance to make the equation and call Ines "Mother." Instead of being the protector of realistic differentiation, she becomes the aggressor in a desire for her own equation—in her own desire to become Mother, to become Marie.

The indications for Nesi wishing to become, or replace, Marie are different from those for Ines, but they cover a similar range. For example, we see Nesi carrying about her schoolbook (281); this recalls not only the depiction of the child Marie "at her school-work" but also Marie's role as the inspirer of Rudolf's imagination—and desire. More tellingly, it is Nesi with her picture-book (*Bilderbuch*) who interrupts the intimate evening alone with Rudolf foreseen by Ines; and while Rudolf ends up with Marie, her picture, and his books, he first leaves with Nesi and her picture-book. The former mediates, or proleptically re-presents, the latter marital breach. Ines herself is not quite clear why she reacts so strongly to Nesi's disruptive presence: "She didn't know herself what all came over her now" (284). But to some extent, she seems subconsciously to realize that she is also competing with Nesi for her husband's (erotic) affections; and equally, that she is competing with Nesi for the role of successor to Marie.

The competition posed by Nesi's desire is even more explicit in relation to the role of "Mother." One of the first images of Nesi (recounted by Rudolf) is with her doll carriage, pulled by "the monster," Nero (278). The doll carriage explicitly portrays Nesi appropriating Marie's role as mother; but so implicitly does Nero. The figural language used to describe him, his role in Ines's dream, and Storm's use of the dog motif in other novellas: all point to Nero as embodying a basic, animalistic vitality, somehow inherited into but unfixed within the family structure.[56] And like the equally erotically figured rose, Nesi seems inappropriately to appropriate that vitality for herself: the yoking of this power (*Macht*) to the doll carriage merely doubles the figure by which Nesi attempts to assume Marie's role as mother.

The first efforts at reappropriation and frustration of Nesi's desire come in the brief scene placed, significantly enough, between the dream sequence and the childbed/deathbed scene. The placement of the scene suggests both the relation of Nesi's desire for repetition and Ines's, and the similar "realist" need for its disruption; but like Ines's desire, Nesi's is not easily untracked. Ines takes over Nesi's playroom and "the things still left from Nesi's babyhood [literally, "cradle-time": *Wiegenzeit*]" (294), which had become part of Nesi's doll playthings; that is, she reappropriates those figures of motherhood and Marie that Nesi had fantastically taken as her own. But Anne still finds Nesi like a controller (*wie ein Kontrolleur*), looking for "my cradle" (295); it remains pointedly unclear whether her claim to possession is as child or as "mother" to her dolls. When Anne then explains that the stork might be coming, Nesi feels herself insulted. She claims not to be a child and to know where children come from; she and father would both rejoice over the new child, except that "then of course the child would have no mother!" (295). Her pretensions to carnal knowledge have their comic effect, but they are nonetheless not completely innocent. Even as the designation "my cradle" proves double-edged, so too does the logic behind "the child would have no mother." It is not only that Nesi considers Marie as the only mother, and so cruelly excludes Ines. It is also that she considers herself as the only successor to the role of Mother, and so again excludes Ines: since she, Nesi, will not be the mother, the child will have none at all.

This is the tangle of competing desires for repetition between Nesi and Ines that leads Ines to say to Nesi at the gate to the garden, "[We] two must get in there and set things in order" (282)—the garden that is semanticized with two different patterns of succession, but whose roses have become so entangled that entry is impossible for either Nesi or Ines. It is not easy to trace exactly how that order is achieved, how the patterns are separated, then pruned and set aright; nor is it clear that order is completely achieved. However, some moments stand out that at least point to the effort to work things through. To begin, we note that Rudolf's "baby solution" turns out to be far more relevant to Nesi's crisis that to Ines's. Nesi is the one whom we see bent over the cradle, and whose gaze and delight are redirected at the newborn child. In fact, for the rest of the narrative it is far more Nesi than Ines who seems occupied with the baby. Perhaps we can explain this by saying that, whereas for Ines the baby to some extent still represents repetition, for Nesi the baby introduces the principle of difference. That is, the baby frustrates her exclusive relationship with her father, in such a way that Nesi is forced to recognize herself as other than this other child. The constitution of herself as different (as sister) would also entail the recognition of her necessary difference from, and so inability to repeat, Marie; and it is perhaps the letting go of her desire to repeat Marie that allows Nesi to recognize Ines in all her difference, as "my dear, sweet Mama." The recognition of both her own and Ines's reality-in-difference also allows for the redirection of her desire, away from Marie and Rudolf and toward her new half-sister. The incestuous patterns of repetition and desire have been broken: desire is realigned within generational bounds; someone "different" is desired within each generation; and the familial plot has quietly dissolved its hold over the future generation.

Another crucial moment in the creation of order to the competing patterns of succession can be detected in the strategy of renarration (*wiedererzählen*).[57] Ines tells Rudolf that he must recount to her his past life with Marie, and adds, "And Nesi! I in turn will recount to her what I have heard from you about her mother—what suits her age, Rudolf, only that—" (300). Paradoxically, in the renarration repetition is employed in the effort against repetition. We note the disruption and reordering of relations: how Rudolf's recounting displaces Marie, as the portrait is removed from his private study to their "common room"; and how Ines's re-recounting also displaces Marie, as she situates herself between Nesi and her mother. In this way, telling and retelling establishes a new order of succession between Marie, Ines, and Nesi, that separates out the two different orders and reasserts the "natural" pattern of past, present, and future. And it does this by reasserting the principle of difference, and especially by reasserting it into the structures of desire. The story that Ines will repeat will not be the same as the one Rudolf repeats. Rather she will retell to Nesi only what suits her (implicitly sexual) maturity as child. Ines's insistence on Nesi and herself as different "receivers" of Marie, and on herself as the controller of that difference, point to a frustration of the unspoken, illicit desire for repetition and re-presentation of Marie in Nesi. And although this renarration is never actually enacted in the story, we do have its functional equivalent in the garden at the end, when "the joyful future [i.e., Nesi with the baby] . . . made its entrance into the garden of the past" (303)—but not before Ines, and Rudolf, have established their interceding presence.

Finally, we note that the refusal to name the newborn baby Marie (or Ines) also aims at disrupting an illicit repetition across generations; at denying the romantic, fairy-tale happy ending based on mirroring and sameness and insisting on one based on difference and freedom from the familial plots of the past. And perhaps we can even conclude that the realist impulse finds one last, oblique expression in the fact that, at the end, the baby still has no name and the last sounds we hear are "sounds that were not yet words" (303). Not only has the present struggled successfully to overcome the dominating conventions of the past; the future is also left undetermined, unbound by the language and formulae of the present "realist" world.

# DOUBLE-DEALINGS

Trading Places in Meyer's 'The Marriage of the Monk' ('Die Hochzeit des Mönchs')

> Truly I saw, and seem to see it still:
> a body with no head that walked along
> the same as the others of that sad herd;
> He held the severed head up by the hair,
> swinging it like a lantern in his hand,
> and as it looked at us it said: "Oh me!":
> Of his own self he made himself a light,
> and they were two in one, and one in two—
> how this can be, he knows who rules.
> —*Inferno*, XXVIII, 118–26

> Why can't we lead our own life under our own warm sun?
> Why this nebulous phantom of government, which restricts our very breath?
> —*The Marriage of the Monk*

> Good God, Colonel, you are lying up there under a pall with seven fatal wounds, and here you are conducting a conversation with me! Are you doubled? Is that reasonable? Is that logical?
> —*The Shot from the Pulpit*

Midway through C. F. Meyer's novella *The Marriage of the Monk* (*Die Hochzeit des Mönchs*, 1883/84), the ruler Cangrande Scaliger exchanges places with his narrator-guest, Dante. Cangrande takes him by the hand and leads him to his own place by the fire: "'It befits you,' he said, and Dante did not contradict him."[1] For his part, Cangrande takes Dante's vacated stool and watches him as he continues his narration. This is arguably the only real action or event in the novella, or rather, in its frame. As such, it invites some crucial questions. What is at stake in the exchange of places? Why does it take place just at this point in the narrative? What does it have to do with the story Dante is telling? with the story Meyer is telling? And since this is our special concern, let me also add the question: What can it tell us about the realism, or rather, the poetic realism of which this novella is such a central, if eccentric example?

To begin we can note how, at least indirectly, the principle of exchanging places characterizes the chief feature, and problem, of Meyer's peculiar variant of poetic realism—namely, of his so-called historical realism. Rather than grounding itself in the depiction of contemporary and local characters and events, Meyer's realism enacts a displacement, or transference, to a remote historical setting, usually that of the Renaissance or Reformation, although sometimes, as here, to the Middle Ages. This deployment of history is usually considered to contribute a certain objectivity to Meyer's writing: so, for example, the authenticity to the figures of Ezzelin, Petrus Vinea, and Friedrich II in the story, or of Cangrande and Dante in the frame, establishes an objective, historical basis for Meyer's tale.[2] However, such authentic characters do not exclusively dominate either the story or the frame, but rather in each case share the stage with obviously invented figures, including the story's protagonist, Astorre. Clearly, then, objectivity alone cannot account for the realist intent of Meyer's use of history.

A more adequate account for the realism to Meyer's use of history avoids the issue of objectivity and foregrounds instead the principle of exchange inherent to the displacement into the past. Historical reality, after all, consists of more than just authentic figures, settings, and facts. It also includes the emotions and intentions that motivate and govern those figures and connect those facts.[3] Much like his contemporary Nietzsche, Meyer was aware that this motivation is largely the invention or interpretation of the contemporary writer, whose fiction constructs the forces moving the figures and connecting events, and so comprises their significance, that is, their reality. He was also aware that this motivation—or regulation—is more or less displaced, or transferred, from the writer's own present back into the place of his historical representation.[4] As Meyer puts it at the beginning of his first novella, *The Amulet*, "I translate old and yellowed pages into the language of our time." While such an "exchange" undoes any effort to ground Meyer's historical realism in some ideal of objectivity, it does allow us to reformulate the issue of his realism in other terms—in terms very close, in fact, to those we developed to describe Stifter's chiastic projection of his social program into, and then out of, the natural realm in the preface to *Many-colored Stones*. First, even as Stifter's chiastic tactic had us look for his "realism" in the normative ideals or laws (*Gesetze*) governing his representation of Nature, so does Meyer's principle of exchange allow us to look for his realism in the invention, or perhaps better, in the controlling motivation to the historical figures and course of events itself; that is, to consider the question of what constitutes realistic motivation or, more generally, what is the real motivation governing or regulating the events in the novella.[5] And second, even as Stifter's tactic had us look for the "laws" as proper to the social rather than the natural sphere, so too does Meyer's procedure allow us to look for that realistic motivation as proper to the narrating present rather than the narrated past. Finally, even as Stifter's practice forced us to consider why the projection into the natural realm might prove necessary for the realization of his social program, so does Meyer's practice require us to consider how or why the historical displacement might be necessary for the realization or representation of his present reality.[6]

Despite this high degree of congruence to the general terms of approach for Stifter's and Meyer's realisms, our initial response to this last-mentioned issue in Meyer's work leads us in a slightly different direction from the one we took with Stifter, and so too toward a slightly different model for realism. Certainly one reason for Meyer's practice of displacement can be found by considering his use of history not as primarily an approach to the real but rather its *avoidance*, that is, as an avoidance of the contemporary real. This formulation implies a more complex structure for Meyer's realism than one based simply on standards of "objectivity" or even objectified "normativity," but it also more fully motivates both the peculiar mix of fiction and fact to his poetic realism and his principle of exchanging places. Perhaps the best description of this alternative account comes in the story itself, in the description of Astorre just before his betrothal to Diana:

The pressure of the attention directed at him and the forms and demands of society that were, so to speak, palpable in the air, let him feel that he could not express the reality of things [*die Wirklichkeit der Dinge*], forceful and sometimes ugly as it is, but rather that he had to give it a mild and pleasing form. So he involuntarily kept himself in the middle between truth and good appearance and spoke irreproachably. (59)

With minor adjustment, this contemplation on truth, reality, and representation can be shown to apply to Meyer's own performance, his own realism. Paradoxically, we are told how the given, present reality of Astorre's situation prevents the simple representation of the "real"—*die Wirklichkeit der Dinge*—and necessitates instead its fictional displacement or veiling. And we note how realism is thus described as necessarily split, defined by its contradictory structure: an unspoken, unspeakable reality, a censoring reality, and a resultant representation between truth and fair appearance (*zwischen Wahrheit und schönem Schein*) that has its own claims to reality—a necessarily poetic reality. From this perspective, too, the principle of exchanging places proves central to Meyer's historical realism, even if in a way that stresses more the needed fiction to his realism than the realism to his fiction, and more the sense of involuntary compulsion than conscious control to his part in the exchange.

These are some of the more abstract ways in which the principle of exchanging places can be shown to characterize Meyer's own writing practice. A far more concrete example comes in the introduction of the figure of Dante as a substitute stand-in for Meyer's own role as narrator. This repetition, or transference, of the narrative act into the novella engenders the frame structure that comprises one of the novella's most notorious, and mannered, features.[7] However, as we know from the discussion of Stifter's *The Mountain Forest*, the frame structure itself also comprises one of the most characteristic, even defining features of many works of poetic realism, including many of Meyer's other historical novellas. In this instance, too, Meyer's tactic of exchanging places takes us simultaneously into questions about his novella in particular, and about realism in general.

There are a number of ways that the device of the frame contributes to the effect of realism. In relation to the embedded narrative, the frame conventionally, as both here and in *The Mountain Forest*, functions as the "real": as the setting into and against which the story proper is introduced and tested. The fact that in so many of Meyer's works the frame also reproduces the act of narration adds to the realistic effect in a manner quite different from that in Stifter, insofar as it self-consciously draws in the practice of writing and reading, or more generally, of narration and reception, which of course constitutes the actual, real condition of the story's production.

In addition to this, the frame itself often conveys a certain reality onto the main story. For instance, the narrative is sometimes presented as coming from a document that a character in the frame has found, read, or heard about; or as deriving from an oral report, either of an individual or of a folk tradition known by someone in the frame; or as remembered by a frame-figure, and reproduced as his or her own, subjective experience. Each of these arrangements contributes a certain credibility or authenticity to the embedded narrative; in fact, the arrangement actually reinforces the reality of both the narrative and the frame. This latter effect is often enhanced if, as in *The Mountain Forest*, certain details, settings, figures, or facts are repeated in both the story and frame: the exchange signals a common ground underlying both realms that further confirms the authenticity of each.[8]

In *The Marriage of the Monk*, however, this second realistic effect, that of the frame on the story, is not operant. Whereas the frame itself is presented as real—and its mode of representation accepted as realistic—the embedded narrative is not. When asked whether his story is "a true story . . . based on documents? Or a legend told by the people? Or an invention of your wreathéd brow?" (11), Dante does not answer directly, but the emphasis is clearly on the latter. As Meyer says, Dante functions more as inventor (*Erfinder*) than as narrator (*Erzähler*).[9] Moreover, the way that certain details and figures are repeated or exchanged between the story and frame does not immediately reinforce the effect of realism to the tale as, for instance, it does in *The Mountain Forest*: Dante borrows the names and relations of characters in the frame as his mode for inventing his story. This not only undercuts the authenticity of the figures in his narrative: it also tends to destabilize the reality of the figures in the frame, insofar as it constantly and self-consciously reflects their own fictive status in Meyer's novella.

Several critics, and most recently Holub, take this emphasis on invention as effectively negating the value of the novella for approaching questions of realism. While noting that the novella consistently focuses on the central issue of narration and representation, Holub claims that it comments "only marginally on the ability of the narrative to capture that elusive quantity we call reality."[10] To some extent, this position is unassailable: but to an equal extent, it seems beside the point of attack. What the narrative's status as invention does foreground is the very process of realistic invention, that is, motivation, or, as we've also called it, regulation. It foregrounds how that motivation or regulation is more properly a property of the narrating present (of the frame) than of the narrated story; and it foregrounds the key question of how the fictional displacement can uniquely represent or realize the present reality (of the frame). That is, it comments on almost all the issues that become central to realism once the simple ideal of objectivity or authenticity is abandoned—an ideal that even in cases such as Stifter's preface, where the subject matter is ostensibly completely nonfictional, we have long since given up.[11]

In any case, the unusual, fictive status of the embedded story in *The Marriage of the Monk* indicates some parameters for our opening inquiries into the realism at stake in the novella, on which I would like now more concretely to focus. Let me begin by asking: What constitutes the reality of the frame? What constitutes the principle of invention or motivation, and how is that principle related to the reality of the frame? and, How do both that frame-reality and that principle of invention incorporate and further the principle of exchange?

I

The most prominent and significant feature to the reality of the frame is its opening association of desire and narration. The first paragraph presents "a group of young courtiers of both the male and female sexes," sitting before a fire and around "an equally young ruler and two, fresh-glowing women" (7). We are apprised that "stories were being told with knowing looks [*bedeutsamen Blicken*] and barely suppressed laughter": that is, stories are exchanged along with glances, the former no less than the latter part of the erotic play, and the latter no less than the former part of the play of meaning.[12]

The arrival of the solemn Dante is initially in marked contrast to this sensuous play; however, the reigning principle of exchange accompanies him, too, and soon brings him into the equation of desire and narration. Cangrande tells Dante, "We are telling stories here [*Hier wird erzählt*]," and bids him exchange his weighty verses for the plaything of an entertaining story: "'Grant leave to the goddesses'—he no doubt meant the Muses—'and amuse yourself with these two lovely mortals'" (7), namely, with Cangrande's two female companions.[13] By trading his genre—one might say, his profession (and women)—Dante is asked to join in the association of narration and desire, in which the act of storytelling is, in its way, depicted as a form of double-dealing, or *Zweiweiberei*. Not only is Dante offered the same two women as inspiration for the "plaything" of his story as Cangrande takes for the "play" of his affections—an exchange based on a certain equatability—but the very act of narrating is depicted as a falling out of the customary, strict moral order that governs Dante's primary world—namely, the *Divine Comedy*—into a kind of trifling self-indulgence. The significance of this last point is further underscored a moment later, in the contrast between Dante's *Scholastik* and his present tale: the transfer in genres will also entail a transfer in the rules for judging and interpreting the actions and motives of the various characters; that is, it will entail different rules governing and regulating the story's reality.

The trade of genres is not the only way that the principle of exchanging places enters the scene with Dante, plays on the theme of desire, and determines the active conditions of the frame. Besides the implicit exchange with Cangrande (suggested by his offer of his female companions) there is also that with the fool, Gocciola, who, we are told, "saw in Dante his rival [*Nebenbuhler*] for the not particularly discriminating favor of the master" (8). Although here the perspective is attributed to Gocciola, Dante also experiences Gocciola as something of a displaced, distorted image of himself, as a double, and he experiences the same sense of threat and violation to his own position at the thought of their equatability. On the other hand, in seeming contrast to Dante's displeasure at the sight of Gocciola is his obvious pleasure in Ascanio's flattering address: "Do not disdain, you Homer and Virgil of Italy, to join in our harmless play" (8). However, it is the same logic of exchange that would delightfully identify Dante with Homer or Virgil and maliciously identify him with Gocciola. Both desire and threat are incited by the possibility of exchanging places,

Double-Dealings 177

and to mix in this play seems by no means as harmless as Ascanio initially assumes.

The same principle that engenders the petty pleasures and violences in the frame also engenders the stories being told. The common theme for the various tales is *plötzlicher Berufswechsel,* the sudden exchange of profession: when Dante asks, he is informed that two examples of the defrocked monk have already been told. In each, the narrator has told a story that reflects his or her person and desire: Germano that of the monk Manuccio, who leaves the cloister to become a soldier; and Issote that of the nun Helen Manente, who breaks her vows to reunite with a long lost lover.[14] That is, each narrates a tale that functions as something of a repetition, or projection: the principle of being able to identify or trade places with the character in one's tale simply extends the logic of desire and exchange that dominates the reality of the frame into the sphere of narration.

The significance of this logic (for both the novella and for realism) and its potential for both pleasure and violence emerge more clearly in respect to Dante's narrative. Dante proposes to develop his story out of a gravestone inscription that reads *hic jacet monachus Astorre cum uxore Antiope. Sepeliebat Azzolinus* (11). While the status of the inscription itself is an issue, falling as it does somehow between the frame and story, the more pressing issue is how Dante's starting point immediately calls for translation, interpretation, and development—that is, for motivation. As we quickly see, the primary basis for interpretation—even conflicting interpretations—seems to be the individual subject, who is however partially checked, or governed, by the outside authority of "history." So, for example, after one reading of the inscription by Cangrande's friend Antiope, Dante demurs and replies, "It has assumed a different form in my mind [*hat sich in meinem Geiste anders gestaltet*] and according to history is also improbable" (12). Perhaps more tellingly, when Dante offers his own, more generous interpretation, Cangrande declares, "Correct, you think as I do!" (12): his own interpretation of the significance, that is, the reality behind the inscription, is explicitly based on his understanding of Ezzelin, which in turn is based on his personal desire to identify with the character. "Reality" in the story seems from the outset to be a function of interpretation, based on the peculiar way the individual displaces himself, by way of desire, into the story. We might even say that reality is a function of desire and the logic of exchange—although again, not without the outside pressure of an historical or *geschichtlich* authority.[15]

Desire and the logic of exchange, and their role in creating a sense of reality, become in fact the ground for Dante's narratorial invention. After implying a substitute identity, that is an exchange of identities, between Cangrande and Ezzelin, Dante expands the tactic to strategy: "'As for the remaining figures in the tale,' he continued, with smiling threat, 'I will, if you allow it'—and he turned himself toward those sitting about him—'take them, too, out of your midst and give them your names; your inner lives [*euer Inneres*] I will leave untouched, for therein I cannot read'" (12). The complex of themes announced in this program is crucial for the subsequent course of Dante's narration. To begin, we note that whereas Cangrande feels flattered, Dante also hints at the threat to his procedure. Again, both pleasure and violation attend the possibility of transposition; but this time, the equally attendant issues of power and control are brought to the fore. That power and control, firmly linked with both desire and violation, should attend the project of imposed re-presentation we know already from the cases of her father and Clarissa, Aquilinus and Eugenia, and Rudolf and Inés; but Dante's relation with his audience proves notably more complicated in this regard, primarily because the centers of both desire and power prove more contested. We see this when Dante asks, "[If] you allow it [*ihr gestattet es*]?" and so focuses attention on the intricate weave of wills involved in his proposed exchange of places. On the one hand, the audience determines and desires its participation in the scheme, and so assumes responsibility for entering into the substitutive chain. On the other hand, this self-determination is obviously compromised by the commanding, even threatening position of Dante, who in asking his question also denies any possible answer: the audience is placed, as it were, "under the pressure of an outside will [*unter den Druck eines fremden Willens*]" (9) in entering into the system of exchange. However, it is neither the one nor the other, but rather both, the split condition of will and desire, that is key to Dante's narrative technique.

This is made clear in the last, most noted point to Dante's program, which again touches on questions of authority, namely in Dante's claim that "your inner lives I will leave untouched, for therein I cannot read." The claim is often accepted by critics, accepted in fact as a statement about realism: they cite the

Double-Dealings

limitation of narrative authority in reading the psychological makeup of other minds as evidence for Meyer's (or Dante's) rather modern realism, even perspectivism.[16] It is, that is, a realism based on an *inability* to trade places. However, the claim is just as often denied by critics, denied in fact as a disingenuous deceit on Dante's part; they see it as a feint aimed at disguising his power, which in the following course of his narration truly does "touch" the inner lives of his audience.[17]

While admitting the latter point, I think we can still entertain the validity of Dante's claim; we can even entertain it as evidence for the realism at stake in the novella, although not in the usual sense. Dante's claim is true, that is, insofar as where the "touching" does occur, it results not from Dante's narration reading into his listeners' inner lives but rather from their reading their inner lives into his narrative: it is at least as much a result of their willing desire and identificatory participation as his perhaps sovereign authority.[18] Moreover, Dante's narrative strategy exploits this impulse for displacement, which is at once enabling and endangering for his auditors, as crucial to his achievement of the effect of realism.[19]

Of course, at first glance the opposite seems to be the case: that Dante's narratorial strategy of exchange is motivated more by malice than desire, depends more on his authority than their will, and aims more at breaking the illusion to his narrative than at effecting its realism. So, for instance in the first example of Dante's procedure, we are told, "In the midst of speaking, Dante sought out from among his listeners the genteel priest, who hid himself behind his neighbor." Dante immediately transposes him into the story as "a wretched creature, an apostate monk named Serapion" (19). The priest seems the unwitting victim of Dante's revenge, punished for his previous, incautious remarks regarding monks: his own desire seems hardly to figure in the equation. And yet, interestingly enough, Dante picks Serapion for a role as something of a would-be double—for Astorre, his brother-monk (*Mitbruder*). The exchange of places that Serapion himself would effect is based on a certain (jealous) desire; equally important, it structurally repeats the exchange between the nameless cleric (in the frame) and his double, Serapion. Dante underscores the structural repetition by straightaway casting Serapion in the role of reader, in fact, as reader of his double. Dante describes how "he lay in wait for Astorre returning home, in order to scrutinize Astorre's face and *therein to read* [darin zu lesen] what Astorre had decided to do for himself. His eyes devoured the woman [Diana]" (19, my emphasis). Desire, doubling, and reading openly interplay in this description, where understanding a character and his motivations depends on wanting to exchange places with him, on reading one's own desire and self into his place—on repetition.

The example of Serapion also raises issues about Dante's authority as opposed to the cleric's self-determination: this is more acutely the case with Burcardo, Cangrande's majordomo, whom Dante also transposes into his tale: "[W]hen he now heard himself named and unexpectedly saw himself, life-size, in the mirror of the novella, he found this misuse of his honorable person insolent and thoroughly improper. . . . [W]hat the others suffered with a smile, he took as an offence" (44f.). Here Dante seems to exercise his power and authority over the powerless, even resisting Burcardo. Still, Dante's very authority and strategy depend on Burcardo, as listener, exercising a certain power of his own. At its simplest, Burcardo must be both willing and able to see himself in the mirror of the novella before Dante's supposed sovereignty can have any effect.[20] Nor is there any reason why this power of Burcardo, as listener, need remain so impotent.

The argument for how Dante's strategy of exchange breaks the illusion to his narrative is obvious: by continually and ostentatiously calling attention to the characters in his story as but fictive representations of his "real" models, Dante underscores the necessary invention to his tale. But the opposite effect is also operable, that of realism: and again, the effect is dependent on the movement of desire within the established structure of exchange. This is best seen in relation to the pair of women, Diana and Antiope, neither of whom hesitates to exercise that readerly power from which Burcardo apparently only passively suffers. Each is intimately involved with her fictive representation: each willingly projects herself and her own desire into the place of her namesake. And it is just this displacement that allows the listener to determine the emotions, intentions, and actions of the character. It is the animating, interpreting projection of her own inner life into the somewhat flat, cartoonish fiction that makes the latter "real" to its auditor.[21] So Antiope is able to anticipate and interrupt Dante with her declaration of Astorre's love for her namesake (63). Her own displaced desire provides the basis for her determination of the real motivations, or forces, governing the tale.

Diana also, and at the same point, interrupts Dante with her interpretation of the story, based on her displaced identification: here too desire transferred is the basis for the realistic effect. Notably, her interpretation differs from Antiope's: the nature of the story's reality depends upon the reader's peculiar desire, self, or place. The result, of course, is a multiple or split reality, based on multiple desires, perspectives, and interpretations; a reality that in its very character as split and multiple has its own claims to realism.[22] More immediately important for us is that, on the basis of her desire and self, Diana claims a special authority over the reality of the story—a critical, readerly authority that directly challenges Dante's own narratorial control. She says, "[H]ave you not noticed, Dante, that Antiope is a little manipulator? You know little about women! In truth, I tell you," etc. (64). Desire and self-transference engender a specific authority, which in turn determines the truth and reality to the tale—although again, not unchecked by the outside pressure of Dante's own challenged, but hardly eliminated, narratorial privilege.

We need also to note that the real-making effect to the exchange between the frame and story works in the other direction as well, insofar as the substitutive mode of "reading" the tale allows for an interpretation, or more simply, for a recognition of the reality behind the reality of the frame. Indeed, this self-revelatory effect to the "mirror of the novella" first completes Dante's hermeneutic strategy and might well be considered the most important, potential realism at work in the exchange; it is, as it were, the functional equivalent to the chiastic strategy for achieving the realist effect we first described for Stifter's preface in chapter two, and have seen deployed in each of the works subsequently discussed.[23] We see this effect indirectly here, in how the process of entering into the story has brought out the true feelings of the two women for each other, a truth or reality initially repressed in the frame and only released through the fiction, or rather, through the displaced investment of reality into the fiction. We see it more directly in Cangrande, who in observing Diana transpose the fictional reality of the story back into the actuality of the frame suddenly comes to a recognition of his own, true desire—which interestingly deviates from that in the tale (64).[24] He realizes his greater attraction to his wife than her rival: he is brought to himself. Even as the selves and desires in the frame clarify, interpret, even create the reality of the fiction, so does the fiction clarify, interpret, even create the reality of the frame—including its selves and desires. And of course, both effects are consequences of the strategy of trading places.

11

Cangrande does not simply function as but another character in Dante's substitutive scheme. Rather, he plays a privileged role in it by virtue of both his power and his desire. Most notably, in his position as ruler (*Herrscher*) in the frame, Cangrande creates the conditions that necessitate the narrative strategy of substitution to begin with. That is, he establishes the initial rules governing expression—and repression: "[At] this court the most audacious speech concerning ecclesiastical matters was tolerated, even smiled at, but a frank or even incautious word concerning the ruler, his person or his politics, could be ruinous" (10). Cangrande's commanding, censoring authority prevents simple, immediate, free representation of the reality surrounding his person and, for him who would express it, necessitates a strategy of fictional displacement, or veiling; necessitates a detour around the reality to express the reality, a detour that as such has its own claims to reality, a necessarily displaced and unreal reality.[25] The circumstance, in fact, is identical to that of Astorre before his betrothal to Diana, which I already described as identical to that of Meyer's own historical realism; however, here the relation between reality and authority is made explicit. There we noted how realism is necessarily split, defined by its contradictory structure: here we note how the same holds true for authority.[26] Dante's narrative authority, for all its apparent sovereignty, still operates under the pressure of Cangrande's, which first requires, even invents, the strategy of displacement; and Cangrande's tyranny, for all its apparent sovereignty, is nonetheless subjected to Dante's, whose power might be described as that of hermeneutic displacement itself—that is, the power not only to move reality along a substitutive chain but also thereby potentially to expose the repressed reality to the repressor himself.

In keeping with his privileged position, Cangrande is not only responsible for the initial strategy of displaced representation to the story. Dante also makes him—or partly makes him—responsible for the regulative forces shaping the story. This is related to, but of a different order from, the control over the story exercised by each of the principal listeners. Whereas their authority is basically limited to determining what motivates, or characterizes, the psychological reality of the individual characters, his is expanded to include what motivates or governs the entire narrative world. We see this modestly, but significantly, when, after announcing his narrative theme, Dante asks Cangrande, "But tell me, my Patron and Protector, how does such a thing end?" (9). Cangrande gives both the answer—"Necessarily badly"—and the gnomic truth that motivates or justifies the proposed, governing necessity. And we see it quite patently when Dante makes Ezzelin Cangrande's representative in the story, Ezzelin who assumes command, both actively and reflectively, for what controls events in the story. What interests me at this point is how, even as Dante assigns Cangrande a kind of absolute, overriding power, he also destabilizes or splits it with his own. So, for example, Cangrande at one point playfully tries to determine the further course of events: "But Dante took from him the word" (44). In respect to the narrative world itself, then, the conditions of control are also presented as split, incomplete, and conflictual.

This is not the only way that Cangrande is uniquely split in Dante's narration: he is also, uniquely, split between two characters in the story, doubled in his doubling. As is made clear through his place between the two women, Cangrande is transposed not only into Ezzelin but also into the protagonist, Astorre. Thus, he is given not only authority over the general rules that govern the story; he is also given the desire that, perhaps in a different sense, governs and moves the story. What concerns me is not simply identifying the double displacement but also noting what that doubling indicates for the operant conditions of the story, namely: how authority and desire are split from and even in conflict with one another and with them, how the self too is split and in conflict with itself.

In mentioning the matter of Cangrande's authority and of his double place in the story, we touch on another, or rather the, central point to the frame: Dante's own authority and his own place in the story. Critics often stress Dante's absolute narrative power (cf. Dante as Fate [*Parze*], 8) and pair it with that of Cangrande. They also usually stress Dante's likeness to either Ezzelin (on the basis of commanding authority) or Astorre (as defrocked monk), or to both, which in turn leads them to argue for an involved, double doubling with Cangrande in the characters of the tale.[27] But in their zeal to establish these truths, such critics efface a more important one: that Dante denies, or at least does not openly acknowledge, either his authority over or his identity in the tale. We might even say that, even as Dante uses Ezzelin and Astorre to displace Cangrande, so he uses Cangrande to displace himself from his own system of displacement—without however admitting that this is what he is doing. This denial, or repression, of the reality of his own prerogative and place is its own reality, and it needs to be recognized if we are to follow the course of the novella. It is in many ways the most remarkable aspect of the frame: Dante looks at the others, but he does not see himself.[28]

The denial of his narratorial control expresses itself not only in Dante's deferral of place to Cangrande (or for that matter, to his listeners) but also concretely in his narrative method. Far from adopting an omniscient, privileged standpoint, Dante narrates from a perspective conspicuously occluded. He denies any special power to interpret or evaluate the actions or psychologies of his characters, either refraining from judgment altogether or offering multiple, alternative possibilities. He even sometimes denies any special access to information about his tale that might clarify its significance. Hans and Rosemarie Zeller take this renunciation of narratorial privilege and control as absolutely central to the story's realistic effect: it results in that ambivalence and perspectivism that most critics, especially since Jeziorkowski, have identified as the signature of Meyer's realism.[29] But without denying the possible, eventual truth to this claim, I think we can still see that in this particular novella the techniques of occlusion, ambivalence, and perspectivism first function as a dodge, a feint disguising Dante's actual sovereignty over his invention.[30] Put more pointedly, we can say that the realistic effect is based on an initial repression of the reality of author-ity; it is a fiction devised to obscure the source of the fiction.[31] This is after all what the unique emphasis on Dante's story as an invention rather than "recounting" makes evident, and intrinsic.

Equally important, it is not only his privileged, objective authority that Dante denies but also his own subjective engagement in his narrative. As the

Double-Dealings 185

Zellers put it, "[We] are dealing with a text without a speaker," or more precisely, "[I]ts subjectivity consists in the refusal of subjectivity."[32] But as we've seen in the examples of the two stories told before Dante's, the story told seems always to reflect something about the person, and desires, of its narrator. It functions as something of a transference, or projection, of the subject onto his or her material—as an exchange. (As the character Ascanio puts it here, "The temperament of the ruler colors court and city" [36], and that of the narrator colors characters and plot.) Moreover, Dante's own narrative strategy vis-à-vis his audience exposes that the motivation to the story's events depends on the individual's self, desire, and identificatory participation; that is, their "reality" is an effect of the individual's projected or transferred subjectivity. But whereas these are also explicitly the initial conditions of Dante's own narration—it is after all "an invention of his wreathéd brow," and the dependence of its rendering on his own person is underscored early on when he declares, "It has assumed a different form in my mind [*in meinem Geiste*]" (12)—nonetheless, Dante denies these very conditions, conditions that he himself in large part sets up. He does not see himself in his tale.[33] But what is crucial here is that the tale he undertakes to tell is precisely that of a self-less soul (*selbstlose Seele*, 10). We might say that the initial point of identity between Dante and his protagonist, Astorre, is nonidentity, nonself. And as we will see, it is not without significance that this nonself status is identified, in the case of Dante and Astorre, with both nondesire and nonauthority.

III

The correspondence between Dante and Astorre over the issue of nonself is but one of the ways that the conditions of narration are transposed into the narrative itself. What we need now to address more fully is how Dante's story itself repeats, or represents, the conditions of narration and principles of invention; how in fact these same conditions and principles motivate the narrative, govern its course, and constitute its reality.[34] But let us first be clear on two points. First, the conditions of narration, as we have seen, are basically twofold. There is Dante's strategy of exchange, with its consequent, complex engagement of his audience's desires, selves, and various authorities; and there is the (would-be) denial of this exchange and engagement, both on the part of the somewhat resisting auditors, who would deny their willing participation in Dante's scheme, and more significantly on the part of Dante himself, who would apparently deny his own subjection to his scheme at all. Both the scheme and its denial can be expected to help shape the course of Dante's narrative; for the same reason, its governance can be expected to be both (self-consciously) overt and (unconsciously) disguised—to be in fact a reality that the story both expresses and refuses to name.[35]

Second, the repetition, or displacement, of the conditions of narration into the story itself—that is, the repetition of the principle of repetition, the displacement of the system of displacement—not only provides a way for understanding the narrative's (hidden) motivations and reality. It also, crucially, provides a reflective way for eventually understanding the narrator's motivations and reality, insofar as these too remain hidden, unconscious, or repressed by him. It is precisely in this function of *double* exposure that the principle of trading places is most decisively at work in shaping reality and affecting a poetic realism in Meyer's novella—in shaping the reality of *both* the story and the frame, where the reality of the frame affects the fiction of the story, which then in turn can again affect the reality of the frame. The chiastic, mutually implicating arrangement is, of course, basically the same as that which we encountered in both Stifter and Keller—Stifter in his employment of the virgin woods vis-à-vis Johanna and Clarissa, and Keller in his use of Aquilinus's statue vis-à-vis Eugenia. But Meyer's text also introduces a crucial, new self-reflective dimension into the equation which, we'll see, allows for a slightly different realist effect to emerge. Moreover, this self-reflective function or effect of the doubling in Meyer's, or rather, Dante's tale is not a singular, but instead a repeating, ongoing effect; and as such, it can be expected to open up the possibility for further exchanges and further (re-)shaping of the story's reality, not least through the move from denial to recognition, from unconscious to conscious representation of the reality governing the narration.

Let me begin with the first point, the first exchange: how the issues that animate the frame and constitute its principles of invention also comprise the reality of Dante's story. The simplest, most significant point is that Dante's tale is actually about the process of transference or substitution; that just as his narrative strategy is based on characters trading places, so is his story.³⁶ The process in fact begins before the start of the story, or rather, it is the reason the story begins where it does. Umberto Vicedomini has suffered the loss of his first wife. Her death initiates the need to find a substitute, and this substitution is the occasion for the wedding party that opens the tale. That is, the origin of the story is itself displacement, re-placement, and re-presentation; it is the installation of Diana Pizzaguerra as substitute (*nur als Ersatz*, 17) that motivates or structures the action.

This beginning of the story with the replacement of the dead first wife links it, of course, with *Viola tricolor*; but unlike in Storm's novella, the process of substitution does not end with the one wife. Rather, the same basic pattern immediately repeats itself at the moment of the wedding party. Indeed, as a pattern, it can only define itself by repeating, by continuing its chain of substitutions. By the accident that brings the party out of balance (*aus dem Gleichgewicht*, 13), the (shadowy) brother dies, and this initiates the need to find a (shadow) substitute for him. The subsequent exchange is the occasion for the sudden change of profession of Dante's story, for Astorre's displacement into "the world . . . which follows its own laws [*die ihre eigenen Gesetze befolgt*]" (25).

Moreover, the same "laws," the same regulating pattern, also take hold of Diana, the substitute bride, and move her even further along the chain of displacement. The same stream and accident that kill Umberto "kill" her, too; when she is pulled back into life, she straightaway exchanges clothes with a poor but sympathetic woman among the bystanders (15), who then in turn makes off with the bridal gown for herself. It is in these newly traded, substituted clothes that Diana presents herself to Astorre, a twice substituted bride to the newly substituted husband. And the pattern is repeated yet again with Astorre: at the moment of his "change of profession," he too exchanges clothes to signal his new, displaced position, donning the outfit of his dead brother, "whose size and build were approximately the same as his own" (31). As with Diana, his own discarded clothes are immediately and in turn taken on by another, in this case by the fool Gocciola. That is, the very logic of the substitutive chain that seems so uncontrollably to generate exchanges sequentially seems also to generate doubles simultaneously.³⁷ Both are expressions of the same, representative principle—in fact, of the same representative principle also active in generating Dante's narrative.

A substitutive chain, then, that carries all the various characters and events along, seems to determine the mode in which things link (*die Dinge sich verketten*, 26): where an intervening death, either real or figurative, initiates an exchange between a "real" self and its displaced substitute, even when the original self is already in some sense a substitute;[38] or from another perspective, where an intervening death initiates an exchange between an original, real, and now absent object of desire and its displaced, substituted representation—even when the original object was also already in some sense a substitute.[39] The pattern seems to define a certain constitutive movement to both self-identity and desire in the tale: however, none of the characters actually acknowledges that either his or her person or desire is directly, that is, really involved in the movement to the pattern. Thus, although the events proper are weddings and betrothals, we are told that Umberto did not love Diana, nor Diana him, and the same is true again of Diana and Astorre. Desire seems conspicuously absent from each exchange, as does a willing, identificatory participation in one's allotted, displaced place. Rather, each exchange is experienced as only a forced, even somewhat malicious violation of one's self.

This lack—or more forcefully, this denial of either desire or self-will and self-investment, raises and keeps open the question of motivation and control, as to who or what governs or enforces the movement of the pattern itself. And in raising the question, it exposes another way in which the conditions of narration in the frame are repeated in those of the narrative proper. That is, not only is the strategy of exchange again at work: so too are its accompanying issues of desire, identification, authority—and denial.

We see this repetition right from the outset, in how Dante frames his theme; whereas he is given his general topic, or pattern (the sudden exchange of position), Dante himself poses the particular psychological, or narrative, problem that this topic properly entails. Not surprisingly (but also not explicitly), his posing of the problem reflects both his own, explicit narratorial practice and his own, implicit self-exclusion. In contrast to the just told tale of Helena Manente, whose displacement was enacted "out of the truth of her loving nature [*aus der Wahrheit ihrer verliebten Natur*]," Astorre's involves an exchange that occurs "for the sake of another, under the pressure of an other's will [*einem andern zuliebe, unter dem Druck eines fremden Willens*]" (9). The terms are familiar to us: the audience enters into its exchange (into the tale) under the pressure of Dante's authority, even as Dante invents his tale (= enters on his exchange) under the pressure of Cangrande's; both in their ways initially deny their own, willing participation in their displaced place in the tale. Similarly, we are familiar with the pattern of a given, immediate reality or "truth" that gets repressed by an "other" authority and displaced into a representative chain. The conditions of (fugitive) self-identity given here are clearly parallel to those given above for Meyer's realism and Dante's own narration. But of course, in the case of the frame, we saw that the exchange under pressure of an other's will did not preclude the active participation of the self and its desire, and in fact the exchange only became real, or true, when the latter occurred. And similarly, the initial repression of truth/reality did not preclude the expression of that reality through the process of displacement, which indeed was seen to present that truth for the first time.[40] In fact, in all cases, it was the split condition—of desire, authority, and reality or truth—that proved operable and decisive. However, it is just this complication that is revealingly denied in Dante's initial formulation; and it is just this denial that keeps the issue of authority, or governance, so conspicuous and unstable at the story's outset.[41]

We see this in the very first scene of Dante's story, in which the wedding party of the unloving (and not self-motivated) Umberto and Diana is depicted as floating down the river Brenta: "The bark moved along with its oars pulled up, relinquishing itself to the will of the river [*dem Willen des Stromes sich überlassend*]" (13). By focusing attention on the river itself, and ascribing to it a certain will, Dante first introduces all his characters as, so to speak, under the pressure of an other, outside force, that alone carries the story, controls and shapes the unfolding events, and initiates the story's upcoming exchanges.

The same image of an outside, controlling authority is also repeated in the juxtaposed figure of Ezzelin. Again we see the members of the wedding party yielding themselves to another, alien power, albeit here a human one. And as with the river, we also see Ezzelin, the all-powerful tyrant, depicted as responsible, as the sole author of the chain. So, for instance, Dante describes him as the original cause of the disaster (*Urheber des Verderbens*, 14); in the next scene, the elder Vicedomini says, "[Y]ou have killed these four of mine, no one other than you. . . . [Y]ou drag us all along your bloody track" (20). But unlike in the case of the river, in that of Ezzelin this outside, controlling force is itself portrayed as compromised, split, placed under the pressure of an other outside will. On the one hand, there are the outside, largely uncontrollable desires of those who yield to his tyranny; for although no one actually admits this, the accident clearly emphasizes the characters' will, their active submission to Ezzelin's rule, which in fact is precisely that which brings them "out of balance" and precipitates the ensuing displacements. On the other hand, there is the compromising pressure on his power applied by the other outside power, or reality, to which Ezzelin himself submits: in neither case does he have power over his own power. We see the latter point, for instance, in Ezzelin's rejection of Vicedomini's charge ("no one other than you") with the possibly questionable counterascription of Fate (*Schicksal*): we see it more concretely (and convincingly) in how Ezzelin's politically omnipotent power is always under another power, namely Friedrich's. The result is that, even as both selves and their objects of desire are continually split and displaced along a chain, with characters denying their willing, desiring participation, so too is authority over that chain, its selves, and desires, with characters denying their own control and the effect of their own active submission in constituting the governing force—and so also their responsibility for the resultant reality. And what is crucial, of course, is how exactly this reproduces the conditions of desire, volition, and authority governing Dante's narration itself, both in its actual, complex structure and in its covert, simplifying denial.

The question of authority, desire, and identity—or rather, the question of their denial—is most critically posed in relation to Astorre and his entrance into the substitutive chain. For even as Astorre is initially (if impossibly) defined by his renunciation of desire and self, so too would he be defined by his lack of will in trading places with his brother, Umberto. This is, after all, the operant condition for the story as Dante initially poses it; it is also the operant condition for Dante's own (denied) relation with his protagonist.

The effort to displace the authority for Astorre's exchange, or *Wechsel*, is rather general. The elder Vicedomini asks Ezzelin, "[G]ive him [Astorre] to me in place of the son whom you have murdered," thus explicitly requesting Ezzelin to assume responsibility for the substitutive exchange. But Ezzelin defers and says, "That is not my affair" (21). However, the elder Vicedomini has himself already worked to displace Ezzelin's authority, by introducing another one, namely, a writ from the Pope that authorizes the exchange. Here, too, we witness a certain displacement, or splitting, of governance, a decentering of control as the operant condition ruling—or not ruling—the story. It is under cover of this (split) authority that the elder Vicedomini exerts his own determining desire over Astorre, allowing Astorre to declare, "I submit to your will, Sir [*Ich bin euch zu Willen, Herr*]! Do with me what you want" (28), thus affecting his own displacement of power. That is, like the others, Astorre would define himself more by his passive submission to an outside force and the course of events than by his own active governance or responsibility. He too would experience the substitutive exchange only as a forced, even somewhat malicious violation of his self.

However, it is just this possibility that is uniquely denied to Astorre. For even as the Pope's textual authority intercedes at this moment to permit Astorre to renounce his vows—to renounce his renunciation—and enter into the chain, it still insists that the exchange be made by him of his own free will and as his own decision (*aus freiem Willen und eigenen Entschlüsse*, 20). And while the exact impetus for this directive is obscure, its effect is clear.[42] For although it manifestly disrupts both the general tendency of all the characters to displace authority onto another and the specific terms initially set by Dante for Astorre's pressured displacement, it nonetheless reestablishes the more complicated terms that we know explicitly from the frame as well as implicitly from the first, precipitating accident: that the individual's will, self, and desire are involved in the exchange, and that it is just this involvement that first makes the exchange real. (Thus, the directive truly is to renounce the renunciation, to acknowledge the denied self and its volition.) This is not of course to say that Astorre's "exchange" simply becomes an effect of his self-determination, his choice: the role of outside coercion is too prominent, too central to claim that. Rather, it is simply to impose, or restore, a decisive split to the real motivation at issue. Astorre both does and does not himself motivate or control his entrance into the substitutive chain, even as his entrance is both into himself and away from himself, into the position of re-presentation.

It is also important to note that this contradiction, or split, in control is represented as being as much internal as external to Astorre's person, and how this follows from the fact that his entrance into the real world of the story and his assumption of authority and self is simultaneously an entrance into and assumption of desire. Although the point is revealingly left largely unspoken, Ezzelin's catechizing of Astorre concerning his vows makes clear that the renunciation of self that Astorre now gives up was one of sexual desire, now admitted: that Astorre is released into the world to take himself a wife indicates the same. And this release of desire into the story and its protagonist yields a slightly different reason for the peculiar split of both will and self at issue in Astorre's entrance into the substitutive chain. Just after his father's death and his own betrothal to his brother's bride, we are told, "Now that he was again in control of his own will, the suspicion stole over him . . . that a dying man had taken advantage of his good faith." In the very next moment, "Unwillingly, almost with hostility, he turned his thoughts to the woman who had become his" (30). The juxtaposition of "again in control of his own will [*seines Willens wieder mächtig*]" and "unwillingly [*unwillig*]" underscores how, even when Astorre is in control of himself, he isn't: if in the first case Astorre sees himself manipulated by another's designs, namely his father's, into acting against himself, in the second we see Astorre still manipulated by an "other's" designs, namely those of his own unconscious, into acting against himself. We might say that so long as the entrance into reality and the self is simultaneously an entrance into desire, that is, the unconscious, to come into one's will and self is nonetheless to remain under the pressure of an other's will. We might also say that the basic, split structure of will and desire that Dante makes the basis of his narrative strategy he makes the basis of Astorre's self-identity as well.

If (unconscious) desire has a decisive effect on Astorre's self-identity and control, it has no less decisive, and split, an effect on the intended object of his desire—and again in ways that reflect Dante's narrative practice. Astorre looks at Diana and finds her, especially with her stark love of the truth (*harte Wahrheitsliebe*), far more real, or *wirklich*, than his expectations and the delicate, apparitional figures of legend (*die zarten Erscheinungen der Legende*, 30f.). And just because she is more real, she is also less desirable. That is, the given, present reality of the object defeats, prevents, or represses the expression of true desire, or rather, it moves it along, necessitates its displacement, its survival in a form more expressive of its need for unreal fiction, an unreality to desire that in some ways constitutes its reality.[43] Two points are of special concern to us here. First, we note how this structure of desire repeats that of self-identity: even as in respect to his own person, Astorre finds himself displaced by (and against) his will from "the truth of his nature" into a representative chain, so in respect to the would-be object of his desire Astorre finds himself displaced by (and against) his desire from "the stark truth" into a representative chain. And second, we note how this structure also repeats that of both Meyer's and, more important, Dante's poetic realism. Not only do their peculiarly displaced, fictive mode of realism reflect the peculiar (displacing, unreal) reality of desire; the representation of desire in the tale also exactly represents the structure of narration that governs the fiction.

The structure of desire exposed here in relation to Diana can also be shown to condition Astorre's attraction to Antiope: here too the principle of exchanging places can be seen to govern the course of events. Antiope first enters the scene for Astorre as he sits thoughtlessly and dreamily eating one berry after another, listening to his two childhood friends. She appears as "a picture ... the first outline of which already captivated his entire soul" (46). The absence of, or displacement from, the oppressive reality of, say, Diana—or for that matter, of the very scene he now imagines ("as in truth and reality [*in Wahrheit und Wirklichkeit*] the terrifying scene took place," 49)—into the half-real, half-fictive realm of imaginative memory allows Astorre's desire to emerge. That is, the displacement from "reality" allows the quite different reality of desire to emerge, a reality that necessarily retains a "poetic," unreal dimension.

But the issue of displacement and its role in Astorre's attraction to Antiope is far more basic than that. As her name implies, Anti/ope represents the very embodiment of the principle of substitution on which the structure of desire and narration in the novella is based. The scene that Astorre both dreams and has narrated depicts Antiope placing her neck next to her father's on the execution block, wanting and willing to exchange places with him. It is this concentrated image of love, death, and exchange that defines Antiope's identity and calls forth Astorre's own desire—a desire for desire, so to speak, for the very principle of exchange.

(It is significantly this first, semiconscious display of desire in Astorre that occasions the first, albeit modest exercise of his own authority, or position. The engagement of his desire gives him a certain wish to assume control over both his own role and the course of events, an interest in regulating his reality. His friend Ascanio would prevent Antiope and her mother, Olympia, from attending Astorre's public betrothal to Diana. But with some structural cunning—Astorre appears only to submit to the commanding, textual authority of Burcardo, and so conceals the motive of his person and desires—Astorre ensures that Antiope will attend. Despite the feint of Astorre's apparent deference, Burcardo says, "Your Majesty [*Herrlichkeit*] alone shall be obeyed" [50]: Astorre himself, and alone, assumes governance over this part of the action.[44])

Even more significantly, the inviting of Antiope leads, through repetition, to the confirmation of Antiope's identity as substitute, which in turn finally leads to the full exposure of Astorre's desire, that is, of the principle secretly governing the story. As anticipated by Ascanio, Olympia makes a scene, a scene that provokes Diana to strike her. But as anticipated by the scene with her father, Antiope displaces the blow by intervening and presenting herself in her mother's place. And it is just this act of exchange that inspires Astorre to his own act of exchange, to displace Diana with Antiope—the act of displacement that exposes the governing reality until then repressed, namely, Astorre's desire; even as the desire itself exposes the reality governing it, namely, displacement.

IV

The revelation of Astorre's desire, and the structure of that desire, does much to explain the forces secretly shaping the course of events and determining the reality of the story. However, there are several crucial events for which such a psychological explanation—such a realism—seems inadequate. The most notable of these is the incident on the bridge: Astorre goes to buy a betrothal ring, picks up two and, when jostled by the crowd, drops one, which then ends up on Antiope's hand, which in turn leads to the scene at Diana's and Astorre's betrothal—etc. These linking coincidences seem to indicate the presence of another force, perhaps even of another authority, regulating events, limiting or splitting both the governance of the various characters' desires and

Double-Dealings

the control over events that they can legitimately claim, and thus, too, limiting the apparent realism to the story.

The systems of governance most frequently appealed to by characters in the story to explain such events are those of the fairy tale (*Märchen*) and Fate (*Schicksal*), each of which generically opposes the motivational system of realism. So, for instance, in respect to her understanding of the incident on the bridge, we are told, "[Y]oung Antiope had dipped a fingertip into the sparkling well of fairy tales [*den Märchenbrunnen*]. Had the encounter on the bridge not been marvelous?" (61). Her servant, Isotta, also interprets the events in such "marvelous" terms, as does Antiope's mother, Olympia, upon hearing "the dazzling fairy tale" from Isotta (55 f.).

Of course to some extent, despite the traditional opposition, the invocation of a fairy tale world does not necessarily contradict the peculiar mode of poetic realism we have identified in the story. In fact, it both confirms its characteristic mix of reality and fiction, desire and imagination, and at the same time provides an additional cover for the workings of its hidden desire. So, for instance, Sotte can read the "marvelous" occurrence on the bridge as a surreptitiously intended act betraying Astorre's unconscious will. Again, it is a case of desire reading desire: the fairy tale interpretation exposes the only slightly concealed nature of Sotte's own, personal wishes, but it also insightfully perceives the somewhat irrational, wild workings of Astorre's unconscious, whose governance expresses itself precisely through its apparent coincidence, or uncontrol.[45]

The same is true of the other, related attempt to identify the rules governing the chain of events in terms of Fate. As already indicated in the scene with the elder Vicedomini, Ezzelin is the most conspicuous advocate of this explanation: he especially (but not uniquely) finds the motivating principle secretly governing the course of events in a higher will, a nonhuman authority that determines fate. So, for instance, concerning the incident on the bridge, we are told, "The love story didn't move him, only the rolling ring occupied him for a moment as a new form of Fate" (82). This, too, would seem to invoke an antirealist system of motivation to explain the story's action. However, like the fairy tale world, Fate can also be brought into collusion with the story's realism. So for instance, Ezzelin's belief in (an astrologically based) Fate is questioned in the story itself by Ascanio, who calls Ezzelin's belief in the power of the stars a compound of reason and madness (40). He also complains that astrologers mislead Ezzelin "to heed his moods and inclinations [*seinen Launen und Lüsten*], in the belief that he is doing what is compulsory [*das Notwendige*]" (40). Again, Fate seems but a cover, and but a cover for personal desire: appearing only to submit to an outside force, Ezzelin conceals the motives of himself and his desires, which alone compel his actions and interpretations.[46]

Nevertheless, whereas the invocation of a fairy tale world need not contradict the peculiar version of poetic realism (of unconscious desire) evident in the novella, the events it is called upon to explain, such as those to the incident on the bridge, still exceed the possible realistic limits to the story.[47] And similarly, whereas Fate per se might be negated and reduced to questions of desire and self-determination, that does not negate the events it is called upon to explain, which still exceed individual characters' desires and powers, Ezzelin's included.[48] One does not thus escape the sense of the nebulous phantom of a government (*Nebelphantom eines Reiches,* 39) that intrudes from outside on the story's realm: a straightforward "realist" reading fails adequately to motivate the chain of events.

What these excessive, coincidental events do indicate is indeed a different, higher reality: the reality of Dante. The very unreality or fictionality at the one level of the text necessarily shifts us to the reality at the other, wherein the story's reality truly is unreal and fictional—a fairy tale. In a sense not applicable to Ezzelin, the appeal to an outside governance such as Fate can be but a cover for the secret motives and desires of the narrator, who in a very precise sense functions as the *Nebelphantom eines Reiches* that presses down on the characters' realm, as the "other will" that determines their reality. Moreover, the uncontrolled accidents in the story not only foreground the controlled designs of the narrator: they also lead us to question the moods and inclinations (*Launen und Lüsten*) behind his designs. That is, such "wild and exaggerated" (36) events not only lead us from questions about characters' desires to issues of narratorial power and control; they also lead from questions about narratorial power to issues of narratorial desire and character—to the issue of how "the temperament of the ruler colors court and city." It is no accident or coincidence that at the center of the event that so forcefully foregrounds the issues of Fate and the fairy tale we find the Florentine craftsman: it is he who is foregrounded by them.

What, then, does the way of relating the course of events expose to us about Dante?[49] Even more: What does the course of events itself, or rather, the act of relating it, expose to Dante about himself?

We noted earlier Dante's characteristic ambivalence about his understanding of his story, especially about his protagonist; what we now can note is that this ambivalence is not without a discernible pattern. Contrary to the general claims of renounced privileged insight, there are several key points in the story where Dante is able to say just what Astorre is experiencing. The most important early example comes in the scene between Astorre and his father. Dante relates that Astorre truly believes the elder Vicedomini is willing to condemn himself to hell if his son will not agree to the proposed substitution: "So he thought and was firmly convinced of it, as I, too, would have been in his place" (27f.). Moments later Dante says, "There stole over him [Astorre] the suspicion, what am I saying, there came over him the shocking certainty, that a dying man had abused his good faith" (30). What interests me is twofold: how it is on the basis of his identification, his trading places with his protagonist that Dante claims his authority over and certainty about Astorre's motives and the reality of his situation; and how he makes this identification and exercises this authority just at the moment of their denial—that is, just as Astorre is denying that he is acting "out of the truth of his nature" and instead "under the pressure of an other's will."

The same pattern is also apparent when Dante professes ignorance as to what Astorre is experiencing. So, for example, in the following scene, which depicts Astorre's entrance into the real world of the story, Dante says, "While he thought or dreamt, I don't know what," etc. (32; cf. "so deeply was he sunk in his full or empty dreams," 35). As mentioned, such a limitation of narratorial insight and incapacity to exchange places are often taken as the expression of a certain perspectival realism on Dante's part; but given both Dante's insight and ability to exchange places in the scene just preceding, I think we must consider a different explanation, a different expressed reality. We must, that is, consider what has changed in Astorre's character or situation so that Dante ceases to be able to identify with him and interpret his inner world, or rather, so that Dante is unwilling to do so. We know from what follows that what Dante denies knowing here, that over which he does not claim authority and refuses to identify as his own, is Astorre's desire: he displays the same characteristic silence or repression about the workings of desire as does his protagonist. Thus, Dante expresses his identification with his protagonist and exercises his authority over Astorre's inner reality at the moment of denial of will and desire; he denies the identification and its accompanying authority at the moment of expression and exercise of desire and will. In each case, the governing principle is the same: the increasingly disingenuous denial of authority, desire, and self-involvement. (Cf. also "if I am properly informed": Dante invents an authority under which he narrates, even as Astorre does one under which he acts.)

What emerges, then, is the importance of the discovery and acknowledgment, by Dante, of his own inner reality and subjectivity for the shaping and motivating of the story's reality. It is just this discovery that Cangrande's interruptions at this point aim at. Even as Dante would use the displacing mirror of his fiction to pose a reality for his listeners, so would Cangrande use the same mirroring fictional process to reveal a reality to Dante, namely, the reality of his own subjectivity, and in turn the reality of its effect on the narration.

We see this in a relatively minor way in Cangrande's first major interruption. Dante has just related the historically "real" anecdote concerning Friedrich II and Petrus de Vinea. Cangrande intervenes to ask Dante his evaluation of the principals' guilt—that is, of what "really" happened. Each time Dante replies, "*Non liquet*," it is not clear. Each time Cangrande reformulates his question, "I mean, in your innermost feelings?"; and each time Dante answers in a way that contradicts his judgment or interpretation in the *Divine Comedy* (44f.). As Dante's own explanation makes clear, the ambiguity or uncertainty (the *non liquet*) by which he would limit his authority is a feint, or rather, a consequence of a split in authorities: on the one hand, the outside authority of public opinion or standards of proof to which Dante claims to submit in the *Divine Comedy*; on the other, the authority of his "innermost feelings," which yields or represents a fundamentally different interpretation, or reality. Cangrande's catechism aims at dislodging Dante from his position of ambivalence and deference to an outside authority—significantly the same position Dante is maintaining at this time vis-à-vis his "dreaming" protagonist—and insisting upon a self-conscious representation of the motives and reality of Dante's story as shaped or governed by the authority of his own subjectivity. Moreover, Cangrande's insistence on Dante's acknowledgment of his own feelings as the determining force motivating the reality of his tale has an immediate, if minor effect on Dante's tale. Whereas when Cangrande first would interrupt Dante defers, saying, "You are the ruler" (43), after the exchange Dante does not defer to Cangrande's representation of the story's course but insists on his own, unique understanding. Thus, Cangrande's engagement of Dante's "innermost feelings" gives Dante an added interest in shaping, controlling, and authorizing the reality of his story. And what especially interests me is the further effect: it is just immediately following this break that Dante represents Astorre acknowledging his desire and assuming some modest control over his own representative role and the course of events.

Cangrande's most significant, strategic confrontation of Dante with himself comes just at that point where the story itself most confronts us with Dante, that is, at the point of the marvelous coincidences on the bridge. Both the focus and form of Cangrande's interruption are decisive. First, what occasions Cangrande's interruption is Dante's representation of the Florentine craftsman, insofar as Dante himself is a Florentine craftsman. That is, what is most at issue for Cangrande in Dante's narrative is Dante's self-representation and self-understanding: the reality it represents, or doesn't represent, is that of the narrator himself.[50] Second, the peculiar vehicle that Cangrande uses to bring home this reality (of Dante's self) to Dante is an imagined visit to a puppet theater. He too uses the displacement into the fictional, with all its strategies of identification and exchange, as the means for achieving his realistic effect.[51]

The particular self or reality that Cangrande aims to reveal to and about Dante is essential for an understanding of Dante's narrative, even as Dante's narrative is essential for an understanding of that self. What attracts Cangrande is Dante's bitter, distorted representation of the Florentine, or more precisely, of the relationship between the Florentine and the higher, outside authority of his city, Florence. The very excess, or unreality, of the representation signals its inadequate motivation (or realism) in and by the story, and so again compels one to look for its motivation (and reality) in the teller instead. The Florentine is presented as "banished from his home by a bought and unjust verdict" (51), as displaced into the world, powerlessly and against his wishes, by the pressure of an other's will. For Cangrande, this represents Dante's self-representation, Dante who is similarly without a home, condemned to be continually displaced along an endless chain of hosts, the precarious and unstable alternations of their changing affections, and commands. For us, this also structurally represents both Dante's representation of Astorre and his desire, and Dante's own strategy of narration, of trading places—where in each case an outside power or reality initiates a displacement, which in turn yields an ongoing chain of exchanges, perilously transferable desires, and thus a lack of controlled center, resting or stopping point—of home. In both his narrative and his narration, then, Dante's implicit (if silent) self-understanding determines the represented reality and its governing rules.[52]

Cangrande does not aim to refute or deny the validity of this structure, this reality fashioning both the poet and his self-representation, or fiction. What he does propose is a different attitude toward its conditions. Cangrande uses his fictional diversion of the puppet play to urge Dante, when placed under the pressure of an other's will and so abused, nonetheless to declare, "I want to be beaten [*Ich will geschlagen sein*]!" (57). Dante—and by extension, his protagonist (and audience?)—needs actively to will and desire his own fate, his own displacement, to will that over which he has no control, and thus in a sense to acknowledge this other's will as his own, as part of himself. That is, will and self are required to come together precisely there, where both falter: under the pressure of an "other" force. One acknowledges responsibility for the other in oneself.[53]

One effect of Cangrande's advice is that Dante is urged to will, as it were, a certain homelessness as the condition of self-identity, a certain lack of unity, simplicity, and familiarity to the forces governing him, a certain *Unheimlichkeit* at the center of himself and his desires. Cangrande looks at Dante, recognizing how the pressure of this other force, authority, or reality has displaced his narrator-guest, so that he knows no home of his own but only the changeable favor of changing patrons, and silently declares: "Here sits a homeless one [*ein Heimatloser*]!" (57).[54] As we have seen, this "homelessness" is the very condition for self-identity, desire, and narration; and in taking this thought as the basis for his proposal to exchange seats with Dante and to put Dante in the place of authority, Cangrande engages in a highly significant, but also highly ambiguous gesture. For the point of seating the homeless one can be, and perhaps must be, read in two contradictory ways: as if on the one hand the homelessness is somehow to be overcome, and a center finally found, acknowledged; and as if on the other the homelessness is itself to be acknowledged, authenticated as the true reality governing the tale, the poet—even the listeners themselves.

V

As I said at the outset, the exchange of places that Cangrande proposes and Dante accepts is clearly the most important point in the novella, a turning-point in the frame coming at the turning-point of the narrative. We are now in a better position to understand what, beyond the logic of exchange itself, the exchange signifies, and to pose the further question: How does it affect the relation between the frame and story, between Dante and his narrative? and, How does this affected relation itself affect the continuation of the story, the unfolding of events?

Most obviously, the exchange of seats signals a complex realignment to the representative functions of Ezzelin and Astorre in the tale, of who and what they become displaced representatives for. As mentioned, many critics recognize the chiastic pattern whereby not only Cangrande is represented by Ezzelin and Astorre, but Dante as well. But what they fail to recognize is that this chiastic crossing only really, self-consciously takes place here—can only take place here, as a result of Dante's emerging acknowledgment of the self-representation to his narrative.[55] In any case, in taking over the place of Cangrande in the frame, Dante clearly seems also to take over the position of the ruler, of Ezzelin, in the tale. That is, the trade compels Dante to assume and acknowledge authority over and responsibility for the course of events, for how and why events unfold as they do—or rather, it forces Dante to assume the problem of authority, since as we know, authority remains elusive, split, and out of control. This is, after all, the lesson of both "I want to be beaten" and "Here sits a homeless one."

The exchange with Cangrande also of course explicitly puts Dante in the position of the protagonist, Astorre. He is described as a literary character in his own fiction ("the wanderer through the Inferno," 57), as placed between the two women, and as dislodged from the detached position of outside observer (the position now assumed by Cangrande). That is, the trade compels Dante to enter into his cast of characters and thus into the chain and system of exchange, to acknowledge his substitutive identity in the tale, and thus to acknowledge the operant desire covertly driving the chain of events as his own; compels him to acknowledge the real forces regulating his fiction; to acknowledge himself.

Just how the trade of places here signals Dante's acknowledgment of authority; how the assumption of authority is connected with the acknowledgment of desire; how both are connected with Dante's acknowledging himself in the tale, and how all this affects the further course of his narration—these are made more or less explicit in the next, and final, interruption. Cangrande's female friend interrupts Dante with the revelation that Astorre "loved Antiope" (63), with several other listeners chiming in with their agreement; this soon escalates to the competing interpretations of events posed by Antiope and Diana, discussed above. As I said, their reader-interpretations are based on transferred desires and identities, which in turn engender a specific force determining the fictional reality. Interestingly, this key play of desire, substitution, and identification takes place just at the place where Astorre identifies his desire for the substitute, Antiope.

However, Dante denies his audience's understanding—and by extension, their desires and selves as participant (shapers) in the reality of the narrative—and insists instead on the uniqueness of his own understanding—and by extension, of his own desire and self as participant, indeed determinant, of that reality.[56] This is in keeping with the accompanying, belated recognition of his own tendency to talk to himself, that is, for *Selbstgespräch* (64f.), and his request that, from this point on, no one interrupt him. From this point on, the narration is to be purely self-reflective, a session with his own self, his own desire, and his own telling.[57] And it is no accident that in Dante's self-reflective representation of *Selbstgespräch* with Astorre in the following scene, the monologic meditation is in fact presented as a dialogic exchange with a double, between Astorre and Gocciola, since this is also the form of Dante's own *Selbstgespräch*, between himself and Astorre (or his story). The very structure of self-realization is predicated on the exchange, on the displaced, mirroring double.[58]

How, then, does the continuation of Dante's tale reflect Dante's changed relation to its telling? How does it reflect Dante's acknowledgment of his rightful place and, in its reflection, what does it reveal to Dante about that place?

Most simply, from this point on Dante effects an identity with his protagonist, acknowledges "who he is" in the tale. We see this already in the representation of Astorre addressing his audience at the betrothal, reflecting the (public) conditions or structure of Dante's own narration; and then again in the representation of Astorre's dialogic *Selbstgespräch,* reflecting its other, (private) conditions or structure, those now more or less brought to the fore. But we see it most clearly in the representation of Astorre wooing Antiope, which shows Astorre, too, finally acknowledging "who he is" in his tale.

The attempt is first made to perpetuate the pattern that has motivated both the narrative and narration so far: to deny one's own self and desire while entering into the displacing chain of substitution. But this time, in keeping with the change in the frame, the pattern is undone. Places are exchanged and so rightful places assumed. Germano asks Astorre to woo Antiope in his place— that is, even as Astorre was a re-presentative for his brother in respect to Diana, so now for his friend in respect to Antiope. But despite Astorre's determination to repress both his desire and self, these are found out; and it is Dante who finds them out. Dante displays unusually keen insight into the hidden reality of Astorre's inner world and motives at this point—even as Astorre does into Germano's. Astorre sees Germano's self-deception, his false claim to selfless motivation, and the emerging reality of his desire; what empowers him to determine that reality is, of course, that it is his own. And the same is implicitly, self-reflectively true of Dante; it is his own recognized self-deception and denial of self and desire that authorizes him to determine the reality of his protagonist as the same. (Note, for instance, how Dante punctuates Astorre's insight into Germano and his own into Astorre with a gnomic apostrophe—the only one in the tale—that includes himself [71].) It is precisely this insight that signals Dante's displaced self-reflection in the tale; and it is this same insight that necessarily subverts the strategy of repression and substitution. Antiope asks, "For whom do you woo, Astorre?" (73), and although he first replies, "For this one here, my brother Germano," in the next instant the stratagem is given up. Astorre loses the cover of his displaced position, moves into himself, exposes the reality of his desire, and so assumes his rightful place.

Similarly, even as Astorre would expose his desire and stop the chain by acknowledging "who he is," so too would Ezzelin now assume his authority and stop the chain by assuming his proper role as ruler. And in this, too, we perceive the story reflecting Dante's acknowledgment of his rightful place, his identity in the tale, or rather, over the tale. Ascanio tells Ezzelin, "If you draw the case into your sphere of power, then all is saved" (82), urging Ezzelin to use his authority and power to determine the course of events, and thus to determine reality. When Ezzelin would do so, Ascanio says, "[O]ut of a dangerous story you have made a charming fairy tale with which someday I, a worthy old man, shall delight my grandsons and -daughters at the fireside" (90 f.), making explicit the identity between Ezzelin's governance of the story's reality and Dante's of the narrative—and equally important, making explicit Dante's (self-consciously reflected) recognition of this identity, his own acceptance of the position of control.

Ezzelin's exercise of his control takes two related forms. In the first, he attempts to stop the chain of events by assuming himself as the governing force secretly behind "the entangled affair." As he says, "I, Ezzelino da Romano, am the first to have been responsible and am therefore also the one chiefly responsible" (85). To some extent, this placement of himself—this acknowledgment of himself—as the governing agency behind the many seeming, general coincidences parallels Astorre's acknowledgment of his self and desire as the governing agency to his personal actions; and of course, it parallels even more closely Dante's acknowledgment of his self, his agency.

The second form assumed by Ezzelin's exercise of control is his attempt to enforce his wish. "[L]et each person return to his own place [*jetzt kehre ruhig jeder in das Seinige*]" (91): that is, to assume authority over almost all the pertinent characters, to bind each to a stable position by claiming power over who each one is, and so to stop the chain. Again, the attempt parallels not only Astorre's bid to bind himself and his desire to a stable identity but also and even more Dante's, who now is moved to master not only his own identity in the tale but also his general, narratorial authority over the tale. So, for instance (and especially), Ezzelin exercises his general power over Astorre: "I assume guardianship over this youth," he declares. "I have full power [*Vollmacht*]" (87). Interestingly, this control expresses itself at the level of writing, as Ezzelin forces Astorre to submit to his textual (*schriftlich*) design (88). Ezzelin similarly claims power over Germano by claiming him as his, Ezzelin's, own. He says, "You are not your own man, you belong to the government [*Du bist nicht dein eigen, du gehörst dem Reich*]!" (89). This time it is the elder Pizzaguerra who secures this appropriation as simultaneously one to the "word": he says, "I gave my word, and it includes your word as well. Submit!!" (88). And the same pattern repeats itself in respect to Antiope, this time with Astorre exercising control. She says, "I am nothing more than your property [*Eigentum*].... If you [Astorre] want and command it, then!" (90)—and Astorre does so want, and so command. In each case, the character is asked to bind both self and desire and to submit to the sovereignty of an other will, not however to exchange positions so much as to be stopped and placed in a proper one.

What interests me is how this imposed authority does yield in the characters a sense of proper self identity, or place. We see this particularly with the two women. In respect to Antiope, listening to "the tyrant's decision . . . roused in the young mistress her first sense of self-esteem [*das erste Selbstgefühl*]" (89; cf. 72, where she is described as still without "self-consciousness [*Selbstbewusstsein*]"). The case is even clearer in respect to Diana. Ezzelin orders, "Tonight a wedding feast with masks shall be celebrated. I am giving the feast" (89). When Astorre asks as who she will come, Diana replies, "I shall come as she whom I am named and who I am [*als die, welche ich mich nenne und welche ich bin*]" (90). The wedding feast with masks again presents the pattern for displaced, substituted identities, and especially in its displacement into fiction reproduces the (earlier) conditions of the narration and threatens to continue those of the (earlier) narrative as well. But now Ezzelin emphatically exerts or usurps his authority over the fiction (and reality), and Diana just as emphatically proposes to assume her proper identity. It is just this happy, seeming coincidence of an outside authority that seeks to return "each person to his own place" and the subject that accepts it that would make the whole into "a charming fairy tale" (cf. "I want to be beaten!"). And it is just this fairytale-like representation of both general authority and personal identity that reflects Dante realizing his own proper authority and identity—realizing, that is, the "reality" to his story, earlier denied.

VI

With the return of "each to his own [*jeder in das Seinige*]," a major turning, even stopping point is reached in Dante's narrative. Everyone assumes responsibility or authority for who he or she is, for their place, and Ezzelin for everyone; each in assuming a proper place, or stabilized self, binds desire and so puts an end to the chain of exchange. In so aligning self, desire, and authority, a certain "reality" is attained, not only insofar as each character assumes his or her self, or place, but even more insofar as Dante seems finally to acknowledge and assume his own identity and authority in the tale, his own agency, his own self as the determining reality motivating and governing the course of events. This "reality" thus attained, we should note, has more than a little in common with that *märchenhaft,* or fantastic reality, that Graf Wittinghaus would impose on his daughters or, more trickily, Rudolf on Ines; and as such, it too seems to conform to that stable, self-identical, and secure conception of "realism" that I outlined in chapter one.

Of course, neither Graf Wittinghaus nor Rudolf was able to sustain this stable reality, and in each case a different reality emerged that signaled the failure of this desired control. And the same proves true here: this momentarily achieved "reality" comes up short, and fails quite to stop or end the tale: "Dante took a deep breath. Then he finished with hastening sentences" (91). Rather, the reality revealed as governing the final, rushing sequences is once again that the simple reality of identity and authority is not to be had. For again, other, strange drives control.

There are altogether three different ways in which the major characters become unwittingly alienated from their selves, desires, and authorities at the end of the tale, upsetting the bid to govern reality and suggesting a different, more troublesome reality as governing in its stead. First, there is Ezzelin: "Against his intentions and will he was detained in the castle, many miles distant from the city" (91). What involuntarily keeps him placed at such an unbridgeable distance from the action—from his own fairy tale—is "a message written in the Emperor's own hand, that required an immediate [*umgehend*] answer": "Propping his working brow in his left hand, Ezzelin let his right glide over the parchment, and his stylus drew him from the first point to the second and from the second to a third" (92). In terms reminiscent of Astorre eating berries upon his entrance into the reality of desire—or for that matter, of Dante upon his entrance into the reality of exile—Ezzelin is held back, distanced, and set along an uncontrolled chain that exceeds, belies, or "goes around" (*umgehen*) his conscious will and power by writing—by writing, which is here depicted as the very condition of his authority and power. Given the easy, essential exchange between writing and narrating in the novella, and the equally essential exchange between Ezzelin and Dante in this part of it, this seeming accident exposes a necessary reality: the very conditions of writing, narration, or representation dictate a certain distance or alienation, an ongoing exchange or relay; the very conditions of Dante's authority defeat that authority. This is the self-conscious realization of the reality of the fiction: that it remains fundamentally "other," subject to forces not in the author's conscious control.[59]

The second instance of subversion to the arranged reality comes in relation to Diana. She had announced her intention to come to the masked ball "as she whom I am named and as who I am": to stop the chain of substitutive identities—enginging the strategy of narration, the course of narrated events, and now, implicitly, the masked ball itself—by assuming one stable, self-designating identity: her reality, "the simple truth [*die einfache Wahrheit*]" (29). And it seems appropriate that it should be Diana who would do so, insofar as she has always been the would-be embodiment of a certain, simple "reality" principle. But as Diana makes her way through the wild, bacchantic crowd, she is knowingly and amorously accosted: "You are not Diana, you are an other [*Nicht Diana bist du, du bist eine andere*]!" (93). The "other" so recognized is Aphrodite, or desire itself: and despite, even because of her denial, there is an essential truth to this observation. Diana is also an "other," and that other is unconscious desire: the attempt to be only oneself by denying or repressing that other cannot succeed (cf. Astorre: "If you look on me as someone unstable, as someone robbed of his senses, that doesn't anger me, for a powerful god, whom I denied because I could not recognize his existence, has exacted his revenge and overpowered me," 87). Rather, even as writing intervenes and distances Ezzelin from his own fairy tale, and so subverts his governance and mastery of reality, so does "Aphrodite" intervene and distance Diana from her own fiction of self-identity, and so subvert her governance, her mastery of herself.

Significantly, this identification (and denial) of the "other" to Diana by the anonymous crowd-member issues in a stabbing that foreshadows Diana's revenge on Antiope, a revenge that clearly exposes the continued, uncontrolled reality of desire. Even more significantly, this same identification of the "other" exposes certain continued, ineradicable difficulties for interpretation in relation to that revenge. Because of the presence of that "other" in herself, Diana can never truly determine the reality of her own actions or motives, including her revenge. And because the same conditions necessarily hold for Dante as well, he can never really determine the significance, the reality of his own representation. In keeping with this, he refuses to interpret the scene between Diana and Antiope: "Did Antiope imagine it? or did Diana really play this game? How slight a thing is a crooked finger! Cangrande, you have accused me of being unjust. I shall not decide" (96). The "other" in him dictates that he cannot control his own fiction, that he cannot know his own meaning. The reality here is that reality can never be grasped, or governed, neither in respect to one's self, nor to one's story.

The third instance is somewhat more indirect; it comes in relation to Astorre and Antiope. Even as they are inside binding themselves and their desire—binding so to speak their meaning—there appears outside a pair of (fictive) doubles, who unbind, alienate, or split the protagonists from control over their identities: "A large, wild woman of ruined beauty went arm in arm with a drunken monk in a tattered cowl" (94). Even as writing deprives Ezzelin of control over his author-ity (his fairy tale) and unconscious desire deprives Diana of control over her actions, so does outside doubling deprive Astorre, and Antiope, of control over their self-identity. What interests me particularly is how, in splitting them from their identities, this doubling—this taking someone else's place—also splits them from their meaning. As Antiope's "shameless" double says, "We give the name to what the nobles do. We put the labels on the apothecary's vials!" (94). This power or authority of "those outside" to determine the significance, indeed the reality of the characters inside, through the distorting, wild lens of their own desires and selves, by means of doubling; this uncontrollable invasion of the "other," of "the other's will," with its splitting of authority and its destabilizing of "reality" by moving or relaying it outward along a substitutive chain—this too has important consequences for understanding the realism at stake in Dante's narration. It reasserts what, in the interest of self-understanding and acknowledgment, Dante had repressed, namely, the nonexcludable participation of his (outside) audience. For all the (therapeutic) reality to the narrative as a monologue, or *Selbstgespräch,* leading to the recognition of Dante's own shaping motivation of the fiction, this other reality—both contrary and parallel—of the narrative does not disappear. The significance, indeed the reality of Dante's tale and characters ultimately still partially rests in the interpretive power and determinative authority of his outside, intrusive "others," who interpret by doubling, by displacing their own selves and desires, splitting authority and so decentering and destabilizing reality, by moving it outward along a substitutive chain. And it is surely worth noting that these doubles are especially associated with the line "In a little while the monk Astorre shall lie beside his wife Antiope" (94). The line deliberately and distortively repeats the initial, inciting gravestone inscription, and it is itself repeated, the second time with a different, distorted (and double) meaning. Readers, that is, doubles, always repeat the "line," and so distort, that is, double its meaning. This is another part of Dante's lesson in realism: the very conditions that achieve the realistic effect subvert the stability of that effect; subvert, that is, the identity of that reality.[60]

Ezzelin through writing, Diana through unconscious desire, and Astorre and Antiope through outside doubles: each exposes a central truth about the pressure of an other's will, about the inability to assume control, by one's self, of one's self and one's truth; and each exposes this as perhaps the tragic condition of the story's reality, and of its narration. But Antiope exposes another, and in some ways contrary truth: that even if one cannot, one also cannot not assume control of oneself. One still must take one's place. As Antiope is preparing for her part in the masked ball, "she looked into her own fearful eyes, which confronted her out of a mirror's glass" (95). Her anxiety leads her to try to take recourse in the tactic of exchange that from the outset has powered the story, and its narration, and that has proved so unstoppable, despite the efforts of Ezzelin, and Dante. She says to her attendant, Sotte, "[Y]ou resemble me and have my build; change costumes with me, if you love me!" (95). But this solution, this practice, is explicitly put to a stop by Astorre, as earlier by Ezzelin (cf. "each return to his own place, if you love me!"). Antiope still must take her own place, no matter how dangerous or endangered. One must, as it were, still pay for one's place by the fire (*am Feuer*): this is its own truth and, in its way, its own tragedy as well.

VII

By all accounts, we should now be at the end; however, it is now the end for which we must account. To maintain even a limited mastery over the meaning and reality of this story has required our own, impossible repression of one of its chief, unspeakable realities or truths, namely, the reality and truth of death (the ultimate exchange, or exchanger). That besides the impetus of desire that of death might be a motivating factor to Dante's narrative is hinted at in Cangrande's opening words: "[A]muse yourself with these two lovely mortals [*Sterblichen*]" (7). It is far more forcefully insisted on by the fact that Dante has another source besides that of the various selves and desires of his audience for the invention of his narrative, namely, that of the gravestone inscription (*Grabschrift*) with which the story begins and, in a sense, ends.

The gravestone inscription is important for an understanding both of the generation and motivation of Dante's narrative and of its realism in several ways.[61] First, it constitutes a reality that belongs to neither the frame nor the story, but rather falls not so much outside as between them, and so in between the exchanges between frame and story, between self and re-presentative substitute. Second, although the inscription thus functions as a somewhat autonomous, given reality, its more important function comes in that Dante and his audience must themselves discover or invent the "reality" of the inscription, must transform this beginning into an appropriate, authoritative end through the introduction of a credibly motivated, realistic middle.[62] As such, the epitaph can be seen to condition the issues of both authority and desire: authority is defined as the ability or right to lead the story to its proper end, or death, as the power over the deferred end of the story, over the detour or displacement between the (supposedly) same-state beginning and end; and similarly desire is defined as a desire for the end, as a curiosity about how the story will properly "die" (and so prove real), a desire that draws all the auditors into and along the unfolding chain. Finally, the epitaph foregrounds a certain reality of writing, not only through its own scriptive character but also through Dante's otherwise peculiar wish to put the gravestone itself somewhere in a library. This underscores how the condition of narration, the reality of writing is always as it were one of death, of the nonliving and the unreal.

The *Grabschrift*, then, functions alongside the selves of Dante's audience as the principle, or source, for his invention. Even as the latter generates a crucial equation of narration and desire, so the former between narration and death, and as a result desire and death both compete and collude in motivating Dante's narration and in establishing its motivation and peculiar realism. Moreover, even as we saw how the conditions of narration in terms of Dante's strategy of exchange were transposed or displaced into the narrative itself, so too can we see how the conditions of narration in terms of the epitaph are similarly transposed and represented—or perhaps better, how the collusion and competition between the two sets of terms are represented in the story.[63] And finally, we can see how in all these respects—the equation of death and narration, the conjunction of both with desire, and their common transposition into the thematic concerns of the story proper—we are returning to matters that engaged us in *The Mountain Forest*, in "Eugenia," and in *Viola tricolor*; over and again, death proves of inescapable importance to our understanding of realism.

The most obvious and significant example of how the conditions of Dante's narration in terms of the gravestone inscription are transposed into the narrative itself has already and unavoidably been suggested in my description of the pattern of substitution or displacement in the story. Even as the reality of the *Grabschrift* falls between those of the frame and the story, and so in between the exchanges between the frame and story, between the selves and their representative substitutes, so does the reality of death fall between the many various exchanges in the story between the characters and their displaced, substitutive roles. More tellingly, the governing principle to this pattern of exchange can as justly be described in terms of death as desire, or rather, in terms of deferral of death instead of deferral of desire. To do so, we need only focus on the family thematics. However passively, both Umberto and Diana and then again Astorre and Diana enter into the chain of substitutions in order to postpone the end of their family line, to sustain an identity that subsists only through the chain of succession. This governing principle finds its active embodiment in the figure of the elder Vicedomini, all of whose powers of will (*Willenskräfte*) are devoted to the arguable necessity of the prosperous growth of his family stock (17), and whose mastery-of-exchange (Vice-domini) ensures the continued dominance of that stock. Moreover, his own death, which falls as much at the moment of Astorre's entrance into the chain as does Umberto's, signals this slightly different, and perhaps competing, pattern of substitution (a pattern that would also include Astorre's three older and now dead brothers). In this pattern, the movement of characters is, as it were, end-determined, death-determined, or more precisely, determined by the desire and will for the deferral of death, of the end—for its displacement. I mention this not only to suggest the complex interplay between desire and death in motivating the story's chain of traded places, but even more to recall how here too the narrative is repeating and replicating the conditions of Dante's narration, whose unfolding course and system of substitutions seem also to be engined simultaneously from two different ends: from an initiatory, displaced desire and from an anticipated, but (masterfully) deferred endpoint.[64]

Not surprisingly, the same interplay of death and desire governs the more specific story and chain of Astorre and his desire. Not only does Astorre himself experience a kind of incipient, figurative death at each instance of his own substitutive exchanges. He also finds himself attracted to women who incorporate (intervening) death into their peculiar representation of (deferring) exchange. This is true of his first encounter with Diana, whom he pulls "dead" from the stream at the moment of his brother's death; it is even more true of his first encounter with Antiope at the moment of her father's execution, which as we said associates her figure with a concentrated pattern of love, (intervening) death, and (deferring) exchange. David Jackson acutely observes the perhaps perverse mixture of death and erotics in Astorre's character and attractions;[65] what he does not observe is how this mixture just repeats in condensed form the pattern that motivates the general chain of events apart from Astorre, and how this in turn just repeats the pattern that motivates the narration itself. And yet this last point is critical: it is the reality of narration itself that finds itself actively reflected in the selves, desires, and events of the story, and that reality includes a perhaps unavoidable mix of desire and death.

Even as death is built into the structure of Astorre's desire, so too into the structure of Ezzelin's authority. Not only does he claim for himself the privilege of closing the eyes of the dead, and so controlling the end of "this sorrowful action [*diese traurige Handlung*]" (40), in a way that for all its gruesomeness nonetheless closely parallels Dante's control of the end (and so meaning) of his "action."[66] It is also Ezzelin who inscribes and signs the gravestone itself, and so asserts specific authority over the final significance of Astorre's tale.[67]

Death also plays a crucial part in the consideration of the regulation of events over and above Ezzelin's authority and Astorre's desire, especially in relation to the two antirealist governance-systems of the fairy tale and Fate. One of the key motifs to the story is that of a shadow world and ghosts, a motif closely associated with that of the fairy tale world and in tension with the story's simple realism. One can read this in terms of the workings of either desire or death, or both: where in the substitutive chain everyone is at least partly a shadow or ghost, a representation "between truth and appearance," necessarily displaced from simple reality by the operations of desire; or alternatively, where the deferred but anticipated deadly end preemptively traces or inscribes its controlling reality onto the major characters. Both are true, both expressive of a reality beyond that of the simple, given reality; but the "ghosting" is also obviously expressive of the reality of the fictionality of the various characters, of their narrative status. This crucial mix of desire, death, and fiction is represented in Abu Mohammed's words: "Let the shadows embrace!" (79), where Ascanio wonders whether this reflects Mohammed's belief in the unreality of the world or in the impending reality of death. But the two go together; the unreality of the fictional world is the reality of death, and—in this tale at least—both are part of the equally unreal reality of desire. Moreover, Dante indicates something similar when, defending his unique understanding of the nature of desire and course of his story, he asserts, "Everyone speaks of spirits, but few have seen them" (63). He alone is authorized to speak of ghosts, because he alone sees that these are ghosts, and knows the necessary death that lies behind their narration, and desire.

Death, or rather the structure engendered by death, also constitutes a significant part of Fate, quite apart from, although still in connection with, Fate as but the moods and desires (*Launen und Lüsten*) of the relevant ruler. This is made especially clear in the "gruesome tale" narrated near the end of the story (83): that tale in which the story itself repeats itself, finds its double, which signals its death, its fate. Ezzelin had conquered a citadel and condemned the rebels to death by sword at the hands of one of his soldiers. Among the rebels is a boy whom Ezzelin thinks to recognize as his illegitimate son, and so has spared; when later on the boy seeks the motive for Ezzelin's action and so discovers the truth of his origin, he is driven to attack the tyrant again, and in the course of that attack is killed at the hand of the same soldier and by the same sword to which he was originally condemned. While this is clearly a story of "moods and desires" and of confounded love and revenge much like Astorre's, the "fateful" part clearly lies in the matter of repetition, or rather, in that of deferral. The repetition brings the deferred beginning to its proper, delayed end, which is the same as the beginning, which Ezzelin's interceding authority has only postponed. Interestingly, it is the boy's curiosity about the origin (*Ursprung*) that leads to his ending by the same hand and sword. And while, again, the representation of love and revenge and Ezzelin's personal intercession clearly reflects Astorre's story, so does that of beginnings as endings, of repetitions as deferrals, of death as prescribed—but, again, at a level that exceeds the narrative itself and resides instead in its narration, in the movement from the first, original presentation of the gravestone inscription to its awaited repetition at the end, with the story in between as but its deferral, its detour, and yet nonetheless the detour that distinguishes the end from the beginning, not least by providing its meaning, its reality.

There is, then, this second source for Dante's narration in the gravestone inscription that both competes and colludes with that of the selves and desires in Dante's audience, and like the latter generates its own system of exchange, that is, between itself as origin and as end. Like the latter, it too is transposed directly into the narrative itself and there determines the course of events; as such, it also clearly determines the end of the story, exposes its significance, makes it real. But the point I would like to make is this: although death thus constitutes another governing pattern, it does not provide any more secure or stable a final significance or reality to the story.[68] The story's truth or meaning cannot be reduced to the ambivalent tension between the doubled patterns of desire and death, nor to death alone as a final, comprehending reality or truth.

Perhaps the best place to see this is precisely there, where it seems most contested, namely, in the repetition of the initial epitaph at the story's end. As mentioned, Antiope's double shouts out before the wedding, "In a little while the monk Astorre will lie beside his wife Antiope [*Über ein kurzes schlummert der Mönch Astorre neben seiner Gattin Antiope*]" (94); after the murders she shouts, "Now the monk Astorre lies beside his wife Antiope [*Jetzt schlummert der Mönch Astorre neben seiner Gattin Antiope*]" (98). The repetition would seem to secure the significance, the reality of the opening epitaph, first in the ambivalent tension between desire and death implicit in "lie [*schlummert*]," and then in the dominant emergence of the latter as its real, true meaning. And yet as the "unrestrained laughter" that accompanies the repeated line might seem to confirm, it fails adequately to contain or comprehend the story's course—the sense of truth and closure that it presents is indeed a laughable one.[69]

This is made even clearer in Dante's parting words. Dante ends his tale, rises, and voices his intention to go seek "the happiness of slumber [*das Glück des Schlummers*]. May the Lord of Peace protect us all!" (98). The lines explicitly repeat both the *Schlummer* of Astorre and the gesture, "bidding peace," of the ruler Ezzelin, both of which appear at both the beginning and end of the story, and so implicitly signify something about Dante's own lord-ship of the tale. But whereas the repetition surely invests the lines with their significance and sense of closure, it is also surely impossible to determine what that meaning is or to govern its openness. And this is not a simple case of ambivalence, where one hesitates between two or more viable interpretations, an ambivalence we've seen that is so often a touchstone for Meyer's realism. Rather, it is a case where interpretation simply falters, where one must forgo to master meaning. The nature of reality, its meaning, is there, governed by repetition; it is not, however, there for us.

SECONDHAND NEWS

Boredom and a Motive for Murder in Wilhelm Raabe's 'Fatso' ('Stopfkuchen')

"The power of anything is ultimately its ability to hurt."
—Thomas Weiskel[1]

"Everybody must get stoned."
—Bob Dylan

The figure of Dante in Meyer's *The Marriage of the Monk* presents us with a peculiarly aggressive, even malicious narrator, who deliberately spites the conventional relation between literature and pleasure, or between entertainment (*Kurzweile*) and desire. We have a similar figure in Fagon, from Meyer's *The Sufferings of a Boy* (*Die Leiden eines Knabens*, 1883). Both narrators' incivility performs an important part in achieving the works' intended realistic effect, insofar as each (and especially the former) can be seen actively to engage and then frustrate his given audience's desire and sense of both self and world. Each provokes the (repressive) constructions that not only comprise the story's governing reality but also, of course, and simultaneously, deny it. Another and even more telling example of this strategy can be found in Wilhelm Raabe's *Fatso* (*Stopfkuchen*, 1891), which represents a particular mode of narratorial aggression and malice best described as one of deliberate, sustained, and unrelenting boredom, or *Langweile*. This boredom involves a special deployment of repetition, and has special consequences for realism.

I

As Roland Barthes says, "It can't be helped: boredom is not simple."[2] So let me begin by laying out something of a poetics of boredom, the aesthetics or, better, the anaesthetics of boredom: its peculiar genealogy, iconography, and constellation of concerns. This is admittedly an extremely large topic: I will be limiting myself to those aspects that are most relevant for an understanding of repetition, of realism, and of *Fatso*.[3]

Boredom is usually considered a modern, especially nineteenth-century phenomenon.[4] However, part of that modern phenomenon is the prehistory it posits or projects for itself, a sort of positive utopia or idyll of boredom, perhaps best articulated by Walter Benjamin in his essay "The Storyteller [Der Erzähler]." Benjamin describes boredom as the primary condition for the now vanishing art of storytelling, or narration: "If sleep is the apex of bodily relaxation, then boredom is that of mental relaxation. Boredom is the dream bird that hatches the egg of experience. A rustling in the forest's leaves drives it away. Its nests—the activities within which boredom secures itself—are already dead in the cities, and are decaying in the country as well."[5] Benjamin situates this productive boredom in a time of unified community and agreement about the nature and meaning of reality and experience (*Erfahrung*), a time embedded in a quasi-mythical natural history, outside of all real historical categories—a time before the rise of modernity, of capitalism, and of the novel. In keeping with the positive evaluation of boredom is the concomitantly positive role of repetition: the iterative rhythm of work engenders the requisite boredom in both the speaker and listener, letting the one practice the art of repeating stories, and the other listen in such a way that the gift of retelling them comes to him all by itself.[6] One might say that, between them, boredom and repetition secured the web of tradition and community that preserved and extended the significant, shared, and somewhat idyllic social world, a world equally and identically represented in the community and its stories.[7]

With the move into modernity proper, Benjamin describes not only an unraveling of the "original" conditions for boredom but also the plaiting of new conditions; and parallel with this, he describes both a decline in the art of storytelling and communicable experience, as well as a rise in the art of the novel.

In the new context, both boredom and narrative acquire new functions in the constitution of reality, significance, and experience. To a large extent, the new functions for both are predicated on the same conditions: both arise out of the fall from (idyllic) natural history into real historical categories. That is, both the new boredom and the novel arise out of the same loss of unified community and of agreement about the nature and meaning of reality and experience. As opposed to its previously positive character, boredom now becomes defined as the experience of emptiness, as pure negativity. At the same time, however, Benjamin also describes this boredom as the new condition or expression of the individual subject, abandoned and challenged to make meaning, pleasure, entertainment (*Kurzweile*), indeed reality for himself—a task most characteristically achieved and reflected in the newly dominant literary genre of the novel.[8]

Benjamin doesn't imagine modern boredom and its corresponding narratives to arise solely out of what has disappeared from the social landscape, but also out of what has appeared in its place. He sees both to be effects of the introduction of new modes of production by capitalist society, of new conditions of work, and so too new forms of indifference, monotony, and repetition. These conditions disrupt the previous repeated chain of tradition (i.e., of repeated, secured reality). They also necessarily impose their own monotonous rhythm and shape on narration and the contemporary world. In many ways what Benjamin describes is a new dialectic of boredom, a dialectic newly engaging *and* disengaging the individual and society: wherein truly communal society is lost, and so the individual rendered isolated, aimless, and bored, but wherein the prototechnological society is rendered omnipresent and uniformly monotonous, and so the individual assimilated and lost.[9] Gone is the easy collusion and shared simple boredom of individual and community to the "prehistorical" world.

One consequence of the modern dialectical conception of boredom is a new and equally dialectical conception of the relation between *Langweile* and *Kurzweile,* boredom and pleasure. This new conception is perhaps first—and certainly best—represented by Soren Kierkegaard in his essay "The Rotation Method" (1842).[10] Kierkegaard begins his essay by adopting the principle that "all men are bores," but he quickly makes a subdivision that becomes characteristic for almost all nineteenth-century discussions of boredom, its primary form of nonsimplicity: a division between those who bore others—"the mob, the crowd, the infinite multitude of men in general"—and those who bore themselves—"the elect, the aristocracy," the would-be individuals.[11] The first group, centrally represented in *Fatso* by both the philistines of the Brummersumm tavern and the postman Störzer, is described by Kierkegaard as believing that "the end and aim of life is work." They do not bore themselves because they do not recognize their own boredom; rather, in one way or another they keep themselves extremely busy, fearing idleness as the root of all evil. "[T]hese people are precisely on this account the most boring, the most unendurable."[12] That is, in order to avoid potentially productive or at least disruptive boredom by means of work, the mob becomes boring, also by means of work. Work-boredom actively represses individual boredom.[13]

Kierkegaard notes that the mob has "an extraordinary talent for transforming everything into a matter of business, whose whole life is business, who fall in love, marry, listen to a joke, and admire a picture with the same industrious zeal with which they labor during business hours."[14] This is basically the same insight expressed by his contemporary Georg Büchner when in *Lenz* he writes, "Most people pray out of boredom, others fall in love out of boredom," and so on (and on).[15] The extension of the conditions of both work and boredom into the lifestyle and aesthetics of the mob ("how they admire a picture") begins to produce those cultural conditions that in a somewhat more exaggerated state become the focus of Frankfurt School theorists such as Horkheimer, Adorno, and Kracauer.[16] They emphasize how the leveling, indifferent, standardizing monotony of modern work eventually imposes a similar (and similarly repressive) standardization on those cultural products—that is, on that entertainment, or *Kurzweile*, by which the mob would divert itself from the monotony of its work: it seeks relief from monotony in monotony. So, for example, the masses seek escape from the boring repetitiveness of their real lives in fictions, but these fictions must display a certain predictability, redundancy, or repetition of convention if they are to provide the required pleasure. *Kurzweile* is reduced to an identical *Langweile,* an identical monotony and redundancy.[17] Moreover, the very monotony, indifference, and repetition of these fictions has the anaesthetic effect of convincing the mob that "reality" repeats, corresponds, is monotonous with them. The fictions comprise a generally shared, perpetuating web or chain that is real without being true, that repeats society's conventions but not its reality, which in fact they repress.

The second group identified by Kierkegaard, namely the aristocratic elite—represented, albeit problematically, by both Eduard and Fatso, each of whom in his own way would distinguish himself from the common herd of men—acquires a more positive evaluation of boredom. This derives first and foremost from the belief that the end and aim of life is not work, but pleasure. This in turn entails a rejection of work, or more precisely, of work without pleasure; but work for its own sake is considered boring, and these privileged individuals reject its occupation and accept the popularly feared idleness even at the risk of boredom. As Nietzsche will put it: "They do not fear boredom so much as work without pleasure; in fact, they need a good deal of boredom if their work is to succeed. For the thinker and for all sensitive spirits, boredom is that unpleasant, windless calm of the soul that precedes the happy voyage and joyous winds; he must endure it, must wait out its effect on him."[18] The need, or if you will, the work of boredom for these "artists and contemplatives of all kinds" is actually twofold. First, this elite group would not only exempt itself from the anaesthetizing ethics of utility and engagement of the common herd; it would also detach itself from the common, anaesthetizing aesthetics of the "interesting," from those normed conventional standards of the entertaining and meaningful that broadly count not only for taste but also for "reality"—herd discourse, as it were, Brummersumm culture. The sovereign indifference, the stoic detachment of *nil admirari*, the egotistic boredom toward everyday accepted pleasures and rituals, even toward their own everyday selves—this is the boredom with boringness that distinguishes the elite individuals from the herd and that constitutes the first work of their boredom.

The boredom of the elect does not, however, work only to cure them from the common aesthetics or anaesthetics of the "interesting," of *Kurzweile*. This group also does not tolerate its boredom, does not remain in a Romantic idyll of inactivity. Rather, boredom again, though differently, works as a negative motor, as an irritant driving the subject in pursuit of new pleasures, different and untried forms of the amusing and interesting. Such is the dialectic of *Lang-*

weile and *Kurzweile* most often associated with the figures of the artist and aesthete in the nineteenth century: rejecting the common, mundane "reality," he is isolated and bored and so motivated both to interrupt the common, boring pleasures and to find his own new, interesting pleasures—his own reality. With all his characteristic irony, Kierkegaard displays the evident paradox here: for all its disdain for the conflation of *Langweile* and *Kurzweile* of the mob, the elite group ends up with its own related equation, with *Kurzweile* again, though differently, a product and expression of boredom.

Kierkegaard also makes a further division in his analysis, one based on the different methods chosen by the would-be elect to escape from their boredom; and while the precise situation of Eduard and Fatso (or rather of their boredoms) within Kierkegaard's categories of the mob and the elect proves crucially problematic, they themselves correspond fairly exactly to the terms of this second division. Kierkegaard distinguishes between what he calls the extensive and the intensive approaches, roughly corresponding to the literary motifs of the journey and of *Bildung* and to the chosen paths of Eduard and Fatso, respectively. According to Kierkegaard, the extensive is "the vulgar and inartistic method, and needs to be supported by illusion. One tires of living in the country, and moves to the city; one tires of one's native land, and travels abroad; one is *europamüde* and goes to America, and so on."[19] The method defeats itself. The remedy against boredom also serves to produce boredom: its result is endless repetition, both of its technique of interruption and of its "new" pleasure. That is, for all its desire to escape from the monotony and predictability of the mob's mode of life and of entertainment, this vulgar aristocratic approach falls prey to a similar monotony and predictability. In the long run, the aesthetics of interest, whether driven by a demand for ever-sameness or ever-difference, ends up the same: with oversameness, repetition, and boredom. (The further irony, though not explored by Kierkegaard, is close at hand: that nothing seems more heavily coded as common and cliché than this notion of the exotic and unusual; even that the notion of escape from bourgeois reality is itself a reflex of that same reality.)

The intensive method—Fatso's own method—of escaping boredom follows a different principle, that of limitation, "the only saving principle in the world."

In Kierkegaard's scheme, it is the privileged and seemingly correct method:

> The more you limit yourself, the more fertile you become in invention. . . . How entertaining to catch a fly and hold it imprisoned under a nutshell and watch how it pushed the shell around; what pleasure from cutting a hole in the desk, putting a fly in it, and then peeping down through a piece of paper. How entertaining to listen to the monotonous drip of water from the roof![20]

This method begins with a consequent detachment from all connections to common reality, not only social and official but also to a certain extent from desire and pleasure themselves—as if in recognition of the fact that the simple disjunction of boredom/pleasure, like that of boredom/work, necessarily issues in the same boredom. Rather, this method is largely self-contained. In the words of Fatso, it is primarily a matter of perspective, or *Anschauung*. One creates, as it were, one's own mode of the interesting through contemplation, through perception of the given: one manufactures what Benjamin calls one's own meaning of life (*Sinn des Lebens*) out of the meaninglessness, emptiness, and boredom with which the given common world presents one.[21]

For all its advantages and privileges, however, the intensive delimiting mode of perceptual self-cultivation still "conceals boredom in its own depths and gradually works it out toward the surface, thus revealing itself as that which it immediately is." For our purposes—that is, for an understanding of Fatso—there are two key expressions of this underlying disruptive boredom. First, insofar as the intensive method is based on limitation, it not only assumes the indifference and abiding insignificance of the world itself. It also assumes the limits, even triviality and broader insignificance, of one's own world, interests, and achieved reality. The recognition of the self-imposed indifference and inconsequentiality of one's world always looms, and its threat is boredom with that world; and whereas that recognition and threat often remain successfully repressed, they are nonetheless consequences of the very conditions on which the method is based.[22] Thus for Kierkegaard—in his ironic detachment from the personic narrator of "The Rotation Method"—the very attempt to forge meaning or reality at the site of the isolated individual is implicitly an admission of the aimlessness and perplexity of living, a symptom of hidden despair, of the incapacity of men to escape their boredom with themselves.

For Benjamin, too, this ideal proves suspect, although his point of critique is slightly different. For Benjamin, the ideal of an individually forged "meaning of life" raises not only the problem of the general indifference or insignificance of the world or society itself. It also, crucially, raises the problem of why this achievement should be of concern to anyone else; why, for instance, Fatso's life and *Weltanschauung* should be of interest to Eduard as narrator—or to us as readers. He argues that the "meaning of life" uniquely achieved by an individual or a character in a novel speaks to the other out of the emptiness of his own: "It is a dry material on which the burning interest of the reader feeds."[23] That is, the reader's (or more specifically, Eduard's) interest in this ideal is not an immediate expression of his desire but of his boredom, of his lack of significance in himself. It is, as it were, the search for, the desire for desire. Thus, if the mob reads novels that must express a certain uniformity, even banality in order to escape its boredom, the elite read (or recount) novels that must express a certain different uniqueness and meaning in order to escape theirs: but the motive and ultimate futility remain the same in both cases.[24]

We should, I think, note how this account of the modern reality or condition of boredom also seems to reverse that attributed to the mob. There, boredom produced an endless uniformity, generality, and monotony of lives and cultural products; here, it produces an endless incommensurability, uniqueness, and difference.[25] One might argue that, through the very mirror of its reversal, the ideal of the isolated self-made individual comes to resemble or repeat the assimilated society-made mob, namely through its endless propagation and so monotony, repetition, and universality. Or, conversely, the uniform norm—which is after all that of bourgeois individualism—realizes itself most forcefully at the site of its supposed opposite, the isolated individual. In any case, the possibly collapsing distinctions between the individual and the mob, between multiplicity and uniformity, between nonidentical and identical realities, seem also to suggest a certain oversameness, which both results from and yields the same, overriding boredom—the same entrapment in a fiction, the same isolation from reality.

The second key expression of the boredom still at work in the intensive method and that keeps its ideal so ambivalent in a figure such as Fatso is its latent cruelty, or malice. It is no accident that Kierkegaard chooses as his first example of the pleasures and entertainment opened up by this approach the imprisonment and slightly sadistic torturing of a fly. The image is but the obverse, displaced expression of the practitioner's own imprisonment: the pain and pleasure he indifferently lumps together and deposes from himself, he imposes, similarly lumped and still indifferently, on his world and others. The callous indifference toward common, shared desire and pleasure he systematically exercises on himself becomes the mode of pleasure he then systematically exercises on, or shares with, others. As in Benjamin's analysis of the modern reason for reading, boredom replaces desire here, but in a far more potentially dangerous form: as the active elimination of desire—as sadism.[26] As we will see, the constellation of boredom and cruelty is a complex one, but even at this point we can distinguish two different though often overlapping configurations. First, the consequent attack against the general boringness of cultural reality by the individual's boredom represents its own violence, an attack against the indifference of power by the power of indifference. But second, there is the boredom, even the self-imposed boredom with himself that the individual can maliciously turn back against the world; this violence becomes the surest expression of the reality of the boredom still at work behind his self-created ideal. Strangely enough, he ends up doing precisely what he perceives vulgar culture to do: forcefully imposing his own condition on others, he initiates and perpetuates a chain of similitude. The result might well be shared reality, but it is again a reality negatively defined.

I I

Such, then, are the poetics of boredom as they emerge to shape the reality, or at least the iconography of reality, to nineteenth-century culture and society. But as already intimated by Benjamin, the poetics of boredom have special relevance for the formal consideration of the novel, quite apart from and yet in necessary affinity with the more thematic concerns addressed above.[27] Most basically, the long form of the novel, its unique investment in time—"its defining expansiveness, its long windedness, its 'good time'"[28]—introduces its own new dialectic of *Langweile* and *Kurzweile,* where one's amusement takes a long time, and where one must enjoy the time taken getting there—and yet where the very strategies mobilized to achieve pleasure share an intimate identity with those that occasion boredom instead, or as well. So, for example, and as Roland Barthes notes, the novellistic mode for generating and maintaining suspense, interest, or *Spannung*, is actually a mode of continual retardation and deferral, of putting off the final revelation or solution that will establish the significance, indeed the reality of the preceding narrative.[29] But this same device of repeated retardation that consigns the reader to waiting can also lead to a loss of interest, to *Entspannung*. As Adam Phillips puts it, the "experience of waiting for something without knowing what it could be" always hovers somewhere between boredom and desire; but if kept waiting too long, one's desire dissolves and leaves nothing but the boredom of discontent and, finally, of disappointment and even anger.[30]

What is true of the novel in general is true of the realist novel in particular: boredom is inseparable from its poetics of representation. This is true in two ways that often converge but just as often conflict in their effect, even in their intended effect. First, as I noted in chapter one, the realist novel is heavily dependent on a certain redundancy that ensures its readability.[31] It displays a foreseeable predilection for the reproduction of the ritualized activities of everyday life, or more generally, it reproduces the widely disseminated iconography of daily "real" life as its own, indeed as the security for its own reality. As Maupassant and Flaubert observed, this often calls for a kind of willed mediocrity, an embeddedness in the commonplace and even trivial. Both the reader's pleasure and sense of reality derive from this artificially achieved redundancy, but so too does his potential boredom (and sense of artifice: predictability). Quite apart from the effect of its long, retarded form, then, the realist poetics of novellistic *Kurzweile* threaten *Langweile*; even apart from the prescribed engagement with trivial, mediocre reality, the ideal of redundancy, mono-tony or "monosemesis" with extratextual reality invites a potentially fatal anaesthetic oversameness. Moreover, the fact that the things repeated are themselves repetitious—daily rituals, recognizable because recurrent types, events that always turn out "as expected"—and are then themselves often repeatedly represented in the narrative in order to secure the redundantly real effect—this merely increases the same effect of oversameness: a semantic saturation of significance, predictability, and monotony.

Second, and as also noted in chapter one, the realist novel is often characterized by a superfluity of detail, an excess of description often manifested in catalogues and collections of "things" whose enumeration can easily induce something akin to museum fatigue in the reader.[32] And whereas the effect is similar to that of the tendency described above, its aesthetic intent is not—at least not initially. Rather, the evocation of the discrete detail or list of details is intent on challenging or resisting meaning, on opposing functional assimilation to established (fictional) systems of intelligibility. Thus while this tendency also deploys a certain redundancy in its reference to the reader's extratextual reality, the deployment is actually aimed against readability, against the *vraisemblable*, and it is at least as much if not more this alleged resistance to or frustration of conventional structures of the sensible as its supposed extratextual referentiality that achieves the realistic effect. Of course, and as also already noted, the interruption of readable structures by extraneous, excessive detail nonetheless eventually evinces its own structure of intelligibility, its own conventionality; the need to impede convention becomes its own convention, and develops a redundancy and predictability remarkably similar to those it supposedly opposes. More centrally for our present purposes, it also falls prey to a similar degree of induced boredom. Again, the very strategy deployed for achieving the effect of the real—here, resistance to traditional structure, evocation of endless superfluous details—shares an intimate identity with that which achieves boredom as well. And again, the supposed opposite to the oversame (the traditional structures) turns out to result in a similar oversameness, and the collapse of the alleged difference to the one and of the distinction between the two yields even more oversameness, monotony, and potential for boredom.[33]

It might seem to go without saying that the *Langweile* so inseparable from realist aesthetics is detrimental to the pleasure and effect it intends.[34] However, the an-aesthetic effect of boredom and oversameness can also be deliberate, its hypertrophy of redundancy a conscious realist strategy rather than an unwanted or merely tolerated by-product. This was recognized, for example, by Thomas Mann in the case of Stifter, whom he called "one of the greatest and most inspiring vindicators of the honor of boredom [*Langenweile*]."[35] And it has also been recognized, for example by Jeffrey Sammons, in the case of Raabe, whose narratives were (and still are) often perceived to be as boring as those of Stifter, but with an even greater degree of deliberate maliciousness and, more important, with an even greater amount of explicit thematization and self-conscious representation of his practice.³⁶ The latter point is evidenced in Raabe's berating narratorial apostrophes to his implied readers and their insipid, interest-driven expectations, and even more so in his use of dramatized character-narrators such as both Eduard and Fatso, who thrust their own boringness forcefully into the discursive foreground. Like Stifter, Raabe *aims* at the effect of boredom and oversameness, and as we will see, he does so as part of his realist project.³⁷

One last general point about the poetics of boredom and the novel, and especially the realist novel. In availing himself of the device of the overtly boring narrator, Raabe situates his work within or against another novellistic tradition particularly prominent in, if not unique to, the nineteenth century. No doubt the best known early representative of this tradition is Goethe's Wilhelm Meister, who at the beginning of the *Apprenticeship* (*Lehrjahre*, 1795/96) narrates episodes out of his bourgeois childhood and in doing so manages to put his listener, Mariane, to sleep. Similarly, in Heine's *Florentine Nights* (1825/35), the narrator Max's droning monologue lulls his female listener, Maria, to sleep, this time perhaps even to death. We find several examples in the realist period beside *Fatso*, such as Keller's *Pankraz the Sulker* (*Pankraz der Schmoller*, 1856) or Raabe's own *Pfister's Mill* (1884); and on the far side of realism we find another in chapter eighteen of Kafka's *The Castle* (1926), where the official Bürgel drones on and on in a conscious and successful effort to put K., and perhaps himself, to sleep. In each case, there is an evident, albeit underlying aggression toward the listener manifested in the narrator's boring discourse, and the intentionality to the boredom and its aggression seem to become increasingly overt as the tradition develops. As we will see, *Fatso* clearly promotes this move toward overt intentionality, and adds some key realist features to the tradition, namely a certain characteristic pettiness and deployment of redundancy in effecting his aggressive boringness. For now I want merely to note the existence of this narrative mode and its marked contrast to the more familiar tradition of narration most often associated with the figure of Scheherazade. In the latter, more "normal" case, the point is ever to recapture the interest of the reader, to ward off boredom and so to ward off death, with tales repeated with endless variation. Here the point seems to be to lose, even to kill the reader's interest, to invite boredom and so too death, with tales repeated without variation. In this respect, too, the poetics of boredom and oversameness has its own secure place in the tradition of the novel, and vies with that of a competing poetics of interest, or *Kurzweile*. And in this respect, too, boredom becomes inseparably linked with a certain calculated cruelty, a deadly intent to its pleasure and its narratorial practice. Which brings us to Fatso.

III

The problem of monotonous repetition and its consequent boredom is present in almost every aspect of *Fatso*; in and between each of the various textual levels of the story and its frame, in and between the various figures, even in and between almost every sentence.[38] But as I hope to show, this pervasive, sustained, and repeated effect is not or is not only an unfortunate, unintended, unaesthetic one. Rather, the repetitions and their boredom are complexly overdetermined by both the unconscious and the highly questionable conscious impulses loose in the text. And as I also hope to show, each aspect of the conscious and unconscious motivations of the repetitions and their tedium—and especially perhaps their contradictions—has consequences for the realism at stake in the novel.

Let us begin with the character of Eduard. Eduard is important not only as character and as auditor of Fatso's embedded narration but also as the *target* of Fatso's narration and as the narrator of the frame. As Ohl insists, this targeting of Eduard is essential to an understanding of the entire novel, and explains why a discussion of repetition and boredom must also begin with his character. For whereas the other central figures of Störzer, Quakatz, and Fatso are all explicitly inscribed in patterns of a repetition-of-the-same, that is not the immediately apparent case with Eduard. However, what the novel (and not only Fatso in the novel) aims to reveal is precisely how Eduard is so inscribed, both as character and as narrator. Even if initially least obvious and most banal, Eduard's stakes in the poetics of boredom and repetition and their relation to realism prove most central and complex. It is no accident, then, that the first word of his narration, and of the novel, is "Again."

The most palpable basis for Eduard's boringness consists in his conventionality, in his immersion in a more than somewhat banally bourgeois, philistine reality—in his entrenched position in Brummersumm culture. And it is only an apparent paradox that Eduard exposes his inscription in this everyday social reality most through his tendency to sentimentalize and idyllize that world, for his literalization always takes place according to an established iconography of the interesting and real, which constantly reveals its conventional philistine basis. This is perhaps most patently revealed in Eduard's nearly insipid description of Fatso's farm, the so-called Red Bank (*Rote Schanze*), in terms of the widely known and popular "pretty, old, and heart-warming pictures" such as Spitzweg sketched (51). But even if not so highly signaled, it is no less evident in his description of his boyhood walks with the postman Störzer, which must be quoted at some length to convey the characteristic effect of Eduard's narration:

What did I care about the correspondence of the farmers, the landowners, the manufacturers that he carried in his satchel across the country? There were far too many more important matters that crawled, flew, ran, buzzed, glowed, fluttered and shone along both the highway and the byways for me to be concerned about. Yes, if the cuckoo, the sparrow, the hedgehog, the hare and the rest of the company, including the sun, the shadow, the wind, the rain, the lightning and the thunder, had all entered into written communication among themselves through Störzer's mediation, then perhaps it would have been even more marvelous. But it was also altogether good how all around the rye and the wheat, the cornflower and the cornpoppy got along without ink, quill, and paper and, without any advanced education . . . knew how to live together in a friendly and sociable manner. (20)

For all the repetition and rhythmic monotony to the several lists of nouns and verbs, the primary source of repetition and monotony here is not really in the lists themselves but rather, I think, in the clichéd sensibility they represent. In fact, even the device of the list, with its sentimental particularization of its iconographic arsenal, seems more monotonous in its conventionality than in its particularity. And in the same way, for all the apparent contrast to the paper-world of the bourgeois carried about in Störzer's satchel, Eduard's "real" natural world—his "more important matters"—seems just as papered and just as bourgeois. It is just this conventionality of the interesting, this mobilization of an established iconography of the real that is the first mark of Eduard as boring—and as a "realist," as a reproducer of that normed discourse that simply assumes itself to be identical with external, extratextual reality.

Eduard's conventional construction of reality is not only enforced in the novel; it is also placed under attack, and not so much by any external reality as by and from within his construction itself.[39] So, for instance, despite Eduard's pronounced idyllization of his hometown (*Heimatstadt*), it is also coded by him as almost exaggeratedly normal and unchanging. In part this is precisely what is idyllized and valorized as real about the hometown culture, the firm if false sense of established repeated norms and coded perceptions. But in part this normalization is instead in the service of Eduard's idyllization and valorization of himself as opposed to his hometown. This opposition to the idyll by its seeming own proponent and participant is the occasion for the recognition of his hometown's boring, trivial, even stupefying nature: "Where in all the world is it easier than in the Brummersumm to turn the point around and let the boring, the stupid, the tasteless, the malicious, the envious world stick it to itself? (12). Eduard of course would exempt himself from this attack against the boring and malicious philistine world—a world coded and attacked as such precisely in the service of his self-exemption, of the self-idyllization that requires his exemption, his difference and distance from the hometown reality and idyll.[40] That is, Eduard conceives of his life "away" in distant Africa as far removed from the trivial redundancy of bourgeois reality and as firmly situated in a quite different life of significant accomplishments and authentic experience. So, for example, Eduard imagines, "as what a hero and with what a wealth of experiences and achievements under my belt I am now returning!" (160), a sense of real adventures and experiences that would elevate him to an elite, even aristocratic status and that would invest him with a privileged "realism" that, by virtue of his familiarity with a certain otherness, permits him to see through the limited, exclusive codes that count for hometown reality.[41]

Eduard's self-idyllization, however, his sense of himself as both more interesting and somehow more weighted with the real than others, is itself subject to collapse from two different directions. First, for all its would-be distance and exoticism, Eduard's life in Africa proves on closer examination to be itself thoroughly bourgeois; it proves a repetition of the near and conventional. His inscription in the same is most clearly indicated by the Spitzweg painting over his wife's sofa and by the name of his "new" homeland, Neoteutoberg; but it is also present in most every detail of his domestic setup "down yonder, out there" (57).[42] Second, even insofar as his life and reality are truly different—as represented for example by the lion-skin rug beneath the Spitzweg painting—they are so in thoroughly conventional terms. As evidenced both by its original source in the travelogues of LeVaillant ("how pleasant it is to read, because he describes it all so pleasantly at home," 18) and by its association with the figure of Störzer, the iconography of an escape from bourgeois norms realized and invoked by Eduard proves relentlessly bourgeois: not only the idea of Africa or the sense of exotic adventures but even the notion of escape itself.[43] Nothing seems quite so normed as Eduard's sense of the abnormal, of his own "otherness": nothing shows his entrapment as much as his mode of escape; nothing seems so banally conventional as his understanding of the unconventional and interesting. Both aspects—his redundant normalcy and his equally redundant mode of otherness—are symptomatic of his faithful adherence to the coded discourse of his philistine world, the latter no less and perhaps more expressive of his representation of a deeply conventional "poetic" realism.

Each of these tendencies toward monotonous redundancy that manifest themselves in Eduard's represented character also and even first manifest themselves in his narration. Much like Dante in *The Marriage of the Monk* (and despite the more pronounced objective nature to the represented world), the true reality represented or repeated by the narration here is that of the narrator, whose representation—again like Dante's—often seems geared to conceal rather than reveal the actual story.[44] In this case, not so much due to the objective nature of the represented reality as to the inevitable grounding of Eduard's character in the fictions of that represented world, the self-revealing, often obscuring narration also displays the same symptoms of poetizing—of clichés, conventions, deployed iconography, etc.—that manifest themselves in or as the story's poetic reality. That is, Eduard's narrative seems redundant of its own redundancy; it presents us with ever more of the same.

And yet this is not quite the case, or rather, it is the case, but in a more complex form of sameness or repetition. For some reason, Eduard is made to experience the potential tension between the desired conventional idyll and his actual disappointment or disenchantment with it, both in respect to his hometown and the disillusionment of his return to it (56; cf. 123) and in respect to himself and his personal achievements (cf. 60, 67).[45] At the level of Eduard's narration, this gap opened up by the failure of his poetic representation expresses itself in several apparently similar but different forms. First, the repetition of the idyll-making becomes all the more insistent, that is, repetitive, in a somewhat desperate effort to reconstitute the lost or at least threatened idyll. A note of both panic and aggression enters into Eduard's idyllizing, which however must be neutralized or repressed in order to preserve the idyll. Thus, while his redundancy of established representational conventions becomes more or less consciously redundant, more or less consciously a fiction, the conscious fiction to the redundancy must be hid, and the idyllizing presented as "still the same," that is, disguised as boring, monotonous, unchanged—as real. In this way, Eduard's boringness, monotony, and redundancy become something quite different from their original role as signals of his embeddedness in conventional reality or fictions; they become a cover, a repression of that reality turned fiction, unreal fiction. We see this for example in Eduard's first mention of Störzer: "My old friend Störzer. My good old friend from the highway of childhood" (7). The very threat to the reality of Eduard's idyllic image of his "friend" leads him to repeat the "old" image even more insistently, with the increase in the conventionality ("my good old friend") both increasing Eduard's (same old) boring redundancy and expressing its loss, its lack of redundancy, mono-tony, reality.[46]

Second, at some equally conscious and unconscious level (and equally though differently expressive of his realist enterprise), Eduard also seems engaged in something of an exploratory exorcism of his tendency to create illusions and idylls, or rather, his tendency to reproduce established idylls. In this case, too, his repetition of the redundancies—of the idyll-making—becomes all the more insistent, and aggressive; but here in the service of dismantling, rather than restoring, the normed discourse or iconography of philistine "reality." Again, the aggression and repetitions are involved in rendering the redundancies boring and monotonous, but not so as to hide them, but to expose them, as fictions, to both himself and his reader. By consciously and repeatedly repeating the repetition, it becomes emptied of its identity and exposed as what it is: a redundant representation with no claim of commensurability with reality.

We can see this apparently contradictory tendency toward increasing the redundancy, repetitiveness, and fictionality to his narration most clearly in respect to the frame story of Eduard's seafaring journey back to Africa. For whereas Eduard seems primarily committed to the idyllic representation of the embedded narrative set in his hometown—both naively and self-consciously repressively—and only secondarily to its deconstruction, he seems not at all committed to the idyllic, conventional treatment of the framing sea story (*Seegeschichte*), and it is only indirectly that its conventional and idyllizing function comes into play. Eduard does not reproduce or repeat the common literary conventions of the adventure story in his narration of his life at sea. Rather, parallel and only apparently reversing the earlier distinction between the philistinism of his hometown and his own distanced, uniquely interesting life, Eduard consciously rails against its established iconography as boring and untrue. He deliberately and aggressively counters the implied reader's expectations for an eventful, "interesting" sea story by insisting that the reality is itself boring—normal, monotonous, and unchanging—as are too the reader's normal, conventional standards of interest or significance: "It is a great and disappointing mistake to suppose that something remarkable occurs every moment on the high seas, and that a German group of traveling companions is always uncommonly humorous, affable, tasteful, and—*interesting*" (60, Raabe's emphasis).

Admittedly, the reasons are complex for Eduard's contradictory narratorial procedure in aggressively marshaling literary clichés for the representation of his hometown and just as aggressively assaulting them for that of his sea voyage. As we will have occasion to address later on, the shift to a more dominantly deconstructive and disenchanted mode in the temporally subsequent frame story is certainly at least in part symptomatic of the effect Fatso's assault on Eduard has had in the embedded narrative. But in part it is also symptomatic of Eduard's own, uneffected tendency toward self-idyllization, which is only apparently threatened by his attack on the very type of adventure story on which he bases his self-importance. Rather, by distancing himself from and deliberately disappointing the poetics of interest he associates with the common herd ("a German group of traveling companions"), Eduard once again works to maintain his own sense of privileged exceptionalism and realism.

We can see Eduard's frustration of the reader's expectations for the frame story and his concomitant assertion of his own elite vantage in his report of the storm at sea. Rather than describing it, he simply says: "See *The Tempest*, an enchanted fairy tale by William Shakespeare, but see it—if you are at all able—only from a reserved box seat, somewhere comfortable" (101). An "exciting" account of the storm is short-shrifted, reduced to mere complacent literary cliché, as a deliberate affront to the philistine, standardized, and "false" sense of the interesting and real; at the same time, Eduard asserts both his superior, elite culture (quoting Shakespeare in the original) and his superior knowledge of the world, his freedom from the poetic illusions of his "comfortable" bourgeois readers.

Still, for all Eduard's apparent assault on the standardized literary conventions of his hopelessly philistine audience, he himself does not seem fully to escape that same conventionalism. We can see this in three ways. First, even while parodying the clichéd conventions of his reader's expectations, Eduard nonetheless uses them and so maintains or repeats the standard illusion; as with the idyllization of his hometown, the repeated fictions seem simultaneously to be dismantled and reinforced in Eduard's representation. This is perhaps most evident in his notably conventional strategy of juxtaposition between events and motifs in the frame and in the story proper. For example, he follows his deflating description of "Fire on board!" as nothing but a cook's smoldering socks with the exclamation, "Just as if the cry had also rung out from the house, 'Fire! Fire at the Red Bank!', I sprang to my feet" (93); whereas the first case thwarts the reader's established expectations, the second reinforces the norm of significant correspondences between the narrative's textual levels. The same standard use of the juxtaposed stories is apparent in the coordination of the rising sea storm in the frame with the rising tension in the primary narrative, and less climactically but just as conventionally, in the coordination of the meals to the two stories or of their conclusions. In both respects, insofar as he intentionally frustrates the anticipated redundancy to the literary convention and intentionally deploys or repeats it, Eduard proves boring; but the latter case is different, and it begins to undermine the undermining effect of the former.

Second, even to the extent that Eduard does truly challenge the standardized values of the adventure story and their claims to represent "reality," the reality with which he opposes those values and claims is itself still completely bourgeois. For instance, he avoids the disappointing mistake (*Täuschung*) of his traveling companions who await something interesting and remarkable on deck because, as he says, "I have been on board a ship often enough in my life to know what is the more agreeable way to pass one's time on an extended voyage" (60); his disillusioned, more experienced realism is still based on the same philistine ideal of comfort or agreeability (*das Behaglichere*) that he mocks in the others (cf. 101). The same is true when Eduard rhetorically inquires "whether it is not remarkable for a man to be writing on a ship, on the so-called high seas . . . about the so-called familiar philistine life of the fatherland" (81); he counters the one philistine convention of "the remarkable" with an identical interest in philistine convention. Thus the distance he introduces proves no distance at all, the opposition just ever more of the same.

Finally, even to the extent that Eduard does just oppose, interrupt, or frustrate the clichéd expectations of his implied reader, he does so *repeatedly*, and the mere hypertrophic repetition of the device, technique, or operation effectively negates and reverses its function. It becomes its own cliché, its own convention, its own source of boredom and monotony.

The consequences of Eduard's use of literary clichés for our problem of poetic realism are worth considering. To some extent, Eduard's usage can be seen quite neatly to conform to the dual-natured models of realism proposed by Jakobson and Barthes that I described in chapter one and that I have deployed throughout this study. But Eduard's practice also radically draws these same models into question On the one hand, in his naive, redundant adherence to conventional representational modes, Eduard expresses the reality (if falseness) of these conventions, and himself as "really" embedded in their reality or, rather, in their modes of representation. However, and at least partially indicative of the by now relatively late realism of Raabe (1890s), this redundant adherence to convention is no longer truly naive on Eduard's part, and so no longer clearly expressive of their reality, but rather of their more or less consciously repressive fiction. On the other hand, in Eduard's efforts to frustrate the automatization of conventional clichéd expectations, whether his own or the reader's, he is engaged in the typical realist task of defamiliarization or disillusionment, through the overt literalization and conventionalization of devices and tropes, resulting in the disjunction of their identification, redundancy, or monotony with "reality." However, and again indicative of the late realism of Raabe, even this disillusioning or impeding function has become more or less a recognizable literary convention, and so no longer automatically a realist operator; the fact that Eduard invokes the technique so repeatedly contributes to its automatization even within the novel.

One obvious corollary of this is that it is unclear how much Eduard is self-deceived in his illusion-breaking, whether or not, like the supposed difference between the conventional philistine of the hometown and the exotic adventurer out of Africa, the difference between the redundancy of and the interruption of the conventional doesn't itself dissolve into a redundancy of oversameness: nothing seems quite so (and becomes more) tropological than Eduard's de-troping, and the convention it represents seems not another but rather still the same convention, that of poetic realism itself. This is, then, the counterpart to the undermining of the first mode of "realism" to Jakobson's model: even as Eduard's adherence to the conventional representational modes of his time proves no longer naive but self-deceptive, and so no longer a mark for their "realism" but rather for their repressive fiction, so his deautomatization of those same modes proves no longer different and so again self-deceptive and no longer a mark for its realism but rather for the same ongoing fiction. And to some extent, it is in just this double self-deception that the new dialectic of fiction and reality to the novel's poetic realism emerges: where the continued, repeated efforts at idyll-making become symptomatic of the repressed failure to maintain the illusion or reality, and where the continued, repeated efforts at idyll-breaking become equally symptomatic of the repressed failure to escape the same illusion/reality. For all their apparent opposition, Eduard's (main-story) efforts at preserving the idyllic illusion and his (frame) efforts at destroying the exotic illusion are motivated by the same reality, and express the same fiction-making drive: the reality of the failure of both efforts, the fiction of both their "realities."

IV

Whereas the repetitive boredom of Eduard and his primary narrative often seems naive, unacknowledged, or at best aggressively hidden, that of "the frightful bore" (73) Fatso and his narrative seems just the opposite: sophisticated, self-conscious, and aggressively exposed. As with Eduard, there might well be a certain original basis for the boringness to Fatso's character. But just as Eduard's monotonous redundancy quickly becomes no longer simply naive but instead complexly motivated by a kind of willed blindness and insecure fear, so too does Fatso's, primarily by a unique kind of self-achieved insight and confident anger. This is not to say that there isn't also a complexity of unconscious motivation to Fatso's tedium equal to Eduard's—far from it: and as we will see, both the conscious and unconscious determinants of his poetics of boredom have consequences for realism every bit as important as Eduard's.

Certainly the first function and primary conscious motivation to Fatso's poetics of boredom is deliberately to frustrate and target Eduard: to confront and expose the latter's supposedly unacknowledged boringness with his own self-conscious and exposed boringness; to break down Eduard's self-image and world(s) through retardation, redundancy, and monotony. As Fatso ironically declares, "But if I'm boring you, I'll stop at once, O most interesting of all Africans and best of all old friends" (65), where the purpose of his boringness is precisely to question and impede Eduard's understanding of himself as interesting and his childhood idyllic; to make what is comfortable uncomfortable, what is canny uncanny, and what is familiar strange (cf. 196).[47]

To accomplish this, Fatso has recourse to an extremely limited but effective arsenal of boring devices. Significantly, the majority of these are the same devices employed by nineteenth-century novelists to sustain interest and the illusion of reality, here deliberately applied to achieve apparently opposing results. So for example, there is the matter of pace. Fatso says, "Oof! Go slow now. No need to hurry. Why shouldn't we take our time?" to which Eduard remarks, "I was so intent [*gespannt*] now on what he had to show me that it took me some real effort to moderate my pace from the gold fields of Kaffraria to his pace at the Red Bank" (61). As mentioned above, "taking one's time" in the novel is not traditionally opposed to its mode of interest and narrative continuity, and is in fact indispensable to its characteristic mode of achieving an aesthetic effect of realism (through detail, elaboration, and so forth). Nor is the strategy of retardation traditionally something other than its mode of suspense, or *Spannung*. But Fatso practices a particular mode of slowing things down—one perhaps best characterized by degree, that is, by the sustained superfluity of retarding repetitions and repeated retardations—which seems specifically calculated to thwart traditional narrative continuity and its conventional aesthetic mode for establishing the illusion of reality, to deny the anticipated aesthetic satisfaction of interest to which Eduard has grown accustomed and on which apparently his own illusions of reality (interest) depend. Fatso does not, that is, simply push the standard poetic devices of repetition to the point where they are rendered unpoetic and monotonous. Rather, his hypertrophy of repetition aims to expose the oversameness and monotony to the accepted poetic deployment of these same devices.

Certainly the excessively retarded and monotonous pace of Fatso's narration contributes greatly to its tediousness and to Eduard's almost desperate irritation and defensive boredom. But these are also the result of Fatso's strategic use of superfluity and redundancy, in ways that reflect more directly on the conventions of the realist novel and more specifically on Eduard's stake in "reality." Fatso has a pronounced propensity for re-presenting, and repeatedly representing, the seemingly obvious and often trivial: the self-evident (*selbstverständlich*, 69,123), the already known, "as if he were pointing out something completely new" (125), and such instances typically call forth responses from Eduard such as, "It was entirely unnecessary for my friend Schaumann to seem to consider it necessary to further arouse my attention" (56; cf. 75). A similar tendency might be seen in the exaggerated emphasis Fatso places on his repeated daily rituals, such as meals, walks, the lighting of his pipe, or his wife Tina's knitting; it can also be seen in his constant narrative repetition of what he has already established in his story. In the realist novel, such a redundant, repeated representation of the everyday, familiar *Selbstverständliche* is of course part of the pleasure and of the easy, ongoing security of its reality; and while the strategy risks a potential monotony of the obvious, it does so to achieve a certain desired mono-tony, i.e., a mono-semesis between these redundant representations and "reality." But as Eduard's responses make clear, while Fatso's hypertrophic use of redundancy initially calls forth the easy security of reality that traditionally answers it, it hardly does so in a way that produces pleasure; and if Fatso's strategy seems actively to invite a usually avoided sense of monotony, this is because it would disrupt the usually desired monotony—that is, the identity or repetition between these self-obvious representations and "reality."

Another way in which Fatso's hypertrophic redundancy would break down Eduard's sense of reality comes in what it opposes, what Eduard does not consider self-evident or redundant, what instead he feels to be significant, the "real" matter at hand that the redundancies merely postpone or suppress: the narrative. However, Fatso aims to reveal this too as a mode of redundancy, in fact as the same mode of redundancy that his hypertrophy of the obvious displays. He does so in two ways: in terms of the story he tells and the one he won't let be told, namely Eduard's own. On the one hand, the "real" story of himself, Tina, and her father that Fatso's dilations on the obvious interrupt is itself couched in the sentimental, idyllic conventions of the obvious, of the "readable" that are so prominent in his nonnarrative dilations: what is interrupted is often made to seem as monotonous, trivial, and obvious as what interrupts—and just as fictional. (The same of course is true of the "real" story of Kienbaum's murder that Fatso so successfully defers: it too is saturated with literary convention and banality.)[48] On the other hand, although the double topos—itself repeated to the point of monotony—is that Fatso keeps interrupting his own story and Eduard (and Tina) keep interrupting his monologue, it seems clear that part of the point of Fatso's deliberately trivial, redundant monologue is continually, even permanently, to disrupt Eduard's story, not to allow him his narrative—which we know is the truly monotonous, unbroken monologue, the monologue of philistine convention. That is, Fatso uses one form of drowning redundancy not only to suppress his own narrative and Eduard's but also to suggest their identity, their eventual oversameness.

Fatso's use of redundancy and repetition to break down Eduard's sense of reality also extends to his somewhat parodic repetition of Eduard's own conventional language and attitudes. This includes not only Fatso's use of literary clichés (e.g., 45) but also certain conventions of behavior and appearance, such as his frequent sighs of self-contentment or his overall apparent representation of a certain philistine ideal. One particularly telling instance of this comes just at the end of Eduard's account of their boyhood parting, as Fatso prepares to kiss Tina on the wall of the Red Bank:

> "And you, my good Eduard, be so kind as to look out once more at the lovely landscape and your beloved hometown—a shame, really, that the bells aren't ringing right now, too. That's how it should be, you embarrassed young boy—"
>
> I really did look around—intimidated, distracted, and embarrassed. I looked out at the landscape and the city down in the valley—in short, I looked away, and, behind my back, with my ears ringing and buzzing, I heard a quick succession of sounds. (48)

This is admittedly a complicated moment: let us just concentrate on Fatso's conscious strategy, his knowing triviality, and its target, Eduard. Fatso's use of "the lovely landscape," "your beloved hometown," and "the bells ringing, too," exposes and exploits his friend's tendency to poetize his perceptions and to indulge in a certain conventional unreality; Fatso uses, that is repeats, this tendency to get Eduard to look away from the "real" event (the kiss), even as he, Fatso, calls attention to the view as a convention, as a looking away. Thus, at its simplest, Fatso's re-presentation of Eduard's poetic reality aims at revealing it as a representation, as an avoidance of reality. But it is more than this: the "reality" that Eduard senses going on behind his back, that dislodges both his conventional, sentimental worldview and his sense of self, comes to him in tones just as sentimental and clichéd—and just as exaggerated. We see this repeatedly, and we see it exploited by Fatso repeatedly: Eduard is most prone to feel disrupted from his conventional poetic reality not by or into a different less scripted "reality" but rather by and into the same conventional poetic reality: the supposed disruptor proves equally monotonous, trivial, and boring. Thus, Fatso's parodic repetitions of Eduard's clichés aim not only to expose them as conventions and not reality; they also aim to expose Eduard's "realist" sense of disillusionment as a convention, one that, far from dislodging, would leave Eduard and his philistine reality even more solidly and monotonously in place on the other side, bolstered precisely by a clichéd sense of lost illusions.

V

Fatso's project of disillusionment is, of course, very much a realist project; that he would challenge not only the conventional "reality" but also the conventional realist disabusement doubles the assault, directs it more pointedly at the institution of poetic realism itself, while still remaining faithful to basic principles of its project. But Fatso's repetitions and boringness (*Langweiligkeit*) are not only engaged in the service of dismantling Eduard's philistine illusions and reality. They are also engaged in the service of establishing Fatso's own illusion or reality: a quasi-historical, mythical reality that devalues the present by introducing both a sweeping historical, even prehistorical expanse of time (a *Lang-weile*) and a set of endlessly repeating, almost archetypal patterns of human behavior.[49] Even as he assaults the redundancy and monotony of Eduard's philistine world by means of his endless repetitions, Fatso also seems to propose redundancy, monotony, and repetition as the nature of reality itself—that is, behind or beyond these same features in bourgeois reality.

We can see, for example, this illusion-breaking and -making in Fatso's prolific use of epic formulae, such as those recurrently applied to his own name, to Quakatz, to Prince Xaverius, and of course to the Red Bank. Certainly one function of these repeated, pleonastic, and somewhat anachronistic epic formulae is to bore and irritate Eduard, deliberately to impose on the traditional, realist-novellistic construction of "reality," to call attention to the hidden, unacknowledged contemporary convention by the exposed, self-conscious noncontemporary one. But another function is to further Fatso's attempt to break down narrative reality into something like mythical reality, to create a sense of "timeless" repetitions that themselves re-present reality: where a structure of repetition unites Fatso to Quakatz, and behind him to Prinz Xaverius, and beyond them all to the prehistoric sloth (*Olimfaultier*) Fatso unearths beneath the Red Bank (cf. 111f.).

Fatso's conception of reality as grounded in a quasi-mythical, redundant principle of repetition clearly represents a threat to any traditionally conceived realist aesthetic, and this threat has often gained added strength for critics from the resonances of a similar postrealist conception of "mythical" reality evident in the late works of Fontane, especially *Stechlin* (1897), and of course in those of Thomas Mann. Both this conception and its threat are perhaps most readily illustrated in respect to the issue of description, for instance in the following view from the Red Bank:

The view to the north, south, east, and west had mostly remained as it was in our childhood. There far below was still the town, there to the side the village of Maiholzen, there the forest, there the open field, and there the distant blue mountains. Therein and thereunder lay comfortably sleeping Heinrich Schaumann's flora and fauna of all the various geological eras, formations, and transitional periods, the giant sloth included and sleeping, too. Over it the late afternoon summer sunshine. Only now one or two railways lines cut across the plain. (122 f.)

Only the first two sentences would satisfy the simplest conception of the realist program as an objective, that is, superficial representation or repetition of the visibly present—or, if we choose to stress the identity of this description with Eduard's normed idyllizing discourse ("as in our childhood"), of realism as the faithful representation of a conventional ideology disguised as the objectively real. In either case, we are still dealing with the simple re-presentation of a stable, present world. And only the last sentence, with its challenge to the nostalgic idyll of the first two lines posed by the train lines of a new reality that cut across and through the supposedly unchanged scene—only this sentence represents the other standard conception of realism that we have focused on, which stresses instead the perceived gap between the normed representation and the present reality, the necessary inadequacy of the convention to the given presence. But this conception, too, is still grounded in a notion of present reality; it is simply that the convention no longer adequately represents it.[50]

However, it is just this ground, this notion, that Fatso's worldview as presented by the middle sentence challenges, and with it the entire realist enterprise. For if reality is palimpsestic, multistriated, subsumed, and shaped by the nonpresent, then a strategy of objective or superficial representation of the present is no longer adequate to "reality"—not because the representation is necessarily just that, a re-presentation and so not "there," but because reality itself is necessarily a representation, and so not "there."[51] It is the repetitive nature of reality that the simple repetition of realism cannot represent.[52]

Still, if Fatso's mythical-historical conception of reality calls realism into question, a realist conception also calls his representation into question—and it is essential that we evaluate Fatso's use of repetition, including its challenge to realism, within the context of realism. First, as Julia Hell observes, Fatso's repetitive conception of reality is to a large extent engaged in the attempt to preserve a certain feudal, provincial ideal and to ignore the present bourgeois reality; to deploy history and repetition so as to establish an imaginary identity between himself and Prinz Xaverius that situates him as something of a romanticized feudal lord, far removed from the pettiness and concerns of the present (cf. 61).[53] That is, Stopfkuchen's notions of historical repetition and *Lang-weile* are to some extent a *denial* of reality, a repression of the difference between now and then (cf. 41). In fact, and only apparently paradoxically, Fatso's personal version of repetitive reality is ultimately extremely similar to Eduard's conventional, redundant one. Both would ignore or overlook any troublesome present reality in favor of some earlier provincial idyll; both would replace the immobility of an ever-identical repetition for temporal development.[54] That is, each proves "untimely" (*unzeitgemäss*) in similar ways, and this "untimeliness" is symptomatic of each one's "timeliness," of Eduard's and Fatso's embeddedness in the present, repressive, and fictionalizing "reality" of bourgeois culture. Both employ an imperfect strategy of fictional redundancy to conceal from themselves the given, and both in using repetition to deny reality by constructing a fictional reality nonetheless still repeat the same—that same philistine reality that constructs its sentimental, self-deceiving idylls. Where Fatso sees difference and dissonance, we see sameness and monotony; the function of his oversameness repeats that of the oversameness he would oppose.[55]

A second point of critique is somewhat more difficult to formulate, but even more consequential. In consciously developing a conception of reality as palimpsestic, multistriated, and subsumed by the nonpresent in ways that challenge realism, Fatso ends up denying the one conception of reality as multistriated, nonidentical and subsumed by the nonpresent that is in fact embraced by realism, namely the conception of unconscious reality. This is especially conspicuous in respect to Fatso's notion of the dissipative effect of his repetitive worldview. Fatso's claims to authority and privileged insight rest on his belief in his power to dissipate (or disenchant) not only the superficial conventional reality of the adult Eduard but also the effective power of their shared eventful childhood past, by assimilating its supposed uniqueness and topicality to his regime of repetition and *Langweile*. But his strategy of dissipation of present reality and its immediate formative past through repetition overlooks the possible, indeed inevitable emergence of a nonpresent, unconscious reality through those same repetitions: his notion of *Langweile* as dissipating interest overlooks the possibility of *Langweile* as secretly sustaining it instead. And yet as we will see, it is at the level of the unconscious dimension of his narration that Fatso's model of nonpresent, nonrepresentable reality proves itself the real—and in so doing, subverts his conscious conception of repetitive reality.

VI

The questionable character of Fatso's boring repetitions as well as their own layered psychological reality are perhaps most pronounced when we consider his repetitions not in the service of realist disabusement, nor in that of a construction of a new alternative reality, but rather in the service of revenge—in fact, repetitions in the service of revenge for repetitions, and of the most banal type: for name-calling. Repetition and revenge are linked throughout the novel, and in several ways. First, we note how monotonous repetition, mostly in the form of name-calling, stone-throwing, and finger-pointing accusations, is the primary form of abuse and vexation throughout the childhood recounted by Fatso. In true realist fashion, the vexation is most often an effect not only of the repetition itself but also of its very triviality, or sustained triviality. But a third factor, the insistent misdirectedness of the repeated, insipid abuse, also contributes to the real effect, and introduces a new and finally most consequential play to the poetic realism at stake in the novel.

This effect is perhaps most prominently thematized in respect to the figure and nickname of Fatso himself, where we are made to sense the force of the banal abuse to which Heinrich Schaumann was repeatedly subjected as a child by means of this nickname, whose effect was real, regardless of whether it corresponded to any prior reality. But it is also the central experience or reality of both Tina and her father, Quakatz—and again, the effect is real regardless of its reality; in fact, its noncorrespondence with any reality constitutes a basic aspect of the real effect of this form of repetition. The latter finds himself over and again summoned before the authorities for his supposed crime, and the very meanness and repetitiveness of the summons, coupled with its misdirectedness, comprises its own form of tortuous, vexatious reality, quite apart from the actual nature of the summons (37). Similarly his daughter, Tina, must listen daily to the taunts of her village classmates: "Cut off her head, cut off her head! Kienbaum! Kienbaum! Tina Quakatz, cut off her head, cut off her head!" (84; cf.

105f.). And she must also suffer the same name-calling and taunting repetitions later on—and equally undeservedly, that is, misdirectedly—from her supposed ally, Fatso himself (e.g., 154). It is repetitions such as these that seem to form the underlying reality of the novel, far more than either Eduard's repeated conventions or Fatso's grandly mythical repetitions: the fact that this pattern is repeated in respect to so many of the principal characters confirms this. And again, it is a reality (and banality) that creates itself through repetition itself, without the requirement of correspondence with or representation of some prior reality, as with Fatso's mythical repetitions, nor for that matter with the falseness resulting from the lack of correspondence with some given reality, as with Eduard's conventional redundancies. On the contrary, this reality exists almost as much because of as in spite of its lack of correspondence with "reality."

If the relatively trivial repetitions of name-calling constitute the primary form of psychological abuse and realism in the story, we should also note that the primary effect of this banal monotony is to reduce its victim(s) to a similar, indeed identical form of monotony and banality, or rather, both to reduce the victim to monotonous repetition and, as an effect of the same reduction, to call forth a murderous, vengeful impulse that is itself always expressed in terms of multiples—that is, of repetition. We see the first effect most plainly in respect to Quakatz, where the repeated taunting charges lead him to his own insipid, repetitive, and repressed behavior: to the worn rut in the kitchen floor (44), to his cry, "It's the *Corpus Juris*, the *Corpus Juris*, the *Corpus Juris*!" (91), even to his last remnant of consciousness, shouting out, "Kienbaum! Kienbaum! Kienbaum!" (127) and, "[It] wasn't me, not me, not me! It wasn't me!" (138f.). The effect also extends to Tina, especially when thinking about her father, "who had no one, no one, no one with whom he could talk" (93) and "who had to hold his head and his heart together with both hands for years and years and years" (109; cf. 118)—so that in fact the (name-calling verbal) repetitions not only call forth (stuttering verbal) repetitions but seem also to initiate an ongoing repeated chain of similitude, reproducing the repetitious behavior in other, contiguous figures as well.

The second effect of the taunting, insipid repetitions is also most evident in respect to Tina—is also, that is, caught up in the chain of repetition, namely the calling forth of an equally violent reciprocal murderous impulse. Repeatedly she recounts how the verbal abuse she suffered for her father's supposed murder nearly led her to become a murderer "a hundred times over" (103 f.; cf. 105; 78 f.; 86). And the child Fatso displays the same impulse as a result of his being repeatedly taunted; he, too, often expresses the impulse to retaliatory violence in terms of multiples (e.g., 27, 96, 119). In some ways, it is this repetitiveness to the murderous impulse that seems most interesting and decisive. First, it parallels the repetitiveness to the reduced insipid behavior of the same person, bringing out the repressed aggressive reality behind or within each petrified stuttering repetition: the murderous impulse both expresses and represses itself in the same redundant symptom. Second, it results in an even more pronounced oversameness with its (opposing) cause, or rather, in a repeated, ongoing oversameness. Even as the initial abuse combines repetition and violence, so does its response, in such a way as to engender an additional monotony, a further redundancy and dissipation of difference—not so as to cancel out the violence but rather so as to guarantee its ongoing effect, its unabated reality.

Third, the ongoing effect and unrelieved reality of the violence seems itself to necessitate the repetitive nature of the murderous impulse in Quakatz, Tina, and Fatso. That is, repetition (in the form of name-calling) is not only the reason each would kill, nor is it only the way each would kill ("a hundred times"). It is also an expression of the fact that what they would kill does not die, cannot die, but necessarily keeps coming back to life, and so must be killed again—and again. The murderous repetition is an expression of its futility, its futility an expression of the returning ineliminable reality of that which it would annihilate.

Finally, the most pressing reason for the necessary repetition and futility to their violence is its lack of target, its unavoidable misdirectedness. The chafing repetitions are never singularly "there" where they can be properly represented and confronted, so that any attack is an improper one, a failed one, and so needs to be repeated. This is as it were the psychological equivalent to the point made above about realist descriptive representation, that it is the repetitive nature of reality that the simple repetition of realism cannot represent. So too, it is the repetitive nature of the abusive violence that the simple answering attack on a single representative cannot touch. The monotonous repetitions that Tina, Quakatz, and even the child Fatso are opposing are both too real and too ghostly, too tenacious and too evasive, ever-present and nonpresent, ever to be successfully defeated. And so their own repetitions, their own violence, must go on as well.

The same pattern that we see repeatedly represented in Fatso's narrated account we also find repeated in and as his narration itself: *Langweile* as revenge, as payback (*heimzahlen*, 96; cf. 196), a revenge perpetrated through repetitions and banality and their equally anaesthetic and irritating effect—all as repayment for and as a repetition of the same suffered earlier by Fatso. Over and again we witness Fatso reducing others to repetition through his own repetitions and repeated retardations, and by so doing provoking both boredom and reciprocal violence (e.g., Eduard, 94, 104, 96; Tina, 117f., 143; the barmaid, 173; cf. also 65, 69, 94, 42). But for all the undeniable success to these attacks, there is also a curious sense of their perpetual failure, as is perhaps most evident precisely where the retaliatory motivation to Fatso's repetitions is also most evident, namely in the insults, or rather, in the repeated insults that Fatso levels against Eduard during the course of his one afternoon visit. As Schweckendieck notes, these insults are incessant and their accusation simple, indeed monotonous: that Eduard and the others abandoned Heinrich Schaumann "under the hedge" and, by designating him as Fatso, misconstrued his true nature.[56] But the motivating reality behind the insults is more forcefully represented by two of their formal features than by the accusations themselves. First is their very repetitive nature: "I can only repeat it again and again Eduard: you [all] misunderstood me" (116). It is not only that the repetitions constitute their own blunt form of violence but also that they reveal Fatso's *need* to repeat, a need created by the previous (and equally banal and malicious) repetitions. The very need to keep repeating the same charge shows that its reality does not go away, but continually and futilely seeks after adequate representation. The second and largely identical feature is the only half-precision of these taunts, their partial misdirectedness; for this aspect of the violence and realism both to the Quakatz/Tina story and to Fatso's own childhood is also reproduced or repeated in the attack on Eduard. Over and again, Eduard is insulted as *ihr* ("you [all]"), as a plurality "without exception," where he is held responsible for, solely representative of all the name-calling, all the misrecognition and misrepresentation of Fatso's true nature. To some extent, this can perhaps be justified insofar as it is precisely this generality, this unacknowledged redundancy and embeddedness-in-the-same in Eduard that is under attack by Fatso in his conscious realist disabusement. But to an exactly equal extent, this attack seems unjustified and imprecise: for again, what is attacked by Fatso are the repetitions themselves, which can only be mislocated, indeed missed at any one site such as Eduard.[57]

Thus, Fatso's repeated attacks indicate not only the tenacity to the conventional, redundant reality there in Eduard's character, nor only the tenacity to the repressed, psychological reality there in Fatso's. They also indicate the vacuity, the nonpresence or representability to the engaged reality, the lack of a real, proper target for the attack: each single attack is false, failed, inadequate, and so needs to be repeated. Again, it is the repetitive, layered nature of the past reality itself that the simple present target of his revenge cannot represent. Stopfkuchen's revenge is, finally, grounded in the same flawed logic of representation as the realism he attacks. The misrepresentation of reality he would undo returns in the reality of misrepresentation he enacts.

VII

The tension between the ongoing revenge through repetition and *Langweile* and the problematic dismantling of different or singular positions occasioned by the same repetition and *Langweile*—this tension is brought to a head in the long-deferred center of the story, namely, the revelation of Kienbaum's murder. The representation of this primal scene is in itself hardly significant, is actually somewhat boring and banal. As Störzer says, "[T]hat's just the thing, that there really isn't much to tell, even though it turned out so badly" (187). What significance it has derives primarily from its foregrounding and recasting of the principal features and motivations to the repetitions and monotonies functioning throughout the text. And in this respect, perhaps more significant than its representation has been its *non*representation, its sustained repression or deferral through Fatso's endless repetitions and *Langweile*. For it is this repression that not only (re-)produces the reality that motivates the Kienbaum tale but that also and in turn comes to be motivated by that same tale. In a way, the Kienbaum story functions much like the penny print of Cain and Abel that suddenly appears and just as suddenly disappears from the set of pictures on Quakatz's kitchen wall (91). Its appearance seems to signal a pattern, indeed a primal mythical pattern that repeats itself throughout the text—in the figures of Kienbaum and Störzer, Quakatz and Kienbaum, Fatso and Eduard, etc.—and so signals the abiding "reality" of such mythical repetitions themselves. But its disappearance, its subsequent repression, not only conceals but also fundamentally reformulates the operant pattern, the operant reality—which thereafter can no longer be explained in terms of this penny print, this simple representation.

Right away, however, I should qualify something I just claimed. Whereas it is true that Störzer's account of Kienbaum's murder is in itself banal and lacking in striking significance, it is also true that this emphatic triviality to the story is part of its significance, indeed its realism: it underscores the motive of the murder itself in realist triviality, monotony, and banal repetition. Störzer explains the conditions underlying and following the murder in terms of the same pattern of repetition as torture and answering revenge that we have seen operant throughout. In his case, the initial motivating repetitions and monotony are actually twofold. First, there is the repeated name-calling, the taunting nicknaming repeated unendingly against him "from earliest childhood on" by the sadistic Kienbaum; and second, there are the repeated work-rounds, the incessant routine sameness of his postal route that continually brings Störzer back into contact with the name-calling torturer (189). Both patterns of repetition reduce Störzer to a similar, even identical state of repressed banality, but both also and simultaneously call forth an answering violence, a reciprocating murderous impulse on the fateful day of Störzer's crime (190). Monotony, repetition, and *Langweile* themselves occasion the "real" event, call forth all by themselves the violent reality at the center of the novel's concerns.

Whereas the murder itself clearly reveals the operant pattern of repetition as torture as its motivating reality, so too does the following concealment of the crime, as Störzer suppresses his role in Kienbaum's death. In fact, one could argue that the concealment or repression—"the one night between the one evening and the one morning" (186)—far more constitutes the original crime than the original blow, which was after all banally accidental. This would be in keeping with the point made above, that in some ways it is Fatso's deferral of rather than telling of the (equally banal) story that comprises its more central significance. In any case, Störzer's repression of the story results in its own identical pattern of repetition as torture. We see the monotony in cause and effect of the crime, for example, in their exactly analogous registration in Störzer's language. At first, Störzer wonders why God "had to bring me together with Kienbaum and his mockery and scorn and arrogance every, every day, every day, every day [*immer tagtäglich, tagtäglich, tagtäglich*]" (189). Afterward he laments, "O Herr Schaumann, Herr Schaumann, because of my job I also had every day, every day, every day [*tagtäglich, tagtäglich, tagtäglich*] to pass by the place where—where I did it" (185).[58] And the same monotony is implicit to the continued boring ritual of Störzer's postal rounds before and after the crime, the very monotony that in fact first occasions the crime and then successfully keeps it from being discovered. The routine repetitions that used secretly to expose him to Kienbaum's taunting repetitions now both help to repress or conceal his crime and still continually, repeatedly expose him to its unrelieved reality. Monotonous repetition proves the motive for the crime, the repression of the crime, and the punishment or revenge for the crime, and the crime itself apparently does nothing to diminish the pattern of repetition and violence.

In fact, if anything the crime increases the pattern of repetition and violence, or rather, the repression of the crime does. Due to the concealment or deferral of the truth or reality of his deed—"I wanted to [give myself up], but I put it off—and I kept putting it off, further and further, and the years passed" (193)—Störzer actually doubles the repetitive tortures by displacing the blame for the deed onto the apparently innocent Quakatz. This not only doubles the repeated torture for Störzer himself, as he must daily pass by both the place where the violence "really" occurred and the place (the Red Bank) where it was represented as having occurred. It doubles the pattern of repetition as torture by also and in turn engaging Quakatz in the same persecuting repetitions to which he, Störzer, was originally engaged by Kienbaum—repeating the repetitions, creating ever more of the same banal conditions, the same reality through the same repeated misrepresentations. And, as I said, this displacement of the violence and its reality resulting from the initial repression and deferral is perhaps the real crime, the true reality represented by the Störzer and Kienbaum story, and is what makes this primal scene so radically different from the penny print of

Cain and Abel (85) to which one might otherwise wish to reduce it. Rather, the real crime is the (inadvertent) creation of the fiction of Quakatz as the guilty party, the fiction that nonetheless engenders a reality, a "poetic reality," for both Störzer and Quakatz. We might say that the true reality or crime represented by the Kienbaum tale is, or rather, already is the moment of displacement and subsequent repetition, already the problem of misdirectedness and misrepresentation as the basic causes and characteristics of the ever-repeating violence.[59]

We see this in almost every detail of the crime scene itself. The mistargeting and only half-precision of the fateful interaction is most graphically thematized in that, when Störzer is hit by Kienbaum's whip, it is because the blow was mis-aimed, or at least partially mis-aimed, and the same is true of Kienbaum when struck by Störzer—"I didn't aim, but it hit" (192). But it is most decisively thematized in that, when Kienbaum taunts Störzer with his repeated name-calling, it is itself a mis-placed, deferred repetition-revenge for the taunting, repeated name-calling between himself and Quakatz earlier in the day. In this scene, Störzer is himself *already* a substitute, a misrepresentative, a deferred target for the real absent source of Kienbaum's anger: as Kienbaum's greeting puts it, "That's right, Mutton Legs! Well, well, is he sitting there again and hatching other people's eggs?" (191f.). The real target seems always already absent from the present scene, even from this "first" scene, which is clearly already a displacement and misrepresentation, a misprision, a fiction; already palimpsestic, multistriated, subsumed, and shaped by the nonpresent.

VIII

Of course, the most important aspect of the story Fatso tells about Kienbaum's murder, its most central displacement, comes with its revelation of the figure of Störzer as one repeated not by Eduard's character—who in becoming a world traveler imagined himself to be following in Störzer's imaginary footsteps—but rather by Fatso's own. Fatso says about Eduard, "He is personally much more deeply involved in this than he presently suspects" (151), but roughly the same proves even truer of Fatso himself. The sameness or monotony between Störzer and Fatso is made obvious in any number of ways (although for puzzling reasons only Eisele seems to note them). We see it in Storzer's childhood pairing with his torturing nemesis; we see it in the nickname whose repetition "from earliest childhood on" (187) proves the primary tactic of banal monotonous torture; in "the difference . . . between a slow sensibility and a quick wit, which he [Kienbaum] with his big mouth and spitefulness let me know about" (187); even and most centrally in the murder scene itself as "where I paid him back [*wo ich's ihm heimgezahlt habe*] for all the wrong he'd done me from earliest childhood on" (186), proleptically repeating Fatso's narratorial revenge on Eduard.

But even as the revelation of Störzer's story as Fatso's own exposes Fatso's narratorial practice as a repetition or continuation of Störzer's crime, the complex nature of that crime seriously problematizes and even subverts that same practice. Ulf Eisele has argued that the reason Fatso can "discover" the story of Kienbaum's murderer is that the story is, finally, his own: that just as with Fatso's other discovery, the prehistoric sloth, Fatso only ever discovers representations of himself. To some extent, this is no doubt true, but if it is accurately to account for Fatso's relation to his Kienbaum story, we must add the condition that he only discovers the self he hides and would not re-present (cf. 178).[60] Störzer's hidden reality—his concealed torture, provoked violence, and subsequent repression or deferral—is Fatso's own, and this is the reason that Fatso can not only discover the story but also continue and repeat its repression, its nondiscovery. And even as Störzer's real crime was not so much in the murder as in its concealment, so too Fatso's real identificatory repetition of Störzer's story lies not so much in its discovery (as Eisele would have it) as in its deferring repression. After all, both the original crime and its discovery were largely accidental, without intention (*ohne Zutun*), and allegedly not in the "nature" of the actant. But the concealment in both cases is purposive and most symptomatic of each one's nature, indeed of their same nature (as a "quiet man [*stiller Mensch*]" 188). Each one's monotonous, repetitive reality conceals another, and Fatso's both; each one's boringness, or *Langweiligkeit*, bespeaks a similar repression, indeed the repression of a similar reality of monotony, repetition, and hidden violence.

Fatso's repression of Störzer's repressed crime is possible to read—and is so read by both Fatso and Eduard—as done in the service of a certain healing anaesthesia. But of course in the "first case" of Störzer, the subjection of his crime to such a repressive regime did not end the violence, but simply continued it in a changed, displaced, indeed multiplied form. And the same seems true in the second case of Fatso, too. In Fatso's repression of Störzer's crime story—and especially because it is his, Fatso's, own story—the regime of *Langweile* does not simply yield a benevolent dissipation of its relevance and reality (cf. 180), but rather instead an active, ongoing, and violent effect. Just because it *is* his story, Fatso can not only discover the "crime," and more important repress it; he must also repeat it, in fact repeat it in the telling, in the repeating of it. Fatso's narration represents the story's "primal" ongoing reality not so much in what it says as in what it does—insofar, that is, as in the telling Fatso repeats the crime of stoning his childhood tormentor, in this case Eduard.

Even that is not quite accurate, however, or rather, not quite the end of it: for in his narration Fatso seems compelled not only to repeat its crime but to repeat both its crimes.[61] Even as the original story is not really played out according to the simple script of Cain and Abel, but is "really" a complex play of deferrals and misrepresentations, so necessarily too is Fatso's own deferred representation, or repetition, of the script. Hence, Fatso's repetition of Störzer's original crime includes not only the revenge against Eduard as his childhood tormentor—Eduard as a repetition of Kienbaum—but also the crime of misplaced accusation against the wrong, "unreal" target—Eduard as a repetition of Quakatz. Like Quakatz, Eduard is assaulted not for anything he really did but rather partly for what it was in his "nature" to do, and partly as the singled-out representative for a more disseminated, elusive, nonpresent reality. Like Quakatz, Eduard is assaulted as representative, which necessarily never is quite reality.[62] Thus, Fatso not only repeats the "reality" of the Kienbaum story in and as his narration, in his payback assault on Eduard; he also necessarily repeats its fiction, its gap between reality and representation, its flawed logic of displacement and mistargeting—its real crime.[63]

IX

The obvious consequence of this resolutely temporal, unstoppable even if (or because) aimless pattern of violent repetitions and imposed similitudes is that, despite his claims to the contrary, Fatso does not end the cycle through his *Langweile*, but rather perpetuates it and its several crimes precisely through his *Langweile*. If there is to be any adequate dissipation of the repetition compulsion, it is left not to Fatso and his narration but to Eduard and his (194f.). And so it is to Eduard's repetition of Fatso's repetition, to his boringness and its several different functions that we must look to find a possible way out.

Let us consider how Fatso's revenge complicates our understanding of Eduard's narration. I have already discussed the two dominant realist impulses to Eduard's way of writing: his philistine tendency to produce idylls through a redundant deployment of clichéd conventions that secure and stabilize his place in banal bourgeois reality; and his more self-conscious tendency to disrupt the effective power of the same conventional idyll through a consequent exorcism of its familiar but false fictions. And I have also already suggested that Fatso's narration, especially his revelation of Störzer's crime, seems clearly to intensify both tendencies. On the one hand, his revelation calls forth a notable repressive impulse in Eduard, who deliberately attempts to reconstitute the threatened illusion through an even more insistent repetition of his redundant conventions. On the other hand, Fatso's attack seems also to reinforce and perhaps even to occasion in Eduard his apparently opposite disenchanting impulse, which leads to its own more aggressive and monotonous deployment of his redundant conventions, not so as to conceal their recognized fictionality and so prolong their threatened life, but rather to expose the one and kill the other.

Both of these "works" of boredom and repetition that Eduard's narration performs are, then, greatly increased as a result of his exposure to Fatso's narration. But because of that same narration of Fatso, Eduard also takes on another "work" of boredom and repetition, the work of needed revenge. Himself reduced by Fatso's taunting, violent, and boringly repetitious narration to a state of repetition—in fact to a forced repetition of Fatso's repetitions, to the recounting of his monologue (58)—he is also charged with, loaded with its accompanying, reciprocating violent and even murderous impulse, with the tendency to boring and violent repetitions in turn.

What we need to account for, then, is what happens to the violent impulse Eduard takes on from Fatso: most generally what he does and does not do with it, and more particularly how it engages the other two impulses behind his narration, toward idyll-making and toward disenchantment. What we realize first is that Eduard clearly does not seek to wreak his revenge directly on his tormentor, Fatso; several times while listening to Fatso, Eduard represses the urge to strike out, and the same repression seems active in Eduard's writing. That is, as with his efforts to preserve his threatened idyll, Eduard's first impulse seems to be to repress the violence done to him. But the intention behind the repression is not—or at least not immediately—seen to repeat Eduard's tendency toward idyll-making but rather to repeat its opposite, his efforts at disenchantment. That is, just as in Fatso's own case, Eduard's repression of the violent impulse is intended, however problematically, to put an end to the violence, to exorcise its redundant reality by submitting it to yet another regime of *Langweile* and repetition; so that just as the work of boredom and repetition in Eduard's narration is in one respect aimed at dismantling his investment in idyllizing philistine conventions, in another it is aimed at dismantling the pattern of revenge: two works of disenchantment, dissipation, nonrepresentation, of the fiction of the one, and of the reality of the other. It is this second work that, as we have seen, Fatso fails to accomplish, leaves in fact to Eduard to accomplish; and the question becomes whether Eduard can succeed at either work in his repetition, his turn.

Eduard's narratorial attempts at this double dissipation take two different forms in the novel, and in each case the examples of both Störzer and Fatso caution us that his attempts are as likely to have failed as to have succeeded. In the first, we might look for the failure precisely in the appearance of success, by considering how in the very act of exposing and discrediting his own idyll-making through his narration, Eduard also continues or repeats it—repeats it by shifting the idyll away from his homeland, his self, and his own discounted claims to "realism" and onto the Red Bank, Fatso, and his now valorized claims instead. We see this particularly at the end, when Eduard apparently confirms as authoritative Fatso's worldview, self-image, and even his image of Eduard (197), and we see it perhaps even more specifically in his concentrated valorization of Tina, whom Fatso himself holds up—repeatedly holds up—as the chief example of the success of his efforts to unburden the world of its past repressions and violence: "I found that, in a curious fashion, I had actually been thinking only about Frau Valentina Schaumann, née Quakatz, and relatively little about Kienbaum, Störzer, Papa Quakatz, and Fatso. The dear woman! The poor, dear woman!" (196). Far from appearing to take revenge on Fatso, and far from expressing the violence done to himself, Eduard instead engages in a new idyllization, one largely based on and affirming Fatso's strategy of *Lang-weile* and concomitant claim to having ended the cycle of violence, both in himself and others.

Of course, a good part of this new idyllization is at Eduard's own expense; and yet Eduard appears only to sacrifice his self-image—and world!—in order to preserve them both at the site of Fatso. We see the self-sacrifice, for instance, in the depiction of himself as entangled in redundant conventions and destroyed by Fatso's "realist" disabusement; we see it in the downplaying of the interest to the frame sea story and hence to himself, a downplaying that also (however feebly and disingenuously) functions as a repetition and hence confirmation of Fatso's "realist" program of deconventionalization. But there is an essential ambiguity to this depiction of Eduard and his bourgeois idyll destroyed or lost and of Fatso and his (mythical) realism confirmed, even repeated by Eduard, and it is the same ambiguity that adheres to the image near the end of Eduard "becoming" Fatso: "I put myself completely in the fat man's place, inside his skin, that is: I found myself put there. I was swollen out to the girth of his body and I had risen to the heights of his comfortable disdain for the world" (196). Contrary to his overt claim, it seems not so much that Eduard becomes Fatso here at the end as that he makes Fatso into himself, into the new repository for the idyll, the homeland, and the hero. Eduard's discredited conventionalism at the hands of the "realist" Fatso becomes a way of maintaining the convention, his lost fictions a way of staying in the fiction. Earlier we noted how, even as the differences between the "hometown" and Africa dissolved into a sameness and monotony that effectively negated Eduard's illusion of having escaped the illusions of the former, so too did the differences between Eduard the idyllizer and Eduard the disabused dissolve into a monotony that negated Eduard's sense of movement into a different, more "real" reality. Now we can see that the same also holds true for the evident redundancy of Eduard's converted worldview and Fatso's, their seeming agreement on the structure of reality or meaning that emerges at the end. Rather than evidence for its mono-semesis with the true nature of reality, the agreement becomes merely evidence for its mono-semesis with Eduard's earlier, "false" conventions or idyll.

Certainly one reason, then, for the inadequacy of this manifestation of Eduard's disenchantment, of his work of mourning (*Trauerarbeit*) for the idyll lost, is that in embracing Fatso's poetics of mythical repetition and *Langweile,* Eduard does not seem to get any closer to reality, nor further away from his original fictions, but rather remains in a certain unreal, fictionalizing, and idyllizing mode, in fact the same idyllizing mode he supposedly is forced to abandon. The monotonous hegemony of the idyllizing impulse proves inescapable, the realist operation of disillusionment proves part of the machinery for maintaining the illusion, and "reality" proves as elusively inaccessible as ever. But another reason for its inadequacy is that Eduard enshrines Fatso's poetics of repetition and *Langweile* in order to repress or deny a quite different reality that has not and will not go away, that of the ongoing, immediate, and hopelessly banal violence. By idyllizing Fatso and his handling of the Kienbaum story, Eduard would deny not only the all-too-evident repressed violence to Fatso's character but also the violence awakened in his own character by Fatso's handling of him. His new mode of idyllizing proves as reality-denying as that of Störzer and Fatso, his claim, "Well, the affair has certainly made itself altogether tolerable" (198), just as questionable as theirs because motivated by the same willed repression (cf. 186). But if on the one hand reality seems something Eduard can never get to, on the other it seems something he can never get away from, either: Fatso doesn't succeed at stopping the violence and dismantling the reality of the affair by subjecting it to his regime of repetition and *Langweile,* and neither does Eduard by adopting and repeating Fatso's *Weltanschauung.* As Eduard admits, "Of course, I wasn't really done with it yet, with the affair" (198).

If in its first form Eduard's narratorial efforts at the double dissipation—of the fiction of his idyllizing, and the reality of his violence—fail because, in yielding his place to Fatso, Eduard seems merely to maintain the idyll, in the second form we can say that Eduard actively assumes (repeats, doubles) the place of Fatso himself, and actively maintains the violence, indeed the violence in the form of boredom and repetition—not only boring naively or surreptitiously through his idyllizing but also consciously, directly, even maliciously through his berating taunts. Even as Fatso attacks Eduard, so in turn Eduard attacks—continually attacks—his reader. But as with Fatso's, the real motivation for Eduard's narratorial assaults is perhaps not so much the conscious and aggressive realist disabusement of his audience's conventions, his or her boring (and false) standards of interest, significance, and realism, but rather the aggressive, symptomatic expression of Eduard's denial of his own violated and now violent reality. Or, more precisely, perhaps the real motivation is the violent reality that Eduard both suppresses with the fiction of attacking the reader's fictions, and nonetheless expresses, represents, or realizes beneath and within that same covering fiction. As with Eduard for Fatso's narration, the reader becomes not so much the real, proper target of Eduard's assault (and so all the less his or her fictions of "reality") as the necessarily misplaced, displaced, improper, and (mis)re-presented site.

If we situate the decisive point to Eduard's repetitions and *Langweile* that comprise his repetition of Fatso not in some positive ideal of a shared, enlightened mythical outlook on reality but rather in the negative, unacknowledged reality of the ongoing violence, then the crucial question for the dissipation of the chain becomes what becomes of the object of Eduard's "revenge," or rather, of the reader of his manuscript, and hence the site of its realistic effect—its perpetuating chain of similitude, its ability to hurt, and to rouse the desire to hurt in turn. When we consider this issue, we note that in Eduard's mind at least, there is a continually changing characterization of this projected reader, from the head of the African colony, through his fellow ship passengers, to his hometown contemporaries, each time with the possibility of access to the manuscript made more remote and less likely, until finally Eduard fends off a would-be reader, the ship's captain, with the words and gesture, "'It really would interest you very little, Captain. A purely private matter!' I said, and closed my manuscript" (207). In the end, the written narrative, the very instrument of Eduard's violence, seems destined to remain as closed and secret as the letters Störzer carries throughout the tale, and relegated to the same basic state of indifference (177, 186).

This fate of the reader in the novel has crucial consequences for our understanding of the fate of the work's realism, of its realistic effect. On the one hand, we can speculate that Eduard's written narrative can have no true object, in a way that could never be said of Fatso's spoken monologue: that precisely because it has no direct connection to its target, it becomes the privileged site for the death of the violence, the *Trauerarbeit* of the real. This would be the exactly opposite conclusion to that of Eisele, who maintains that in Eduard's writing, Fatso and his story live on (*überleben*) in a way impossible in speech alone; it would also be the opposite project of that normally associated with poetic realism, namely the necessarily impossible attempt to bring the real to life in its written representation. But maybe the hope, the project here is this: that it is, finally, writing that can render the "real" truly dead, harmless, and unreal fiction; that the work's poetic realism is not meant to bring reality to life or to preserve it, but to bury it, at long last to lay it to rest—the problem being not an impossible access to reality but an equally impossible excess of reality. Eduard's narration with all its repetition and boredom would then best be understood as a form of *Trauerarbeit*: of mourning, letting go, of killing off the already dead.[64]

On the other hand, this speculation seems to be refuted by the text. The lack of a true object or possibly accurate representation does not derail the patterns of violence in the novel, and there is no reason to assume it does in the case of the violence that is the novel, either. Rather, much like Fatso's petrified coprolites, which no longer give offense, Eduard's dead words might yet prove another missile to perpetuate and keep alive the hurt. For what the novel shows us is that what is dead and no longer real can still really injure again, even a world, a time, a language away—and like Eduard's half-breed Dutch African children, we too will suffer and perpetuate the reality, if ever we encounter the fiction. The work's realistic effect is not, that is, maintained in any disenchantment of our own (boring) conventional reality, nor in our persuasion to a new broader reality, but rather in our ongoing entanglement in the woven chain of violence.[65] We might never be able to arrive at anything real about the novel; we certainly will never be able to escape its real, either.

8 (IN) CONCLUSION
Second Thoughts

I began this study by proposing a twofold, conflictual model for analyzing poetic realism, in which each part of the model was defined largely in terms of its relation to the principle of repetition. On the one hand, in its dependency on redundancy of the established iconographies of social and literary conventions, poetic realism was seen as firmly grounded in repetition as part of its efforts to maintain and convey a uniform, regular version of the world "as it is." On the other hand, in its intended resistance to such inherited social and literary codes, realism was also seen as opposing repetition and basing its claim to "the real" on its achieved break with the dominant modes of representation and signification. I traced the various modulations of this basic paradigm as they occurred in the theoretical discourses of narratology, Critical Theory, psychoanalysis, and, later, feminist gender studies. A rather surprising consensus about the mechanisms of reality formation and the role of repetition therein emerged, which seemed to confirm the viability of our model. But so too did a challenge to it, proposed first by Frankfurt School critics and then seconded, albeit from a slightly different point of attack, by more Foucauldian minded critics, all of whom suggested that such a dual, conflictual, and to some extent self-subversive structure of realism still might turn out to be in the service of sustaining a single, uniform, normed aesthetic discourse identifiable as "realism."

My subsequent analyses of poetic realist fictions seems to confirm both the viability of such a twofold model and the challenge to it. Each separate claim to realism could be seen to dominate the work of individual authors, from Stifter's conservative efforts to maintain a heavily redundant and static world by means of the repetition of established codes and conventions, through Storm's—and Keller's—struggles to break with the authority of such conventions, to frustrate repetition, and to introduce difference as the authenticating mark of the real. More often, however, and even in the instances just mentioned, both claims appeared simultaneously and inseparably operant in the same texts. This was perhaps most clearly the case in the stories of Stifter, Storm, and Meyer, each of which initiated an attempt to impose a stabilizing mimetic re-presentation or equivalence on the textual world so as to control and determine its governing reality, only to have that effort frustrated by the emergence of other, controlling forces. In each of these cases, realism came in large part to be associated with the realization of the failure of the work's mimetic program and compulsion to repeat, a failure more or less affirmatively embraced in Storm's novella, and more tragically acknowledged in those of Stifter and Meyer.

The decisive and highly self-conscious failures of the realist projects in these works would seem to undercut the more or less monological model of realism proposed by such Frankfurt School critics as Berman and Holub without necessarily discrediting the understanding of realist discourse proposed by my own model. Indeed, in staging such failures of their totalizing mimetic programs, these works foreground one of the chief operators in my twofold scheme, namely the competing but complementary claim to realism as the subversive disruption of such an established order in favor of a different and ostensibly more authentic reality. And this holds true whether those unsettling forces were conceived as arising from some "other" domain repressed or excluded by the would-be dominant discourse or representation, or from within that dominant world itself, as an inherent consequence of its own designs and deployed forces. In either case, the identification of realism solely with an achieved moment of stabilizing uniformation and imposed equivalence necessarily and often even spectacularly fails.

Far more challenging to my initial analytical scheme—and hence seemingly far more supportive of the critique leveled by the Frankfurt School critics—were the failures of the dual model evident in the presented works of Raabe and Keller. In Raabe, the model failed—which is to say, "realism" failed—because it proved incapable of generating the desired disruptive and disenchanting difference and instead constantly collapsed back into an all-encompassing (but still false) sameness; neither the effort to maintain an established stable world as "real" nor that to thwart such a world and to attain to a new, different, and more authentic perspective proved possible. In Keller, the model failed because it proved incapable of generating any uniform program at all and instead continually yielded an ineradicable duplicity; every effort to impose a normative ideological or aesthetic program seemed simultaneously to occasion its disruptive transgression, and every effort to defamiliarize and frustrate the established norms and signifying practices seemed instead also to reinforce and further their hold. Indeed, if repetition seemed to induce an inescapable sameness and determinacy into every would-be discrete and differentiated realist claim in Raabe's world, it seemed to induce an ineliminable multiplicity and indeterminacy into every such claim in Keller's. In each case, for all its foregrounded evocation, the dual conflictual model of realism as either a faithful adherence to literary and ideological codes or a conscious disruption of them failed to sustain itself, and instead collapsed under the pressure of its own internal contradictions.

Even these failures, however, can hardly be taken to disavow the realist aesthetic project implied by my twofold model. Still less can they be taken to confirm a reading of realism as singularly in the service of manufacturing and maintaining a uniform normed aesthetic and ideological discourse. At best, only Raabe's *Fatso* could be held up as supporting this conclusion, and even then it emerges as only one conclusion, only one negative (and relatively late) manifestation of the realist problematic that could be (retroactively) extended to encompass the whole range of poetic realism only at the expense of an unjustifiably distorting and leveling uniformation of its own. The example of Keller's *Seven Legends*, in fact, for all its dismantling of the operant distinctions between normative reinforcement and subversive transgression, nonetheless points to a strictly opposite conclusion. It insists on the impossibility of any realist discourse, whether conceived in primarily literary or ideological terms, to produce or impose any single uniform program at all. And I would insist that this, too, is but one conclusion, and that to represent the phenomenon of poetic realism fully and accurately, we cannot afford to identify it only with its more or less negative or wholly dismantled moments, but must be able to account for its more positively constructed ones as well. The realist difference achieved in Storm's *Viola tricolor* is, I believe, real enough, and certainly deserves to figure in the realist equation. And the more tragically but still self-consciously staged failures of Stifter's *The Mountain Forest* and Meyer's *The Marriage of the Monk* cannot be reduced to such a state of in-difference, either. The failures of the stable realist fictions they intend and the accompanying realizations they invite depend as much on a possible subversion of the settled world as they do on such a settled world that can then be subverted—and in the case of Stifter, that can then uncannily reappear. Far from yielding either a depressingly uniform program or—perhaps more depressing—no coherent program at all, a reading of realism in terms of this dual conflictual model has produced a wide, varied, and irreducible array of responses to a common problematic.

The mythological image of the Hydra was introduced in the opening paragraph of this study as an icon for the fate of almost every discussion of poetic realism, and it has proved the fate of this one as well. Out of the struggles with poetic realism in terms of my initially proposed twofold model there has emerged a second, equally contentious model, namely the model of realism that I have designated as a chiastic strategy of mimetic equivalence, itself deeply embedded in the problem of repetition. It emerged alongside my initial model in all but the last of my analyses, and in each case it initiated an engaging and highly complex interplay between the poetic and the real: from Stifter's projection of his "gentle law" and ideal of virginity onto the natural realm in order to have it reflectively imposed on the human realm and, more specifically, on the female figures of Johanna and Clarissa; through Keller's use of Eugenia's statue and Storm's of Marie's portrait to determine the realities of their respective female characters; to Meyer's use of Dante's embedded narrative to determine the reality not only of Dante's audience but also of Dante himself. In each case, this imaginary, mirroring mechanism was seen to reverse the mimetic relations of model and copy, original and representation traditionally assumed to obtain in realist discourse, in such a way as to reassert the necessarily poetic dimension to its project. And in each case, this chiastic tactic was seen to be intrinsically involved both in the various attempts to control "reality" through a mimetic re-presentation in order to achieve a stable, well-regulated world, *and* in the consequent failure of such attempts, the failed equivalence between the representation and real, which, affirmatively or tragically, proved its own reality. For all its repeated failures to secure and determine the desired stable and enduring reality, this chiastic logic also proved tenaciously unsubdued in its drive repeatedly to reassert itself. Indeed, like the Hydra and so much of poetic realism itself, this aspect of realism seems not only to survive its defeats, the repeated demonstrations of its flawed and fictive double nature, but even, repeatedly, to thrive on them.

NOTES

NOTES

CHAPTER 1: THEORETICAL INTRODUCTION

1. Rene Wellek, *Concepts of Criticism*, ed. Stephen G. Nichols, Jr. (New Haven: Yale University Press, 1963), 238.

2. Lilian R. Furst, *Realism* (London: Longman, 1992), 1. In confirmation of her claim, we might note that the same image crops up again in George Levine, *Realism and Representation* (Madison: University of Wisconsin Press, 1993).

3. Cf. J. P. Stern, *On Realism* (London: Routledge & Kegan Paul, 1973), 28.

4. Roland Barthes, "The Reality Effect," in *French Literary Theory*, ed. Tzvetan Todorov, trans. R. Carter (Cambridge: Cambridge University Press, 1982). Reprinted in Furst, *Realism*, 135–41.

5. A similar point is made by Martin Swales, *The German Novelle* (Princeton: Princeton University Press, 1977). For the relevance of Swales's description of the novella to the description of poetic realism, see below.

6. Again, see Swales's account of the defining operation of the novella.

7. Roman Jakobson, "On Realism in Art," in *Readings in Russian Poetics: Formalist and Structuralist Views*, ed. L. Matejka and K. Pomorska (Cambridge: MIT Press, 1971), 38–46.

8. This point is well made by Robert Alter in *Partial Magic: The Novel as Self-Conscious Genre* (Berkeley: University of California Press, 1975), x.

9. J. Hillis Miller, *Fiction and Repetition* (Cambridge: Harvard University Press, 1982).

10. Gilles DeLeuze, *Difference and Repetition*, trans. Paul Patton (New York: Columbia University Press, 1994).

11. Indeed, even Nietzsche's own thought depends on a far more conflicted attitude toward the relation of repetition and the real than Miller's description allows, for his notoriously difficult notion of eternal recurrence must be poised against the model of endless difference singled out here.

12. Robert C. Holub, *Reflections of Realism: Paradox, Norm, and Ideology in Nineteenth-Century German Prose* (Detroit: Wayne State University Press, 1991); Russell Berman, *The Rise of the Modern German Novel: Crisis and Charisma* (Cambridge: Harvard University Press, 1986). I need to acknowledge my own particular debt to Holub, both to his published work and to our personal correspondence and dialogue; this

study is in good part a continuation of that dialogue. I should also mention the stellar work on realism from a Frankfurt School perspective done by Eva Geulen, most especially in *Worthörig Wider Willen* (Munich: Iudicum, 1992). I omit discussion of her argument here primarily because it does not represent the problematic assumptions about realism by Frankfurt School critics with which I wish to take issue; see below.

13. Max Horkheimer and Theodor W. Adorno, *Dialectic of Enlightenment*, trans. John Cumming (New York: Continuum, 1972). Parenthetical references in the text refer to this edition. I should emphasize that, in singling out the influence of Horkheimer and Adorno, I am not denying that of Georg Lukacs; I simply prefer to concentrate on what I take to be the more intriguing representation of the Frankfurt School model.

14. Do note Holub's wonderful evocation of Odysseus, especially in his chapter on "The Realist Education," which subtly alludes to Horkheimer's and Adorno's discussion and gently reasserts their more embracive focus.

15. See Horkheimer's letter of June 2, 1942, to Leo Lowenthal, quoted in Martin Jay, *The Dialectical Imagination: A History of the Frankfurt School and the Institute of Social Research, 1923–1950* (Boston: Little, Brown & Co., 1973), 213.

16. This apparent reversal in the qualities of the model is not entirely absent from Barthes or Jakobson; it is perhaps more a matter of different emphases than qualitative disagreement.

17. And we might note here the obvious, that the relation between myth and enlightenment in Horkheimer and Adorno often reappears in other more literary critics as that between romanticism and realism; even as the former pair functions within enlightenment, so too the latter within realism. See the discussion of Jakobson above.

18. The exception is Eva Geulen, *Worthörig Wider Willen*.

19. Berman, *The Rise of the Modern German Novel*, 2. Cf. 16 and his description of the "monological structure of contemporary [nineteenth-century] culture" and "the reduction of the diversity of life to a one dimensionality."

20. Ibid., 62 f.

21. Ibid., 2, 23.

22. Holub, *Reflections of Realism*, 18.

23. Cf. Frederic Jameson, *The Political Unconscious: Narrative as a Socially Symbolic Act* (Ithaca: Cornell University Press, 1981), 152.

24. Such a redefining includes as one of its first gestures the discarding of the by now traditional distinction between realist and what Robert Alter has called "self-conscious" texts; for while the distinction has productively served to increase our appreciation for nonrealist works that flaunt the conditions of their artifice and, in so doing, inaugurate an exploration into the complex relations between fiction and reality, it has disastrously served to diminish our appreciation for realist works and the

ways—different but no less consequential—they display their fiction and initiate their own probing inquiries into the limens between literature and life.

25. For a concise account of the differences between immanent and transcendent critique, as well as of the problems that adhere to each position, see Andrew Arato, "Esthetic Theory and Cultural Criticism: Introduction," in *The Essential Frankfurt School Reader*, ed. Andrew Arato and Eike Gebhardt (New York: Continuum, 1982), 197–207.

26. Swales, *The German Novelle*, 19–59.

27. This is primarily in response to Berman's argument for the centrality of Freytag's novel to any discussion of realism. And yet such an argument ignores the point made by Horkheimer and Adorno, that inferior works are not to be taken as representative of how art works: "That factor in a work of art which enables it to transcend reality certainly cannot be detached from style; but it does not consist of the harmony actually realized, of any doubtful unity of form and content, within and without, of individual and society; it is to be found in those features in which discrepancy appears: in the necessary failure of the passionate striving for identity. Instead of exposing itself to this failure in which the great work of art has always achieved self-negation, the inferior work has always relied on similarity with others—on a surrogate identity" (131). Again, Holub's practice transcends the possible limits of his theory here: he frequently engages aesthetically accomplished novellas, and even fairly eccentric ones, as the subject matter for his analyses, and this contributes to the overall superiority of his study.

28. Let me acknowledge the seminal influence here of Shlomith Rimmon-Kenan's article "The Paradoxical Status of Repetition," *Poetics Today* 1, no. 4 (1980): 151–59.

29. Cf. Leo Bersani, "Realism and the Fear of Desire," in *A Future for Astyanax* (Boston: Little, Brown & Co., 1969), 51–88; Richard Brinkmann, *Wirklichkeit und Illusion: Studien über Gehalt und Grenzen des Begriffs Realismus für die erzählende Dichtung des neunzehnten Jahrhunderts*, 2d ed. (Tübingen: Niemeyer, 1966).

30. This is, however, the paradox inherent to Freud's model: the repetition of the latter is an expression of the continued repression of the former, is a structural effect of the former—even as, in Jakobson's historically extended model for realism, every newly triumphant and stabilized set of realistic conventions was fated to produce its own subversive resistance, resulting in a similarly ongoing, sustained repetition of the disruptive "reality." Or similarly how in Lacan's model, desire itself is only an effect, a consequence of repression: see below.

31. Sigmund Freud, "Jenseits des Lustprinzips [Beyond the Pleasure Principle]," in *Studienausgabe*, ed. Alexander Mitscherlich, Angela Richards, and James Strachey (Munich: Fischer Verlag, 1982), 3:228. The emphases are Freud's own.

32. Cf. Barbara Johnson, "The Frame of Reference: Poe, Lacan, Derrida," *Yale French Studies* 55/56 (1978): 499.

33. Freud, "Jenseits des Lustprinzips," 229.

34. See especially Rimmon-Kenan's application of this to the question of narration as production rather than reproduction in Rimmon-Kenan, "From Reproduction to Production: The Status of Narration in Faulkner's *Absalom, Absalom!*" *Degrés* 16 (1978): f1–f19.

35. Peter Brooks, "Freud's Masterplot: Questions of Narrative," in *Literature and Psychoanalysis. The Question of Reading: Otherwise*, ed. Shoshana Felman (Baltimore: Johns Hopkins University Press, 1982), 280–300.

36. Freud writes, for example, "We consider as in the highest degree significant the fact that this function of the germ-cell [i.e., the furtherance of life] is strengthened, or even only made possible, if it melds with another cell similar to itself and yet also different from it" ("Jenseits des Lustprinzips," 249 f.). As we will see, this desire for difference is central to the "life" impulse, and the realist impulse, in many of our narratives as well, although not at the cellular level.

37. It is, however, arguably also implicit in Horkheimer's and Adorno's notion of enlightenment's pursuit of a uniform, same-state stasis.

38. For Brinkmann and Bersani, see above (note 29).

39. This point is well made by Samuel Weber, *Return to Freud: Jaques Lacan's Dislocation of Psychoanalysis*, trans. Michael Levine (Cambridge: Cambridge University Press, 1991), and deserves emphasis throughout this chapter.

40. Lacan alternatively describes this mirroring process as between the child and the eyes, or desire, of the doting mother, who is placed in this position by the historical contingencies of the bourgeois nuclear family. The difference between the two descriptions can at least partly be ascribed to the genealogical processes between Lacan's notion of the mirror-stage and his later identification of it with the Imaginary; for my purposes, the distinction is negligible. See Weber, *Return to Freud*, 7–19; 99–119.

41. Weber, *Return to Freud*, 106. Weber also stresses that the Imaginary is contradictorily based on both a recognition of difference (where the mirror image possesses a unity and stability that the self itself lacks) and on an effacement of difference (where the child sees itself as the image), a contradiction that necessarily and even fatally imperils the reality of the subject in the Imaginary, which is constantly threatened by its own internal mechanisms for sustaining its fiction of stability, its reality (12–18). The point is important for us insofar as it confirms the inherent, intrinsic instability of the operations of poetic realism.

42. Again, the link between Lacan and Jakobson is shrewdly explored by Weber, *Return to Freud, passim*.

43. Roman Jakobson, "Two Aspects of Language and Two Types of Aphasic Dis-

turbances," in Roman Jakobson and Morris Halle, *Fundamentals of Language*, Janua Linguarum, Series Minor, 1 (1956), 69–96.

44. Jaques Lacan, *The Four Fundamental Concepts of Psycho-Analysis*, ed. Jacques-Alain Miller, trans. Alan Sheridan (New York: W. W. Norton & Co., 1981), 91–119. For a concise exegesis, see Elizabeth Wright, *Psychoanalytic Criticism: Theory in Practice* (London: Methuen, 1984), 113–22.

45. For the relation between mourning and the dismantling of narcissistic mechanisms, see Freud, "Trauer und Melancholie [Mourning and Melancholy]," *Studienausgabe*, 3:193–212.

CHAPTER 2: THEMATIC INTRODUCTION

1. Roland Barthes, *Roland Barthes*, trans. Richard Howard (New York: Hill and Wang, 1977), 85.

2. Adalbert Stifter, *Werke und Briefe. Historisch-Kritische Gesamtausgabe*, ed. Alfred Doppler and Wolfgang Frühwald (Stuttgart: Kohlhammer, 1982), 2:2. All parenthetical references in this chapter are taken from this edition and refer exclusively to the *Vorrede* to *Bunte Steine*. For the English, I have consulted the translation by Jeffrey L. Sammons in Jeffrey L. Sammons, ed., *German Novellas of Realism* (New York: Continuum, 1989), 1:1–7. My discussion in this chapter is in many ways intended as a dialogic response to the model of realism proposed, and defended, in Holub, *Reflections of Realism*, which begins with a close reading of Büchner's "Kunstgespräch." Hence my decision to place Büchner's text in dialogue with Stifter's here. For more on Holub's model, see chapter one.

3. I am however in essential agreement with Russell Berman, *The Rise of the Modern German Novel*, 105–33, that Stifter's politics are more accurately described as those of a cautious liberalism, as cognizant of the terrors of conservative order as of those of revolutionary upheaval. For more on the polemical character of the preface, and Stifter's own, hardly one-sided position, see F. J. Stopp, "Die Symbolik in Stifters *Bunten Steinen*," *DVjS* 28 (1954): 165–93.

4. Walter Benjamin, "Karl Kraus," in *Gesammelte Schriften*, ed. Rolf Tiedemann and Hermann Schweppenhäuser (Frankfurt am Main: Suhrkamp, 1980), 2:334–67, here 340 f.

5. The echoes of Schillerian aesthetics in these projected principles are clear. For more on the intellectual tradition behind the preface, see Sepp Domandl, "Die philosophische Tradition von Adalbert Stifters 'Sanftem Gesetz,'" *VASILO* 21 (1972): 79–103.

6. Cf. Holub, *Reflections of Realism*, 16–18.

7. Cf. Karl Mautz, "Das antagonistische Naturbild in Stifters *Studien*," in *Adalbert Stifter: Studien und Interpretationen*, ed. L. Stiehm (Heidelberg: Lothar Stiehm, 1968), 23–57.

8. The basic claim here for the "nonpolitical" strategy of realist politics owes much to D. A. Miller's analyses of English and French realist texts in *The Novel and the Police* (Berkeley: University of California Press, 1988). The peculiarities of the German poetic realist tradition, where the overt, official political culture is displaced into "natural," religious, and familial discourses and not only or even primarily into other social discourses, as is the case with most of the "social" realist texts discussed by Miller: these peculiarities are addressed below.

9. For more on the pre–1848 relevance of the preface, see Eugen Thurnher, "Stifters 'sanftes Gesetz,'" in *Unterscheidung und Bewahrung: Festschrift für Hermann Kunisch*, ed. Klaus Lasarowisz and Wolfgang Kron (Berlin: de Gruyter, 1961), 381–97.

10. Cf. Terry Eagleton, *The Ideology of the Aesthetic* (Oxford: Basil Blackwell, 1990), 26–28. Eagleton rightly gestures at Horkheimer in support of this point. See esp. Max Horkheimer, "Begriff der Aufklärung," in *Gesammelte Schriften*, ed. Alfred Schmidt and G. Schmid Noerr (Frankfurt am Main: Fischer, 1987), 5:25–66. As I indicated in chapter one, Horkeimer also emphasizes the broader but related point that poetic realism might necessarily prove as subversive as it is redundant of the bourgeois ideology it mimetically reproduces in its own, different discursive field, and not least through its acknowledged fictional character, a point ignored by Berman and relegated to the inadvertent by Holub. See also Miller, *The Novel and the Police*, 93–101.

11. Eva Geulen, *Worthörig wider Willen*, 94, invokes the term "chiasmus" in a different though related context in her discussion of descriptive practices in Stifter's *The Mountain Forest*.

12. My discussion in subsequent chapters will elaborate further on this recursive rhetorical structure of realism.

13. For the dual-natured, conflictual model of realism in general, see chapter one; also Philippe Hamon, "On the Major Features of Realist Discourse," in *Realism*, ed. L. R. Furst, trans. L. R. Furst and Sean Hand (London: Longman, 1992), 166–85.

14. The term "shudder [*Schauern*]" again recalls Schiller, in particular the experience of the sublime, and so again reminds us that the origin of the laws—and violence—supposedly regulating Nature derives from elsewhere—that is, from the moral and aesthetic sphere. For the immediate context as well as for a reading of Stifter in general, the association between the sublime and the Freudian uncanny articulated by Thomas Weiskel, *The Romantic Sublime: Studies in the Structure and Psychology of Transcendence* (Baltimore: Johns Hopkins University Press, 1976), seems especially appropriate.

15. Cf. the model for the deployment of power elaborated by Michel Foucault in volume 1 of *The History of Sexuality*, trans. R. Hurley (New York: Vintage, 1978), and his critique therein of "The Repressive Hypothesis." My own dialogue with Holub can be seen in the mutual challenge and collaboration between these two models. See also the discussion of the relation between "law-preserving [*rechtserhaltend*]" and "law-making [*rechtssetzend*]" violence in Benjamin, "Zur Kritik der Gewalt [Critique of Violence]," *Gesammelte Schriften*, 2:179–203.

16. Cf. J. P. Stern, *On Realism*, 44–51; also Holub, *Reflections of Realism*, 49. The same conflict is also central to the discussion of realist aesthetics in Keller's *Green Henry* (*Der Grüne Heinrich*).

17. Martin and Erika Swales, *Adalbert Stifter: A Critical Study* (Cambridge: Cambridge University Press, 1984), 39–41; Berman, *The Rise of the Modern German Novel*, 114f.

18. We might just note two primary reasons why Stifter particularly requires the Christian concept of God to represent the unseen forces that uphold his realist natural world, despite realism's apparent (and not only apparent) antipathy to transcendent other-worldliness. First, he requires it to ensure that natural forces (*Kräfte*) function as laws (*Gesetze*) as principles of meaning or intelligibility and not just of power, and, further, to ensure that these "laws" function as "*the* law," as expressions of a single, uniform reality. Second, as Benjamin notes and as is only apparently unrelated, Stifter requires the concept of God to ensure that his natural world functions as an expression of fundamentally *patriarchal* law, or power (Benjamin, "Karl Kraus," 2:365). In fact, and as we shall see, this gendering of natural reality, or law, is perhaps the most decisive aspect of Stifter's realism and the most pressing motivation for his appeal to God as the law behind his natural world.

19. Certainly we shall see that in *The Mountain Forest* it is not at all clear that the various pieces and discourses of meaning are all harmonious, all one, even as the attempt to make them so *is* clear. Stifter's much later novella *Descendants* (*Nachkommenschaften*, 1864) comically captures the dilemma in its opening image of wagonloads of different realist paintings purportedly representing the same "thing."

20. The violence at issue is a slightly different one from that discussed above, aimed not so much at negating the disruption of individual upheaval as at constituting its own inclusive, uniform order, but the self-conscious awareness of the violence and its possible futility remain the same, and retain the same intrinsic place in Stifter's program.

21. The literature on Stifter as painter is vast, as is that on his descriptions of nature (*Naturbeschreibungen*). For the move toward spatial stasis, see, e.g., Peter Küpper, "Literatur und Langweile: Zur Lektüre Stifters," in *Adalbert Stifter: Studien und Inter-*

pretationen, ed. L. Stiehm (Heidelberg: Lothar Stiehm, 1968), 171–89. For realism's appeal to painting to support its project of literary mimesis, see Jakobson, "On Realism in Art"; Holub, *Reflections of Realism*; and my discussion of Storm's *Viola tricolor* in chapter six. For Benjamin's observation, see Benjamin, "Stifter II," in *Gesammelte Schriften*, 2:609 f.; for its decisive refutation, see Geulen, *Worthörig wider Willen*. For the topos of vision in general, see further Jürgen Manthey, *Wenn Blicke zeugen könnten* (Munich: Carl Hanser, 1983), 261–86; and Erika Tunner, "'Zum Sehen geboren, zum Schauen bestellt': Reflexionen zur Augensymbolik in Stifters *Studien*," *Etudes Germaniques* 40 (1985): 335–48.

22. The dehistoricizing quality of the scientific gaze is thus a key feature of its realist function, as well as another important aspect of the collaborative relation in realism between science and religion, which similarly dehistoricizes its world.

23. For more on this process, see Roland Barthes, "Myth Today," in *Mythologies*, trans. Annette Lavers (New York: Hill and Wang, 1983), 109–59; Miller, *The Novel and the Police*, 26 f.; Bersani, "Realism and the Fear of Desire," 51–88.

24. Benjamin, "Stifter I," in *Gesammelte Schriften*, 2:608 f.; see also his January 1919 letter to Schoen (*Briefe*, 205–7), cited in *Gesammelte Schriften*, 3:1416 f. See, too, Peter Demetz, "Walter Benjamin als Leser Adalbert Stifters," in *Adalbert Stifter Heute: London Symposium 1983*, ed. J. Lachinger, A. Doppler, and A. Stillmark (Linz: Wimmer, 1985), 38–43; and Dagmar Lorenz, "Stifters Frauengestalten," *VASILO* 32 (1983): 93–106. I should stress that when claiming Nature here becomes "a reality that excludes reality," I also mean it becomes a reality that produces through its process of exclusion this other reality, this other fiction, this other nature. Or in other words, "female sexuality" need not be considered some original reality that Stifter's realist fiction excludes, but rather itself a product of that fiction and as such a part of realist fiction.

25. For more on the topos of the Medusa's head in nineteenth-century literary representation, and especially its complex gender politics, see Catriona MacLeod, *Embodying Ambiguity: Androgyny and Aesthetics from Winckelmann to Keller* (Detroit: Wayne University Press, 1998); also Holub, *Reflections of Realism*, 55 f.

26. Cf. William Collins Donahue, "The Kiss of the Spider Woman: Gotthelf's Matricentric Pedagogy," *German Quarterly* 67, no. 3 (1994): 304–24. Hebbel's *Agnes Bernauer* and Fontane's *Effi Briest* are further classic examples of this fatal dilemma; on a less obvious, more insidious register, so too is Heyse's *L'Arrabiata*.

27. Both Swales and Holub assume only the exclusive reading, the former for Stifter in particular and the latter for realism in general. My argument with both is not simply for the inclusive reading and against the exclusive one, but rather, in however self-contradictory a fashion, for both readings together.

28. I should add that the paradox is clearly inherent to the rhetorical strategy of

repetition deployed by Stifter to develop his realist program. The very separation and connection of the natural and the human, of the two chiastically arranged halves of the preface, are based on a mutual exclusion as well as inclusion. The very structure of repetition between the two worlds is predicated simultaneously on their differentiation and their both presupposed and eventual identity. One might say that in its own division of the two spheres, Stifter's preface proves to be the dreaded "lightning-blast that splits apart houses" (10).

29. Georg Büchner, *Sämtliche Werke und Briefe*, ed. Werner R. Lehmann (Hamburg: Christian Wegner, 1967), 1:87.

30. Note how this yields a notion of "real" individuals who are anything but whole, but rather necessarily, even if impossibly, partial—characters who are ironically as one-sided (*einseitig*) as those violent individuals whom Stifter opposes as "small" and somehow unreal just because they are one-sided, but also characters whose one-sidedness or flatness can be considered neither an artistic failing nor a falling short of the demands of realism, but rather an ideological requirement for its achievement. Note, too, how it is not only community but also communication itself—that is, representability, that is dependent on submission to this common law. We might even say that the very principle of communicability thus becomes a mechanism for the maintenance of reality: that is, not that reality predicates representability, but the reverse.

31. The sentence continues: "in the industriousness that sustains us, in the activity through which one works for those in his own circle, for those far away, and for mankind, and finally in the order and form with which whole societies and states surround and conclude their existence" (13).

32. This is the position articulated by Holub, *Reflections of Realism*, 91f., in his analysis of love and desire in Stifter's *Indian Summer* (*Der Nachsommer*, 1857).

33. Catriona MacLeod points out to me that the behavior of the content of this sentence parallels that of its rhetorical structure in this regard, with "the sweet inclination of both sexes" situated at the maximum distance from "the love of spouses for one another" and immediately followed by a swerving away to more abstract, depersonalizing terms.

34. Again, the clearest example of this will come in *The Mountain Forest*, with its complex revelations of incest. For more on the theme of incest in Stifter's programmatic works, see MacLeod, *Embodying Ambiguity*, 185–206; and Manthey, *Wenn Blicke zeugen könnten*, 279–84. For more on incest and realism, see my discussion of Storm's *Viola tricolor* in chapter six.

35. Cf. the second essay, sections 16–18, of Friedrich Nietzsche, *Zur Genealogie der Moral* (*On the Genealogy of Morals*), in volume 5 of *Sämtliche Werke: Kritische Studienausgabe in fünfzehn Einzelbände*, ed. Giorgio Colli and Mazzino Montinari (Munich:

Deutscher Taschenbuch Verlag, 1988). Note too that Stifter seems here to make the connection between the individual and social or general forces (*Kräfte*) that he earlier denied and only rhetorically (re-)claimed.

36. That the new "realist" desire and imagination remain highly, even forcibly embedded in convention is no argument against their existence. For as Stifter represents them, those of his allegedly more wild and fantastic literary predecessors and rivals prove equally if not more conventional and artificial. In true realist fashion, it is simply one set of conventions against another: see Jakobson, "On Realism in Art."

CHAPTER 3: DOUBLE VISIONS

1. Cf. *Granite*, the first story in *Many-colored Stones,* where the tale of the Knight of Wittinghausen is recapitulated as something of an exemplum for the new story itself, thus indirectly securing the exemplary status of *The Mountain Forest* for the later volume and program as well.

2. At first sight, the confusion seems to arise from the excessive attention paid to specific details, from a superfluity of particular *realia* that risks a loss of the sense for the intelligible whole, precisely that whole (and intelligibility) that Stifter apparently desires his description of Nature to represent. This is a danger often associated with realism in general and especially with Stifter's: however, at second sight, this turns out not to be the major problem here. Rather, the confusion at the outset of *The Mountain Forest* arises not so much from the overabundance of details as from the overabundance of meaning; the multiple specifics do not so much overwhelm the structures of intelligibility as those structures overwhelm the few, relatively simple "facts." But this, too, would seem a consequence of Stifter's realist intent: that the natural details must be made to signify, must themselves carry the burden or inscription of their meaning.

3. Of course, this move into the remote reaches of the woods and from there into a nebulous, fairytale-like past is also invested with its *avoidance* of reality—that is, of the narrator's contemporary social-historical world, which goes all but unmentioned in the frame. As I said in the preceding chapter, this avoidance of the (politically) real, or rather, this mode of presenting the "real" in nonpolitical and nonhistorical terms, is characteristic of poetic realism. And as we will see, it remains a significant part of the reality of the woods in the story our narrator tells as well.

4. For the "two points" (*zwei Punkte*), see Adalbert Stifter, *Werke und Briefe. Historisch-Kritische Gesamtausgabe*, 1:4:211. All parenthetical references in this chapter are taken from this edition and refer exclusively to *Der Hochwald* (*The Mountain Forest*).

5. While the strain between the pattern and subject matter certainly accounts for part of the perplexity encountered here and avoided in the more abstract context of the preface to *Many-colored Stones*, we should note that it also arises from the narrator at-

tempting to make explicit what in the preface to *Many-colored Stones* Stifter deliberately attempts to expunge. As we saw, in the latter Stifter projects certain human and social values onto the site of Nature, but then (partially) effaces their origin before projecting them back, as natural laws, onto the human world, which however he treats divorced from nature itself. In *The Mountain Forest*, the narrator instead actively evokes a human world in his description of Nature through metaphors such as "granite blocks, like pale skulls" (212), or "a branchless trunk, like a solitary antique column" (213); and in his subsequent description of the human realm, he also evokes a natural one through such imagistic, reversing repetitions as "Granite forms, which lay sown about on the lawn" (215). The result is a far busier play of the reflective repeating relations between the natural and the human worlds than in the preface to *Many-colored Stones*, a play at once more contrived and sincere, even realistic; however, it is basically still the same play, the same back and forth, mirroring structure of repeating realities. For more on the evocation of a human world within the natural, see Roy Pascal, "Die Landschaftsschilderung im 'Hochwald,'" in *Adalbert Stifter: Studien und Interpretationen*, ed. Lothar Stiehm (Heidelberg: Lothar Stiehm Verlag, 1968), 57–68; Karl Mautz, "Das antagonistische Naturbild in Stifters 'Studien,'" in *Adalbert Stifter: Studien und Interpretationen*, 69–88; Erich Heintel, "Natur und Geschichte in Stifters 'Hochwald,'" in *Wiener Jahrbuch für Philosophie* (1973): 7–41.

6. These two contradictory movements are imposed and maintained not least through his chapter titles, which follow the same double movement, similarly parceled between the natural and human-historical spheres: 1. *The Forest Castle* (*Waldburg*); 2. *The Forest Trek* (*Waldwanderung*); 3. *The Forest House* (*Waldhaus*); 4. *The Forest Lake* (*Waldsee*); 5. *The Forest Meadow* (*Waldwiese*); 6. *The Forest Crag* (*Waldfels*); 7. *The Forest Ruins* (*Waldruine*).

7. Cf. John Reddick, "Mystification, Perspectivism and Symbolism in *Der Hochwald*," in *Adalbert Stifter Heute: Londoner Symposium 1983*, ed. Johann Lachinger, Alexander Stillmark, and Martin Swales (Linz: OÖ Landesverlag, 1985), 44–74, who at one moment seems to recognize that virginity is a "positive projection" onto the site of nature, but for the most part assumes that nature "really is" virginal, and that the story records the tragic human violation of that natural reality qua virginity.

8. Cf. 234, where the stream is subject to a different law from the rest of the forest; also 214 f., where the castle ruins are found downstream.

9. This is perhaps best formulated in the more religious terms that always inhabit the natural ones in the story: "like a beautiful thought of God the wide expanse of the forest sank itself softly into Clarissa's soul, which, knowing nothing of that, in a still and gentle and beautiful feeling surged toward it" (237).

10. For the interchangeability, see 220, 223 f., 232, 236, 237, 241 f. Of particular inter-

est is the description on 241f., when Johanna and Clarissa are first entering the high woods and are represented "as they sat there in their sedan chair [*ihrer Sänfte*] and, like two pictures of angels [*zwei Engelsbilder*] in a frame, looked out." This *Sänfte* is subsequently described as "the narrow, bearable prison [*das enge tragbare Gefängniss*]" (248), and its coincidence with the gentle law (*das sanfte Gesetz*) that similarly equates and imprisons the women by making them angelically pure "pictures" seems hardly, well, coincidental.

11. We see this throughout the *Studies*, in both its achieved design and its disrupting failure. For example in *The Castle of Fools* (*Die Narrenburg*), where the painting in the green hall of Chelion, whose sexuality fatally disrupts the serene stability of the entire Scharnast family, cannot be left out to view, lest it incite the disruptive desire of yet another male, that is, where the failure to contain female sexuality is reflected in the medium habitually invoked to control it: Happiness, and viewable pictures, are restored only when the more manageable Anna is restored in Chelion's place. The pattern that *The Castle of Fools* asserts in its violation dominates *The Album of My Greatgrandfather* (*Die Mappe meines Urgrossvaters*) in a more characteristically secured mode, although here an effigy (*Bildnis*) or statue (*Bildsäule*) replaces the more usual painting: after a jealous, disruptive outburst of passion, the beloved Margarita is replaced by the narrator/protagonist with a statue (*Standbild*) in his house, which he gazes at constantly until both his desire and its (absent) object have been properly trained, mastered, and restored, at which point the real Margarita can safely reappear and the appointed course of their happiness be fulfilled.

12. As I said in the last chapter, something similar is also evident both in Lenz's figure of the Medusa's head and especially in Heinrich Lee's paintings of Anna and nature scenes. It is just this pattern, this mode of fixing female reality through visual representation, that Johanna seems to embody: a representation that excludes, and so contains, reality.

13. Cf. Reddick, "Mystification, Perspectivism and Symbolism in *Der Hochwald*," 53, who finds the papers and parchment scrolls inexplicable.

14. We will see a similar collapse of narrative and history (of *Geschichte* and *Geschichte*) as almost identical expressions of the disruptive and would-be excluded reality later on in the figure of Ronald, Clarissa's beloved, whose narrative of the war intrudes into the speech (*Reden*) or narrative (*Erzählung*) of the mountain forest—that speech or narrative by which Gregor, the father's friend, works to present the natural world as a stable, controlled, secure, and beloved realm. It also appears for a final time, its opposition to the visual project captured in the accompanying image of "the window plastered with worthless paper [*das mit schlechtem Papiere verklebte Fenster*]" (211) in Bruno's report of what actually happened to Ronald and the father, a narrative of the

historical, real event that leaves Johanna like a deceased angel (*wie ein gestorbener Engel*) and Clarissa's tears "like the blood of a slaughtered animal" (315).

The dual nature of language in general and writing in particular is evident not only in *The Mountain Forest* but throughout the *Studies* and *Many-colored Stones* as well. In its record-keeping function, as for instance in the doctor's medical charts in *The Album of My Greatgrandfather* or in Maria's estate-planning in *Two Sisters*, writing complements the visual project of stabilizing mastery of the given. This is perhaps best seen in *Many-colored Stones*, in the figure and activity of the surveyor-narrator of *Limestone* (*Kalkstein*), whose visual measurements of the initially forbidding landscape transpose unproblematically into his written records, transforming the scene into something realized, mastered, and beloved—much like the narrator's transformation here of the woods and of Johanna. But in another aspect, writing in Stifter's early work seems radically opposed to the project of mastered stability, and that opposition seems inseparable from an ineradicable temporality that adheres to writing (this second dimension to writing is not recognized by Holub in his reading of *Indian Summer*, perhaps because it is not there; see Holub, *Reflections of Realism*, 69–78). We see this most overtly in two of the *Studies*, *The Castle of Fools* and *The Album of My Greatgrandfather*. In the former, the founder of the family Scharnast decrees that each ruling family member must completely write out the unfolding course of his life, and then deposit his report in the red-rock chamber built for just this purpose; he must also agree to read all preceding, similarly stored reports (this red room for the writings is explicitly contrasted with the green room for the paintings: see above, note 11). The express purpose is to achieve a stable moral order or control, but the effect is the opposite: the writings not only record but actually instigate an ongoing history of moral dissolution in the family. In *The Album of My Greatgrandfather*, the "gentle colonel" persuades the narrator-protagonist to follow him in the repeated practice of first writing down all the thoughts and events of his present life and then sealing the book and reading it for the first time years later. Here the express purpose, and effect, is to convince oneself of the unreality of one's supposedly accurate and informed representation: the actual unfolding of time and history undoes the expected sense of mastery, and confirms the insight voiced in *The Castle of Fools*—"What I here write, is not I—I cannot write me [*Was ich hier schreibe, bin nicht ich—mich kann ich nicht schreiben*]" (448). In both cases writing is associated with a sense—its own sense—of inevitable temporality and uncontrol, an ineradicable historicity that is held up as reality; a reality that frustrates the effort after a stable, uniform, equivalent representation.

15. Music occurs only rarely in Stifter's works (indeed in poetic realist texts in general)—prominently in *Two Sisters* and *Tourmaline*, more suggestively in the aeolian

harp of Prokopus in *The Castle of Fools*. When it does, it generally functions as it does in *The Mountain Forest*, as a disruptive, threatening element.

16. Cf. Susan Buck-Morss, *The Origin of Negative Dialectics* (New York: Free Press, 1977), 43. I would like to thank Jiro Tanaka for this reference.

17. Reddick reads this quite differently: see "Mystification, Perspectivism and Symbolism in *Der Hochwald*," 56.

18. Cf. Eva Geulen, *Worthörig wider Willen*, 97.

19. Cf. Konrad Steffen's comment on *The Castle of Fools*: "Although heroically carried out, Jodokus' attempt to be doubly considerate toward Chelion after that night in which he forced from her her confession, is useless. Once the husband confronted her, albeit with gentle words, still with the eyes of a murderer; now every day she expects a new outbreak of the rage and jealousy she once thought impossible, and she no more believes in the overcoming of the instinctive drives than did the early Stifter himself." In Konrad Steffen, ed., *Adalbert Stifter. Gesammelte Werke* (Basel: Birkhäuser, 1962), 1:497f.

20. This is brought out again in the father's own depiction: he too is assimilated to a world of painting, "as if his figure had stepped out of one of Van Dyk's frames," and, in keeping with his more active role, to a world of *seeing* as well, to "that time of seers and prophets" (cf. "an eye, strongly arched and speaking"). Moreover, the holding off of time and change implicit in both the still-life painting and the transport (*Hinüberhebung*) from "that time" is further accentuated by the narrator's metaphorical portrayal of the father as *wie eine Zeitlose* (literally, "like a timeless [flower]," 224f.).

21. This inherent futility of the father's visual project and its immutable ideal is also brought out in the narrator's initial description of him, especially insofar as it is made to register effects very different from those evoked earlier about Johanna, and much closer to those he described as symptoms of the loss of the intended, immutable purity and the fall into (historically real) time—of the reality evoked about the figure of the other daughter, Clarissa. So, for instance, whereas Johanna is oddly enough figured as a house, even as his house, the father is "a ruin of powerful manly strength and size": whereas Johanna "grows" a blooming rose to suit her in some sense ever-present and at-home father, he himself is "one of those figures of the knighthood whose bloom was past [*des abgeblühten Rittertums*], so rarely still seen at that time and so unsuited for the contemporary world" (224f.). His out-of-placeness and -timeness, which is perhaps retrospectively strengthened by his association with "that time of seers," seems tragically to belie the promise embodied both in the (static) image of Johanna and in his own image, "like a timeless flower," and to show instead the traces of the feared and even denied (historical) reality embodied in Clarissa. In a contradictory and already

doomed fashion, the description of the father seems to combine both of the "realities" associated with his daughters.

22. This is further emphasized by the absent mother.

23. Note the present tense, which conveys the collaborative supervision of the narrator, whose collusion with the father (and Gregor) continues to be a central part of the story.

24. This apparently contradicts Holub's analysis of *Indian Summer*, where love and desire are depicted as without relation: see *Reflections of Realism*, 92. It is worth emphasizing the parallel here with the related omission in his reading of the novel, namely of the threatening, nonvisual aspect of language. Certainly both omissions are as attributable to Stifter's text as to Holub's analysis; but the point remains that an analysis of *The Mountain Forest* reveals an intrinsic complexity to Stifter's realism that one of *Indian Summer* fails to foreground.

25. The introverted erotics are perhaps especially conspicuous in Clarissa's relation with Johanna: "Clarissa kissed her twice with true passion on her child's lips, on whose unconscious swelling beauty she delighted like a lover [*wie ein Liebender*]" (220). But they are no less there in both daughters, as for instance when they sit together "like two lovers, consciously resting in the boundless inclination of the other [*der gränzenlosen Neigung des Andern*]" (260; cf. 249 f.). Reddick insightfully points out the gender confusion in both passages: see "Mystification, Perspectivism and Symbolism in *Der Hochwald*," 69.

26. As such, the father is also the major source for the patriarchal character of the hidden order behind the natural world, linked here, as in the preface to *Many-colored Stones*, with that of the Christian God.

27. This deletion might be seen repeated in the replacement of the novella's original title with the subsequent one of *The Mountain Forest*.

28. Cf. the Adamic language taught by men to women in other Stifter stories, e.g. *The Album of My Greatgrandfather*, *The Village on the Heath* (*Das Haidedorf*), *The Castle of Fools*, and so on.

29. This last point touches on one of the chief paradoxes about Gregor's figure and what might well be read as one of the novella's chief flaws. Gregor is simultaneously identified as a poetic visionary, or *Fantast*, deeply invested in the religious and fairy-tale-like, and as a demystifying realist, indeed as the most outspoken representative of a realist aesthetic in the novella. This paradox, however, is intrinsic to the *kind* of realism Gregor would represent, and can be read as a studied response to the same paradox and flaw at the heart of all poetic realism. So for instance we have seen how the father's realistic determination of the woods is still very much a fantastic fiction, both in its ini-

tial projection of his desire and in its intended representative effect for his daughters. However, in his case the fantastic basis of the fiction is also denied by the fiction itself, which seeks to efface all traces of fantasy both from its represented world, the woods, and from its recursive target, the daughters. Its fiction is that there is no fiction, its fantasy that there need be no fantasy; and while this contradictory, repressive denial might seem characteristic of realism, it also proves characteristically impossible to maintain, indeed has already proved a fatal flaw in the father's exclusionary designs. Gregor's inclusionary realism seeks to avoid this flaw. When he describes the woods it is "as if one were reading from an old, beautiful book of poetry" (244), and the woods literally and fantastically come to "speak" as if human on his watch ("Everything speaks, Everything narrates"): through his eyes the woods are transformed into a fairy tale, or *Märchen,* for Clarissa and Johanna, and they in turn are turned into a matching *Märchen* in the eyes of the woods (259). The very nature of the new attempt forces Gregor to become more fantastic than the father, even if, finally, no less disastrously disappointed (see below).

30. Cf. Geulen's brilliant reading of this passage: see *Worthörig wider Willen,* 104 f.

31. The association of the prerealist natural world with the feminine or matriarchal, represented here by the grandmother, is characteristic of Stifter: cf. *The Castle of Fools, Mica (Katzensilber).* But that the patriarchal realism only succeeds by denying what it is supposed to contain, namely the same feminine—this is thematized as a problem (as a failure) only here.

32. This raises the extremely interesting issue of the paradoxes to realist allegory: the inherent allegorical dimension of all realism, and its built-in failure—not because of the allegory, but because of its realism.

33. Although the reference is obviously to Gustav Adolf, Stifter deliberately avoids specifying this in order to keep in play the more abstract or allegorical resonances evoked by his command; the generality is deliberate, as evidenced by Stifter's reworking of the "Journalfassung."

34. As I said before (see above, note 14), Ronald's intrusive appearance on the forest meadow is, as much as anything, that of language itself, of language as *Geschichte* and *Geschichte* in all its *Geschichtlichkeit*: in its abrupt beginning, its powerfully onrushing narrative flow, and its equally sudden end; in its evocation of a past and future tense, and its insistent push to traverse the path between them, etc. As Clarissa says to Gregor, "He urgently desires to speak with us" (280); and to Ronald himself, "I believe you want to speak with us—we have come—so speak" (282), and what follows is his narrative of past, present, and future. His speech or narrative radically disrupts that of the forest, or rather of Gregor's inscription of the forest; but it nonetheless emphatically remains the same medium, that of Gregor's own stories, of the novella itself, and

of all poetic realism. It simply recalls the linguistic reality of temporality, or *Geschichtlichkeit,* that confronts and opposes all efforts to achieve a stable, uniform representation through language. Thus too the logic to the subsequent exchange between Clarissa and Johanna, "How beautifully he speaks our language." "But one day he will go [*wird er fortgehen*]" (302 f.): the one entails the other.

Similarly, but more prominently thematized, Ronald's volatile love, which so radically disrupts the seemingly calm love of the father and of the forest realm, reasserts the necessary temporality and movement of all desire, including the father's. As the narrator tells us, "It was precisely that last quality, which every moment threatened the loss of love, which so magically bound Clarissa" (285). For more on narrative, desire, and temporality, see below.

35. The inherence of the reality of temporal movement represented by Ronald and its threat to the ongoing "realist" desire for mimetic stability (still most represented by the father) are even more conspicuous in the scene immediately preceding that on the forest meadow, where Ronald sings his song, and in the subsequent one at the father's castle, both of which also more graphically highlight the issues of repetition at stake in his appearance. When Clarissa first sang a broken verse from this song at the beginning of the story, Johanna let us know its perceived threat to the father; when Ronald sings the song in its entirety, we learn that it is centrally concerned with a moment of succession, with death as its intervening term. The song begins, "Once upon a time there was a king / He wore a golden crown," and ends, "And again there was a king / He rode beside the rock: / There lay the whitened bones / Beside the golden crown" (277). Although the more or less Oedipal structure to the song should require no comment, we should note that Reddick somehow manages to misread the function of this song, failing to recognize its relevance to the father. But then he seems to miss the role of the father throughout, which leads to similar misreadings: e.g., his reading of the forest lake qua *Naturauge* as associated with Clarissa: see "Mystification, Perspectivism and Symbolism in *Der Hochwald,*" 55.

In the scene at the father's castle, the death threat against the father implicit to Ronald's song becomes explicitly realized. The sexual symbolism to the encounter between the father and Ronald again requires no comment: the father espies Ronald, suddenly the sole representative of the threatening armed forces, riding toward his house: "Without saying a syllable, he suddenly slung his lance at the rider, not considering that at this distance it couldn't possibly reach its mark—and the poor, weak, innocent lance, it didn't reach its mark" (314)."

Even as, in the woods, the real threatening historical forces were not so much the external ones of the war as the internal ones of love, so here the real historical forces at work seem less externally political (which are in fact merely a covering fiction) than internally familial—and in this, the threat Ronald embodies seems again an intrinsic one. He represents history, movement as succession—the same movement-as-succession that the father deploys to try to maintain a stable, continuous world, by reducing all such movement to mimetic repetition. From himself, the father would have Clarissa's love transferred to his representative-substitute, Gregor, and from Gregor to his next representative-substitute, Bruno, the *Reiter/Ritter* (rider/knight) whose generic designations overlap so curiously and significantly with the father's own. Ronald represents this same ongoing, succeeding movement, but in its threat to stability and mimetic equivalence, in its introduction of difference rather than (or along with) sameness. However, it is still the same chain of substitution that underlies both conflicting realities, as we see in the king in the song or the rider in the quote above: and so again, the reality Ronald represents seems at once to be other and the same—in some ways, a paradox of repetition itself.

36. This point is explicitly represented in the novella itself, in Bruno's report of the destruction of the father's house. What Bruno says first is, finally, most revealing: he says, "The real misfortune was a forest [*Ein Wald war das eigentliche Unglück*]" (313). He explains that the father's house, their house, would never have been destroyed—"Not a finger would have touched it"—but for their own defensive strategy, their own risky decision "to throw up fortifications in that forest and turn back the enemy." The passage (*Übergang*) of the Swedish forces would have proceeded peacefully through the woods, "harmlessly, like a band of pilgrims with songs resounding," but for the *Schanzen*, the fortified woods themselves, which stopped the forces' forward course, not so much throwing them out as keeping them trapped within the forest, behind the line the father's side itself had drawn. This imposed, displaced blockade causes the Swedish forces to swell and build up to the point that they overcome the resistance, rupture the barrier "like broken glass," and destroy the father's house, before proceeding on their course. In a very real way, the father's house can be seen to have brought about its own destruction; but it does so indirectly, by having first projected itself and its defenses into the woods.

It is not difficult to draw the parallel's between this decisive vignette and the whole novella, to see the mountain forest (*Hochwald*) itself as the fortified forest (*Schanzenwald*) and as "the true misfortune." As in the *Schanzenwald*, so too in the *Hochwald* all the various forces fighting on the father's side—the father himself, Gregor, the narrator, in some sense Stifter himself—transform the forest into a defensive realm by drawing or constructing a line, a line meant to keep the various human forces out of the woods, or in the woods—either way to stop them, define them, and contain them. And even as the Swedish forces simply move along, a movement as essential to their identity as to the songs they are singing, so too Clarissa's self and desire: it is no more the course of the one than the other which occasions the tragedy, but rather the ill-advised attempt to stop them; only then and only thus does the human movement become disruptive. In both cases, this stoppage was, or is, the woods, which are meant to achieve a stasis that can then be defended and deployed to control, govern, or confront the human world. But the strategy turns against itself: the father's house is destroyed, and the whole bid to govern and maintain the world "the way it is" is destroyed not so much by the movement it feared as by the stasis it desired all along.

37. Even if we admit that the disruptive forces of desire, history, and so on have proven themselves to be a reality that cannot be repressed, in either the woods or Clarissa, and so also that the destruction of her childlike virginity, of the forest's static uniformity (*Einformigkeit*), even of the father's house could not "realistically" be prevented; even then, if we admit that the narrator's—and Gregor's—reinscription of the poetically real, natural, and divine order to include these forces and that destruction seems both justified and necessary, an honest, acknowledging, and timely self-conscious response to the way the world "really is"; even so, we would still have to admit that the attempt at reformulation seems hopelessly belated and artificial, and moreover to contradict itself in its very intent. The belatedness and artifice are perhaps best seen in how Johanna "clearly felt that she had lost something, however overwhelming the proofs of her sister's love, and perhaps for that very reason. Often, like a child, there came over her heart a homesickness for the past" (298). The very excessive and even violent insistence on the continued reality of their common bond betrays its loss, and so too its unavoidable fiction. And the inherent self-contradiction is perhaps best seen in how the attempt to maintain the embracing reality or order of nature ("the former calm [*die alte Ruhe*]") goes against what is trying to be embraced, namely change, movement, disruption, and destruction; or conversely, in how the very fact that it is a third attempt, a third formulation of "the way things are" that at least in part supersedes and abandons the previous ones (the father's exclusive one and Gregor's inclusive but still atemporal one), belies the immutability of the poetically real world, whose laws or principles of governance need constantly to be reconceived in order to achieve the continued, desired effect of mimetic equivalence between the natural and human realms. In both respects, we seem thrown back—or forward—into the necessary violence and fiction posed earlier by the narrator as the unavoidable conditions of all belatedly imposed uniformity and order in the post-Edenic, real world of desire and history.

As for the second point, regarding the narrator in particular: there is, I believe, an inherent ambiguity to his reformulation of the natural world that is absent from Gregor's, one that calls into question both his acceptance of Clarissa's self-assertion and the supposedly realistic basis of his natural world. Each of the changes in the reality of the woods—the approaching winter, the obscuring fog, the wasting hoarfrost, the bloodied leaves, and so on—each of these can be read as the registered, projected effects of Clarissa's "crime," as the symbolic indices not of her continued conformity with its laws but of her fatal and so condemned disruption of its previously pure, maintained, stable reality. And to some extent, this clearly is the case, and is clearly in keeping with the acknowledged fantastic character of all the previous inscriptions of the woods, which have always seemed as allegorical, fictional, or representative as they have real. Even as the father first projected his law of virginity onto the forest, so now do we find Clarissa's transgression of that virginity projected onto and realized in that same forest, which comes to reflect the violent violation of the previous natural order, or what amounts to the same thing: of the father's, Gregor's, and the narrator's own systems of governance over that order, that reality.

But an insuperable problem arises here for the narrator's attempt to record Clarissa's "crime," one that threatens to undo his entire enterprise. For by the same recursive structure that has grounded the novella's realisms throughout, the woods that now record the disruption of the determining system of governance become in turn, that is, in the chiastic return, just that determining system of governance. Even as the father, Gregor, or the narrator projected their laws onto the woods so that they would then be reflected back as "reality" onto the nature of the women, so now the effects of Clarissa's transgression, projected as they are onto the woods, become reflected back *as* reality onto her, who suddenly again finds herself in accord with the natural realm, and so the effect of her transgression effectively effaced. The very gesture or strategy that establishes the realism of the novella by inscribing and then (partially) effacing the fantasy of the patriarchally projected virginity also (partially) effaces the transgression of that projection, once it has been similarly inscribed. The very strategy of chiastic repetition that was to enforce the first projected fantasy as real, natural, and lawful also enforces its registered disruption as real, natural, and lawful—indeed as necessarily the same reality, nature, and law: the same woods. Like a figure before a mirror, the mimetic equivalence simply cannot be broken; the novella's "realism" becomes constitutionally incapable of violation. Or to put it more fully: the narrator can depict Clarissa's emergent self-identity and sexuality as violations of the common reality only by himself violating the mimetic, reflective system for generating that common reality. To show her bad faith, he must first break with his own.

38. For a reading of Stifter's telescopes as conveying such a narrative perspectivism, see Gerald Gillespie, "Space and Time Seen through Stifter's Telescope," *German Quarterly* 37, no. 2 (1964): 120–30.

39. For one of the most recent and best elaborations of this position, see Lilian R.

Furst, "Figuring the Pretense," in *All is True: The Claims and Strategies of Realist Fiction* (Durham, N.C.: Duke University Press, 1995), 146–73.

40. In a letter to B. Landucci of the Venetian Senate, August 11, 1609. Quoted by Gebler, *Galileo and the Roman Curia* (London, 1879), 19, and cited by Arthur Koestler, *The Sleepwalkers: A History of Man's Changing Vision of the Universe* (London: Penguin, 1959), 369.

41. In a letter to Gustav Heckenast, July 29, 1858. See Adalbert Stifter, *Werke*, ed. Uwe Japp and Hans Joachim Piechotta (Frankfurt am Main: Insel, 1978), 4:333. The potential antipathy of astronomical investigations to any realist program is perhaps best attested to by the fictional productions of Kepler himself, whose *Somnium*, written in 1609 and published in 1634, is arguably the first major work of science fiction in Western literature. See Karl S. Guthke, *The Last Frontier: Imagining Other Worlds from the Copernican Revolution to Modern Science Fiction*, trans. Helen Atkins (Ithaca: Cornell University Press, 1990), 84–93. On the other hand, Svetlana Alpers, *The Art of Describing: Dutch Art in the Seventeenth Century* (Chicago: University of Chicago Press, 1983), 30–38, argues for Kepler's investigations into the more earthbound functioning of the human eye, which he conceived in terms analogous with a lensed instrument, as providing the theoretical basis for seventeenth-century Dutch realist painting. For Alpers, the realist mode is the Keplerian mode.

42. Martin Selge, "Der Blick durchs Fernrohr: Teleskopische Vermittlung in *Der Hochwald*," in *Adalbert Stifter: Poesie aus dem Geist der Naturwissenschaft* (Stuttgart, 1976), 22–36, also links the figure of Kepler with the telescopes of this novella, and he also links the telescopes with the problem of lawfulness, or *Gesetzlichkeit*. However, the "law" he sees telescopes to incorporate is that of Kepler's orbital ellipsis—i.e., a transposition of the skybound to the earthbound. I argue for a quite different incorporated *Gesetzlichkeit* and a quite different appreciation of Kepler's relevance. Selge does not mention the letter cited above (see note 41).

43. Jonathan Crary, *Techniques of the Observer: On Vision and Modernity in the Nineteenth Century* (Cambridge: MIT Press, 1990), also argues for the importance not only of vision as normativizing but also for the normativizing of vision in mid-nineteenth-century culture. However, Crary's study does not address the "forms by which the dominant practices of vision were resisted, deflected, or imperfectly constituted," primarily because he considers such forms "marginal and local" (7). My argument is that, quite to the contrary, the "resistance" to and failures of the normativizing practices of vision in this period are intrinsic, systemic, and impossible to leave out of account.

44. Both the *Naturauge* and the telescope can be seen as participating in the project

of what Martin Jay calls "monocularity": see Martin Jay, "Scopic Regimes of Modernity," in *Vision and Visuality*, ed. Hal Forster (Seattle: Bay Press, 1988), 3–27.

45. Catriona MacLeod points out to me the need to differentiate between the mode of telescopic power elaborated for realism here and that of panoptic power elaborated for realism by theorists such as David Miller in *The Novel and the Police*. Unlike Bentham's (or rather Foucault's) Panopticon, the apparatus of the telescope does not see "everything." Rather, it presents a selected field that it magnifies to fill the available space. Thus exclusion remains a fundamental part of its power.

CHAPTER 4: DOUBLE TAKES

1. Walter Benjamin, "Gottfried Keller," in *Gesammelte Schriften*, ed. Rolf Tiedemann and Hermann Schweppenhäuser (Frankfurt am Main: Suhrkamp, 1980), 2:291.

2. This opening paragraph has been meticulously analyzed by Holub, *Reflections of Realism*, 101–31.

3. Gottfried Keller, letter to Friedrich Theodor Fischer on May 19, 1872, *Sämtliche Werke*, ed. Dominik Müller (Frankfurt am Main: Deutscher Klassiker Verlag, 1991), 6:818. All parenthetical references in the text are taken from this volume, and refer exclusively to the *Sieben Legenden* (*Seven Legends*). For the English I have consulted Martin Wyness's translation of "Eugenia" in Frank G. Ryder, ed., *Gottfried Keller: Stories* (New York: Continuum, 1982), 333–46.

4. Müller, *Keller: Sämtliche Werke*, 6:822, 6:819.

5. Ibid., 6:820.

6. Ibid., 6:824.

7. For a detailed reading of the *Seven Legends* in terms of Keller's Feuerbach reception, see Christine Renz, *Gottfried Kellers "Sieben Legenden": Versuch einer Darstellung seines Erzählens* (Tübingen: Niemeyer Verlag, 1993).

8. Cf. the fourth legend, "The Virgin and the Nun" ("Die Jungfrau und die Nonne"), about a nun who leaves the cloister to explore the "real" world, but who almost immediately meets a man with whom she gladly rides away: "Under such circumstances they saw nothing of the countryside nor of the light that spread across it; and the nun, who had just been yearning for the wide world, now closed her eyes before it and confined herself to the territory that could be carried on a horse's back" (6:51).

9. The failure to distinguish clearly between the concepts of desire and gender, frequently conflated in the term "sex," has been a fruitful point of criticism for feminist theorists, especially in considering psychoanalytical readings; cf. Valerie Traub, *Desire and Anxiety: Circulations of Sexuality in Shakespearean Drama* (London: Routledge, 1992). As will become clear, I wish to associate the desire/genre pairing identified here in the foreword with a desire/gender pairing operant in the stories: my own "failure" to

distinguish firmly between the latter terms reflects not only Keller's refusal to do so but also the overlay with the desire/genre terms I wish to emphasize and explore.

10. For a brilliant theoretical reading of how this representational coincidence works in a slightly different context, see Benjamin's analysis of the role played by gesture in Kafka's work in Walter Benjamin, "Franz Kafka," *Gesammelte Schriften*, 2:409 ff.

11. Gerhard Kaiser, *Gottfried Keller, Das gedichtete Leben* (Frankfurt am Main: Insel Verlag, 1981), associates the self-conscious representation of the tale's artful dimension solely with the figure of the Virgin Mary, especially her statues (417). But this leaves out of account the function of the statue in the first story, "Eugenia": see below.

12. Judith Butler, *Gender Trouble: Feminism and the Subversion of Identity* (New York: Routledge, 1990), 136.

13. Ibid.

14. Ibid.

15. Ibid.

16. Ibid.

17. For a brilliant analysis of the normative, regulating function of transvestism in late-eighteenth- and early-nineteenth-century German literature, see Catriona MacLeod, *Embodying Ambiguity* (Detroit: Wayne State University, 1998).

18. Butler, *Gender Trouble*.

19. Ibid.

20. Keller's sixth legend, "Dorothea's Flower-Basket" ("Dorotheas Blumenkörbchen"), explicitly thematizes the possible impossibility of successfully distinguishing the parodically from the "really" intended, as the intended mockery and mischievousness to Dorothea's words and actions are continually missed by Theophilus, and not just because he is a naive reader. The relevance of this aspect of the legend to the case of the *Seven Legends* itself is patent. Butler herself in her more recent work has come to acknowledge the difficulties in the position described here. In *Bodies That Matter* (New York: Routledge, 1993), she writes, "Although many readers understood *Gender Trouble* to be arguing for the proliferation of drag performances as a way of subverting dominant gender norms, I want to underscore that there is no necessary relation between drag and subversion, and that drag may well be used in the service of both the denaturalization and the reidealization of hyperbolic heterosexual gender norms. At best, it seems, drag is the site of a certain ambivalence, one which reflects the more general situation of being implicated in the regimes of power by which one is constituted and hence of being implicated in the very regimes of power that one opposes" (125). Although I believe these many readers correctly understood the argument proposed by *Gender Trouble*, I also believe her retelling of it here to be more persuasive, even if arguably fatal for her original model. For a most subtle reading of the necessary hesitancy

of any representation between the reinforcement of and resistance to the political reality it engages, see Eva Geulen, "Resistance and Representation: A Case-Study of Thomas Mann's 'Mario and the Magician,'" *New German Critique* 68 (1996): 3–29.

21. For the ineliminable vagaries of this term, see Terry Eagleton, *Ideology: An Introduction* (London: Verso, 1991).

22. During at least one point in the rather complicated and drawn-out history of their composition, the *Seven Legends* were intended by Keller to be part of *The Epigram* (*Das Sinngedicht*, 1881) and so apparently to be narrated by the more or less openly (and naively) misogynistic figure of Reinhart. The extent to which this intention influenced the fashioning of the narratorial perspective in "Eugenia" is open to interpretation; Müller finds the narratorial attitude toward women to be both more negative and more dramatized here than in any of the other legends (6:800).

23. Walter Benjamin, "The Storyteller" ("Der Erzähler"), associates this function of narrative repetition with the reality formation of stories in particular, and would probably distinguish it from that of novellas, or *Novellistik*. Although in the case of this deliberately hybrid form the distinction might seem moot, it does encourage Rudi Bentz, "Form und Struktur der 'Sieben Legenden' Gottfried Kellers" (Ph.D. diss., Zürich, 1979), to read these opening paragraphs as merely imitative of inherited narrative conventions (110), and so perhaps as even more open to question, especially in regard to their adequacy for explaining the subsequent story, than they already are.

24. Both Renz, *Gottfried Kellers "Sieben Legenden"*; and Kaiser, *Gottfried Keller, Das gedichtete Leben*, productively identify the intended parallel between the legends of "Eugenia" and "The Naughty-Holy Vitalis" ("Der schlimm-heilige Vitalis"), and I will at times refer to the latter to help clarify the former.

25. The all-important duplication in the names of Eugenia's companions is Keller's innovation: Kosegarten identifies them as Prothus and Hyanzinthus. See Müller, *Gottfried Keller, Sämtliche Werke*, 6:837.

26. Cf. Kaiser, *Gottfried Keller, Das gedichtete Leben*.

27. This is not to ignore but to highlight the obvious resultant problem of Aquilinus's (or the bookworms') attraction to Eugenia; despite all the normative authority invested in male desire, it still seems unable to shed its own perverseness—i.e., its own attraction to the perverse. But more on that below.

28. Marjorie Garber, *Vested Interests: Cross-Dressing and Cultural Anxiety* (New York: Routledge, 1992), 16f.

29. Cf. Renz, *Gottfried Kellers "Sieben Legenden."*

30. The shift in power to the male control of the mirroring arrangement also marks the decisive difference between this and the comparable moment in "Regine," where

the male protagonist, Erwin Altenauer, discovers his wife, Regine, imitating in the mirror the statue of Venus de Milo situated in the next room, turning herself into a reflective copy of its aesthetic ideal (6:183). For all the repetition, this moment in "Regine" is as reviled as the one here is valorized; the crucial distinction between the two being that whereas here the statue and its imitative incorporation are arranged by Aquilinus, in "Regine" they are arranged by the transvestite female painter. And we see something remarkably similar in "The Lost Smile" ("Das verlorene Lachen," 1874), where the operant doubling is not between the woman Justine and a statue but more directly between her and the male protagonist, Jocundus, whose smile exactly reproduces hers (for the statue in "Eugenia" as Aquilinus, see below). The mirroring is an increasingly disastrous one as long as Justine remains the force in control of their mimetic marriage; order (and the smile itself) are only "properly" restored once Jocundus seizes power over the conditions of their happiness, which is to say, over the conditions governing their reflective, replicative smiles.

31. It is perhaps not inappropriate to point out the parallel between Keller's and Aquilinus's strategy for legitimating the "reality" of their construct of Eugenia by means of the (phantasmatic) production of an anterior identity that never existed but can now be restored and much of the rhetorical language of "reunification" that dominated the formation of a new German national identity in the more recent past. The bad faith and efficacy of this mechanism remain evident whether we are speaking of the "reality" at stake in nineteenth-century fiction or twentieth-century politics.

32. Cf. the further association of the scene with a "return" to an earlier Eugenia: "She easily found her way into the part of the city, all glimmering with marble, where the temples and public buildings were situated and where she had passed her youth" (19). But note too those public edifices (*öffentlichen Gebäude*).

33. The unexpected convergence is almost inadvertently signaled by the *Nachtwache* (literally, "night-watch") that appears twice here, first as the policeman who almost surprises Eugenia with the statue, and then as the spiritual vigils the monks think Eugenius is keeping at this time (20). Both as statue and as monk, Eugenia is subject to a similar, and similarly vigilant, policing.

34. Cf. Antje Harnisch, "'Die Sucht, den Mann zu spielen' in Gottfried Kellers Realismus," *German Quarterly* 68, no. 2 (1995): 153; Kaiser, *Gottfried Keller, Das gedichtete Leben*. Even Renz, *Gottfried Kellers "Sieben Legenden,"* who wields a sophisticated, nonpsychological apparatus of Feuerbachian projection to analyze the encounter between Eugenia and the statue, still concludes that here "Eugenia worships herself; she returns, out of her perversion, to herself [*sie kehrt aus der Verkehrung zu sich selbst zurück*]" (150).

35. Cf. "[It] was a more noble feeling than vanity through which she now recog-

nized her better self [*ihr besseres Selbst*] in the magical moonlight" (19), wherein the "noble" (*edel*) rather than the vain (*eitel*) should properly arouse our critical suspicions. For all the undeniable and prescient embeddedness of Keller's fiction in Freudian psychoanalytic structures, it should be pointed out that doubles in Keller are almost always more openly politically contrived; cf. "Regine" and "The Lost Smile" (both discussed in note 30 above), and also "Clothes Make the Man" ("Kleider Machen Leute," 1874).

36. For a more detailed discussion of the process by which a male narcissistically constructs his identity through the detour of a female image, see my *Artificial I's: The Self as Artwork in Ovid, Kierkegaard, and Thomas Mann* (Tübingen: Niemeyer, 1993), 101–12. I also discuss there the "anti-Pygmalion" impulse to turn not a statue into a woman but a woman into a statue, an impulse with obvious applicability to Aquilinus; cf. the wonderfully damning line, "Not a soul stirred in the still marble world [*Keine Seele rührte sich in der stillen Steinwelt*]" (19). For an opposite reading, of Aquilinus as Pygmalion, see Renz, *Gottfried Kellers "Sieben Legenden*," 176–78; Harnisch, "'Die Sucht, den Mann zu spielen,'" 153.

37. That Eugenia loses in this encounter is further stressed by the narrator's anachronistic card smile, "That made her feel just as if she had played the wrong card" (19).

38. The gender, or *Gattung*, ambiguity that adheres to the statue here also occurs in the fountain frieze in "The Virgin and the Devil," where the marble figures shift uncannily between seeming male devils and female angels; and again in the statue in "The Naughty-Holy Vitalis," which shifts between representing the pagan goddess Juno and the Christian Virgin Mary.

39. That it is Aquilinus to whom Eugenia must prove her femininity is Keller's innovation; Kosegarten has the analogous moment in his tale played out between Eugenia and her father. See Müller, *Gottfried Keller, Sämtliche Werke*, 6:839 f.

40. Renz, *Gottfried Kellers "Sieben Legenden*," also analyzes the encounter with Aquilinus as a repetition of the statue scene, although for different reasons (151 ff.). The move in the repetition toward the more fleshly and the more narrative continues the direction already begun by Eugenia's encounter with the widow and by the widow's Potipharian retelling of that encounter, both of which repeat and replace the function served earlier by the statue, the former in its erotic disciplining of Eugenia, the latter in its functional parallel with Keller's project. The most important point to the movement is perhaps this, that both Eugenia and the self-conscious reflection on poetic realism are being simultaneously brought on to their "proper" spheres and identities.

41. The repetition of the statue scene in Eugenia's encounter with the widow is most forcefully maintained through the depiction of Eugenia arriving "with her

thoughts dwelling more under the pillars of the midnight temple than on the matter that lay before her" (20), and these "far other thoughts" incite Eugenia to linger in the widow's embrace before finally awaking and breaking free. The suggestion that she is thinking of Aquilinus while kissing the widow not only repeats the superimposition I described for Eugenia kissing the statue, it also echoes the widow's own illusion and doubles the fictive heterosexual nature of the encounter. Nonetheless, in a manner repeated several times in the *Seven Legends*—most notably in the erotic contacts of the Virgin Mary with the (feminized) Devil and with Bertrade in the following two tales— the deviant homoerotic nature of the encounter permeates and complicates this cover. The two women are depicted locked in wild embrace (*wilder Umhalsung*, 21), and while Eugenia remains mostly passive, distracted, and surprised, the narrator still insists on her more than partial complicity and also leaves crucially ambivalent—again through the device of shifting grammatical cases, this time for Eugenia/Eugenius—whether her pleasure comes as a woman kissing a man (the widow as Aquilinus), a man kissing a woman (Eugenia as Eugenius), or a woman kissing a woman. In any case, the moment can be seen as emphatically one of per-version, of category-crisis, of conventional desire and gender roles flagrantly transgressed; but the moment can also be seen to follow not only from her disruptive shift into the Christian sphere and male clothing but also and no less from her supposedly normalizing re-turn to the profane world and encounter with its disciplinary female statue.

There is, moreover, yet another turn here, another way of figuring the same event. For all the overt wildness of Eugenia's cross-dressed homoerotic tryst with the widow, there is still an important and equally overt corrective impulse at work in the encounter: if the statue scene suggests how even the normative program of realism can yield the disruptive play of desire and gender, this scene shows how even the most deviant display of desire and gender can still serve realism's normative program. The rehabilitative mechanism of the encounter is operant in two ways. First, the covering fiction that Eugenia is kissing Aquilinus (or alternatively, the statue) continues the disciplinary training begun with the statue in the preceding scene. The fact that it is a fiction, a superimposed poetic veil, does not detract from its real effect: the phantasmatic illusion here functions just as clothing and gesture do elsewhere, and seems just as capable of producing its corresponding reality. Second, even beyond this reinforcing repetition, the embrace of the widow represents an advance in Eugenia's re-formation. It signals the emergence of "flesh and blood" desire in Eugenia, precisely the real physical desire both her earlier existences denied, and precisely the desire needed to bind her to Aquilinus and so to realize her "true" femininity. All of which is to say that desire, whatever its gendered direction or "turn," is not only the disruptive element in the realist scheme but also the required element to attain the real. Both here and in the statue scene, the same event proves at once and inseparably normative and transgressive, because in both cases dependent on the same mechanism for realizing its effect: desire.

42. For Aquilinus's assumed coldness, see also 15, 25. For the crucial connection between self-discipline or repression of desire and the discipline/repression of the object of desire, cf. 24: "With every minute it became more difficult to keep hidden his pleasure with the beautiful being who had been found again [*die schöne Wiedergefundene*]. Nonetheless he controlled himself and . . . determined to ascertain whether, in regard to proper discipline [*Zucht*], he had the old Eugenia [*die frühere Eugenia*] before him." We saw something similar in Stifter's preface to *Many-colored Stones*, where the absence of the marvelous in Nature is predicated on the lack of marvel in the self; and we will see much the same in Raabe's *Fatso* (*Stopfkuchen*), where the disciplinary violence Heinrich Schaumann imposes on himself he also imposes on everyone about him.

43. The basic process by which frozen reflecting men can produce marmoreal women is wonderfully described by MacLeod in terms of Perseus and Medusa; see *Embodying Ambiguity*, 167–84.

44. Cf. how it is the "warm" clothing (and not the "sweet" Eugenia who was hidden inside) that is said to have seduced the widow (26).

45. For the evocation of the statue in this simile, cf. the earlier image of Eugenia, "white as marble" (17). The image of the rose is radically ambivalent throughout the *Seven Legends*, especially insofar as it shifts between its sensual profane connotations and its sacred Christian ones. Cf. Renz, *Gottfried Kellers "Sieben Legenden,"* 153 f.

46. That the "real" Eugenia is to be equated here with her clothing—or rather, with Eugenia and her clothing—is neatly conveyed by the verbal echo: her clothes are torn in two (*entzwei*) and she falls together with them (*zusammen-brechend*) in des-pair (*Verzweiflung*). The splitting of Eugenia that accompanies her gendering proves (almost) fatal; her unveiling does not so much reveal the real as it destroys it. And it is worth emphasizing that the narrative realizes this, despite the obvious contradiction with the subversive, liberating program Keller announced in the foreword and, I've argued, translates into the narrative here.

47. For an interesting account of the necrophiliac coupling of women, desire, and death in modernist aesthetics, and especially the way this coupling helps secure the required "masculinity" in the fiction-producing artist, see Maria Tatar, *Lustmord: Sexual Murder in Weimar Germany* (Princeton: Princeton University Press, 1995), 36.

48. Cf. Michel Foucault, *The History of Sexuality: Volume I, An Introduction*, trans. Robert Hurley (New York: Vintage, 1980): "Silence itself—the things one declines to say, or is forbidden to name, the discretion that is required between different speak-

ers—is less the absolute limit of discourse, the other side from which it is separated by a strict boundary, than an element that functions alongside the things said, with them and in relation to them within over-all strategies. . . . There is not one but many silences, and they are an integral part of the strategies that underlie and permeate discourses" (27). We might also note the ambiguity of that "shudder": while one reading of it would register Eugenia's apparent fear, that is, her despairing response to Aquilinus's oppressive, even annihilating exercise of cultural power, another would register her equally apparent arousal, that is, her erotic response to Aquilinus's same exercise of that power. Again, "realist" repression needn't only eliminate desire, it can also produce it—and do so in its very character as a repressive force.

49. This unknown quality of Eugenia that keeps her significantly intact at the end of the tale is furthered by the narrator's unwillingness or inability to enter into Eugenia's inner thoughts from the moment of her collapse into Aquilinus's arms onward. His silence is also her silence, his distance hers as well.

50. Cf. Kaiser, *Gottfried Keller, Das gedichtete Leben.*

51. Cf. 27: "Now after Eugenia had sufficiently investigated the nature of marriage [*das Wesen der Ehe*], she directed her knowledge toward converting her husband to Christianity." This final unexpected "turn" to the tale not only underscores the by now quite darkly ironic reality of the governing similarity between the two spheres, such that Eugenia's and Aquilinus's realization of the profane ideal of erotic love prepares them for assuming the Christian ideal of ascetic denial, because the former is finally as fully restraining and denying as the latter, undermining yet one more time the story's operant distinctions between the regulating and the liberating, the normalizing and the disrupting. It also underscores the decidedly less melancholy conclusion that within the given cultural conventions and discursive practices, power—and that is to say, the authority to determine (and redetermine) the real—remains as tactically available as ever.

CHAPTER 5: SECOND WIVES, SECOND LIVES

1. Theodor Fontane, cited by Peter Goldammer, ed., *Theodor Storm, Sämtliche Werke* (Berlin: Aufbau, 1972) 2:749.

2. Storm also referred to the novella as a "Muster." See Gerd Eversberg, *Erläuterungen zu Theodor Storm. Viola tricolor. Beim Vetter Christian*, Königs Erläuterungen und Materielen, 199 (Hollfeld: C. Bange, 1984), 47.

3. Cf. Theodor Fontane, "Theodor Storm," in *Sämtliche Werke*, ed. Walter Keitel (Munich: Carl Heinser, 1969), ser. 3, 1:273.

4. Wolfgang Tschorn, *Idylle und Verfall: Die Realität der Familie im Werk Theodor Storms*, Abhandlungen zur Kunst-, Musik-, und Literaturwissenschaft, no. 271 (Bonn: Bouvier, 1978), 115 f.

5. All parenthetical references are taken from *Theodor Storm, Sämtliche Werke*, ed. Albert Köster, vol. 3 (Leipzig: Insel, 1919). They refer exclusively to *Viola tricolor*.

6. For a recent sociological approach to the question of the second wife, see the excellent discussion of David des Granges's painting of the Saltonstall family (1636/1637) in Arthur E. Imhof, *Die Lebenszeit: vom augeschobenen Tod und von der Kunst des Lebens* (Munich: C. H. Beck, 1988), 148 f.

7. This is the approach assumed by, e.g., Johannes Klein in his afterword to *Theodor Storm, Sämtliche Werke* (Munich: Winkler, 1951), 2:1030. Klein writes, "With but a few alterations, the subject-matter is taken immediately out of Storm's life." Cf. Goldammer, *Theodor Storm, Sämtliche Werke*, 2:748.

8. It will be remembered that Jakobson insists that these two possibilities are themselves doubled, both being possible perspectives for both the author and the reader, with the latter often situated at a later, and so different, moment in this literary historical process.

9. Jakobson himself does not consider this back-formation and misprision of one's literary forebears, but it seems an indispensable operation in his general model. For more on misprision, see Harold Bloom, *The Anxiety of Influence* (London: Oxford University Press, 1973).

10. Hildegard Lorenz, *Varianz und Invarianz. Theodor Storms Erzählungen: Figurenkonstellationen und Handlungsmuster*, Abhandlungen zur Kunst-, Musik-, und Literaturwissenschaft, no. 363 (Bonn: Bouvier, 1985).

11. This is not to say that *Viola tricolor* is Storm's only "realist" novella. Rather, within his corpus there are a number of tales that similarly disrupt the author's own literary conventions, some of which are discussed below.

12. Holub, *Reflections of Realism*, 135; Fritz Martini, *Deutsche Literatur im bürgerlichen Realismus 1848–1898*, Epochen der deutschen Literatur (Stuttgart, 1962), 2:631.

13. Cf. Berthold Auerbach, "Die Stiefmutter," in *Zur Guten Stunde* (Stuttgart: Hoffman, 18—?), 54–124, where several characters, and especially the stepdaughter, are explicitly governed by the fairy-tale conventions about stepmothers that shape their psyches (see esp. 81, 85). Storm refers to this tale as a poorly done precursor to *Viola tricolor*. See Eversberg, *Erläuterungen zu Theodor Storm*, 47.

14. Storm certainly intended the story to have such an underlying social dimension. He wrote that it was "written with the conviction that in it I had something to say to my nation." Quoted by Eversberg, *Erläuterungen zu Theodor Storm*, 51.

15. Jakobson, "On Realism in Art," 39.

16. Shlomith Rimmon-Kenan, in her seminal article "The Paradoxical Status of Repetition," 151–59, formulates this idea somewhat differently as "Paradox 2: Con-

structive repetition emphasizes difference, destructive repetition emphasizes sameness (i.e. to repeat successfully is not to repeat)" (153).

17. This reversal of the traditional view is certainly the approach adopted by Roland Barthes in his "Introduction to the Structural Analysis of Narratives" in *Image-Music-Text*, trans. Stephen Heath (New York: Noonday Press, 1977), where he claims that literary realism is based on "the necessity to vary and outgrow the first *form* that man ever came by, namely repetition" (124). Conversely, other French structuralists have followed the Frankfurt School theorists and argued that the (narrative) desire for repetition belongs not to the realistic but to the mythical impulse; see Terence Hawkes, *Structuralism and Semiotics* (Berkeley: University of California Press, 1977), 39–49. Holub, in his discussion of Keller's *A Village Romeo and Juliet*, seems also to conclude that the crucial issue of repetition is, finally, a mythical rather than realist one: see *Reflections of Realism*, 101–31. And as I argued in chapter one, the issue of repetition can be shown to underlie Jakobson's other model for realism, namely his association of metaphor with romanticism and metonymy with realism. By emphasizing the desire for repetition (identity, substitutability, etc.) in the former and to avoid it in the latter, we can see the relevance of this model not only to Jakobson's literary historical model and to these other theoretical musings, but to Storm's novella as well.

As I also discussed in chapter one, J. Hillis Miller, while advancing from a different direction, arrives at a fairly similar conclusion in his study *Fiction and Repetition* (Cambridge: Harvard University Press, 1982). For example, in his discussion of Hardy's *The Well-Beloved*—the novel thematically closest to *Viola tricolor* in his study—Miller stresses the tension between a reality conceived according to his Nietzschean model, in which there are no repetitions, and characters falsely inclined, in the very act of seeing, to trace likes in unlikes. "Such a vision," he writes, "sees things in their metaphors, or rather it sees things as metaphors, as the transposition of the same pattern from one episode or event . . . to another." A character who sees things in this way "sees things and persons not in their substantial uniqueness but as signs pointing back to earlier things or persons 'standing for' them. . . . He lives his life as metaphor, that is as mistake" (13). The overcoming of that mistake, and the thwarting of the repetition that leads to that mistake, would be evidence of a "realistic" impulse; my analysis of *Viola tricolor* follows a similar line.

18. For the correspondences between this and the psychological model for Freud's repetition compulsion as elaborated in "Jenseits des Lustprinzips [Beyond the Pleasure Principle]" in *Studienausgabe*, 3:213–72, see chapter one.

19. See Elisabeth Bronfen, *Over Her Dead Body* (New York: Routledge, 1992), 324–48, which also discusses Georges Rodenbach's *Bruges-la-Morte* and focuses on the the-

matic constant of the death of the second wife. An earlier version of her discussion also included an analysis of Arthur Schnitzler's *Die Nächste*; I would like to thank her again for the many stimulating conversations that contributed to this chapter.

20. In between, we have many realist works that follow the same basic paradigm as *Viola tricolor*, such as Fontane's *Delusions, Confusions* (*Irrungen Wirrungen*, 1887) and *Schach von Wuthenow* (1882); Meyer's *The Marriage of the Monk* (*Die Hochzeit des Monchs*, 1883/84); and, with the return of Judith at the end, Keller's *Green Henry* (*Der Grüne Heinrich* 1879/80). In an indirect but important way, *Effi Briest* (1894/95) can also be seen to enact the realist version of the topos of the second wife (see below, note 55).

Overall, one of the noticeable differences between romantic and realist texts is the tendency of the former to present pairs of women in juxtaposition (*nebeneinander*) and the latter in succession (*nacheinander*). (Keller's novel has it first the one way, then the other; Stifter's *The Mountain Forest* has it more in the "romantic" mode.) As in *Viola tricolor*, and as we'll see again in *The Marriage of the Monk*, the representation of successive pairs of women often allows for the thematic incorporation of realist concerns into the narrative itself.

21. For the relation of doubles, revenants, and repetition to the uncanny, see Freud, "Das Unheimliche [The Uncanny]," *Studienausgabe*, 4:257–74. For a reading of the uncanny in Storm, see Andrew Webber, "The Uncanny Rides Again: Theodor Storm's Double Vision," *Modern Language Review* 84, no. 4 (1989): 860–73.

22. We might take this as an acute instance of Lacan's dictum that "man's desire is the desire of the Other." See Lacan, *The Four Fundamental Concepts of Psycho-Analysis*, 38.

23. E.g., Eversberg, *Erläuterungen zu Theodor Storm*: "The exceptional thing about Storm's handling of the theme is to be seen in how the poet does not proceed from the suffering child of the first marriage nor from the disappointed husband, but rather tackles the problem from the perspective of the second wife" (50).

24. This linkage of the dead woman and painting, or representation, also applies to Anna in Keller's *Green Henry* and her literary precursor, Ottilie, in Goethe's *Elective Affinities* (*Die Wahlverwandtschaften*).

25. Holub, *Reflections of Realism*, 55 f.

26. Ibid., 147.

27. See Hartmut Vincon, *Theodor Storm mit Selbstzeugnissen und Bilddokumenten*, Rowohlt Monographien (Hamburg: Rowohlt, 1972), 136.

28. For more on the eyes and the uncanny in *Aquis submersus*, see Webber, "The Uncanny Rides Again," 869.

29. Desire is again the motivating factor to the movement from representation to realization in Storm's "Künstlernovelle" *Psyche*. Here, the protagonist-artist represents

in a statue his rescue of the girl Marie; the narrative is resolved only when the statue/representation is repeated once more and comes true, that is, when he once again holds Marie in his arms. As in *In the Castle* and *A Corner of the Forest*, the conflation of artwork and life in the moment of repetition subverts the sense of realism and gives way instead to a resolutely poetic, romantic impulse.

30. For dog symbolism in Storm's novellas, see Julia C. Rohwer, "Das Tier als Leitmotiv in den späten Novellen Theodor Storms," *Acta germanica* 10 (1977): 245–63. Although she links the figure of the dog with a certain primal, animalistic vitality, Rohwer unnecessarily makes an exception for *Viola tricolor*.

31. For the methodology to the analysis of literary dreams, see Dorrit Cohn, "Wilhelm Meister's Dream: Reading Goethe with Freud," *German Quarterly* 62, no. 4 (1989): 459–72. She explains that the decoding method is an essentially rigorously intratextual one: "to interpret each oneiric image in its relationship to the life of the fictional dreamer, as it is presented in the surrounding text as a whole" (460).

32. The distinction between painting and photography is an interesting one for realism in general; in this particular case, the distinction merely doubles Ines's fantastic desire for repetition, insofar as, as photograph, she would become at once a picture (*Bild*) and shadow (*Schatten*) (297; for Marie as *Schatten*, 288).

33. Franz Stuckert, *Theodor Storm: Sein Leben und seine Welt* (Bremen: Schünemann, 1955), misses this crucial distinction. He writes, "Nesi, whose shy courting the new mother has always longingly sought for, in the shock of the moment voluntarily finds the name of mother which she had withheld for so long [*den so lange verweigerten Mutternamen*]" (313).

34. See Elisabeth Bronfen, "Dialogue with the Dead: The Deceased Beloved as Muse," in *Sex and Death in Victorian England*, ed. Regina Barreca (London: Macmillan, 1990), 241–59.

35. In this respect, we should note the close association of artists and death throughout the story. The painter of Marie's portrait (273), "the great dead [*die grossen Toten*], Haydn and Mozart" performed at the evening concert (282), and even the insect musicians at the end (302). All are somehow otherworldly, which alerts us that the aesthetic problem associated with Rudolf's psychology is not limited to him alone.

36. See Lorenz, *Varianz und Invarianz*, 208–11.

37. This problem is perhaps most consequently explored in Keller's *Green Henry*, but it informs the thematics of many other self-reflective realist works as well.

38. A similar argument can also be made for *Green Henry*, where the link made between Heinrich's relations with women and with painting points to the same essential identity of imagination and desire as the aporia of the realist enterprise.

39. Again, Rudolf's case goes to the heart of the realist dilemma, as we can see, e.g., in both *Green Henry* and *Effi Briest*, each of whose title figures can, at least initially, imagine and desire only tropologically, i.e., romantically.

40. Here I differ from Holub, *Reflections of Realism*, wherein he suggests that realism "is ultimately synonymous with the repression of desire" (131). For a more detailed account of my difference with his representation of the relation between desire and realism, see chapter three.

41. The imagery of feasting here, in respect to both Rudolf's gaze and Ines's hunger, invites another reading, one that focuses on the realigning of the vampiristic patterns in the story (Marie as vampire; Rudolf as vampire). Such a reading would point in the same direction, away from the metaphoric/fantastic and toward the real as the source of sustenance.

42. In the preface to the first edition of their fairy tales, the Grimm brothers call special attention to the topos of the "harsh stepmother" and add this footnote: "Even flowers have acquired their names from this topos; *Viola tricolor* is called Little Stepmother [*Stiefmütterchen*], because each of its yellow petals has a small, narrow green petal beneath it, which are considered to be the seats that the mother gives to her truly happy children; the two stepchildren must stand above, mourning in dark violet, without a seat." *Kinder- und Hausmärchen, gesammelt durch die Brüder Grimm*, ed. Heinz Rölleke (1812/15; rpt., Frankfurt am Main: Deutscher Klassiker Verlag, 1986) 1:ix. I would like to thank Maria Tatar for this reference.

43. That this new mode of "scientific" vision and naming is still rife with issues of conventionalization and entrapment through conventionalization we know already from our analysis of Stifter; for other indices that the impulses toward convention and its representational threat persist through to the end of this novella, see below.

44. The single-word citation, of course, derives from and points to the end of part one of Goethe's *Faust*.

45. See Lorenz, *Varianz und Invarianz*, 116–18.

46. In keeping with this double designation, the garden also has a double character, in the one case determined by the "black, pyramid-shaped conifers" and in the other by the "long-stemmed centifolious roses" (274). For the roses, see below.

47. Cf. Lorenz, *Varianz und Invarianz*, 186–89. The competing notions of succession are also evident in Auerbach, "Die Stiefmutter," 85.

48. Both the narrator and Rudolf try to prevent us from dwelling too long on this ("quickly looked at"; "but her husband led her hurriedly into the house"). But the language and gesture of the following event—Rudolf's picking up Nesi even as he had just picked up Ines—almost inadvertently repeats the identification.

49. As Thomas Mann gladly reminds us, the sexual attraction to girl children of

thirteen and even ten years of age was very much a part of the biography of Storm himself. See Thomas Mann, "Theodor Storm," in *Gesammelte Werke in zwölf Bänden* (Frankfurt am Main: Fischer, 1960), 9:256.

50. See Lorenz, *Varianz und Invarianz*, 120–23. She also mentions Nesi's red-white dress in this regard.

51. For "patterns of incest," or what he calls "structural incest," see Holub, *Reflections of Realism*, 101–32. The role of incest in Stifter's *The Mountain Forest* has been discussed above in chapter four; as here, it is between father and daughter(s), is indirect and deferred, and ultimately frustrated as a controlling impulse. See below.

52. But see his poem "Sibling Blood" ("Geschwisterblut") in *Sämtliche Werke*, ed. Albert Köster (Leipzig: Insel, 1919), 1:157 ff.; and Vinçon's account of its inception and reception (*Theodor Storm mit Selbstzeugnissen und Bilddokumenten*, 62–66).

53. See Holub, *Reflections of Realism*, 135; Lorenz, *Varianz und Invarianz*, 186; 250.

54. This is true with reservations: see Leonard L. Duroche, "Like and Look Alike: Symmetry and Irony in Theodor Storm's *Aquis submersus*," *Seminar* 7, no. 1 (1971): 1–13.

55. We note a similar pattern, or desire, in *Effi Briest*, where Effi's marriage to Innstetten is meant to repeat the (unfulfilled) marriage to Innstetten of her mother. This unrealized but still functionally active "first" marriage introduces a complex tangle of the "second wife" and "incest" patterns into Effi's and Innstetten's relationship that is every bit as destructive and determinative as that in *Viola tricolor* (cf. also *Schach von Wuthenow*).

56. See Rohwer, "Das Tier als Leitmotiv."

57. Cf. Lorenz, *Varianz und Invarianz*, 188 f.

CHAPTER 6: DOUBLE-DEALINGS

1. Conrad Ferdinand Meyer, *Die Hochzeit des Mönchs*, in *Sämtliche Werke* Historisch-kritische Ausgabe, ed. Hans Zeller and Alfred Zäch (Bern: Benteli, 1961), 12:57. All parenthetical references in this chapter are taken from this volume, and refer exclusively to *Die Hochzeit des Mönchs*. For the English I have consulted the translation of Marion W. Sonnenfield in *The Complete Narrative Prose of Conrad Ferdinand Meyer*, trans. George F. Folkers, David B. Dickens, and Marion W. Sonnenfeld (Lewisburg, Penna.: Bucknell University Press, 1976), 2:105–68.

2. Cf. Beth L. Mugge-Meiburg, *Words Chiseled in Marble: Artworks in the Prose Narratives of Conrad Ferdinand Meyer* (New York: Peter Lang, 1991), 55, 57.

3. Cf. Holub, *Reflections of Realism*, 162.

4. Cf. Marianne Burkhard, *Conrad Ferdinand Meyer* (Boston: Twayne, 1978), 47; Mugge-Meiburg, *Words Chiseled in Marble*, 55, 70.

5. Cf. Holub, *Reflections of Realism*, 166.

6. Zäch, *Meyer, Sämtliche Werke*, notes that Meyer experimented with several different historical settings for the story, including Corsica, twelfth-century Nürnberg, and thirteenth-century Florence before deciding on Padua, which underscores how it is the principle of displacement, rather than any particular time, place, or facts, that most characterizes Meyer's historical realism.

7. For contemporary responses to the mannerism of the frame, see Zäch, *Meyer, Sämtliche Werke*, 12:250 ff.

8. Cf. Holub, *Reflections of Realism*, 137–40.

9. Zäch, *Meyer, Sämtliche Werke*, 12:250.

10. Holub, *Reflections of Realism*, 156.

11. Cf. Sjaak Onderlinden, *Die Rahmenerzählungen Conrad Ferdinand Meyers* (Leiden: Universitaire Pers Leiden, 1974), 124, who argues that the emphasis on Dante's invention of the story actually increases its realism. Even Holub's own analysis of *The Saint* (*Der Heilige*, 1879) points to a similar position: see above, note 3.

12. The situation is quite similar to that in Henry James's "The Turn of the Screw": see the analysis by Shoshana Felman, "Turning the Screw of Interpretation," in *Literature and Psychoanalysis. The Question of Reading: Otherwise*, ed. Shoshana Felman (Baltimore: Johns Hopkins University Press, 1982), 94–207, esp. 119–38.

13. Zäch points out that Meyer, too, exchanged genres for his tale, which was originally conceived as a verse drama, and only transferred into a prose novella at the behest of his publisher, Rodenberg. See Zäch, *Meyer, Sämtliche Werke*, 12:246, 249.

14. Tamara Evans, *Formen der Ironie in Conrad Ferdinand Meyers Novellen* (Bern: Franke, 1980), 127, points out how these two stories correspond to Meyer's own *The Saint* and *Plautus in the Convent* (*Plautus im Nonnenkloster*, 1881), respectively, and how Meyer thus breaks the illusion of his frame narrative, recalls our attention to his own production of fiction, and so keeps the issue of his own writing practice intrinsic to the novella itself.

15. Evans, *Formen der Ironie in Conrad Ferdinand Meyers Novellen*, 122 f., is the only critic I know who quite rightly stresses the split condition of the story's invention, split between the individual's will and the outside authority of history: for the significance of this split, see below. I should note that in positing poetic realism as a function of desire, I am once again challenging Holub's formulation of realism as (only) its repression. See Holub, *Reflections of Realism*, 131.

16. Klaus Jeziorkowski, "Die Kunst der Perspektive: Zur Epik Conrad Ferdinand Meyers," *Germanisch-Romanische Monatsschrift* Neue Folge 17, no. 4 (October 1967): 398–416, here 403; W. D. Williams, *The Stories of C. F. Meyer* (Oxford: Oxford University Press, 1962), 93.

17. Evans, *Formen der Ironie in Conrad Ferdinand Meyers Novellen*, 123 f.; Mugge-

Meiburg, *Words Chiseled in Marble*, 72; Onderdelinden, *Die Rahmenerzählungen Conrad Ferdinand Meyers*, 125; Williams, *The Stories of C. F. Meyer*, 95, 99; Benno von Wiese, "Conrad Ferdinand Meyer: *Die Hochzeit des Mönchs*," in *Die deutsche Novelle* (Düsseldorf: August Bagel, 1962), 2:182.

18. Cf. Ernst Feise, "*Die Hochzeit des Mönchs* von Conrad Ferdinand Meyer: Eine Formanalyse," in *Xenion: Essays in the History of German Literature* (Baltimore: Johns Hopkins University Press, 1950), 224.

19. For realism as an effect, see Holub, *Reflections of Realism*, 14 f. Again, my difference with Holub is in arguing that realism is an effect of desire.

20. Cf. von Wiese, "Conrad Ferdinand Meyer: *Die Hochzeit des Mönchs*," 2:182.

21. This is at least partially in opposition to the claim of Karl Guthke, "C. F. Meyer's Kunstsymbolik," in *Wege zur Literatur: Studien zur deutschen Dichtungs- und Geistesgeschichte* (Bern: Franke, 1967), 187–204: "Art alone secures the 'humanly true' testimony about the human being in his world" (202). Rather, it is first the human being (*der Mensch*) who, through projection, determines the possible truth of the artwork, which only then is chiastically able in turn to project a truth back to him or her. See below. The opposition is more complete to the position of Herbert Fellmann, "Die 'fragwürdige' Erzählkunst C. F. Meyers: Untersucht an der Novelle *Die Hochzeit des Mönchs*," in *Jahrbuch der Wittheit zu Bremen* 9 (1965): 23–45: "These are not figures with whom we are able to identify ourselves," 28.

22. Cf. Brigitte Leuschner, "Erfinden und Erzählen: Funktion und Kommunikation in autothematischer Dichtung," *MLN* 100, no. 3 (1985): 498–513; Holub, *Reflections of Realism*, 166.

23. Cf. Williams, *The Stories of C. F. Meyer*, 94.

24. Ibid., 103.

25. Cf. Friedrich Kittler, *Der Traum und die Rede: Eine Analyse der Kommunikationssituation Conrad Ferdinand Meyers* (Bern: Franke, 1977), 270. It goes without saying that the structure I associate here with Dante's narration, as above for Meyer's poetic realism (and as below for Astorre's self-identity and desire), is equivalent to Freud's structure for the unconscious and dream formation; see chapter one. However, and as I hope will become clear, I am not so much proposing that narration functions like the unconscious in this tale as that the unconscious functions like the narration. See below.

26. For the narrative world as split (*gespalten*), see Fellmann, "Die 'fragwürdige' Erzählkunst C. F. Meyers," 30.

27. For Dante's absolute narrative authority, e.g. Evans, *Formen der Ironie in Conrad Ferdinand Meyers Novellen*, 117. For Dante as Ezzelin, see Feise, "*Die Hochzeit des Mönchs* von Conrad Ferdinand Meyer: Eine Formanalyse," 225. For Dante as Astorre,

see Edward Plater, "The Figure of Dante in *Die Hochzeit des Mönchs*," *MLN* 90 (1975): 678–95; and Kittler, *Der Traum und die Rede*, 257. For Dante as both Ezzelin and Astorre, see Manfred R. Jacobson, "The Two Faces of Dante: Fate and the Artist in C. F. Meyer's *Die Hochzeit des Mönchs*," *Trivium* 16 (May 1981): 99; Evans, *Formen der Ironie in Conrad Ferdinand Meyers Novellen*, 125; von Wiese, "Conrad Ferdinand Meyer: *Die Hochzeit des Mönchs*," 176.

28. Cf. Kittler, *Der Traum und die Rede*, 257.

29. Rosemarie and Hans Zeller, "Erzähltes Erzählen: Funktionen der Erzählhaltungen in C. F. Meyers Rahmennovellen," in *Erzählforschung 2: Theorien, Modelle und Methoden der Narrativik*, ed. Wolfgang Haubrichs, Beiheft 6 of Zeitschrift für Literaturwissenschaft und Linguistik (Göttingen: Vandenhoeck & Ruprecht, 1977), 98–113, here 111. Cf. Jeziorkowski, "Die Kunst der Perspektive"; and Deborah S. Lund, *Ambiguity as Narrating Strategy in the Prose Work of C. F. Meyer* (New York: Peter Lang, 1990).

30. Cf. Williams, *The Stories of C. F. Meyer*, 90.

31. Cf. Holub, *Reflections of Realism*, 16 f.

32. Zeller and Zeller, "Erzähltes Erzählen," 109, 110.

33. Fellmann, "Die 'fragwürdige' Erzählkunst C. F. Meyers," 26, quotes Joseph Kunz to the effect that Dante's nonidentification with his tale seriously compromises its realism.

34. This is precisely the point that most all critics seem to miss. For example von Wiese, "Conrad Ferdinand Meyer: *Die Hochzeit des Mönchs*," who offers a sensitive reading of the narratorial conditions, says that the interest is in how, not what Dante narrates (*wie, nicht was Dante erzählt*, 180) and thus overlooks that the "what" is a representation of the "how." But it is only through a recognition of this repetition that the double, chiastic structure of realism to the novella can also be recognized: see below.

35. The fact that the governing reality of many of Meyer's novellas, including this one, is often hidden from (and even misunderstood by) the characters involved is recognized by other critics. E.g., Dennis McCort, *States of Unconsciousness in Three Tales of C. F. Meyer* (Lewisburg, Penna.: Bucknell University Press, 1988), who describes "tales in which the major characters are shown to be typically, chronically, and [even] fatally unaware of a potent field of reality that constitutes the essential 'world' of the work" (12). For Dante as not overtly recognizing the motivating reality to his own narrative, see David A. Jackson, "Dante the Dupe in C. F. Meyer's Die Hochzeit des Mönchs," *German Life and Letters* 25 (1971–72): 5–25; Michael Shaw, "C. F. Meyer's Resolute Heroes: A Study of Becket, Astorre, and Pescara," *DVjS* 40 (1966): 372–81, here 378. My argument stresses not only that this hidden governing reality derives from the operant

conditions of narration but also that its eventual exposure, i.e., realization, becomes part of the work's poetic realism. See below.

36. This is recognized by Shaw, "C. F. Meyer's Resolute Heroes," who writes: "Critics of Meyer seem to have failed to notice the considerable importance that the substitutability of persons ... plays in the story" (376); what is remarkable is that Shaw himself fails to notice the connection between the substitutability of persons in the story and Dante's strategy of narratorial invention. Sigmund Freud, *Briefe an Wilhelm Fliess 1897–1904* Ungekürzte Ausgabe, ed. Jeffrey M. Masson (Frankfurt am Main: Fischer, 1986), also recognizes that substitution and displacement are the key features to Dante's narrative, but he too fails to see the connection with Dante's narration (but see Kittler, *Der Traum und die Rede,* 263). And yet several of his formulations seem as readily applicable to the latter as the former, for example his description of "the back-phantasizing [*das Zurückphantasieren*] of a new experience into a former time, so that the new persons form a series with the old and furnish the models for them"; or, in a sentence mistakenly left out of the first edition of the letter and that seems precisely to capture the chiastic strategy of Dante's poetic realism, "To see the mirror-image of the present in a phantasized past, which then becomes prophetic for the present" (Letter 171, July 7, 1898, 348–350). However, it is precisely the matter of the repetition of the conditions of narration in the "reality" of the story that seems to me to be most at issue in the story, and that first renders possible the hermeneutic effect of realization that Freud describes.

37. Actually, the doubling is itself doubled in respect to Astorre, as the monk Serapion is also (proleptically) introduced at the (proleptic) moment of Astorre's exchanged position, as he walks back to his father's house with Diana, just after the death of his brother. That is, even as entrance into the sequential chain of substitution seems doubled—first at the death of his brother and then again at that of his father—so too is the generated double doubled.

38. For Astorre himself as already a substitute, cf. 14. We might compare the substitute/representative status of even the original selves with the equally already representative status of the "original" characters in the frame, a status insisted on by Meyer's self-conscious art.

39. Cf. Lacan, desire as an endless relay along a chain of signifiers, engined by an original absence: see chapter one.

40. Cf. Shaw, "C. F. Meyer's Resolute Heroes," who in respect to *The Saint* argues, "Becket shows how a violent, destructive interference in the life of a person may not destroy that life but may, on the contrary, create the conditions of its intensest fulfillment" (371). This sentiment seems to me more applicable to *The Marriage of the Monk*

than Shaw's own reading of Astorre's struggle as the refusal to become an instrument in the designs others have elaborated. Rather, the point seems to me to be to accept the designs of the "other" as somehow one's own: see below.

41. For Dante's formulation as inadequate to his tale, see Shaw, "C. F. Meyer's Resolute Heroes," 378; Jackson, "Dante the Dupe," 6.

42. The requirement to renounce the renunciation and to acknowledge one's own will and resolve (represented by the pope's letter) seems to come from outside Dante's initial motivational scheme and moreover to be without correspondence to a figure in the frame (crudely: who is the pope?). Yet significantly, the directive is represented and prosecuted by Ezzelin, who champions his apparent adversary's cause, that of the Holy Seat (*der heilige Stuhl*). We might compare Ezzelin's catechism of Astorre (concerning his repressed desire) with Cangrande's catechism of Dante (concerning his "innermost feelings" and repressed self), where Cangrande seems actually to take on the cause of his apparent adversary, namely Dante himself (the occupant of the stool)—the cause of getting around the repression and showing the repressor to himself, that is, of getting Dante to renounce his renunciation and acknowledge his will and desire. (As Lacan would say, the letter always arrives at its destination, the sender.) So far as I know, no critic has addressed the issue of the motivation to the pope's directive, and yet it is certainly the most crucial disruption or redirection in the story.

43. Cf. Lacan, *The Four Fundamental Concepts of Psycho-Analysis*, 100–114, especially his notion of the lure and its relation to realism: see also chapter one.

44. Cf. Fellmann, "Die 'fragwürdige' Erzählkunst," who notes that in inviting Antiope, Astorre "acquires solid reality as a human being," 34. Again, "reality" is an effect of desire, identification with one's allotted role, and its correlative authority.

45. Cf. Jackson, "Dante the Dupe," 10, who reads the bridge incident solely in terms of Astorre's unconscious desire.

46. Cf. Feise, "*Die Hochzeit des Mönchs*: Eine Formanalyse," 221.

47. Cf. Jacobson, "The Two Faces of Dante," 102.

48. Cf. Feise, "*Die Hochzeit des Mönchs*: Eine Formanalyse," 221.

49. Cf. Evans, *Formen der Ironie in Conrad Ferdinand Meyers Novellen*, 114, who rightly emphasizes that the figure of Dante is far more humanized (*vermenschlicht*) than one might expect from Meyer's own characterization of him as merely a type representing the Middle Ages: see Zäch, *Meyer, Sämtliche Werke*, 12:251. We might contrast this oft-quoted characterization by Meyer with two other, more revealing formulations: First, "The frame with Dante was toute necessité, in order to place the reader in the proper perspective [*den richtigen Gesichtspunkt*]": and second, "[Dante] also serves to formulate the theme *dictatorially* [herrisch], which in this instance had to be of concern to me" (Meyer's emphasis). See Zäch, *Meyer, Sämtliche Werke*, 12:249, 251.

50. Cf. the fool Gocciola, who talks "not about the tragic fate of the house, but only about his own affairs." So too Dante—and the auditors.

51. Cf. Jacobson, "The Two Faces of Dante," 102.

52. Cf. *The Saint*, where the story of Thomas Becket is characterized as a narratorial confession on the part of Hans the Crossbowman.

53. Just because Dante's response to Cangrande's advice is silence does not mean it has no further effect; far from it. Just as the silent workings of (Astorre's) desire have been shown covertly to govern the story's first half, so might the silent workings of Cangrande's advice its second half. Cf. Burkhard, *Conrad Ferdinand Meyer*: "[S]ilence about a crucial experience is typical" (30).

54. Von Wiese, "Conrad Ferdinand Meyer: *Die Hochzeit des Mönchs*," is apparently alone among critics in stressing, "Above all else, Dante is the homeless one" (179); he does not however explore how this affects either Dante's narration or his story.

55. It is perhaps worth mentioning that two other novellas by Meyer turn on a similar act of substitution, i.e., of the "real" for the counterfeit place-holder. In *The Shot from the Pulpit* (*Der Schuss von der Kanzel*, 1877), the working pistol takes the place of its nonworking double (which was a deceitful dodge); the substitution precipitates the decisive exchange of places between the priest and his successor. And in *Plautus in the Convent*, the real cross takes the place of its lightweight double (again, a deceitful dodge); the substitution precipitates the decisive exchange of places of Gertrude, out of the nunnery and into the world. We might also note the functional identity in engineering the exchange between Cangrande here and the General and Poggio in their respective tales.

56. It is significant that the understanding at issue here is that of the nature of desire and how it has covertly been the force shaping the course of Astorre's fortunes; it is this nature that Dante claims uniquely to know, this understanding that he alone commands. What distinguishes Dante's interpretation of the hidden reality of desire from that of the others is, apparently, its tragic cast: he quotes to (or against) his auditors the maxim "Love is rare and usually has a bad end [*ein schlimmes Ende*]" (63). But what strikes me even more about the maxim than its ominous foreshadowing is its felicitous echoing, namely of the opening exchange between Dante and Cangrande, where Dante asked, "[H]ow does such a thing end?" and Cangrande replied, "Necessarily badly [*Notwendig schlimm*]." Then the issue was acting "for the sake of an other, under the pressure of an other's will," here it is acting out of love, even "out of the truth of a loving nature." The echo is decisive. It secures what was then denied, that is, it shows Dante recognizing what he then repressed, and by this I mean not just the change from denial of desire under pretense of compulsion to acknowledgment of desire and so acceptance of responsibility but even more the acknowledgment of the false

opposition: of the complex, contradictory fact that the course of love is always somehow to be submitted to a will that is both one's own and yet fundamentally not one's own, but other; to be subjected to the unconscious.

57. Cf. Kittler, *Der Traum und die Rede*, 261, who however reads the entire story as Dante's talking to himself, his *Selbstgespräch*.

58. Evans, *Formen der Ironie in Conrad Ferdinand Meyers Novellen*, 120, notes that the monologue is in fact a dialogue, but attributes this to Dante's irony rather than to the very structure of self-realization represented by Dante's narratorial strategy.

59. For the interchangeability of writing and narrating, see for example Kittler, *Der Traum und die Rede*, 255. For writing as subverting the conditions of conscious control, cf. Kittler, Ibid., 256: "[D]iscourse does something other than he who names himself "I" says [*der Diskurs tut etwas anderes, als der sich "ich" nennt sagt*]," under the pressure of "the law of all speech, the affront of the split between the expressed subject and the expressing subject [*des Gesetzes jeder Rede, von der Spaltung zwischen Subjekt des Geäusserten und Subjekt der Äusserung betroffen zu werden*]." Note, too, the multiplicity of languages in the story, i.e., its thematized otherness.

60. It will be noted that besides my implicit difference with Holub's claim that realism is synonymous with the repression of desire, there is my related difference with his claim that realism excludes otherness (*Reflections of Realism*, 17); see chapter one. To some extent, the differences are connected insofar as desire is the "other" on which realism depends, and the reality it needs to acknowledge. But of course, the "other" here is not only desire.

61. It should go without saying that death is also important for an understanding of Meyer's use of (dead) history: see Burkhard, *Conrad Ferdinand Meyer*, on the link between death and objectification in Meyer's poetry, esp. 107ff.

62. Cf. Peter Brooks, "Freud's Masterplot: Questions of Narrative," in *Literature and Psychoanalysis*, 280–300. This essay and that of Freud's on which Brooks's is based, namely "Beyond the Pleasure Principle," have substantially influenced my reading in this last section. For more on Brooks and Freud, see chapter one.

63. Von Wiese, "Conrad Ferdinand Meyer: *Die Hochzeit des Mönchs*," 194ff., perceptively describes the importance of death in the story, without however connecting it with the conditions of narration.

64. For the progressive movement in the story from the double as the guarantor of immortality (e.g., both Astorre and Diana for their family lines) to the double as guarantor of death (e.g., the barefoot man [75] and La Sposina [80], for Astorre and Antiope, respectively), cf. Freud, "Das Unheimliche [The Uncanny]," in *Studienausgabe*, 4:241–74.

65. Jackson, "Dante the Dupe," passim.
66. Cf. Kittler, *Der Traum und die Rede*, 258.
67. Cf. Walter Benjamin, "The Storyteller [Der Erzähler]," in *Gesammelte Schriften*, 2:449–57.
68. Cf. Shaw, "C. F. Meyer's Resolute Heroes," 380, who recognizes and stresses the absurdity of the final deaths as a mode for establishing and controlling a causal nexus in and over the story.
69. Cf. Kittler, *Der Traum und die Rede*, 257, on Dante's self-conscious representation in the story of the ridiculousness, or *Lächerlichkeit*, of his own control over the story. I should perhaps mention that death does not thus function as Holub argues Orientalism does in *The Saint* to stabilize and so, finally, to exclude ambivalence and "otherness." Quite the contrary—and the consequences for our understanding of realism are worth emphasizing.

CHAPTER 7: SECONDHAND NEWS

1. Thomas Weiskel, *The Romantic Sublime: Studies in the Structure and Psychology of Transcendence* (Baltimore: Johns Hopkins University Press, 1976).
2. Roland Barthes, *The Pleasure of the Text*, trans. Richard Miller (New York: Hill and Wang, 1975), 25.
3. All parenthetical references in this chapter will refer to Wilhelm Raabe, *Stopfkuchen*, in volume 18 of *Sämtliche Werke*, ed. Karl Hoppe (Göttingen: Vandenhoeck & Ruprecht, 1963). For the English I have consulted the translation of Barker Fairley, revised by John E. Woods, entitled "Tubby Schaumann" in *Wilhelm Raabe: Novels*, ed. Volkmar Sander (New York: Continuum, 1983), 155–311.
4. For the genealogy of boredom in earlier German literature and thought, see Ludwig Voelker, *Langweile. Untersuchungen zur Vorgeschichte eines literarischen Motivs* (Munich: Fink Verlag, 1975).
5. Walter Benjamin, "Der Erzähler," in *Gesammelte Schriften*, ed. Rolf Tiedemann and Hermann Schweppenhäuser (Frankfurt am Main: Suhrkamp, 1980), 2:446.
6. Benjamin distinguishes two groups of special importance among the premodern storytellers, "which, to be sure, overlap in many ways. . . . 'When someone goes on a trip, he has something to tell about,' goes the German saying, and people imagine the story teller as someone who has come from afar. But they enjoy no less listening to the man who has stayed at home, making an honest living, and who knows the local tales and traditions. If one wants to picture these two groups through their archaic representatives, one is embodied in the resident tiller of the soil, and the other in the trading seaman" (2:440). The applicability of this division to Stopfkuchen and Eduard, respec-

tively, seems patent, along with the caveat of their overlap. But of course, neither Stopfkuchen nor Eduard belongs to this premodern world, and that fundamentally alters the functions of their stories.

7. As Gerhart v. Graevenitz observes in "Der Dicke im schlafenden Krieg. Zu einer Figur der europäischen Moderne bei Wilhelm Raabe," *JbRG* (1990): 1–21, the idyllic boredom that Benjamin posits in the premodern period also figures centrally in Romantic thought. For example, in his "Idyll of Indolence [*Idylle über den Müssiggang*]" in *Lucinde* (1799), Friedrich Schlegel praises the virtues not only of indolence but also of laziness (*Faulheit*), *Passivität*, and *Apathie*: the ideal of "taking one's time" that culminates in pure vegetation (*dem reinen Vegetieren*) that is also so central to Stopfkuchen's *Langweiligkeit* (cf. 98), and that for both is the necessary condition for the production of the poetic; see also Claude David, "Über Wilhelm Raabes *Stopfkuchen*," in *Lebendige Form: Interpretationen zur deutschen Literatur*, ed. Jeffrey Sammons and Ernst Schuler (Munich: Fink Verlag, 1970), 266. But as the not so subtle shift in vocabulary suggests, this Romantic conception is still quite different from Benjamin's, in that it is predicated on a certain lack; that is, its productive boredom is no longer a condition of work and social life but rather a refuge or respite from both—even as is its fiction. And this lack, or disjunction, is further accentuated in that the idyllic boredom is not assigned to some premodern past but rather is to be achieved within, but apart from, the bourgeois present, as a would-be repetition of a now lost paradise, with boredom and idleness as "the only fragment of our likeness to God that still remains to us from Paradise." See Friedrich Schlegel, "Idylle über den Müssiggang," in *Lucinde*, in *Kritische Ausgabe*, ed. Ernst Behler and Hans Eichner (Munich: Schöningh, 1959—), 5:25–29.

The other side to this disjunction of productive boredom from the context of work and social life is the attribution of a new, unproductive form of boredom within that same context. In fact, despite the obvious affinity of indolence, etc., with the poetics of boredom, Schlegel himself reserves the word *Langweile* for the world of "empty, restless activity, . . . of industriousness and usefulness," of "overanxious frenzy" and "work." As in Benjamin, the occupation of employment—"the unquestioning striving and progressing without station or centre [*ohne Stillstand und Mittelpunkt*]"—imposes a certain boredom on its practitioners, through repetition. However, it is a purely empty, repressive boredom, one that alienates from the poetic and, in a sense, from a forgotten "reality" as well.

8. This is basically the condition described by Walter Rehm in *Gontscharow und Jacobsen, oder Langweile und Schwermut* (Göttingen: Vandenhoeck and Ruprecht, 1963).

9. Acknowledgment of this dialectic is what is missing in most works devoted to a discussion of boredom, most notably Thomas Kuhn, *The Demon of Noontide* (Prince-

ton: Princeton University Press, 1976), who concentrates solely on the so-called noble ennui and dismisses the all-too-mundane monotony of the masses as beneath critical respectability, and so ignores the necessary dialectic. So too Rehm, *Gontscharow und Jacobsen*, and even Graevenitz, "Der Dicke im schlafenden Krieg," who in his otherwise excellent account of Schlegel's romantic boredom neglects to mention the competing *Langweile* Schlegel ascribes to the workaday world. See now also Patricia Meyer Spacks, *Boredom: The Literary History of a State of Mind* (Chicago: University of Chicago Press, 1995).

10. Soren Kierkegaard, "The Rotation Method," in *Either/Or: Volume I*, trans. David Swenson and Lillian Swenson (Princeton: Princeton University Press, 1959), 279–96.

11. Ibid., 284.

12. Ibid.

13. Cf. the postman Störzer—a prescient example of what we mean today by being "totally postal"—for whom the monotony of his geography (see below, note 17) not only proves a form of escapism from or repression of the monotony of his everyday routine, but for whom the monotony of that everyday routine also proves a form of escapism from or repression of his everyday, more or less secret desperation. The two repeat each other and display their sameness not only because they express but also because they hide the same reality, because they express the same fiction: because not only does the escapism prove depressingly normal but the normal proves an equally depressing escapism.

14. Kierkegaard, "The Rotation Method," 285.

15. Georg Büchner, *Sämtliche Werke und Briefe*, 1:96. See also Peter Mosler, *Georg Büchners 'Leonce und Lena.' Langweile als Gesellschaftliche Bewusstseinsform* (Bonn: Bouvier, 1974).

16. See Horkheimer and Adorno, "The Culture Industry," in *Dialectic of Enlightenment*, 120–67; Siegfried Kracauer, "Langweile," in *Das Ornament der Masse* (Frankfurt am Main: Suhrkampf, 1963), 321–25.

17. As Störzer explains to the young Eduard, "Just imagine, the same route day after day, year in and year out.... Could you stand that for your whole life, always on the same route, if you didn't have your thoughts and imagination and fantasies and books, Eduard? Wouldn't it have to become boring to you in the long run, without geography?" (21). Because Störzer's initial impulse toward fantastic, imaginative, entertaining, or distracting exoticism lies in the workaday present monotony, it takes its form: it repeats its source both by deploying the same effective strategy of monotony to dull and repress the daily experience of monotony and by inadvertently displacing and representing that would-be repressed reality onto and at the site of its supposed opposite.

This is most clearly seen in Störzer's fascination with Eduard's recounted school lesson in the ancient states of Asia Minor:

> "Well, then: Mysia, Lydia, Karia, Lycia, Pisidia, Phrygia, Galatia, Lykaonia, Cilicia, Kappodocia, Armenia minor, that's all of them."
>
> "My God, Eduard, it's just as if you were listing us Germans in all our subdepartments!" (21)

The escape from boring monotony is sought in a monotony that repeats it: Störzer seeks relief from monotony in the anaesthetics of monotony.

18. Friedrich Nietzsche, *Die Fröhliche Wissenschaft* (*The Gay Science*), Aphorism #42.

19. Kierkegaard, "The Rotation Method," 287.

20. Ibid., 288.

21. It is a peculiar but characteristic strain of the *Bildung* topos to nineteenth-century thought: peculiar because it does not consciously aim at a final assimilation into social reality, convention, and interests—far from it; but characteristic because it throws the individual back upon himself as the site for escape, and not least, for escape from himself.

22. Both Hubert Ohl, "Eduards Heimkehr oder Le Vaillant und das Riesenfaultier. Zu Wilhelm Raabes *Stopfkuchen*," in *Raabe in neuer Sicht*, ed. Hermann Helmers (Stuttgart: Kohlhammer, 1968), 247–78; and Volkmar Sander, "Illusionszerstörung und Wirklichkeitserfassung im Roman Raabes," in *Deutsche Romantheorien*, ed. Reinhold Grimm (Frankfurt: Athenäum, 1968), 262–76, stress this aspect of Fatso.

23. Benjamin, "The Storyteller [Der Erzähler]," 2:456.

24. We might note how Benjamin's argument echoes or repeats, but again in negative form, the structure of multiple, nonidentical realities we discovered in our own reading of Meyer's *The Marriage of the Monk*. There, it was the presence of multiple desires, perspectives, and interpretations or significances among the "readers" that impeded the unity of reality, as well as the presence of his own "other" desire in the creator (Dante) himself. Here, it is the presence of multiple boredoms, lack of perspectives, and personal significances among the "readers" that drives them to seek significance, desire, and reality elsewhere, and the presence of his own haunting (/repressed) boredom in the creator himself that threatens the final significance of his fiction/reality. Boredom replaces desire, and personal unreality replaces personal reality as the motor for investment; the nonidentity and inaccessibility of reality, or significance, remains the constant reality.

25. Holub, *Reflections of Realism*, 217, describes both of these conditions as first

pertaining in the period following realism proper; Raabe's novel, while clearly riding a cusp, somewhat qualifies this division.

26. For more on boredom and cruelty, see the philosopher whom Stopfkuchen holds up as his model, namely Schopenhauer. For a good description of how the violence of repression replaces the desire it represses, see Tatar, *Lustmord: Sexual Murder in Weimar Germany*, esp. 132–52.

27. These formal dimensions of boredom need not, and frequently do not, remain formal, but rather are represented in the very subject matter of the novel. This is especially evident in the nineteenth-century realist novel: see Erich Auerbach, "In the Hôtel de la Mole," in *Mimesis: The Representation of Reality in Western Literature*, trans. Willard R. Trask (Princeton: Princeton University Press, 1953), 454–92. Such a dual deployment to the boredom/reality of the novel is perhaps most famously represented in Goncharov's *Oblomov*. For more on the parallels between Goncharov's novel and Raabe's, see Rehm, *Gontscharow und Jacobsen;* and Graevenitz, "Der Dicke im schlafenden Krieg."

28. Rehm, *Gontscharow und Jacobsen*, 36.

29. Barthes, *S/Z*, trans. Richard Miller (New York: Hill and Wang, 1974).

30. Adam Phillips, *On Kissing, Tickling, and Being Bored: Psychoanalytic Essays on the Unexamined Life* (Cambridge: Harvard University Press, 1993), 77.

31. Hamon, "On the Major Features of Realist Discourse," 166–85. See also Susan Suleiman, "Redundancy and the 'Readable' Text," *Poetics Today* 1, no. 3 (1980): 119–42.

32. Barthes, "The Reality Effect," in Furst, *Realism*, 135–41.

33. Probably the most prominent case study of this in German realism is Adalbert Stifter's *Indian Summer* (*Der Nachsommer*), where the excessive focus on the smallest details in his nature descriptions (which often amount to the repeated description of the same "thing," with only barely perceptible, barely functional differences in emphasis), combined with the enumeration of accumulating things (its own form of repetition, where the monotonous rhythm of the list overrides the concrete specificity of the objects; their repeated enumeration or mention in order to ensure their continued presence in the narrative world merely reinforces the effect)—both of these tendencies constantly threaten to dissolve the usually trivial, mundane, ritualized narrative plot—i.e., the novel's own structure of readability, its most tangible, accessible security for its redundancy of "reality," and frequently its most clichéd, boring component. See Peter Küpper, "Literatur und Langweile: zur Lektüre Stifters," in *Adalbert Stifter: Studien und Interpretationen*, 171–88.

34. Certainly one can readily discover a prejudice against the effect in the criticism, both contemporary and modern, of Stifter; perhaps even more in the lack of criticism,

that is, of interest in him, or Raabe, or most all of German realism. Somewhat more surprising is the take of supposedly neutral literary theory, as evident for example in Rimmon-Kenan's second paradox to the status of repetition in "The Paradoxical Status of Repetition": "Constructive repetition emphasizes difference, destructive repetition emphasizes sameness (i.e. to repeat successfully is not to repeat)." Rimmon-Kenan quotes Brooke-Rose as saying that "theory in theory does not evaluate," but both go on to describe how a hypertrophy of repetition results in "the unpoetic function, or the way the poetic function collapses," and both consider this an intolerable aesthetic weakness. Rimmon-Kenan explicitly identifies the tendency to such hypertrophy with the redundancy at the heart of realist discourse, and writes, "The [aesthetic] danger is that of oversameness, of a repetition that repeats itself without variation." See also Suleiman, "Redundancy and the 'Readable' Text."

35. Mann sees that the *Langweile* at stake in Stifter's works is actively opposed to the aesthetics of interest and, while noting that there is something pathologically aggressive to Stifter's narratorial strategy, he concludes, "The sensationalism of boredom is nonetheless uncanny in the finest sense [*Das Sensationalwerden der Langenweile ist ohnehin im schönsten Sinne unheimlich*]" (from a letter to Fritz Strich, 27 November 1945). Mann's own stake in this positive recognition of aesthetic boredom should also be noted: at the time he was working on his *Doktor Faustus*, which perilously pursues a deliberate, excessive strategy of oversameness, imposing a hypertrophy of redundancy on its material as well as on its formal features, and so adamantly intends an effect of "a repetition that repeats itself without variation." And we might further note that, for the later Roland Barthes, a "certain boredom" is a key effect of his highly valorized poetics of bliss, which is contrasted with that of pleasure, which "comes from culture and does not break with it." See Barthes, *The Pleasure of the Text*, 14.

36. Jeffrey Sammons, *Wilhelm Raabe: The Fiction of the Alternative Community* (Princeton: Princeton University Press, 1987).

37. This last point is crucial. For all the arguable affinity between the boringness of Stifter and, say, Mann's Serenus Zeitblom, or more relevantly, between the deliberately boring mobilization of both clichéd material and vertical time arrays in Raabe's *Fatso* and Mann's *Doktor Faustus*, we are still talking about fundamentally different literary periods and so fundamentally different contexts and functions for the poetics of boredom. Similarly, for all the commonality to the dismantling of "texts of pleasure" to Stifter's or Raabe's practice and Barthes's theory, it would still be a distortion to identify the former's intentions with the latter's poetics of bliss—far from it, since for both their practice is far too grounded in the trivial and in the uncanny, pathological, and somehow violent to qualify as "blissful." In this instance at least, we must forcefully resist any premature collapse into oversameness. Rather, even as we need to demarcate

the poetics of boredom to (Raabe's) realism on the far side of the premodern "prehistory" of Benjamin and of the golden-age, temporally exempt idyll of Schlegel, so too on the near side of the "mythical" modernism of Mann and of the "posttemporal" (and postindividual) postmodernism of Barthes.

38. Many of these repetitions have been enumerated by Christa Hebbel, "Die Funktion der Erzähler- und Figurenperspektiven in WR's Ich-Erzählungen," Ph.D. diss., University of Heidelberg, 1960, 104–16, which she unfortunately and inaccurately designates as *Leitmotive*.

39. Of course, Eduard is often faced with an apparent threat to the identity between his conventional idyllizing iconography and the given external reality, such as when the natural hometown world he describes above is voided by capitalistic "Melioration": the frog pond of his childhood has been filled in, the beech tree cut down (33). But such a gap between iconography and reality does not yield any disruptive, realist disenchantment or disillusionment in Eduard, or rather, it yields only a false sense of disenchantment, without ever truly dislodging Eduard from his iconography. This is because the sense of loss, of a gap of incommensurability, is very much a part of his conventional construction of reality, and the possible disruption is simply recuperated as sentimental cliché—as iconography, as a convention. Not the reality but the sense of its loss is securely assimilated as part of the bourgeois idyll; the supposedly "realist" sense of disillusionment proves itself in this instance at least to be still in the service of maintaining the illusion, the fiction, the sentimental bourgeois fiction of reality.

40. This is another, and slightly different, reason why the depiction of the idyll as a lost idyll is part of Eduard's fiction rather than a challenge to it.

41. This aspect of Eduard's character and realism has well-known correspondences with those of Leonhard Hagebucher from Raabe's earlier novel, *Abu Telfan* (1867), in which the protagonist is similarly returning from Africa and aims his more sophisticated critical eye at the hometown bourgeois reality. Raabe himself calls attention to the parallel between the two figures by naming the boat on which Eduard is returning to Africa the *Hagebucher*.

42. E.g., how he is a well-to-do landowner with wife and family, concerned with important social connections, racist, etc. See Julia Hell, "Wilhelm Raabes Stopfkuchen: Der Ungleichzeitige Bürger," *JbRG* (1992): 165–93.

43. One of the more poignant literary representations of this irony comes in the opening scene of the primary narrative in Theodor Storm's *Immensee*. We might note that several critics have identified Storm himself with the figure of Eduard, e.g., Eckhardt Meyer Krentler, "Stopfkuchen—Ein Doppelgänger. Wilhelm Raabe erzählt Theodor Storm," *JbRG* (1987): 179–204; Mark Leerer, "Der ausgegrabene Heinrich Schliemann und der begrabene Theodor Storm," *JbRG* (1989): 63–90. I do not find the

arguments very persuasive, but I certainly do concur with the identification of Eduard with the poetics of poetic realism.

44. Cf. Shlomith Rimmon-Kenan, "Narration as Repetition: The Case of Günter Grass's *Cat and Mouse*," in *Discourse in Psychoanalysis and Literature*, ed. Shlomith Rimmon-Kenan (London: Methuen, 1987), 176–210.

45. Although one might ascribe this effect to the perceived gaps between Eduard's idyllizing expectations and the "changed" reality of his hometown, or alternatively to Fatso's assault on Eduard's philistine exoticism and self-image, it also seems an inevitable result of the faulty logic of difference and interest to Eduard's self-definition. After all, the conventional reality of his hometown idyll is actually conventioned as disappointment by Eduard in the service of his own personal idyll; but insofar as the latter is still dependent on, even redundant of, the former, Eduard necessarily (even if inadvertently) doubly discredits his own significance and reality in its original construction. In fact, one can justifiably see in the resultant tension between his representation and its failure the motive not only for the recuperative repetition to Eduard's narration on board the ship but also for that to his return home in the first place.

46. Of course, the very act of repressing the consciousness of the failed representation through its re-presentation also yields its unconscious representation, which expresses itself in Eduard's narration as even more repetitiveness. For example, he chooses to represent a typical, banal, childhood idyllic day, but nonetheless a day on which Störzer declares:

> Of course everybody who knows nothing about it still thinks it's a truly fine day; but, but, I won't say a thing about what I know of this area and the weather outlook. For me, even with all this sunshine now, it's clouding up a bit too suspiciously over there and all around, but especially behind Maiholzen, from where our bad weather comes. (17)

Or again (and significantly again), Eduard represents a day on which Störzer would show him "a cuckoo's egg in a hedge sparrow's nest" (16), a motif that is itself repeated at the very beginning in Eduard's seemingly and annoyingly banal account of his stroll with his Brummersumm companions.

> When northern men know how to find the Great Bear, it's quite an accomplishment; but even then many who should know better often make the mistake of attributing the Pole Star to it rather than to the Little Bear. (9)

Both of these latter examples reproduce the structure of misplacement that is of course central to Störzer's secret—and, as I hope to show, to the novel's realism—and so undermine the intended, banal idyll. So in Eduard's manifestly clichéd, conscious, and falsifying attempt to represent his childhood idyll, he nonetheless unconsciously and repeatedly represents details that undermine the desired fiction.

We can also compare this with Störzer's repetition of what he knows and would conceal, for instance in his response to Eduard's account of the earthquake in Chile: "Hm, a couple thousand more or less! One more or less—less" (18; cf. his frequent repetition of "a heavy bag" [19]). Störzer attempts to feign indifference, insignificance, lack of interest: but whereas his effort to conceal, to maintain, even to generate this meaninglessness occasions one form of repetition, the reality he would hide and repress nonetheless keeps breaking through and enforcing its own form of repetition.

47. In this respect, we should note that Eduard's boredom in the face of Fatso's boringness is clearly and again defensive and repressive. The greater the monotony, the greater the resistance, and so the more Eduard's boredom approaches panic: the claim of no-effect (boredom) is Eduard's denial of effect in the increasingly precarious attempt to sustain the threatened reality. We might say that in this case Eduard's boredom is the fiction deployed against the reality of Fatso's monotonous attack, even as monotony proves the reality deployed against Eduard's fiction of reality. For more on boredom as repression, see Rene Spitz, "Wiederholung, Rhythmus, Langweile," *Imago* 23 (1937): 171–96; and Otto Fenichel, "Zur Psychologie der Langeweile," *Imago* 20 (1934): 270–81.

48. We see very much the same strategy in Raabe's *Horacker* (1876) as well.

49. See Roman Guardiani, "Über WR's *Stopfkuchen*," in *Raabe in neuer Sicht*, 12–43; and Hermann Meyer, "Raum und Zeit in Wilhelm Raabe's Erzählkunst," in ibid., 98–129.

50. Cf. Hamon, "On the Major Features of Realist Discourse"; also Ulf Eisele, *Der Dichter und sein Detektiv. Raabes "Stopfkuchen" und die Frage des Realismus* (Tübingen: Niemeyer, 1979).

51. Cf. Graevenitz, "Der Dicke im schlafenden Krieg," 20.

52. Fatso's challenge to realistic representation indicated here in respect to description is also evident in respect to narrativity, to the realist faith in the unfolding of events or reality along a single linear timeline, where their significance and consequence are more or less directly dependent on their observable sequential unfolding. Once repetition breaks down belief in sequence as consequence, the realist strategy of narrativity loses its force. For the relation between such linearity and realism, see Miller, *The Novel and the Police*, 8–10.

53. Part of the imaginary retreat to an earlier period is the "untimely" valorization of a positive conception of *Langweiligkeit* and indolence that resonates with romantic, Schlegelian strains: see Graevenitz, "Der Dicke im schlafenden Krieg." But even as we

must evaluate Fatso's "postrealist" conceptions in a realist context, so too his apparently prerealist ones.

54. Cf. Jay, *The Dialectical Imagination*, 187, 213 ff. We might also note that for both Eduard and Fatso the acknowledged gap between the (lost) idyll and present reality functions as part of rather than as a challenge to their respective idylls.

55. As Claude David puts it, "Philistinism at the beginning, philistinism at the end [*Spiessertum am Anfang, Spiessertum am Ende*]" ("Über Wilhelm Raabes *Stopfkuchen*," 268). For some of the many ways in which the operant oppositions between Eduard and Fatso are dismantled in the novel, and the subversive effect of the resultant monotony on Fatso's project, self-identity, and reality—all of which no less than with Eduard depend on the maintenance of supposed differences—see below.

56. Adolf Schweckendieck, "Wilhelm Raabes *Stopfkuchen*. Eine ketzerische Betrachtung," *JbRG* (1974): 75–97.

57. So that while it is indeed true what Ohl discerns, namely that Eduard is the target of all Stopfkuchen's narration, it is also true that Eduard must be a mistaken target, and this mistakenness is as much the key to the novel as its targeting.

58. Cf. also "O God, God, God, yes there certainly has been a murder that I committed against Kienbaum; but all the little and the littlest things and the crude and the crudest things the man did to me as a youth and as a young man and as a man, that's all part of it, too" (189), where the repetitions can be seen as motivated by either the initial taunting or the following guilt. We might note that the quoted passage (*tagtäglich, tagtäglich, tagtäglich*) is quoted by Hermann Meyer as representative of the limited psychological realist motivation for the novel's repetitions, which he primarily ascribes to the reality of Fatso's mythical worldview. My argument of course is that the former is the reality motivating the fiction of the latter. See Meyer, "Raum und Zeit in Wilhelm Raabe's Erzählkunst."

59. Cf. Rimmon-Kenan's third paradox, "The first time is already a repetition, and the repetition is the very first time" ("The Paradoxical Status of Repetition," 155); also Barbara Johnson (on primal scenes), "The Frame of Reference: Poe, Lacan, Derrida," in *The Purloined Poe: Lacan, Derrida, and Psychoanalytic Reading*, ed. John P. Muller and William J. Richardson (Baltimore: Johns Hopkins University Press, 1988), 245.

60. Eisele's description of the operant structure of realism in Fatso's telling of the "murder story" is obviously quite close to mine for Dante's relation to his story in *The Marriage of the Monk*. Still, both my reading of Meyer's text and my analysis of Raabe's dictate that I qualify Eisele's argument.

61. Cf. Rimmon-Kenan, "Narration as Repetition"; also her "From Reproduction to Production: The Status of Narration in Faulkner's *Absalom, Absalom!*" *Degrés* 16 (1978): f1–f19.

62. In both cases, the representative becomes sacrifice, *das sühnende Opfer* (195), but in a system where the logic of representation and of sacrifice no longer coincide. See Horkheimer and Adorno, "The Concept of Enlightenment," in *Dialectic of Enlightenment*, 10.

63. We can of course go further than even this. In his narration, Fatso seems compelled not only to repeat both of Störzer's crimes in the story but also to commit all three crimes in the story. Insofar as Fatso's peculiar mode of attack—namely repetition, incessant taunting, etc.—repeats that of Kienbaum, so too does his crime, with Eduard now (again) a repetition of Störzer, and especially of Störzer as the indirect, displaced target of abuse: the position Störzer shares with Quakatz, and of course the position Fatso himself would share, or repeat, with both. Both Fatso and Eduard by turns occupy, re-present, and don't represent, each and every primary position in the basic story pattern. The result is that for Fatso and his narration, there no longer seems to be any direction for the violence to take, no access to the desired reality in or through its representatives—and yet no lessening of the violence, the reality to and of his narration itself, which continually regenerates its pattern, no matter how misapplied.

64. For an elegant, insightful reading of boredom as a form of mourning, see Adam Phillips, *On Kissing, Tickling, and Being Bored*, 68–78.

65. This chain is perpetuated by any of the most common responses to Raabe's text. Either one stops reading out of frustration, throwing aside the book in angry vexation at its endless, taunting repetitions, and so reenacts the primal scene of Störzer's crime. Or one endures to the end and somehow feels the violence ended as well: either like Quakatz after his stroke, no longer bored or upset by the tortured experience because rendered helplessly simple-minded by it and so lulled into a perception of a benevolent reality that is in fact the surest evidence of its true violence; or worse, like Eduard, desperately pretending to such an idyllic reality because the truth is too much, too real to bear. Or, finally, like Fatso, one attacks the novel's whole world, armed with the elite weapons of criticism—and so the violence goes on, carried on at another, but ultimately no different, level of attack.

WORKS CITED

Alpers, Svetlana. *The Art of Describing: Dutch Art in the Seventeenth Century.* Chicago: University of Chicago Press, 1983.
Alter, Robert. *Partial Magic: The Novel as Self-Conscious Genre.* Berkeley: University of California Press, 1975.
Arato, Andrew. "Esthetic Theory and Cultural Criticism: Introduction." In *The Essential Frankfurt School Reader*, edited by Andrew Arato and Eike Gebhardt. New York: Continuum, 1982.
Auerbach, Berthold. "Die Stiefmutter." In *Zur Guten Stunde.* Stuttgart: Hoffman, 18—?
Auerbach, Erich. "In the Hôtel de la Mole." In *Mimesis: The Representation of Reality in Western Literature*, translated by Willard R. Trask. Princeton: Princeton University Press, 1953.
Barthes, Roland. *Image-Music-Text.* Translated by Stephen Heath. New York: Noonday Press, 1977.
———. *Mythologies.* Translated by Annette Lavers. New York: Hill and Wang, 1983.
———. *The Pleasure of the Text.* Translated by Richard Miller. New York: Hill and Wang, 1975.
———. "The Reality Effect." In *French Literary Theory*, edited by Tzvetan Todorov, translated by R. Carter. Cambridge: Cambridge University Press, 1982. Reprint, Furst, *Realism.*
———. *Roland Barthes.* Translated by Richard Howard. New York: Hill and Wang, 1977.
———. *S/Z.* Translated by Richard Miller. New York: Hill and Wang, 1974.
Benjamin, Walter. *Gesammelte Schriften.* 12 vols. Edited by Rolf Tiedemann and Hermann Schweppenhäuser. Frankfurt am Main: Suhrkamp, 1980.
Bentz, Rudi. "Form und Struktur der 'Sieben Legenden' Gottfried Kellers." Ph.D. diss., Zürich, 1979.
Berman, Russell. *The Rise of the Modern German Novel: Crisis and Charisma.* Cambridge, Mass.: Harvard University Press, 1986.
Bersani, Leo. *A Future for Astyanax.* Boston: Little, Brown & Co., 1969.
Bloom, Harold. *The Anxiety of Influence.* London: Oxford University Press, 1973.
Brinkmann, Richard. *Wirklichkeit und Illusion: Studien über Gehalt und Grenzen des Be-*

griffs Realismus für die erzählende Dichtung des neunzehnten Jahrhunderts. 2d ed. Tübingen: Niemeyer, 1966.

Bronfen, Elisabeth. "Dialogue with the Dead: The Dead Beloved as Muse." In *Sex and Death in Victorian England*, edited by Regina Barreca. Bloomington: Indiana University Press, 1990.

———. *Over Her Dead Body: Death, Femininity, and the Aesthetic*. New York: Routledge, 1992.

Brooks, Peter. "Freud's Masterplot: Questions of Narrative." In *Literature and Psychoanalysis. The Question of Reading: Otherwise*, edited by Shoshana Felman. Baltimore: Johns Hopkins University Press, 1982.

Büchner, Georg. *Sämtliche Werke und Briefe*. Edited by Werner R. Lehmann. Hamburg: Christian Wegner, 1967.

Buck-Morss, Susan. *The Origin of Negative Dialectics*. New York: Free Press, 1977.

Burkhard, Marianne. *Conrad Ferdinand Meyer*. Boston: Twayne, 1978.

Butler, Judith. *Bodies That Matter*. New York: Routledge, 1993.

———. *Gender Trouble: Feminism and the Subversion of Identity*. New York: Routledge, 1990.

Cohn, Dorrit. "Wilhelm Meister's Dream: Reading Goethe with Freud." *German Quarterly* 62, no. 4 (1989): 459–72.

Crary, Jonathan. *Techniques of the Observer: On Vision and Modernity in the Nineteenth Century*. Cambridge, Mass.: MIT Press, 1990.

David, Claude. "Über Wilhelm Raabes *Stopfkuchen*." In *Lebendige Form: Interpretationen zur deutschen Literatur*, edited by Jeffrey Sammons and Ernst Schuler. Munich: Fink Verlag, 1970.

Deleuze, Gilles. *Difference and Repetition*. Translated by Paul Patton. New York: Columbia University Press, 1994.

Demetz, Peter. "Walter Benjamin als Leser Adalbert Stifters." In *Adalbert Stifter Heute: London Symposium 1983*, edited by J. Lachinger, A. Doppler, and A. Stillmark. Linz: Wimmer, 1985.

Domandl, Sepp. "Die philosophische Tradition von Adalbert Stifters 'Sanftem Gesetz.'" *VASILO* 21 (1972): 79–103.

Donahue, William Collins. "The Kiss of the Spider Woman: Gotthelf's Matricentric Pedagogy." *German Quarterly* 67, no. 3 (1994): 304–24.

Downing, Eric. *Artificial I's: The Self as Artwork in Ovid, Kierkegaard, and Thomas Mann*. Tübingen: Niemeyer, 1993.

Eagleton, Terry. *Ideology: An Introduction*. London: Verso, 1991.

———. *The Ideology of the Aesthetic*. Oxford: Basil Blackwell, 1990.

Eisele, Ulf. *Der Dichter und sein Detektiv. Raabes "Stopfkuchen" und die Frage des Realismus.* Tübingen: Niemeyer, 1979.

Evans, Tamara. *Formen der Ironie in Conrad Ferdinand Meyers Novellen.* Bern: Franke, 1980.

Eversberg, Gird. *Erläuterungen zu Theodor Storm. Viola tricolor. Beim Vetter Christian, Königs Erläuterungen und Materielen.* Vol. 199. Hollfeld: C. Bange, 1984.

Fairley, Barker, trans. "Tubby Schaumann." In *Wilhelm Raabe: Novels,* edited by Volkmar Sander. New York: Continuum, 1983.

Feise, Ernst. "*Die Hochzeit des Mönchs* von Conrad Ferdinand Meyer: Eine Formanalyse." In *Xenion: Essays in the History of German Literature.* Baltimore: Johns Hopkins University Press, 1950.

Fellmann, Herbert. "Die 'fragwürdige' Erzählkunst C. F. Meyers: Untersucht an der Novelle *Die Hochzeit des Mönchs.*" In *Jahrbuch der Wittheit zu Bremen* 9 (1965): 23–45.

Felman, Shoshana. "Turning the Screw of Interpretation." In *Literature and Psychoanalysis. The Question of Reading: Otherwise,* edited by Shoshana Felman. Baltimore: Johns Hopkins University Press, 1982.

Fenichel, Otto. "Zur Psychologie der Langweile." *Imago* 20 (1934): 270–81.

Fontane, Theodor. "Theodor Storm." In *Theodor Fontane, Sämtliche Werke,* edited by Walter Keitel, series 3, 1:273. Munich: Carl Heinser, 1969.

Foucault, Michel. *The History of Sexuality: Volume I, An Introduction.* Translated by Robert Hurley. New York: Vintage, 1980.

Freud, Sigmund. *Briefe an Wilhelm Fliess 1897–1904* Ungekürzte Ausgabe. Edited by Jeffrey M. Masson. Frankfurt am Main: Fischer, 1986.

———. "Das Unheimliche." In *Studienausgabe.* Vol. 4, edited by Alexander Mitscherlich, Angela Richards, and James Strachey. Munich: Fischer Verlag, 1982.

———. "Jenseits des Lustprinzips." In *Studienausgabe.* Vol. 3, edited by Alexander Mitscherlich, Angela Richards, and James Strachey. Munich: Fischer Verlag, 1982.

———. "Trauer und Melancholie." In *Studienausgabe.* Vol. 3, edited by Alexander Mitscherlich, Angela Richards, and James Strachey. Munich: Fischer Verlag, 1982.

Furst, Lilian R. *All Is True: The Claims and Strategies of Realist Fiction.* Durham, N.C.: Duke University Press, 1995.

———, ed. *Realism.* London: Longman, 1992.

Geulen, Eva. "Resistance and Representation: The Case of Thomas Mann's 'Mario and the Magician.'" *New German Critique: An Interdisciplinary Journal of German Studies* 68 (spring–summer 1996): 3–29.

———. *Worthörig Wider Willen.* Munich: Ludicum, 1992.

Gillespie, Gerald. "Space and Time Seen through Stifter's Telescope." *German Quarterly* 37, no. 2 (1964): 120–30.

Goldammer, Peter, ed. *Theodor Storm, Sämtliche Werke*. 4 vols. Berlin: Aufbau, 1972.

Guardiani, Roman. "Über Wilhelm Raabe's *Stopfkuchen*." In *Raabe in neuer Sicht*. Stuttgart: W. Kohlhammer, 1968.

Guthke, Karl. "C. F. Meyer's Kunstsymbolik." In *Wege zur Literatur: Studien zur deutschen Dichtungs- und Geistesgeschichte*. Bern: Franke, 1967.

——. *The Last Frontier: Imagining Other Worlds from the Copernican Revolution to Modern Science Fiction*. Translated by Helen Atkins. Ithaca: Cornell University Press, 1990.

Hamon, Philippe. "On the Major Features of Realist Discourse." In *Realism*, edited by L. R. Furst, translated by L. R. Furst and Sean Hand. London: Longman, 1992.

Harnisch, Antje. "'Die Sucht, den Mann zu spielen' in Gottfried Kellers Realismus." *German Quarterly* 68, no. 2 (1995): 147–59.

Hawkes, Terence. *Structuralism and Semiotics*. Berkeley: University of California Press, 1977.

Hebbel, Christa. "Die Funktion der Erzähler- und Figurenperspektiven in Wilhelm Raabe's Ich-Erzählungen." Ph.D. diss., University of Heidelberg, 1960.

Heintel, Erich. "Natur und Geschichte in Stifters 'Hochwald.'" *Wiener Jahrbuch für Philosophie* (1973): 7–41.

Hell, Julia. "Wilhelm Raabes Stopfkuchen: Der Ungleichzeitige Bürger." *Jahrbuch der Raabe Gesellschaft* (1992): 165–93.

Holub, Robert C. *Reflections of Realism: Paradox, Norm, and Ideology in Nineteenth-Century German Prose*. Detroit: Wayne State University Press, 1991.

Horkheimer, Max. "Begriff der Aufklärung." In *Gesammelte Schriften*, edited by Alfred Schmidt and G. Schmid Noerr. Frankfurt am Main: Fischer, 1987.

Horkheimer, Max, and Theodor W. Adorno. *Dialectic of Enlightenment*. Translated by John Cumming. New York: Continuum, 1972.

Imhof, Arthur E. *Die Lebenszeit: vom aufgeschobenen Tod und von der Kunst des Lebens*. Munich: C. H. Beck, 1988.

Jackson, David A. "Dante the Dupe in C. F. Meyer's *Die Hochzeit des Mönchs*." *German Life and Letters* 25 (1971–72): 5–25.

Jacobson, Manfred R. "The Two Faces of Dante: Fate and the Artist in C. F. Meyer's *Die Hochzeit des Mönchs*." *Trivium* 16 (May 1981): 99–106.

Jakobson, Roman. "On Realism in Art." In *Readings in Russian Poetics: Formalist and Structuralist Views*, edited by L. Matejka and K. Pomorska. Cambridge, Mass.: MIT Press, 1971.

——. "Two Aspects of Language and Two Types of Aphasic Disturbances." In Roman Jakobson and Morris Halle, *Fundamentals of Language*. Janua Linguarum, Series Minor, 1 (1956), 69–96.

Jameson, Frederic. *The Political Unconscious: Narrative as a Socially Symbolic Act*. Ithaca: Cornell University Press, 1981.

Japp, Uwe, and Hans Joachim Piechotta, eds. *Adalbert Stifter, Werke*. Frankfurt am Main: Insel, 1978.

Jay, Martin. *The Dialectical Imagination: A History of the Frankfurt School and the Institute of Social Research, 1923–1950*. Boston: Little, Brown & Co., 1973.

———. "Scopic Regimes of Modernity." In *Vision and Visuality*, edited by Hal Forster. Seattle: Bay Press, 1988.

Jeziorkowski, Klaus. "Die Kunst der Perspektive: Zur Epik Conrad Ferdinand Meyers." *Germanisch-Romanische Monatsschrift* Neue Folge 17, no. 4 (1967): 398–416.

Johnson, Barbara. "The Frame of Reference: Poe, Lacan, Derrida." In *The Purloined Poe: Lacan, Derrida, and Psychoanalytic Reading*, edited by John P. Muller and William J. Richardson. Baltimore: Johns Hopkins University Press, 1988.

Kaiser, Gerhard. *Gottfried Keller, Das gedichtete Leben*. Frankfurt am Main: Insel Verlag, 1981.

Keller, Gottfried. *Sämtliche Werke*. 7 vols. Edited by Dominik Müller. Frankfurt am Main: Deutscher Klassiker Verlag, 1991.

Kierkegaard, Soren. "The Rotation Method." In *Either/Or: Volume I*, translated by David Swenson and Lillian Swenson. Princeton: Princeton University Press, 1959.

Kittler, Friedrich. *Der Traum und die Rede: Eine Analyse der Kommunikationssituation Conrad Ferdinand Meyers*. Bern: Franke, 1977.

Klein, Johannes. *Theodor Storm, Sämtliche Werke*. Vol. 2. Munich: Winkler, 1951.

Koestler, Arthur. *The Sleepwalkers: A History of Man's Changing Vision of the Universe*. London: Penguin, 1959.

Kracauer, Siegfried. "Langweile." In *Das Ornament der Masse*. Frankfurt am Main: Suhrkampf, 1963.

Krentler, Eckhardt Meyer. "Stopfkuchen—Ein Doppelgänger. Wilhelm Raabe erzählt Theodor Storm." *Jahrbuch der Raabe Gesellschaft* (1987): 179–204.

Kuhn, Thomas. *The Demon of Noontide*. Princeton: Princeton University Press, 1976.

Küpper, Peter. "Literatur und Langeweile: Zur Lektüre Stifters." In *Adalbert Stifter: Studien und Interpretationen*, edited by L. Stiehm. Heidelberg: Lothar Stiehm, 1968.

Lacan, Jaques. *The Four Fundamental Concepts of Psycho-Analysis*. Edited by Jacques-Alain Miller. Translated by Alan Sheridan. New York: W. W. Norton & Co., 1981.

Leerer, Mark. "Der ausgegrabene Heinrich Schliemann und der begrabene Theodor Storm." *Jahrbuch der Raabe Gesellschaft* (1989): 63–90.

Leuschner, Brigitte. "Erfinden und Erzählen: Funktion und Kommunikation in autothematischer Dichtung." *MLN* 100, no. 3 (1985): 498–513.

Levine, George. *Realism and Representation*. Madison: University of Wisconsin Press, 1993.

Lorenz, Dagmar. "Stifters Frauengestalten." *VASILO* 32 (1983): 93–106.

Lund, Deborah S. *Ambiguity as Narrating Strategy in the Prose Work of C. F. Meyer*. New York: Peter Lang, 1990.

MacLeod, Catriona. *Embodying Ambiguity: Androgyny and Aesthetics from Winckelmann to Keller*. Detroit: Wayne University Press, 1998.

Manthey, Jürgen. *Wenn Blicke zeugen könnten*. Munich: Carl Hanser, 1983.

Martini, Fritz. *Deutsche Literatur im bürgerlichen Realismus 1848–1898*, Epochen der deutschen Literatur. Stuttgart, 1962.

Mautz, Karl. "Das antagonistische Naturbild in Stifters *Studien*." In *Adalbert Stifter: Studien und Interpretationen*, edited by L. Stiehm. Heidelberg: Lothar Stiehm, 1968.

McCort, Dennis. *States of Unconsciousness in Three Tales of C. F. Meyer*. Lewisburg, Penna.: Bucknell University Press, 1988.

Meyer, Conrad Ferdinand. *Sämtliche Werke*. Edited by Alfred Zäch and Hans Zeller. Historische Ausgabe. Bern: Benteli, 1961.

Meyer, Hermann. "Raum und Zeit in Wilhelm Raabe's Erzählkunst." In *Raabe in neuer Sicht*. Stuttgart: W. Kohlhammer, 1968.

Miller, David A. *The Novel and the Police*. Berkeley: University of California Press, 1988.

Miller, J. Hillis. *Fiction and Repetition*. Cambridge, Mass.: Harvard University Press, 1982.

Mosler, Peter. *Georg Büchners 'Leonce und Lena.' Langweile als Gesellschaftliche Bewusstseinsform*. Bonn: Bouvier, 1974.

Mugge-Meiburg, Beth L. *Words Chiseled in Marble: Artworks in the Prose Narratives of Conrad Ferdinand Meyer*. New York: Peter Lang, 1991.

Müller, Dominik, ed. *Gottfried Keller, Sämtliche Werke*. 7 Vols. Frankfurt am Main: Deutscher Klassiker Verlag, 1991.

Muschg, Adolf. *Gottfried Keller*. Munich: Kindler Verlag, 1977.

Nietzsche, Friedrich. *Die Fröhliche Wissenschaft*. In *Sämtliche Werke: Kritische Studienausgabe in fünfzehn Einzelbände*. Vol. 3, edited by Giorgio Colli and Mazzino Montinari. Munich: Deutscher Taschenbuch Verlag, 1988.

———. *Zur Genealogie der Moral*. In *Sämtliche Werke: Kritische Studienausgabe in fünfzehn Einzelbände*. Vol. 5, edited by Giorgio Colli and Mazzino Montinari. Munich: Deutscher Taschenbuch Verlag, 1988.

Ohl, Hubert. "Eduards Heimkehr oder Le Vaillant und das Riesenfaultier. Zu Wilhelm

Raabes *Stopfkuchen*." In *Raabe in neuer Sicht*, edited by Hermann Helmers. Stuttgart: Kohlhammer, 1968.

Onderlinden, Sjaak. *Die Rahmenerzählungen Conrad Ferdinand Meyers*. Leiden: Universitaire Pers Leiden, 1974.

Pascal, Roy. "Die Landschaftschilderung im 'Hochwald.'" In *Adalbert Stifter Studien und Interpretationen*, edited by Lothar Stiehm. Heidelberg: Lothar Stiehm Verlag, 1968.

Phillips, Adam. *On Kissing, Tickling, and Being Bored: Psychoanalytic Essays on the Unexamined Life*. Cambridge, Mass.: Harvard University Press, 1993.

Plater, Edward. "The Figure of Dante in Die Hochzeit des Mönchs." *MLN* 90 (1975): 678–95.

Raabe, Wilhelm. *Sämtliche Werke*, edited by Karl Hoppe. Göttingen: Vandenhoeck & Ruprecht, 1963.

Reddick, John. "Mystification, Perspectivism and Symbolism in *Der Hochwald*." In *Adalbert Stifter Heute: Londoner Symposium 1983*, edited by Johann Lachinger, Alexander Stillmark, and Martin Swales. Linz: OÖ Landesverlag, 1985.

Rehm, Walter. *Gontscharow und Jacobsen, oder Langweile und Schwermut*. Göttingen: Vandenhoeck and Ruprecht, 1963.

Renz, Christine. *Gottfried Kellers "Sieben Legenden": Versuch einer Darstellung seines Erzählens*. Tübingen: Niemeyer Verlag, 1993.

Rimmon-Kenan, Shlomith. "From Reproduction to Production: The Status of Narration in Faulkner's *Absalom, Absalom!*" *Degrés* 16 (1978): f1–f19.

———. "Narration as Repetition: The Case of Günter Grass's *Cat and Mouse*." In *Discourse in Psychoanalysis and Literature*, edited by Shlomith Rimmon-Kenan. London: Methuen, 1987.

———. "The Paradoxical Status of Repetition." *Poetics Today* 1, no. 4 (1980): 151–59.

Rohwer, Julia C. "Das Tier als Leitmotiv in den späten Novellen Theodor Storms." *Acta Germanica* 10 (1977): 245–63.

Rölleke, Heinz, ed. *Kinder- und Hausmärchen, gesammelt durch die Brüder Grimm*. 1812/15. Reprint, Frankfurt am Main: Deutscher Klassiker Verlag, 1986.

Sammons, Jeffrey. *Wilhelm Raabe: The Fiction of the Alternative Community*. Princeton: Princeton University Press, 1987.

———, trans. "Adalbert Stifter: Preface to Many-colored Stones." In *German Novellas of Realism*. Vol. 1, edited by Jeffrey L. Sammons. New York: Continuum, 1989.

Sander, Volkmar. "Illusionszerstörung und Wirklichkeitserfassung im Roman Raabes." In *Deutsche Romantheorien*, edited by Reinhold Grimm. Frankfurt: Athenäum, 1968.

Schlegel, Friedrich. *Lucinde*. In *Kritische Ausgabe*. 35 vols., edited by Ernst Behler and Hans Eichner. Münich: Schöningh, 1959–91.

Schweckendieck, Adolf. "Wilhelm Raabes *Stopfkuchen*. Eine ketzerische Betrachtung." *Jahrbuch der Raabe Gesellschaft* (1974): 75–97.

Selge, Martin. "Der Blick durchs Fernrohr: Teleskopische Vermittlung in *Der Hochwald*." In *Adalbert Stifter: Poesie aus dem Geist der Naturwissenschaft*. Stuttgart: W. Kohlhammer, 1976.

Shaw, Michael. "C. F. Meyer's Resolute Heroes: A Study of Becket, Astorre, and Pescara." *DVjS* 40 (1966): 372–81.

Sonnenfeld, Marion W., trans. *The Marriage of the Monk*. In *The Complete Narrative Prose of Conrad Ferdinand Meyer*, translated by George F. Folkers, David B. Dickens, and Marion W. Sonnenfeld. Lewisburg, Penna.: Bucknell University Press, 1976.

Spacks, Patricia Meyer. *Boredom: The Literary History of a State of Mind*. Chicago: University of Chicago Press, 1995.

Spitz, Rene. "Wiederholung, Rhythmus, Langweile." *Imago* 23 (1937): 171–96.

Steffen, Konrad, ed. *Adalbert Stifter. Gesammelte Werke*. 14 vols. Basel: Birkhäuser, 1962.

Stern, J. P. *On Realism*. London: Routledge & Kegan Paul, 1973.

Stifter, Adalbert. *Werke und Briefe. Historisch-Kritische Gesamtausgabe*. 8 vols. Edited by Alfred Doppler and Wolfgang Frühwald. Stuttgart: Kohlhammer, 1982.

Stopp, F. J. "Die Symbolik in Stifters *Bunten Steinen*." *DVjS* 28 (1954): 165–93.

Storm, Theodor. *Sämtliche Werke*. Edited by Albert Köster. Leipzig: Insel, 1919.

Stuckert, Franz. *Theodor Storm: Sein Leben und seine Welt*. Bremen: Schünemann, 1955.

Suleiman, Susan. "Redundancy and the 'Readable' Text." *Poetics Today* 1, no. 3 (1980): 119–42.

Swales, Martin. *The German Novelle*. Princeton: Princeton University Press, 1977.

Swales, Martin, and Erika Swales, eds. *Adalbert Stifter: A Critical Study*. Cambridge: Cambridge University Press, 1984.

Tatar, Maria. *Lustmord: Sexual Murder in Weimar Germany*. Princeton: Princeton University Press, 1995.

Thurnher, Eugen. "Stifters sanftes Gesetz." In *Unterscheidung und Bewahrung: Festschrift für Hermann Kunisch*, edited by Klaus Lasarowisz and Wolfgang Kron. Berlin: de Gruyter, 1961.

Traub, Valerie. *Desire and Anxiety: Circulations of Sexuality in Shakespearean Drama*. London: Routledge, 1992.

Tschorn, Wolfgang. *Idylle und Verfall: Die Realität der Familie im Werk Theodor Storms*. Abhandlungen zur Kunst-, Musik- und Literaturwissenschaft. Vol. 271. Bonn: Bouvier, 1978.

Tunner, Erika. "'Zum Sehen geboren, zum Schauen bestellt': Reflexionen zur Augensymbolik in Stifters *Studien*." *Etudes Germaniques* 40 (1985): 335–48.

Vincon, Hartmut. *Theodor Storm mit Selbstzeugnissen und Bilddokumenten*. Rowohlt Monographien. Hamburg: Rowohlt, 1972.

Voelker, Ludwig. *Langweile. Untersuchungen zur Vorgeschichte eines literarischen Motivs*. Munich: Fink Verlag, 1975.

von Graevenitz, Gerhart. "Der Dicke im schlafenden Krieg. Zu einer Figur der europäischen Moderne bei Wilhelm Raabe." *Jahrbuch der Raabe Gesellschaft* (1990): 1–21.

von Wiese, Benno. "Conrad Ferdinand Meyer: *Die Hochzeit des Mönchs*." In *Die deutsche Novelle*. Vol. 2. Düsseldorf: August Bagel, 1962.

Webber, Andrew. "The Uncanny Rides Again: Theodor Storm's Double Vision." *Modern Language Review* 84, no. 4 (1989): 860–73.

Weber, Samuel. *Return to Freud: Jaques Lacan's Dislocation of Psychoanalysis*. Translated by Michael Levine. Cambridge: Cambridge University Press, 1991.

Weiskel, Thomas. *The Romantic Sublime: Studies in the Structure and Psychology of Transcendence*. Baltimore: Johns Hopkins University Press, 1976.

Wellek, Rene. *Concepts of Criticism*. Edited by Stephen G. Nichols, Jr. New Haven: Yale University Press, 1963.

Williams, W. D. *The Stories of C. F. Meyer*. Oxford: Oxford University Press, 1962.

Wright, Elizabeth. *Psychoanalytic Criticism: Theory in Practice*. London: Methuen, 1984.

Wyness, Martin, trans. "Eugenia." In *Gottfried Keller: Stories*, edited by Frank G. Ryder. New York: Continuum, 1982.

Zäch, Alfred, and Hans Zeller, eds. *Conrad Ferdinand Meyer: Sämtliche Werke Historische Ausgabe*. Vol. 12. Bern: Benteli, 1961.

Zeller, Rosemarie, and Hans Zeller. "Erzähltes Erzählen: Funktionen der Erzählhaltungen in C. F. Meyers Rahmennovellen." In *Erzählforschung 2: Theorien, Modelle und Methoden der Narrativik*. Beiheft 6 of *Zeitschrift für Literaturwissenschaft und Linguistik*, edited by Wolfgang Haubrichs. Göttingen: Vandenhoeck & Ruprecht, 1977.

INDEX

In this index an "f" after a number indicates a separate reference on the next page, and an "ff" indicates separate references on the next two pages. A continuous discussion over two or more pages is indicated by a span of page numbers, e.g., "57–59." *Passim* is used for a cluster of references in close but not consecutive sequence.

Abdias (Stifter), 31, 33, 41
Adorno, Theodor, 13, 219, 269n27; *Dialectic of Enlightenment*, 7–10
Adventure stories: Raabe's use of, 230, 233–36
Aesthetics, 25, 34–35, 113
Aggression, 216, 227, 232–34, 258
Album of My Greatgrandfather, The (*Die Mappe meines Urgrossvaters*) (Stifter), 31, 34, 278–79nn11, 14
Alienation, 206–7
Allegory, 282n32; nature as, 64–67, 74–75, 277n9, 285–86n37; portraits as, 141–42
Amulet, The (Meyer), 171–72
Aquis submersus (Storm), 140, 144, 153, 164
Artifact: beloved as, 140–42
Authority: narrative, 178–81, 183–84, 197–99, 282–83n34, 304nn34, 35, 308n58; controlling, 189–92, 199–201, 204–5; and desire, 194–95, 210; and identity, 205–7

Barthes, Roland, 5, 24, 102, 217, 225, 268n 16, 297n17; "The Reality Effect," 2–3
Benjamin, Walter, 11, 25, 91, 273n18, 309–10n6; "The Storyteller," 217–18; on meaning of life (Sinn des Lebens), 222–23

Berman, Russell, 11f, 23, 31, 261, 269n27; *Rise of the Modern German Novel*, 7
Bersani, Leo, 19
Boccaccio, Giovanni: *Decameron*, 92
Boredom, 310–11nn9, 13, 313n27, 314–15nn35, 37; as narrative technique, 216, 226–40, 310n7, 311–12nn13, 17; anaesthetics of, 217–24; and pleasure, 218–19, 224–25; and revenge, 254–59
Brigitta (Stifter), 41, 98
Brinkmann, Richard, 19
Bronfen, Elizabeth, 136f
Brooks, Peter, 18
Büchner, Georg, 25, 36; *Lenz*, 24f, 30, 219, 278n12
Butler, Judith, 98–99, 101–2, 110, 118

Castle, The (Kafka), 227
Castle, In the (*Im Schloss*) (Storm), 137, 143, 164f
Castle of Fools, The (*Die Narrenburg*) (Stifter), 33–34, 79f, 278–79nn11, 14, 280n19
Children: and incest, 162–63; and repetition, 167–68
Christianity, 101; and natural order, 66, 273n18; and fables, 93–95; and gender, 105, 123; and identity, 109–10; and desire, 110–11, 294n45

Community, 36, 56, 74
Condor, The (Stifter), 77f, 79f
Cooper, James Fenimore, 44f
Corner of the Forest, A (*Waldwinkel*) (Storm), 137; repetition in, 143–44; incest as theme in, 162–63
Critical Theory (Frankfurt School), 2, 7, 9, 11, 14, 219, 261, 287n17
Cross-dressing, 102; Keller's themes of, 98–99, 109; defamiliarization and, 100–101; identity and, 117–18; and gender, 120–21

Daily life: reproduction of, 2–3
Darwin, Charles, 2
Death, 152, 308n69; and reality, 89–90, 283–84n35; as theme, 150, 297–98n19, 299n35, 308n61; and desire, 145–47, 158–59, 212–13, 214–15; and substitution, 187f
Death drive, 18–19
Debt and Credit (*Soll und Haben*) (Freytag), 14
Decameron (Boccaccio), 92
Defamiliarization, 100–101
Deleuze, Gilles: Nietzschean and Platonic models of repetition, 6, 21
Demythologization: Enlightenment as, 8–10
Descendants (*Nachkommenschaften*) (Stifter), 78, 81, 273n19
Desire, 22, 37, 40, 42, 64, 72–73, 119, 216, 224, 281n25, 294n42, 299n38, 300n41, 301n55; sexual, 38, 88, 95, 288–89nn8, 9, 290n27, 294n45, 300–301n49; as theme, 53, 61f, 298–99n29, 307n53; and character, 69–70; and patriarchal vision, 82–83; and gender, 106–7, 123; and Christianity, 110–11; and repetition, 137–39, 148–49; and death, 144–47, 158–59, 212–13, 214–15; ambiguity of, 152–53; and fantasy, 67–69, 153–56, 276n36, 300n39; and realism, 95–96, 154–55; incest and, 163–65; and narration, 175–76, 178; and reality, 178, 307–8n56, 308n60; and displacement, 176–77, 192–94, 201–4; and authority, 194–95, 210
Dialectic of Enlightenment (Horkheimer and Adorno), 7–10
Disillusionment, 240–42, 256–57
Displacement, 291–92n34, 305n36; Meyer's use of, 180–81, 182, 186, 192–93, 201–3, 302n6; and desire, 192–94
Divine Comedy, The (Dante), 176, 198
Dreams: as device, 144–48, 303n25
Dress: gender and, 98–99, 101, 120–21, 294n46; identity and, 117–18; eroticism and, 124–25

Eekenhof (Storm), 137, 140, 163, 165f
Effi Briest (Fontane), 134, 300n39, 301n55
Enlightenment, 7–10
Epigram, The (*Das Sinngedicht*) (Keller), 98
"Eugenia" (Keller), 98, 263, 289n11, 291nn32, 33, 292n36, 295n49; repetition in, 103–4, 186, 292–93nn39, 40; gender issues in, 104–6, 107–8, 121–22, 291n33; desire in, 106–7, 290n27, 294n42; identity in, 108–12, 116–17, 125–26, 127–28, 291n31, 294n45; representation in, 112–16, 117–21; genre and gender in, 122–23, 292n37; eroticism in, 123–25, 294–95nn48, 51

Fables: retelling, 92–95
Fairy tales (Märchen), 137, 195, 276n3, 281–82n29, 296n13, 300n42
Family: and society, 36–37; and love, 56–62 *passim*; destruction of, 73, 280–81n21, 284–85n36; and bourgeois society, 130–31

Index

Fantasy, 281–82n29, 299n32; and history, 67–68; repression of, 70–71; and reality, 77, 147–48; as romantic theme, 151–52; and desire, 155–56

Fatso (Stopfkuchen) (Raabe), 216, 262, 294n42, 309–10n6, 315n39, 316–18nn45, 46, 52, 53; boredom as theme in, 219f, 221–22, 227, 228–44, 310n7, 311–12nn13, 17, 317n47; name-calling and revenge in, 244–48, 318n57; murder as repressive theme in, 248–53; repetition and revenge in, 254–59, 318n58, 319nn63, 65

Fiction and Repetition (Miller), 6, 297n17

Flagman Thiel (Bahnwärter Thiel) (Hauptmann), 137

Florentine Nights (Florentinische Nächte) (Heine) 227

Fontane, Theodor, 94, 129, 143, 298n20; *Effi Briest*, 134, 300n39; *Stechlin*, 241

Foucault, Michel, 23

Frame stories, framing: *The Mountain Forest* as, 42–43, 173–74; *The Marriage of the Monk* as, 174–76, 181–82

Frankfurt School, *see* Critical Theory

Freud, Sigmund, 2, 15, 269n30, 270n36, 303n25, 305n36; on repression, 16–17; on repetition compulsion, 17–18, 269n30; on death drive, 18–19

Freytag, Gustav, 269n27; *Debt and Credit*, 14

Furst, Lilian, 1

Gender, 288–89n9; Stifter's interpretations of, 33–34; Keller's use of, 97, 104–12 *passim*, 291n33, 292nn37, 39; and dress, 98–99, 100, 124, 294n46; repetition compulsion and, 101–2; identity and, 119, 121–22, 289–90n20; disavowal of, 120–21; and genre, 122–23

God, 32f, 65–66, 273n18

Goethe, Johann Wolfgang von: *Novella*, 91; *Wilhelm Meister's Apprenticeship*, 227

Green Henry (Der Grüne Heinrich) (Keller), 34, 92, 98, 298n20, 299n38, 300n39

Grillparzer, Franz: *The Poor Musician*, 91

Gustav Adolf's Page (Meyer), 98

Hauptmann, Gerhart: *Flagman Thiel*, 137

Heine, Heinrich: *Florentine Nights*, 227

Hell, Julia, 242

Heredity, 164–68 *passim*

History, 4, 278–79n14; and realism, 26, 85–87; Stifter's characterization of, 33, 42, 47–48, 52–53, 71–72, 283–84n35; and Nature, 43–44, 45–46, 66–67; and vision, 87–88; Meyer's use of, 171–72, 302n6; and identity, 242–43

Hitchcock, Alfred: *Vertigo*, 136f

Hoffmann, E. T. A., 78

Holub, Robert, 11f, 23, 134, 141, 153, 164, 261, 278–79n14, 281n24, 300n40, 302n15, 308n60; *Reflections of Realism*, 7; on Meyer, 174–75

Horkheimer, Max, 219, 269n27, 272n10; *Dialectic of Enlightenment*, 7–10

Identity, 125–26, 127–28, 300n48; mimesis and, 108–9, 290–91n30; transvestism and, 110–12, 289–90n20; and representation, 112–19, 121–22, 291n31; and authority, 205–7; subversion of, 207–10, 305–6n40; substitution of, 211–12; and history, 242–43

Imagination, 39f, 134; as romantic theme, 151–52; and desire, 153–54, 276n36, 300n39

Incest: as theme, 162–63, 275n34, 301n51; Storm's use of, 163–64, 165; repetition and, 164–66

Indian Summer (*Der Nachsommer*) (Stifter), 31, 83, 278–79n14, 281n24, 313n33

Jackson, David, 212
Jakobson, Roman, 2f, 5, 9, 20, 102, 131–32, 134, 268n16, 269n30, 296nn8, 9; "On Realism in Art," 4; "On Two Aspects of Language," 21; on realist defamiliarization, 100–101; on representation, 135–36

Kafka, Franz: *The Castle*, 227
Keller, Gottfried, 1, 32, 91, 260–61, 291n33; *Green Henry*, 34, 92, 98, 298n20, 299n38, 300n39; *A Village Romeo and Juliet*, 92f, 97; *Pankraz the Sulker*, 227; *The Epigram*, 98; *Seven Legends*, 93–127 *passim*, 262f, 289–90n20, 290n22, 291n33, 292n36, 295n49; retelling by, 92–95; on desire, 95–96, 106–7, 110–11, 290n27, 294nn42, 45, 299n38; repetition by, 96–97, 292n39; on gender, 97–99, 104–6, 107–8, 294n46; repetition in, 103–4; on representation and identity, 112–28 *passim*, 290–91nn30, 31; gender and genre in, 122–23; eroticism in, 123–25, 292–95nn40, 41, 48, 295n51; displacement by, 186, 291–92n34
Kepler, Johannes, 80, 287nn41, 42
Kierkegaard, Soren, 2; "The Rotation Method," 218–19, 222; on boredom, 220f, 223–24
Kleist, Heinrich von: *Marquise of O—*, 91
Kosegarten, Ludwig, 93, 100
Kracauer, Siegfried, 219
Kuh, Emil, 94
Kürnberger, Ferdinand, 94

Lacan, Jacques, 19–22, 270n40; the Imaginary and Symbolic, 20f, 270n41

Lenz (Büchner), 24, 219, 278n12; "Kunstgespräch," 24, 30, 34
Ligeia (Poe), 136f
"Ligeia impulse," 137–38, 140, 144
Limestone (*Kalkstein*) (Stifter), 77, 80, 91
Lolita (Nabokov), 136–37
Lorenz, Hildegard, 164; *Varianz und Invarianz*, 133
Love, 37, 64, 275n33; and desire, 38, 307–8n56; and family, 56–62 *passim*; as threat, 58, 282–83nn34, 35; and repression, 70–71

Mann, Thomas, 226, 241, 300–301n49, 314–15nn35, 37
Many-colored Stones (*Bunte Steine*) (Stifter), 39–48 *passim*, 77, 91, 156, 276n1, 276–77n5, 278–79n14; political themes in, 24–26, 172
Marquise of O— (Kleist), 91
Marriage of the Monk, The (*Die Hochzeit des Mönchs*) (Meyer), 91, 216, 263, 298n20, 299n35, 312n24; frame of, 170–71, 181–82, 302nn13, 14, 306n42; historical theme of, 172–73; use of invention in, 174–75; exchanging places in, 175–76, 187, 201–2, 305n37; reality in, 177–78, 196–97, 231; authority of narrative in, 178–79, 183–84, 304nn34, 35, 307–8n56; structural repetition in, 179–80; displacement in, 180–81, 182, 192–94, 202–4; engagement of narrative in, 184–85; conditions of narration in, 185–86, 197–99, 210–11, 306n49; substitution in, 186–88, 211–12, 305n38; repetition in, 188–89; authority as theme in, 189–92, 194–95, 199–201, 204–5; Fate in, 195–96, 213–14; alienation in, 206–7; subversion of identity in, 207–10, 305–6n40; desire and death in, 212–13, 214–15
Martini, Fritz, 134

Marx, Karl, 2
Meyer, C. F., 1, 261, 302n6, 308n61; *Gustav Adolf's Page*, 98; *The Amulet*, 171–72; *The Sufferings of a Boy*, 216; *The Marriage of the Monk*, 91–92, 170–201 passim, 263, 298n20, 302nn13, 14, 306n42, 307n53, 312n24; invention in, 174–75; framing by, 175–76, 181–82; on authority of narrative, 178–79, 183–84, 302n11, 305n34, 307–8n56; displacement in, 180–81, 192–94, 201–4; engagement of narrative in, 184–85; conditions of narration in, 185–86, 197–99, 210–11, 216, 306n49; substitution in, 186–88, 211–12, 305nn36, 37, 38, 307n55; repetition in, 188–89; authority as theme in, 189–92, 194–95, 199–201, 204–5; Fate in, 195–96, 213–14; reality in, 196–97, 304–5n35; use of narrative, 197–98; alienation in, 206–7; subversion of identity in, 207–10, 305–6n40; desire and death in, 212–13, 214–15, 299n35
Miller, J. Hillis, 21, 267n 11; *Fiction and Repetition*, 6, 297n17
Mimesis, 261; mythical, 9f, 263–64; in *The Mountain Forest*, 55, 59; identity and, 108–9, 114–16, 117
Mirroring, 43, 91, 160–61, 270n40, 290–91n30
Mirror of Cyprianus, The (*Der Spiegel des Cyprianus*) (Storm), 137–43 passim, 164f
Mountain Forest, The (*Der Hochwald*) (Stifter), 26, 33, 40, 80, 91, 142, 163, 263, 273n19, 275n34, 276nn1, 2, 3, 277n6, 278–79n14, 301n51; repression in, 35–36, 70–71; as tragedy, 41–42, 75–76; narrative and themes in, 42–48, 49–50, 53–54, 282–83nn34, 35; characters in, 50–53, 54–58, 69–70; use of repetition in, 58–61; protection and desire in, 61–62, 119; poetic realism in, 63–64; allegorical nature in, 64–67, 74–75, 277nn6, 7, 9; history in, 67–68, 71–72, 283–84n35; desire in, 72–73; reality of, 76–77, 86–87; telescopes in, 78–83 *passim*; vision in, 84–85; realism in, 85–86; framing in, 173–74
Mountain Quartz (*Bergmilch*)(Stifter), 91
Mourning, 18, 22
Music, 279–80n15
Myth, 8–10, 11, 263–64

Nabokov, Vladimir: *Lolita*, 136–37
Narcissism, 118, 292n35
Narration, narrative, 2, 263, 278–79n14; and desire, 175–76; authority in, 178–79, 282–83n34, 302n11, 304n34, 307–8nn56, 58; engagement in, 184–85; conditions of, 185–86, 259, 281n23; Meyer's use of, 197–98; reality of, 210–11, 231; aggression in, 216, 227, 232–34, 258; boredom and, 217–18, 227–36, 237–38; repetition in, 225–26; Raabe's style of, 226–27, 319n65
Nature: Stifter's theme of, 27, 39, 42, 50–51, 63, 74–76, 83, 172, 186, 273n18, 276–77nn2, 5; violence in, 28–29, 272n14; and vision, 32–33, 48–49; and history, 43–44, 45–46; virginity of, 46, 61f, 186; and human reality, 53–54; patriarchy in, 64, 281n26; as allegory, 65–67, 74–75, 277n9, 285–86n37; sexuality and, 89, 274n24, 282n31
Neighbor's House to the Left, In the (*Im Nachbarhause links*) (Storm), 140, 165f
Nietzsche, Friedrich Wilhelm, 2, 171, 220, 267n 11
Novella (Goethe), 91

Oval Portrait, The (Poe), 140

Painting, 32, 34, 142–44, 280n20, 299nn32, 38; portrait, 140–44

Pankraz the Sulker (*Pankraz der Schmoller*) (Keller), 227
Patriarchy, 59; in Nature, 64, 281n26; vision and, 82–83, 84–85
Pfister's Mill (Raabe), 227
Phillips, Adam, 225
Pleasure: and boredom, 218–21, 223–25
Poacher, The (*Der Wildschütze*) (Stifter), 60
Poe, Edgar Allan: *Ligeia*, 136f; *The Oval Portrait*, 140
Poor Musician, The (*Der arme Spielmann*) (Grillparzer), 91
Psyche (Storm), 140, 298–99n29

Raabe, Wilhelm, 1, 29, 261, 315n41; *Pfister's Mill*, 227; *Fatso* (*Stopfkuchen*), 216–22 passim, 228–59, 262, 294n42, 309–10n6, 315n39, 316–17nn45, 46, 318n57; use of boredom by, 226–27, 228–40, 310n7, 311–12nn13, 17, 314–15n37, 317n47; illusions of reality in, 240–44, 316–18nn46, 52, 53; repetition and revenge in, 244–48, 254–59, 318nn57, 58; use of repression by, 248–53, 318n58, 319nn63, 65
Realism: poetic, 4–5, 13, 24, 59, 63–64, 131–32; death and, 89–90; social, 130, 133–34; vs. romanticism, 159–60
"Realism in Art, On" (Jakobson), 4
Reality, 40, 104, 121, 260, 300n40, 312n21; repression and, 16–17, 251–53, 318n58; significant, 27–28; dual nature of, 75–76; of woods, 76–77, 276n3, 285–86n37; historical, 86–87; and fantasy, 147–48; desire and, 154–55, 178, 308n60; of frame, 181–82; narrative and, 196–98, 210–11, 234–35, 307–8n56; and authority, 205, 304–5n35; and redundancy, 238–40; illusions of, 240–43; misrepresentation of, 247–48; and disillusionment, 256–57

"Reality Effect, The" (Barthes), 2–3
Redundancy, 260; as narrative technique, 225f, 227–28, 235–36; and sense of reality, 238–40, 243f, 248
Reflections of Realism (Holub), 7
Religion, 277n9. *See also* Christianity
Renarration, 168–69
Repetition, 1–2, 6, 23, 91–92, 148f, 216, 260, 267n11, 297n17, 299n32, 313–14n34; in myth, 8, 10; and psychoanalysis, 15–17; of violence, 28–29, 319n65; in Stifter, 58–61, 62–63, 75, 274–75n28, 313n33, 314n35; Keller's use of, 96–97, 103–5, 108–9, 121; Storm's use of, 133, 140–41, 143–44, 152f, 160; and substitution, 137–41, 143, 161–62; incest and, 164–66, 275n34; children and, 167–68; through renarration, 168–69; and narrative authority, 179–80; Meyer's use of, 186, 215; as narrative method, 225–26, 237–40; Raabe's use of, 228–36, 311–12nn13, 17, 319n63; and identity, 242–43, 300n48; and revenge, 244–48, 254–59; and violence, 248–51
Repetition compulsion, 17–18, 101–2, 269n30
Representation, 92, 135–36, 148; pictorial, 78, 143; and identity, 112–19, 121–22, 290–91nn30, 31
Repression, 16–17, 29, 33, 57, 119, 254, 294n42; law and, 35–36; reality as, 68–69; Raabe's use of, 248–53, 318n58
Retardation, 225, 238
Retelling: of fables, 92–95, 97–98, 128
Rise of the Modern German Novel (Berman), 7
Romanticism, 4, 25, 33, 132, 159–60, 272n14, 298n20, 300n39
Romantic topos: in *Viola tricolor*, 132–36 passim, 140–42, 144–61; repetition in, 137–40, 149; deformation of, 150–57;

haunted garden as, 157–61; portrait as, 140–42
"Rotation Method, The" (Kierkegaard), 218–22 passim

Sadism, 224
Sammons, Jeffrey, 226
Science, 32, 79–80, 274n22, 287–88nn44, 45, 300n43
Seven Legends (*Sieben Legenden*) (Keller), 93–101 passim, 262, 289–90nn20, 22. *See also* "Eugenia"
Sexuality, 38, 88f, 162, 274n24, 275n34, 278n11, 292–94nn40, 41, 300–301n49. *See also* Desire
Shakespeare, William, 92
Solar Eclipse of July 8, 1842, The (Stifter), 79–83 passim
Stechlin (Fontane), 241
Stepmother, The (Auerbach), 91
Stifter, Adalbert, 1, 226, 260–61, 273n18, 274n24, 275n30, 313–14n34; *Many-colored Stones*, 24–26, 39–46 passim, 77, 91, 156, 172, 276–77nn1, 5, 278–80nn14, 15, 19; *Limestone*, 77, 80; *Studies*, 26, 77; *The Condor*, 77–80 passim; *A Walk in the Woods*, 41, 77, 81; *Brigitta*, 41, 98; *The Castle of Fools*, 33–34, 79f, 278n11, 278–79n14, 180n19; *The Album of My Great-grandfather*, 31, 34, 278–79nn11, 14; *Abdias*, 31, 33, 41; *Two Sisters*, 82f, 279–80n15; *The Mountain Forest*, 26, 33, 35–36, 40–91 passim, 119, 142, 163, 173–74, 263, 273n19, 275n34, 276n3, 277nn6, 7, 9, 278–79n14, 283–84n34, 35, 284–85n36; *The Solar Eclipse of July 8, 1842*, 79–83 passim; *Descendants*, 78, 81, 273n19; *Indian Summer*, 31, 83, 278–79n14, 281n24, 313n33; realism of, 27–28, 85–87; use of repetition by, 28–29, 58–59, 62–63, 274–75n28, 314n35; on artist as investigator, 29–32; on vision, 32–33, 78f, 84–85, 87–88, 300n43; on law, 35–36, 38–39; on family, 36–37, 284–85n36; on Nature, 46, 49–50, 186, 276n2; on history, 47–48, 71–72, 283–84n35; reality and fantasy in, 59–61, 67–68, 281–82n29; on protection and desire, 61–62, 119; poetic realism of, 63–64; nature as allegory in, 64–67, 74–75, 277nn7, 9, 285–86n37; desire as theme in, 69–70, 72–73, 281n25; repression in, 70–71, 119; repetition in, 75–76, 149; reality of, 76–77; and telescopes, 77–90; use of framing by, 173–74

Storm, Constanze, 131
Storm, Dorthea Jensen, 131
Storm, Theodor, 1, 29, 261, 296nn11, 13, 14, 298n23, 300–301n49, 315–16n43; *Aquis submersus*, 140, 153, 164; *In the Castle*, 137–43 passim, 164f; *In the Neighbor's House to the Left*, 140, 165f; *A Corner of the Forest*, 137, 143–44, 162–63; *The Mirror of Cyprianus*, 137–43 passim, 164f; *Psyche*, 140, 298–99n29; *Eekenhof*, 137, 140, 165f; *Viola tricolor*, 91, 129–69 passim, 187, 262, 299n30, 300n42; social realism of, 130–31, 133–34; poetic realism of, 131–32; romantic topos in, 136, 150–57; *Märchen*, 137; and repetition and substitution, 137–40, 143–44, 153, 161–62, 167–68; on desire, 144–45, 148–49, 152–53, 154–56, 298–99n29; on death, 145–48; and haunted garden, 157–61; on incest, 162–66, 300n51; renarration in, 168–69
"Storyteller, The" (Der Erzähler) (Benjamin), 217–18
Studies (Stifter), 26, 77
Substitution, substitutability: in Storm's works, 137–42, 143; repetition in, 161–62; in Meyer's work, 186–88, 191, 202,

305nn36, 37, 38, 307n55; identity and, 211–12
Sufferings of a Boy, The (*Die Leiden eines Knabens*) (Meyer), 216
Swales, Martin, 13–14, 31

Telescopes: Stifter's use of, 77–90, 287–88nn44, 45
Transference. *See* Substitution
Transvestism, 98, 102; identity and, 109ff, 289–90n20; gender and, 120–21
Tschorn, Wolfgang, 130, 134
"Two Aspects of Language, On" (Jakobson), 21
Two Sisters (Stifter), 82f, 279–80n15

Urfabel: retelling, 92–95

Varianz und Invarianz (Lorenz), 133
Vertigo (Hitchcock), 136f
Village Romeo and Juliet, A (*Romeo und Julia auf dem Dorfe*) (Keller), 92f, 97
Viola tricolor (Storm), 91, 129, 187, 262, 299n30, 300n42; social realism of, 130–31; romantic motifs of, 132–36 *passim*, 140–42, 150–57; representation in, 135f;

repetition and substitution in, 137–40, 149, 161, 167–68; desire in, 144–45, 152–53; death as theme in, 145–47; fantasy in, 147–48; haunted garden in, 157–58; incest in, 162f, 165–66
Violence, 27, 28–29, 40, 272n14, 273n20, 280n19; and aesthetics, 34–35; and human nature, 38f; and repetition, 246–47, 248–51, 319n65; and revenge, 254–59
Virginity, 46, 277n7; of the woods, 44–50 *passim*, 57–63 *passim*, 73, 186, 285–86n37
Vision, 48–49, 78f, 287n43; science and, 32–33, 287–88nn44, 45, 300n43; telescopic, 80–81, 82–83, 88–89; law and order and, 84–85; history and, 87–88

Walk in the Woods, A (*Der Waldsteig*) (Stifter), 41, 77, 81
Weber, Samuel, 20, 270n41
Wellek, Rene, 1
Wiederholungszwang, 17–18
Wilhelm Meister's Apprenticeship (*Wilhelm Meisters Lehrjahre*) (Goethe), 227

Young Germany (*Junges Deutschland*), 25, 28, 33